A New Woman Reader

A New Woman Reader:
Fiction, Articles, and Drama
of the 1890s

Edited by

Carolyn Christensen Nelson

broadview press

Canadian Cataloguing in Publication Data

Main entry under title:
A new woman reader : fiction, articles, and drama of the 1890s

Includes bibliographical references.
ISBN 978-1-55111-295-4

1. English literature – 19th century.   2. American literature – 19th century.   3. Women – Literary collections.   4. Feminism – Literary collections.   I. Nelson, Carolyn Christensen.

PR1111.F45N48 2000   820.8'0352042   C00-931775-9

Broadview Press Ltd., is an independent, international publishing house, incorporated in 1985.

North America
Post Office Box 1243, Peterborough, Ontario, Canada K9J 7H5
3576 California Road, Orchard Park, NY 14127
Tel: (705) 743-8990; Fax: (705) 743-8353;
e-mail: customerservice@broadviewpress.com

United Kingdom:
Turpin Distribution Services, Ltd., Blackhorse Rd., Letchworth, Hertfordshire SG6 1HN
Tel: (1462) 672555; Fax: (1462) 480947; e-mail: turpin@rsc.org

Australia:
St. Clair Press, P.O. Box 287, Rozelle, NSW 2039
Tel: (02) 818-1942; Fax: (02) 418-1923

www.broadviewpress.com

Broadview Press gratefully acknowledges the financial support of the Book Publishing Industry Development Program, Ministry of Canadian Heritage, Government of Canada.

Typesetting and assembly: True to Type Inc., Mississauga, Canada.

PRINTED IN CANADA

FOR MY SISTER MARGARET

CONTENTS

INTRODUCTION

The term the "New Woman" was coined in England in March 1894 when Sarah Grand, whose well-known novel *The Heavenly Twins* appeared the previous year, published "The New Aspect of the Woman Question" in the *North American Review*. In the essay she uses the phrase "the new woman" to denote the woman who has finally "solved the problem and proclaimed for herself what was wrong with Home-is-the-Woman's-Sphere, and prescribed the remedy." Within two months the phrase the "New Woman," now printed with capital letters, was ubiquitous. It was printed in one journal after another and the comic newspaper *Punch* joined in with its own satiric response to the new creation; it published a so-called nursery rhyme on "The New Woman." In her angry response to Grand, in an essay entitled "The New Woman," published in the *North American Review* in May, the novelist Ouida, the *nom de plume* of Marie Louise de la Ramée, also capitalized the New Woman. On September 1, Sydney Grundy's satirical view of this woman was successfully staged as a play called *The New Woman*, with a run of 173 performances.

A stereotyped image of the New Woman quickly took hold on the public imagination. She was educated at Girton College, Cambridge, rode a bicycle, insisted on rational dress, and smoked in public: in short, she rejected the traditional role for women and demanded emancipation. According to Victorian ideology, men and women were meant to occupy separate spheres that were determined for them from birth according to their biological sex. The woman's sphere was the home while the man's sphere was the rest of the world. The New Woman, arguing that the separate spheres ideology was a construct of society and culture rather than a biological mandate, demanded that women be given the same opportunities and choices as men. Their rejection of the constrictions of the feminine or womanly sphere seemingly aligned the New Women with the decadents of the period because both groups refused to be contained by their culturally assigned gender roles. The decadents, who included such late nineteenth- and early twentieth-century writers as Oscar Wilde, Ernest Dowson, and Aubrey Beardsley, believed in the superiority of art over nature, both biological nature and supposedly natural standards of sexual behavior. Both the decadents and the New Women were treated by their critics with levity; they were mocked in cartoons and in plays such as Grundy's *The New Woman*. Nevertheless, the fear of deviance that was created by the perception that both groups were crossing gender lines and rejecting what was supposedly natural created an anxiety that is obvious in many articles that appeared in periodicals during the 1890s. The New Woman writers' frank discussion of female sexuality and suppressed desire further contributed to the public's unease. In the middle of the decade the trial of Oscar Wilde, which resulted in a conviction for sodomy resulting from his relationship with Lord Alfred Douglas, increased this growing anxiety. Some believed there were even national implications: a country of effeminate men and masculine women must be culturally degenerate and the race itself was in danger of decline. All these anxieties contributed to the distinctive fin de siècle mood of the 1890s.

Despite the popular perception of a mannish New Woman emerging, women of the nineties held a variety of opinions on social and political issues and even the New Women did not see themselves as a monolithic group. What the New Women did share was a rejection of the culturally defined feminine role and a desire for increased educational and career opportunities that would allow them to be economically self-sufficient. This desire for emancipation came at a time when women's lives had already begun to improve. Women were benefiting from the establishment of educational institutions for women and changes in the marriage laws. Girton College (1869) and Newnham College (1871) were founded as women's colleges at Cambridge, while Royal Holloway College (1879) and Westfield College (1882) were established for women in London. The Married Women's Property Acts, passed in 1870 and 1882, somewhat improved women's position in that women now had the right to their own property after marriage. Nevertheless, women desired further emancipation; they wanted to enjoy the same rights and privileges that men had, including the same education, the ability to pursue their own interests, and the right to occupations. Before 1919, almost all the professions, such as the law, were closed to women. Without the opportunity to earn their own living, marriage was an economic necessity for most women. Many of the New Women novels, such as Sarah Grand's *The Beth Book* (1898) and *The Heavenly Twins* (1893), and Iota's *A Yellow Aster* (1894), demonstrate the great disparity between a family's treatment of brother and sister and the vastly different opportunities accorded each.

The marriage question was central to most discussions by and about the New Woman and was an important part of New Woman writing, both fiction and essays. Mona Caird's essay "Marriage," published in 1888, began an important public debate on issues relating to marriage that continued in the periodicals during the next decade. Caird concluded "that the present form of marriage—exactly in proportion to its conformity with orthodox ideas—is a vexatious failure." Many of the New Woman novels, such as Caird's *The Daughters of Danaus* (1894), demonstrate how social and legal forces subordinate women in marriage. However, despite all of the problems relating to the marriage question that women described in their essays and fiction, most of the New Women writers were not opposed to marriage. Rather, they believed that it should be constituted on entirely different terms than it presently was; marriage should be freely chosen rather than imposed on women by social and economic forces.

Another issue related to the marriage question that was important in the New Woman fiction and in women's articles was the sexual double standard for men and women. While women were expected to bring sexual purity to marriage, men's past sexual activities were tolerated by society. Several of the New Woman novels demonstrate the dangers of women's sexual innocence and men's profligate behavior when unsuspecting wives are infected with syphilis by their husbands. Women in Grand's *The Heavenly Twins* and Emma Frances Brooke's *A Superfluous Woman* (1894) contract syphilis from their husbands and die as a result. Sarah Grand, as well as other women writers, believed that men should have to live up to the same moral standards as women and bring the same purity to marriage that was required of women. Further, because women's ignorance about matters of sexuality could have devastating consequences, women should be educated about sexual issues before marriage so they could make intelligent choices about the men they married. Grand's views of sexual purity were not shared by all the New Women. George Egerton, for example, celebrated women's sexuality and depicted women whose lives are as unconstrained by convention as men's. Sydney Grundy's play satirizes this controversy over purity when the dissolute colonel says to the New Women, "To begin with, you must make up your minds whether you wish to regenerate us or to degrade yourselves." In an earlier exchange between two women in the play, Enid says: "And *I* say that a man, reeking with infamy, ought not to be allowed to marry a pure girl—." To which her friend Victoria responds: "Certainly not! *She* ought to reek with infamy as well."

While debates over the marriage question, sexual purity, and the construction of the New Woman were being conducted in periodicals, Blanche Crackanthorpe began another related controversy with the publication of her article in the *Nineteenth Century,* in 1894, called "The Revolt of the Daughters." Crackanthorpe's discussion revisits many of the controversies found elsewhere: the sexual double standard, education for women, and the desirability for unmarried women to own their own latchkey, a symbol of their ability to move freely outside the protection of family and home. While Crackanthorpe believed that "Marriage *is* the best profession for a woman," she acknowledges that not all women will marry and that unmarried women need to have work. Crackanthorpe's article provoked mothers and daughters to respond, and essays on the advisability of daughters revolting against the restrictions on their lives appeared all during 1894 in a variety of periodicals.

While the rebellion of the New Woman during the 1890s was primarily against social and economic restrictions, she saw political change through women's gaining parliamentary suffrage as another means of achieving emancipation. The agitation for the vote began long before the 1890s and continued well into the twentieth century. Proof that women, even educated women, did not share all the same political goals at the end of the nineteenth century is evident in an examination of the suffrage issue. While men had continually blocked the passage of any amendment for women's suffrage in Parliament, many prominent women also opposed it in writing. "An Appeal Against Female Suffrage" was published in the *Nineteenth Century* in June 1889 and was signed by 104 women. Notable among the signatories are Mrs. Matthew Arnold, Mrs. Leslie Stephen (mother of Virginia Woolf), Mrs. Humphry Ward (the novelist), and Beatrice Potter (later Webb). A later "Appeal Against Female Suffrage" was published in July 1889 in the *Nineteenth Century* and signed by more than 1,800 women. They included students from Girton College, Cambridge, as well as the poet Christina Rossetti. The effort by women to gain the vote continued throughout the decade of the 1890s but it was not until the 1918, after years of demonstrations, marches, militant action, and imprisonment, that women of thirty and over who were house-holders or wives of householders were finally able to vote. In 1928 all women twenty-one and over were given the vote. By the beginning of the twentieth century some of the New Woman writers had turned their energies to the movement for achieving political rights. They joined the suffrage cause, forming the Women Writers Suffrage League.

The New Woman fiction did not begin in 1894 when Sarah Grand first used the phrase. Olive Schreiner's novel *The Story of an African Farm* (1883), with its unconventional heroine, is one of the first such novels. Henrik Ibsen's play *A Doll's House* was first produced in London in 1889 and *Hedda Gabler* in 1891; the strong heroines of these plays are types of the New Woman and no doubt influenced the representation of women in the New Woman fiction which followed. Some New Woman writers were men; these include Thomas Hardy, George Gissing, and George Bernard Shaw. However, most New Woman fiction was written by women. Such novels and stories are character-ized by the representation of strong heroines who rebel against the limita-tions placed on their lives and demand the same education and economic opportunities as men enjoy. The fiction also places much greater emphasis on women's sexuality, and the frankness with which the fiction dealt with the psy-chology of women, as well as some very negative portrayals of marriage, pro-voked an angry response from many critics.

Women found it easier to find publishers for their fiction after the demise of the three-volume novel in 1894 broke the power of Mudie's Circulating Library. Mudie's was the largest and most successful of the lending libraries in the nineteenth century, purchasing and lending thousands of volumes a year. Because of its buying power, it was able to exert strict control over the content of books published. When one-volume novels began to be published in the 1890s and people began to buy rather than borrow books, publishers became more willing to publish daring novels and in increasing numbers women began to publish. The fear of women's dominance of the literary market is demonstrated in Grundy's play when one of the men complains: "The theatre is dying!" A woman responds: "The novel will sweep everything before it." Sylvester asks, "You mean, the female novel?" to which another man answers: "Nothing can stop it." This anxiety over fiction by women who wrote so explicitly about marriage and sexual desire is revealed in several of the novels of the decade, when women first began to create heroines who were themselves writers. The husband of Evadne, Grand's heroine in *The Heavenly Twins*, makes her promise that she will not publish books on social subjects during his lifetime. In *Red Pottage* (1899), by Mary Cholmondeley, the brother of Hester Gresley, a writer, burns her book because he believes it to be immoral. Mabel Wotton and Ella Hepworth Dixon also created heroines who struggled as writers. An indication of the number of women writing during the nineties and the following two decades is revealed by *Toward a Feminist Tradition*, an annotated bibliography of feminist novels in English written by women from 1891-1920, compiled by Diva Daims and Janet Grimes: it contains 3,407 titles by 1,723 authors.

The founding in 1894 of a new literary journal, the *Yellow Book*, published by Elkin Mathews and John Lane (after October 1894 by Lane alone) at the Bodley Head and edited by Henry Harland, also was adventitious for new writers, particularly women. It ran as a quarterly until 1897 and eventually comprised thirteen volumes. The *Yellow Book* allowed many women, some unknown at the time, to bring their work to public attention in a prestigious journal. Stories by George Egerton and Ella D'Arcy were included in the first volume, putting them in the company of well-known writers such as Henry James, Arthur Symons, and George Moore. The women writers of the *Yellow Book* were primarily realists but their stories had great variety; some were comic, others fantastic, and many were told from a male point of view.

The year before the first volume of the *Yellow Book* appeared, Lane had begun a Keynotes Series of books, taking the name from George Egerton's collection of stories entitled *Keynotes* (1893), the first book in the series. Both in the *Yellow Book* and in the Keynotes Series Lane published works by a new generation of writers, many of them women. The series eventually had 33 volumes, 13 of them by women, including works of fiction by Ella D'Arcy, Evelyn Sharp, Victoria Cross, Netta Syrett, and Mabel Wotton.

While fiction with feminist heroines continued to be written after the 1890s, by the end of the century the New Woman, as she was constituted in the popular imagination and in the bold fiction of its writers, faded from attention. The New Woman was no longer a shocking figure and many of the social and legal changes which she had desired and written about had been effected. Many of these New Woman writers continued to publish in the twentieth century, but their work did not receive the same attention that it had in the 1890s. Nevertheless, for a few years these writers occupied an important place in the literary and social life of England and they made a significant contribution to the development of the short story and the novel. With its feminist heroines who directly challenged society's construction of the feminine and demanded their emancipation, and its greater emphasis on a psychological exploration of women's inner lives, this fiction provided more authentic depictions of women for its readers. The New Women also developed the forms of fiction in new ways, using dream sequences, stream-of-consciousness techniques, and innovative narrative methods.

Today few of the works by the New Woman writers are in print, making it difficult for readers to have a complete picture of the literature of the 1890s. The fiction by male writers of the period, with its representations of women, is more typically studied and anthologized. However, the fiction of the New Woman and the controversies surrounding her need to be included in any study of the 1890s in order for one to have a comprehensive understanding of the decade. This literature provides the transition from that of the Victorian age to the overtly political suffrage literature of the early twentieth century, and to modern literature.

A NOTE ON THE TEXT

While the term New Woman is also used with American writers of the same period, it is primarily associated with English writers. This text focuses on New Woman writers in England and the response to their writing.

Short stories rather than novel excerpts represent the fiction of the New Woman writers in this book; I believe that the novels are best appreciated by being read in their entirety. The guide to Further Reading (p. 353) provides a representative list of New Woman novels.

Whenever possible, I have provided dates for the writers and their works. Because I could not locate biographical information on a few writers, some dates are missing. I have silently corrected minor typographical errors, such as quotation marks that were omitted.

I have made every reasonable effort to trace the copyright holders of the materials included in this book. I would be pleased to hear from any such holders and credit them in subsequent editions.

I appreciate the information and advice given to me by colleagues, particularly Hayden Ward, whose knowledge of the Victorian period is encyclopedic. I also thank my husband, Byron, for all his help and support.

PART ONE

SHORT STORIES
BY NEW WOMAN WRITERS

INTRODUCTION

The women of the 1890s revolted against their traditional role in society and also in the way they had been represented in fiction. In their novels and stories the New Woman writers began to explore for themselves the lives of women, removing the definition of what was woman's nature and the true feminine from the hands of male writers and replacing it with a more complete and complex view. They do that in remarkably different ways but all of them force us into a reexamination of the representation of women in the fiction of the nineteenth century.

While the New Woman writers were primarily realists and naturalists, many of them experimented with the forms of fiction, altering them in a variety of ways to represent what they believed to be a more authentic picture of woman's true nature. George Egerton was the most stylistically innovative of these writers as her stories included in this text demonstrate. In her essay "A Keynote to Keynotes," Egerton states: "I realised that in literature, everything had been better done by man than woman could hope to emulate. There was only one small plot left for her to tell: the terra incognita of herself, as she knew herself to be, not as man liked to imagine her—in a word, to give herself away, as man had given himself away in his writings."[1] Egerton uses the stream of consciousness to examine women's inner lives, subordinating plot to focus instead on impressions, moments of time, and psychological states. She creates ambiguities in her stories through the use of ellipses and ambiguous pronoun references. Egerton is interested in revealing women's ambitions, desires, and dreams, and she does that by deliberately sacrificing the narrative line of a tightly plotted story.

Egerton's stories demonstrate her disdain for conventional morality, which she believed was constructed by men and imposed on women, narrowing their lives and experiences. In "Now Spring Has Come," she states that "man manufactured an artificial morality ... and established a system that means war, and always war, because it is a struggle between instinctive truths and cultivated lies." She urges women to break free from conventionality and to celebrate their "untamed spirit" and "eternal wildness" ("A Cross Line"). Egerton wanted women to live life fully and to do so they must free themselves from traditional notions about respectability. Egerton did not share the concern other New Woman writers had for opportunities for women in education and careers. Rather she encouraged women to fulfill their lives through maternity and in equal relationships with men; marriage for her was not a prerequisite for woman's happiness or for bearing children.

Grand, just as had Egerton, depicted in her fiction women who refused to be contained by man's definition of the feminine. Her stories demonstrate her belief that women's emancipation will be beneficial and liberating for men as well as for women. "The Undefinable," told from the man's point of

3

view as are many New Woman stories, demonstrates the transformation that takes place in the imagination of the painter when he recognizes his model as an individual and as his equal. She refuses to be the "womanly woman" he always thought was men's object of desire, a woman who existed for man's physical pleasure. Rather than being the passive object of man's gaze, she asserts her individuality onto the created work. When the painter recognizes and accepts the model's more authentic identity as true woman, with her vitality and mystery, he is able to paint with the inspiration he previously lacked. He finally recognizes her as "a free woman, a new creature, a source of inspiration," which is Grand's definition of the New Woman whose emergence will benefit both man and woman. The story also predicts that woman's full emancipation will lead to her becoming man's equal in creative production. As was true of Egerton, Grand was optimistic about the future, believing that more equitable relationships would exist between men and women when women were freed from their oppressed condition.

Victoria Cross's "Theodora: A Fragment" has affinities to the writing of the decadents with its sexually-charged atmosphere and the ambiguity of desire evident in the cross-dressing and in the narrator's sketches of both men and women and men who look like women. A man whose desire for Theodora is enhanced by her androgynous appearance and her donning of men's clothing narrates the story. Further contributing to the mood of decadence is Theodora, who has "a smile that failed to dispel the air of fatigue and fashionable dissipation that seemed to cling to her." The story is more about the narrator's perception of Theodora and his reasons for desiring her than it is about Theodora herself, but she clearly is no traditional woman. Cross creates in Theodora a woman who is vastly different from traditional ideas of the feminine, submissive type that is supposed to be the object of male desire.

The women in Netta Syrett's fiction are in rebellion and in the case of Kathleen Drayton, in "Thy Heart's Desire," that rebellion is against the claustrophobic marriage she endures with her husband, a man of limited intelligence and charm. The desert setting of the Middle East, which isolates Mrs. Drayton from contact with others and from sources of intellectual stimulation, is an image of her arid marriage. Her only chance of conversation comes at the end of the day when her husband returns to their tent, but the poverty of his imagination only increases her misery. Her reasons for marrying such a dull man are similar to those given by many girls: she was ignorant and inexperienced and bored. She thought marriage would be an escape from an unhappy home, but it only provided another setting in which to be isolated and bored. Syrett seemingly provides a way of escape for Mrs. Drayton when Broomhurst arrives and falls in love with her and her husband dies. But another marriage is not the panacea for her situation. Broomhurst's promise to take care of her will not liberate her from the drab boredom of her life but instead trap her in another loveless marriage. Syrett does not provide a happy marriage ending, but in Kathleen Drayton's final look toward the expansiveness of the sea there is the suggestion in the "transient gleams of sunlight" of a more liberating possibility for self-fulfillment.

The problems of marriage as they relate to the condition of women, which Mona Caird describes in her essay "Marriage," are demonstrated in many of the stories and novels written by the New Women writers, including those of Netta Syrett and Ada Radford. When the narrator of Radford's "Lot 99" asks her brother for money so she can get the education necessary to become a teacher, he responds as most brothers would have at that time: she doesn't need an education because she will marry. Education for women was supposedly unnecessary because marriage was women's natural vocation. Without an education or any means of earning money, women entered loveless marriages to escape their homes or poverty, as does Kathleen Drayton, or else they become the so-called odd women who never marry and are left with little means to sustain themselves economically. The odd woman of Radford's story has a small inheritance and thus can avoid poverty after rejecting marriage. She derives her strength of character from her unmarried Aunt Lizzie, a strong, independent woman who raised the orphan children of her brother and passed on to the narrator the independent spirit that helps her endure alone.

Radford's story proves a point made by many New Woman writers: men as well as women pay a price for denying women the ability to be independent and self-sustaining. Men can be also be trapped in loveless marriages as is the case with the narrator's brother, Lionel, whose "unfortunate marriage" to a woman of a lower class than himself results from "his folly" or sexual indiscretions. Mona Caird in her essays linked marriage problems to the more general condition of women, while the distinctly different moral standards by which men and women were judged were repeatedly attacked by Sarah Grand in her essays as well as her fiction, particularly in her novel *The Heavenly Twins*. In Mabel Wotton's "The Hour of Her Life," Annette, with her flower shop, is economically independent. But it is clear that her male admirers, who are socially her superiors, are not supposed to marry her, but rather visit her in her "inner sanctum." In Wotton's story as well as Radford's, men exploit women sexually while women use their sexuality in an attempt to rise socially and economically. Without the ability to improve their condition through education, women are forced to use their sexuality as a commodity in the marriage market. Even Aunt Lizzie, an independent woman, fails to see the larger issue as it relates to women's condition; she doesn't blame men for their behavior and thinks it is not right "to chain a young man to his folly."

Ella D'Arcy seemingly takes a male point of view in many of her stories, disparaging the behavior of women. In "White Magic," Mauger relates a story to the narrator to support his belief that women are hopelessly irrational and willingly believe old wives' tales. But such a belief results in a situation in which the lovers appear destined to live happily ever after, a rare ending for a New Woman story. Is D'Arcy validating Mauger's and the narrator's point of view or rather showing that these men are misinterpreting the evidence? Mauger's assessment of women, that they are "wonderful enigmas," is surprisingly close to the view of Egerton, whose stories celebrated women's intuitive, mysterious nature. Mauger intends to demean women by his assessment of them as irrational creatures; in Egerton's view it is this more primitive spirit of woman, with its ability to go beyond the rational and respond to more vital life forces, that makes woman man's superior. The woman in "A Cross Line" laughs "to herself because the denseness of man, his chivalrous conservative devotion to the female idea he has created, blinds him, perhaps happily, to the problems of her complex nature." D'Arcy may also be laughing in such a way at Mauger and his companion for their confidence at assessing a woman's real nature.

As the short fiction included in this text demonstrates, the New Woman writers represented the psychological nature and social conditions of women in many different ways, on occasion even having a man tell the story to create an ironic perspective on a woman. Some of the writers, most significantly George Egerton, experimented with narrative techniques to provide a more complete representation of women's inner lives. All of their stories focus on women who have abandoned their traditional sphere to lead more complex lives. While some stories have happy or uncertain endings, few end in a traditional marriage.

NOTE

1. "A Keynote to Keynes," *Ten Contemporaries*, ed. John Galsworthy (London: Ernest Benn Limited, 1932).

GEORGE EGERTON
(MARY CHAVELITA DUNNE BRIGHT, 1859-1945)

George Egerton (Mary Chavelita Dunne Bright) was born in Melbourne, Australia, daughter of a mother of Welsh descent whose maiden name was George and an Irish father, John Joseph Dunne, who was known for his book, How and Where to Fish in Ireland *(1887). Because Dunne provided little financially for his large family, Egerton's early years were spent in poverty. She went away to school in Germany and then tried various means of employment. In 1887, Egerton went to Norway with a married man, Henry Higginson, who deserted his wife. They lived together in Norway for two years. Because he was abusive and alcoholic, Egerton's years with Higginson were unpleasant, but she stayed with him until he died in 1889.*

While living in Norway, Egerton learned Norwegian and read the works of various Scandinavian writers, notably Henrik Ibsen, August Strindberg, and Knut Hamsun. She had a brief relationship with Hamsun which provided the basis of her story "Now Spring Has Come," and, after returning to London, translated Hamsun's novel Hunger. *Egerton then married George Egerton Clairmonte, who, like Egerton's father, took little financial responsibility for his family. Egerton began writing to provide a means of support for her family. Her first collection of short stories,* Keynotes, *after being rejected by William Heinemann, was published by John Lane and Elkin Mathews at the Bodley Head in 1893. It was a literary success and became the first book in Lane's Keynotes Series. Aubrey Beardsley designed a cover and a keynote monogram for each book in this series.* Keynotes *was followed by another collection of stories,* Discords, *in 1894, the sixth volume of the Keynotes Series. Two of Egerton's stories also appeared in the* Yellow Book. *Stories in both* Keynotes *and* Discords, *often drawn from Egerton's own experiences, explored psychological states of women, their dreams and fantasies, including their erotic desires. Their frank depiction of marriage and women's sexuality shocked some critics.*

Egerton published two more volumes of stories, Symphonies *(1897) and* Fantasias *(1898), but they did not live up to the promise of her earlier volumes and were poorly reviewed. Her autobiographical novel,* The Wheel of God, *also published in 1898, received favorable reviews but Egerton no longer enjoyed the fame that her earlier volumes brought her. Her marriage to Clairmonte, never successful, ended in divorce in 1901. That same year she met and married Reginald Golding Bright, a drama critic who was fifteen years her junior. Egerton then began writing plays but only three were ever performed and they were not successful. World War I began just as Egerton's only child, George Clairmonte, was about to enter Cambridge; he was killed in action in 1915. Bright, her husband, died in 1941.*

7

A CROSS LINE

[*Keynotes*. London: Elkin Mathews & John Lane, 1893]

The rather flat notes of a man's voice float out into the clear air, singing the refrain of a popular music-hall ditty. There is something incongruous between the melody and the surroundings. It seems profane, indelicate, to bring this slangy, vulgar tune, and with it the mental picture of footlight flare and fantastic dance into the lovely freshness of this perfect spring day.

A woman sitting on a felled tree turns her head to meet its coming, and an expression flits across her face in which disgust and humorous appreciation are subtly blended. Her mind is nothing if not picturesque; her busy brain, with all its capabilities choked by a thousand vagrant fancies, is always producing pictures and finding associations between the most unlikely objects. She has been reading a little sketch written in the daintiest language of a fountain scene in Tanagra, and her vivid imagination has made it real to her. The slim, graceful maids grouped around it filling their exquisitely-formed earthen jars, the dainty poise of their classic heads, and the flowing folds of their draperies have been actually present with her; and now?—why, it is like the entrance of a half-tipsy vagabond player bedizened in tawdry finery—the picture is blurred. She rests her head against the trunk of a pine tree behind her, and awaits the singer. She is sitting on an incline in the midst of a wilderness of trees; some have blown down, some have been cut down, and the lopped branches lie about; moss and bracken and trailing bramble, fir-cones, wild rose bushes, and speckled red "fairy hats" fight for life in wild confusion. A disused quarry to the left is an ideal haunt of pike, and to the right a little river rushes along in haste to join a greater sister that is fighting a troubled way to the sea. A row of stepping-stone crosses it, and if you were to stand on one you would see shoals of restless stone loach "Beardies" darting from side to side. The tails of several ducks can be seen above the water, and the paddle of their balancing feet and the gurgling suction of their bills as they search for larvæ can be heard distinctly between the hum of insect, twitter of bird, and rustle of stream and leaf. The singer has changed his lay to a whistle, and presently he comes down the path a cool, neat, grey-clad figure, with a fishing creel slung across his back, and a trout rod held on his shoulder. The air ceases abruptly, and his cold grey eyes scan the seated figure with its gipsy ease of attitude, a scarlet shawl that has fallen from her shoulders forming an accentuative background to the slim roundness of her waist.

Persistent study, coupled with a varied experience of the female animal, has given the owner of the grey eyes some facility in classing her, although it has not supplied him with any definite data as to what any one of the species may do in a given circumstance. To put it in his own words, in answer to a friend who chaffed him on his untiring pursuit of women as an interesting problem:

"If a fellow has had much experience of his fellow-man he may divide him into types, and, given a certain number of men and a certain number of circumstances, he is pretty safe on hitting on the line of action each type will strike; 't aint so with woman. You may always look out for the unexpected; she generally upsets a fellow's calculations, and you are never safe in laying odds on her. Tell you what, old chappie, we may talk about superior intellect; but, if a woman wasn't handicapped by her affection, or need of it, the cleverest chap in Christendom would be just a bit of putty in her hands. I find them more fascinating as problems than anything going. Never let an opportunity slip to get new data—never!"

He did not now. He met the frank, unembarrassed gaze of eyes that would have looked with just the same bright inquiry at the advent of a hare, or a toad, or any other object that might cross her path, and raised his hat with respectful courtesy, saying, in the drawling tone habitual with him—

"I hope I am not trespassing?"

"I can't say; you may be, so may I, but no one has ever told me so!"

A pause. His quick glance has noted the thick wedding ring on her slim brown hand, and the flash of a diamond in its keeper. A lady decidedly. Fast? perhaps. Original? undoubtedly. Worth knowing? rather.

"I am looking for a trout stream, but the directions I got were rather vague; might I—"

"It's straight ahead, but you won't catch anything now, at least not here,— sun's too glaring and water too low; a mile up you may in an hour's time."

"Oh, thanks awfully for the tip. You fish then?"

"Yes, sometimes."

"Trout run big here?" (What odd eyes the woman has, kind of magnetic.)

"No, seldom over a pound, but they are very game."

"Rare good sport isn't it, whipping a stream? There is so much besides the mere catching of fish. The river and the trees and the quiet sets a fellow thinking—kind of sermon—makes a chap feel good, don't it?"

She smiles assentingly. And yet what the devil is she amused at, he queries mentally. An inspiration! He acts upon it, and says eagerly:

"I wonder—I don't half like to ask—but fishing puts people on a common footing, don't it? You knowing the stream, you know, would you tell me what are the best flies to use?"

"I tie my own, but—"

"Do you? how clever of you! wish I could," and sitting down on the other end of the tree, he takes out his fly book, "but I interrupted you, you were going to say?"

"Only," stretching out her hand (of a perfect shape but decidedly brown) for the book, "that you might give the local fly-tyer a trial, he'll tell you."

"Later on, end of next month, or perhaps later, you might try the oak-fly, the natural fly you know; a horn is the best thing to hold them in, they get out of anything else—and put two on at a time."

"By Jove, I must try that dodge!"

He watches her as she handles his book and examines the contents critically, turning aside some with a glance, fingering others almost tenderly, holding them daintily and noting the cock of wings and the hint of tinsel, with her head on one side; a trick of hers he thinks.

"Which do you like most, wet or dry fly?" (she is looking at some dry flies.)

"Oh," with that rare smile, "at the time I swear by whichever happens to catch most fish. Perhaps, really, dry fly. I fancy most of these flies are better for Scotland or England. Up to this March-brown has been the most killing thing. But you might try an 'orange-grouse,' that's always good here; with perhaps a 'hare's ear' for a change—and put on a 'coachman' for the evenings. My husband (he steals a side look at her) brought home some beauties yesterday evening."

"Lucky fellow!"

She returns the book. There is a tone in his voice as he says this that jars on her, sensitive as she is to every inflection of a voice, with an intuition that is almost second sight. She gathers up her shawl. She has a cream-coloured woollen gown on, and her skin looks duskily foreign by contrast. She is on her feet before he can regain his, and says, with a cool little bend of her head: "Good afternoon, I wish you a full basket!"

Before he can raise his cap she is down the slope, gliding with easy steps that have a strange grace, and then springing lightly from stone to stone across the stream. He feels small, snubbed someway, and he sits down on the spot where she sat and, lighting his pipe, says "check!"

🌸 🌸 🌸

She is walking slowly up the garden path. A man in his shirt sleeves is stooping amongst the tender young peas. A bundle of stakes lies next him, and he whistles softly and all out of tune as he twines the little tendrils round each new support. She looks at his broad shoulders and narrow flanks; his back is too long for great strength, she thinks. He hears her step, and smiles up at her from under the shadow of his broad-leafed hat.

"How do you feel now, old woman?"

"Beastly. I've got that horrid qualmish feeling again. I can't get rid of it."

He has spread his coat on the side of the path and pats it for her to sit down.

"What is it" (anxiously)? "if you were a mare I'd know what to do for you. Have a nip of whisky?"

He strides off without waiting for her reply and comes back with it and a biscuit, kneels down and holds the glass to her lips.

"Poor little woman, buck up! You'll see that'll fix you. Then you go by-and-by and have a shy at the fish."

She is about to say something when a fresh qualm attacks her and she does not.

He goes back to his tying.

"By Jove!" he says suddenly, "I forgot. Got something to show you!"

After a few minutes he returns carrying a basket covered with a piece of sacking. A dishevelled-looking hen, with spread wings trailing and her breast bare from sitting on her eggs, screeches after him. He puts it carefully down and uncovers it, disclosing seven little balls of yellow fluff splashed with olive green. They look up sideways with bright round eyes, and their little spoon bills look disproportionately large.

"Aren't they beauties (enthusiastically)? This one is just out," taking up an egg, "mustn't let it get chilled." There is a chip out of it and a piece of hanging skin. "Isn't it funny?" he asks, showing her how it is curled in the shell, with its paddles flattened and its bill breaking through the chip, and the slimy feathers sticking to its violet skin.

She suppresses an exclamation of disgust, and looks at his fresh-tinted skin instead. He is covering basket, hen, and all—

"How you love young things!" she says.

"Some. I had a filly once, she turned out a lovely mare! I cried when I had to sell her, I wouldn't have let any one in God's world mount her."

"Yes, you would!"

"Who?" with a quick look of resentment.

"Me!"

"I wouldn't!"

"What! you wouldn't?"

"I wouldn't!"

"I think you would if I wanted to!" with a flash out of the tail of her eye.

"No, I wouldn't!"

"Then you would care more for her than for me. I would give you your choice (passionately), her or me!"

"What nonsense!"

"May be (concentrated), but it's lucky she isn't here to make deadly sense of it." A humble-bee buzzes close to her ear, and she is roused to a sense of facts, and laughs to think how nearly they have quarrelled over a mare that was sold before she knew him.

🐝 🐝 🐝

Some evenings later, she is stretched motionless in a chair, and yet she conveys an impression of restlessness; a sensitively nervous person would feel it. She is gazing at her husband, her brows are drawn together, and make three little lines. He is reading, reading quietly, without moving his eyes quickly from side to side of the page as she does when she reads, and he pulls away at the big pipe with steady enjoyment. Her eyes turn from him to the window, and follow the course of two clouds, then they close for a few seconds, then open to watch him again. He looks up and smiles.

"Finished your book?"

There is a singular soft monotony in his voice; the organ with which she replies is capable of more varied expression.

"Yes, it is a book makes one think. It would be a greater book if he were not an Englishman. He's afraid of shocking the big middle class. You wouldn't care about it."

"Finished your smoke?"

"No, it went out, too much fag to light up again! No (protestingly), never you mind, old boy, why do you?"

He has drawn his long length out of his chair, and, kneeling down beside her, guards a lighted match from the incoming evening air. She draws in the smoke contentedly, and her eyes smile back with a general vague tenderness.

"Thank you, dear old man!"

"Going out again?" negative head shake.

"Back aching?" affirmative nod, accompanied by a steadily aimed puff of smoke, that she has been carefully inhaling, into his eyes.

"Scamp! Have your booties off?"

"Oh, don't you bother, Lizzie will do it!"

He has seized a foot from under the rocker, and, sitting on his heels, holds it on his knee, whilst he unlaces the boot; then he loosens the stocking under her toes, and strokes her foot gently.

"Now, the other!" Then he drops both boots outside the door, and fetching a little pair of slippers, past their first smartness, from the bedroom, puts one on. He examines the left foot; it is a little swollen round the ankle, and he presses his broad fingers gently round it as one sees a man do to a horse with windgalls. Then he pulls the rocker nearer to his chair and rests the slipperless foot on his thigh. He relights his pipe, takes up his book, and rubs softly from ankle to toes as he reads.

She smokes and watches him, diverting herself by imagining him in the hats of different periods. His is a delicate-skinned face with regular features; the eyes are fine, in colour and shape with the luminous clearness of a child's; his pointed beard is soft and curly. She looks at his hand,—a broad strong hand with capable fingers,—the hand of a craftsman, a contradiction to the face with its distinguished delicacy. She holds her own up with a cigarette poised between the first and second fingers, idly pleased with its beauty of form and delicate nervous slightness. One speculation chases the other in her quick brain; odd questions as to race arise; she dives into theories as to the why and wherefore of their distinctive natures, and holds a mental debate in which she takes both sides of the question impartially. He has finished his pipe, laid down his book, and is gazing dreamily, with his eyes darkened by their long lashes, and a look of tender melancholy in their clear depths, into space.

"What are you thinking of?" There is a look of expectation in her quivering nervous little face.

He turns to her, chafing her ankle again.

"I was wondering if lob-worms would do for—"

He stops. A strange look of disappointment flits across her face and is lost in an hysterical peal of laughter.

"You are the best emotional check I ever knew," she gasps.

He stares at her in utter bewilderment, and then a slow smile creeps to his eyes and curves the thin lips under his moustache, a smile at her.

"You seem amused, Gipsy!"

She springs out of her chair and seizes book and pipe; he follows the latter anxiously with his eyes until he sees it laid safely on the table. Then she perches herself, resting her knees against one of his legs, whilst she hooks her feet back under the other—

"Now I am all up, don't I look small?"

He smiles his slow smile. "Yes, I believe you are made of gutta percha."

She is stroking out all the lines in his face with the tip of her finger; then she runs it through his hair. He twists his head half impatiently, she desists.

"I divide all the people in the world," she says, "into those who like their hair played with, and those who don't. Having my hair brushed gives me more pleasure than anything else; it's delicious. I'd *purr* if I knew how. I notice (meditatively) I am never in sympathy with those who don't like it; I am with those who do. I always get on with them."

"You are a queer little devil!"

"Am I? I shouldn't have thought you would have found out I was the latter at all. I wish I were a man! I believe if I were a man, I'd be a disgrace to my family."

"Why?"

"I'd go on a jolly old spree!"

He laughs: "Poor little woman, is it so dull?"

There is a gleam of devilry in her eyes, and she whispers solemnly—

"Begin with a D," and she traces imaginary letters across his forehead, and ending with a flick over his ear, says, "and that is the tail of the y!"

After a short silence she queries—

"Are you fond of me?" She is rubbing her chin up and down his face.

"Of course I am, don't you know it?"

"Yes, perhaps I do," impatiently; "but I want to be told it. A woman doesn't care a fig for a love as deep as the death-sea and as silent, she wants something that tells her it in little waves all the time. It isn't the love, you know, it's the being loved; it isn't really the man, it's his loving!"

"By Jove, you're a rum un!"

"I wish I wasn't then. I wish I was as commonplace as—. You don't tell me anything about myself (a fierce little kiss), you might, even if it were lies. Other men who cared for me told me things about my eyes, my hands, anything. I don't believe you notice."

"Yes I *do*, little one, only I think it."

"Yes, but I don't care a bit for your thinking; if I can't see what's in your head what good is it to me?"

"I wish I could understand you, dear!"

"I wish to God you could. Perhaps if you were badder and I were gooder we'd meet half-way. You are an awfully good old chap; it's just men like you send women like me to the devil!"

"But you are good (kissing her), a real good chum! You understand a fellow's weak points. You don't blow him up if he gets on a bit. Why (enthusiastically), being married to you is like chumming with a chap! Why (admiringly), do you remember before we were married, when I let that card fall out of my pocket? Why, I couldn't have told another girl about her. She wouldn't have believed that I *was* straight. She'd have thrown me over. And you sent her a quid because she was sick. You are a great little woman!"

"Don't see it! (she is biting his ear). Perhaps I was a man last time, and some hereditary memories are cropping up in this incarnation!"

He looks so utterly at sea that she has to laugh again, and, kneeling up, shuts his eyes with kisses, and bites his chin and shakes it like a terrier in her strong little teeth.

"You imp! was there ever such a woman!"

Catching her wrists, he parts his knees and drops her on to the rug. Then, perhaps the subtle magnetism that is in her affects him, for he stoops and snatches her up and carries her up and down, and then over to the window and lets the fading light with its glimmer of moonshine play on her odd face with its tantalising changes. His eyes dilate and his colour deepens as he crushes her soft little body to him and carries her off to her room.

✻ ✻ ✻

Summer is waning and the harvest is ripe for ingathering, and the voice of the reaping machine is loud in the land. She is stretched on her back on the short heather-mixed moss at the side of a bog stream. Rod and creel are flung aside, and the wanton breeze, with the breath of coolness it has gathered in its passage over the murky dykes of black bog water, is playing with the tail fly, tossing it to and fro with a half threat to fasten it to a prick-ly spine of golden gorse. Bunches of bog-wool nod their fluffy heads, and through the myriad indefinite sounds comes the regular scrape of a strick-le on the scythe of a reaper in a neighbouring meadow. Overhead a flotil-la of clouds is steering from the south in a north-easterly direction. Her eyes follow them. Old time galleons, she thinks, and with their wealth of snowy sail spread, riding breast to breast up a wide blue fjord after victory. The sails of the last are rose flushed, with a silver edge. Somehow she thinks of Cleopatra sailing down to meet Antony, and a great longing fills her soul to sail off somewhere too—away from the daily need of dinner-getting and the recurring Monday with its washing; life with its tame duties and virtuous monotony. She fancies herself in Arabia on the back of a swift steed. Flashing eyes set in dark faces surround her, and she can see the clouds of sand swirl, and feel the swing under her of his rushing stride. Her thoughts shape themselves into a wild song, a song to her steed of flowing mane and satin skin; an uncouth rhythmical jingle with a feverish beat; a song to the untamed spirit that dwells in her. Then she fancies she is on the stage of an ancient theatre out in the open air, with hundreds of faces upturned towards her. She is gauze-clad in a cobweb garment of wondrous tissue. Her arms are clasped by jewelled snakes, and one with quivering dia-mond fangs coils round her hips. Her hair floats loosely, and her feet are sandal-clad, and the delicate breath of vines and the salt freshness of an incoming sea seems to fill her nostrils. She bounds forward and dances, bends her lissom waist, and curves her slender arms, and gives to the soul of each man what he craves, be it good or evil. And she can feel now, lying here in the shade of Irish hills with her head resting on her scarlet shawl and her eyes closed, the grand intoxicating power of swaying all these human souls to wonder and applause. She can see herself with parted lips and panting, rounded breasts, and a dancing devil in each glowing eye, sway voluptuously to the wild music that rises, now slow, now fast, now deliriously wild, seductive, intoxicating, with a human note of passion in its strain. She can feel the answering shiver of feeling that quivers up to her from the dense audience, spellbound by the motion of her glancing feet, and she flies swifter and swifter, and lighter and lighter, till the very ser-pents seem alive with jewelled scintillations. One quivering, gleaming, dar-ing bound, and she stands with outstretched arms and passion-filled eyes, poised on one slender foot, asking a supreme note to finish her dream of motion. And the men rise to a man and answer her, and cheer, cheer till the echoes shout from the surrounding hills and tumble wildly down the crags. The clouds have sailed away, leaving long feathery streaks in their wake. Her eyes have an inseeing look, and she is tremulous with excite-ment. She can hear yet that last grand shout, and the strain of that old-time music that she has never heard in this life of hers, save as an inner accompaniment to the memory of hidden things, born with her, not of this time.

And her thoughts go to other women she has known, women good and bad, school friends, casual acquaintances, women workers—joyless machines for grinding daily corn, unwilling maids grown old in the endeavour to get settled, patient wives who bear little ones to indifferent husbands until they wear out—a long array. She busies herself with questioning. Have they, too, this thirst for excitement, for change, this restless craving for sun and love and motion? Stray words, half confidences, glimpses through soul-chinks of suppressed fires, actual outbreaks, domestic catastrophes, how the ghosts dance in the cells of her memory! And she laughs, laughs softly to herself because the denseness of man, his chivalrous conservative devotion to the female idea he has created blinds him, perhaps happily, to the problems of her complex nature. Ay, she mutters musingly, the wisest of them can only say we are enigmas. Each one of them sets about solving the riddle of the *ewig weibliche*—and well it is that the workings of our hearts are closed to them, that we are cunning enough or *great* enough to seem to be what they would have us, rather than be what we are. But few of them have had the insight to find out the key to our seeming contradictions. The why a refined, physically fragile woman will mate with a brute, a mere male animal with primitive passions—and love him—the why strength and beauty appeal more often than the more subtly fine qualities of mind or heart—the why women (and not the innocent ones) will condone sins that men find hard to forgive in their fellows. They have all overlooked the eternal wildness, the untamed primitive savage temperament that lurks in the mildest, best woman. Deep in through ages of convention this primeval trait burns, an untamed quantity that may be concealed but is never eradicated by culture—the keynote of woman's witchcraft and woman's strength. But it is there, sure enough, and each woman is conscious of it in her truth-telling hours of quiet self-scrutiny—and each woman in God's wide world will deny it, and each woman will help another to conceal it—for the woman who tells the truth and is not a liar about these things is untrue to her sex and abhorrent to man, for he has fashioned a model on imaginary lines, and he has said, "so I would have you," and every woman is an unconscious liar, for so man loves her. And when a Strindberg or a Nietzsche arises and peers into the recesses of her nature and dissects her ruthlessly, the men shriek out louder than the women, because the truth is at all times unpalatable, and the gods they have set up are dear to them...

"Dreaming, or speering into futurity? You have the look of a seer. I believe you are half a witch!"

And he drops his grey-clad figure on the turf. He has dropped his drawl long ago, in midsummer.

"Is not every woman that? Let us hope I'm, for my friends, a white one."

"A-ah! Have you many friends?"

"That is a query! If you mean many correspondents, many persons who send me Christmas cards, or remember my birthday, or figure in my address-book? No."

"Well, grant I don't mean that!"

"Well, perhaps, yes. Scattered over the world, if my death were belled out, many women would give me a tear, and some a prayer. And many men would turn back a page in their memory and give me a kind thought, perhaps a regret, and go back to their work with a feeling of having lost something—that they never possessed. I am a creature of moments. Women have told me that I came into their lives just when they needed me. Men had no need to tell me, I felt it. People have needed me more than I them. I have given freely whatever they craved from me in the way of understanding or love. I have touched sore places they showed me and healed them, but they never got at me. I have been for myself, and helped myself, and borne the burden of my own mistakes. Some have chafed at my self-sufficiency and have called me fickle—not understanding that they gave me nothing, and that when I had served them, their moment was ended, and I was to pass on. I read people easily, I am written in black letter to most—"

"To your husband!"

"He (quickly)—we will not speak of him; it is not loyal."

"Do not I understand you a little?"

"You do not misunderstand me."

"That is something."

"It is much!"

"Is it? (searching her face). It is not one grain of sand in the desert that stretches between you and me, and you are as impenetrable as a sphinx at the end of it. This (passionately) is my moment, and what have you given me?"

"Perhaps less than other men I have known; but you want less. You are a little like me, you can stand alone. And yet (her voice is shaking), have I given you nothing?"

He laughs, and she winces—and they sit silent, and they both feel as if the earth between them is laid with infinitesimal electric threads vibrating with a common pain. Her eyes are filled with tears that burn but don't fall, and she can see his somehow through her closed lids, see their cool greyness troubled by sudden fire, and she rolls her handkerchief into a moist cambric ball between her cold palms.

"You have given me something—something to carry away with me—an infernal want. You ought to be satisfied. I am infernally miserable."

"You (nearer) have the most tantalising mouth in the world when your lips tremble like that. I...What! can you cry? You?"

"Yes, even I can cry!"

"You dear woman! (pause) And I can't help you!"

"You can't help me. No man can. Don't think it is because you are you I cry, but because you probe a little nearer into the real me that I feel so."

"Was it necessary to say that? (reproachfully). Do you think I don't know it? I can't for the life of me think how you, with that free gipsy nature of yours, could bind yourself to a monotonous country life, with no excitement, no change. I wish I could offer you my yacht. Do you like the sea?"

"I love it, it answers one's moods."

"Well, let us play pretending, as the children say. Grant that I could, I would hang your cabin with your own colours; fill it with books, all those I have heard you say you care for; make it a nest as rare as the bird it would shelter. You would reign supreme; when your highness would deign to honour her servant I would come and humour your every whim. If you were glad, you could clap your hands and order music, and we would dance on the white deck, and we would skim through the sunshine of Southern seas on a spice-scented breeze. You make me poetical. And if you were angry you could vent your feelings on me, and I would give in and bow my head to your mood. And we would drop anchor and stroll through strange cities, go far inland and glean folklore out of the beaten track of everyday tourists. And at night when the harbour slept we would sail out through the moonlight over silver seas. You are smiling, you look so different when you smile; do you like my picture?"

"Some of it!"

"What not?"

"You!"

"Thank you."

"You asked me. Can't you understand where the spell lies? It is the freedom, the freshness, the vague danger, the unknown that has a witchery for me, ay, for every woman!"

"Are you incapable of affection, then?"

"Of course not, I share" (bitterly) "that crowning disability of my sex. But not willingly, I chafe under it. My God, if it were not for that, we women would master the world. I tell you men would be no match for us. At heart we care nothing for laws, nothing for systems. All your elaborately reasoned codes for controlling morals or man do not weigh a jot with us against an impulse, an instinct. We learn those things from you, you tamed, amenable animals; they are not natural to us. It is a wise disposition of providence that this untameableness of ours is corrected by our affections. We forge our own chains in a moment of softness, and then" (bitterly) "we may as well wear them with a good grace. Perhaps many of our seeming contradictions are only the outward evidences of inward chafing. Bah! the qualities that go to make a Napoleon—superstition, want of honour, disregard of opinion and the eternal I—are oftener to be found in a woman than a man. Lucky for the world perhaps that all these attributes weigh as nothing in the balance with the need to love if she be a good woman, to be loved if she is of a coarser fibre."

"I never met any one like you, you are a strange woman!"

"No, I am merely a truthful one. Women talk to me—why, I can't say—but always they come, strip their hearts and souls naked, and let me see the hidden folds of their natures. The greatest tragedies I have ever read are child's play to those I have seen acted in the inner life of outwardly commonplace women. A woman must beware of speaking the truth to a man; he loves her the less for it. It is the elusive spirit in her that he divines but cannot seize, that fascinates and keeps him."

There is a long silence, the sun is waning and the scythes are silent, and overhead the crows are circling, a croaking irregular army, homeward bound from a long day's pillage.

She has made no sign, yet so subtly is the air charged with her that he feels but a few moments remain to him. He goes over and kneels beside her and fixes his eyes on her odd dark face. They both tremble, yet neither speaks. His breath is coming quickly, and the bistre stains about her eyes seem to have deepened, perhaps by contrast as she has paled.

"Look at me!"

She turns her head right round and gazes straight into his face. A few drops of sweat glisten on his forehead.

"You witch woman! What am I to do with myself? Is my moment ended?"

"I think so."

"Lord, what a mouth!"

"Don't, oh don't!"

"No, I won't. But do you mean it? Am I, who understand your every mood, your restless spirit, to vanish out of your life? You can't mean it. Listen; are you listening to me? I can't see your face; take down your hands. Go back over every chance meeting you and I have had together since I met you first by the river, and judge them fairly. To-day is Monday; Wednesday afternoon I shall pass your gate, and if—if my moment is ended, and you mean to send me away, to let me go with this weary aching..."

"A-ah!" she stretches out one brown hand appealingly, but he does not touch it.

"Hang something white on the lilac bush!"

She gathers up creel and rod, and he takes her shawl, and, wrapping it round her, holds her a moment in it, and looks searchingly into her eyes, then stands back and raises his hat, and she glides away through the reedy grass.

❋ ❋ ❋

Wednesday morning she lies watching the clouds sail by. A late rose spray nods into the open window, and the petals fall every time. A big bee buzzes in and fills the room with his bass note, and then dances out again. She can hear his footstep on the gravel. Presently he looks in over the half window.

"Get up and come out, 'twill do you good. Have a brisk walk!"

She shakes her head languidly, and he throws a great soft dewy rose with sure aim on her breast.

"Shall I go in and lift you out and put you, 'nighty' and all, into your tub?"

"No (impatiently). I'll get up just now."

The head disappears, and she rises wearily and gets through her dressing slowly, stopped every moment by the feeling of faintness. He finds her presently rocking slowly to and fro with closed eyes, and drops a leaf with three plums in it on to her lap.

"I have been watching four for the last week, but a bird, greedy beggar, got one this morning early—try them. Don't you mind, old girl, I'll pour out my own tea!"

She bites into one and tries to finish it, but cannot.

"You are a good old man!" she says, and the tears come unbidden to her eyes, and trickle down her cheeks, dropping on to the plums, streaking their delicate bloom. He looks uneasily at her, but doesn't know what to do, and when he has finished his breakfast he stoops over her chair and strokes her hair, saying, as he leaves a kiss on the top of her head—

"Come out into the air, little woman; do you a world of good!" And presently she hears the sharp thrust of his spade above the bee's hum, leaf rustle, and the myriad late summer sounds that thrill through the air. It irritates her almost to screaming point. There is a practical non-sympathy about it, she can distinguish the regular one, two, three, the thrust, interval, then pat, pat, on the upturned sod. To-day she wants some one, and her thoughts wander to the grey-eyed man who never misunderstands her, and she wonders what he would say to her. Oh, she wants some one so badly to soothe her. And she yearns for the little mother who is twenty years under the daisies. The little mother who is a faint memory strengthened by a daguerreotype in which she sits with silk-mittened hands primly crossed on the lap of her moiré gown, a diamond brooch fastening the black velvet ribbon crossed so stiffly over her lace collar, the shining tender eyes looking steadily out, and her hair in the fashion of fifty-six. How that spade dominates over every sound! And what a sickening pain she has; an odd pain, she never felt it before. Supposing she were to die, she tries to fancy how she would look. They would be sure to plaster her curls down. He might be digging her grave—no, it is the patch where the early peas grew; the peas that were eaten with the twelve weeks' ducklings; she remembers them, little fluffy golden balls with waxen bills, and such dainty paddles. Remembers holding an egg to her ear and listening to it cheep inside before even there was a chip in the shell. Strange how things come to life. What! she sits bolt upright and holds tightly to the chair, and a questioning, awesome look comes over her face. Then the quick blood creeps up through her olive skin right up to her temples, and she buries her face in her hands and sits so a long time.

The maid comes in and watches her curiously, and moves softly about. The look in her eyes is the look of a faithful dog, and she loves her with the same rare fidelity. She hesitates, then goes into the bedroom and stands thoughtfully, with her hands clasped over her breast.

She is a tall, thin, flat-waisted woman, with misty blue eyes and a receding chin. Her hair is pretty.

She turns as her mistress comes in, with an expectant look on her face. She has taken up a night-gown, but holds it idly.

"Lizzie, had you ever a child?"

The girl's long left hand is ringless, yet she asks it with a quiet insistence as if she knew what the answer would be, and the odd eyes read her face with an almost cruel steadiness. The girl flushes painfully and then whitens, her very eyes seem to pale, and her under lip twitches as she jerks out huskily—

"Yes!"

"What happened it?"

"It died, Ma'm."

"Poor thing! Poor old Liz!"

She pats the girl's hand softly, and the latter stands dumbly and looks down at both hands, as if fearful to break the wonder of a caress. She whispers hesitatingly—

"Have you, have you any little things left?"

And she laughs such a soft, cooing little laugh, like the churring of a ring-dove, and nods shyly back in reply to the tall maid's questioning look. The latter goes out, and comes back with a flat, red-painted deal box and unlocks it. It does not hold very much, and the tiny garments are not of costly material, but the two women pore over them as a gem collector over a rare stone. She has a glimpse of thick crested paper as the girl unties a packet of letters, and looks away until she says tenderly—

"Look, Ma'm!"

A little bit of hair inside a paper heart. It is almost white, so silky, and so fine, that it is more like a thread of bog wool than a baby's hair. And the mistress, who is a wife, puts her arms round the tall maid, who has never had more than a moral claim to the name, and kisses her in her quick way.

The afternoon is drawing on; she is kneeling before an open trunk with flushed cheeks and sparkling eyes. A heap of unused, dainty lace trimmed ribbon-decked cambric garments is scattered around her. She holds the soft scented web to her cheek and smiles musingly. Then she rouses herself and sets to work, sorting out the finest, with the narrowest lace and tiniest ribbon, and puckers her swarthy brows, and measures lengths along her middle finger. Then she gets slowly up, as if careful of herself as a precious thing, and half afraid.

"Lizzie!"

"Yes, Ma'm!"

"Wasn't it lucky they were too fine for every day? They will be so pretty. Look at this one with the tiny valenciennes edging. Why, one nightgown will make a dozen little shirts—such elfin-shirts as they are too—and Lizzie!"

"Yes, Ma'm!"

"Just hang it out on the lilac bush; mind, the lilac bush!"

"Yes, Ma'm."

"Or Lizzie, wait—I'll do it myself!"

Now Spring Has Come

[*Keynotes.* London: Elkin Mathews & John Lane, 1893]

A Confidence

"When the spring time comes, gentle Annie, and the flowers are blossoming on the plain!
Lal, lal, la, la, la, lallallalla, lal, lal, lal, la, la, la, la, la,
When the spring time comes, gentle Annie, and the mockin' bird is singing on the tree!"...

"I don't believe that mocking-bird line belongs to the song at all, Lizzie, you never do get a thing right!"

The words have a partly irritated, partly contemptuous tone that seems oddly at variance with the size of the child who utters them. She is lying flat on her stomach on the floor, resting her elbows at each side of a book she is reading, holding her sharp chin in the palms of her hands, waving her skinny legs in unconscious time to the half tired, half feverish lilt of the nurse as she jogs the baby in time to the tune. She gazes, as she speaks, at the girl with a pair of unusually bright penetrating eyes. This mocking-bird line never fails to annoy her.

"Troth, an if I cud get the young limb to slape I wouldn't care if 'twas mockin'-birds or tom-cats!" is the indifferent answer.

☀ ☀ ☀

Strange how some trivial thing will jog a link in a chain of association, and set it vibrating until it brings one face to face with scenes and people long forgotten in some prison cell in one's brain; calling to new life a red-haired girl, with sherry-brown eyes, and a flat back, pacing a nursery floor in impatient endeavour to get a fractious child to sleep—ay, her very voice and her persistent mixing of mocking-birds and spring time. So muses the child twenty years after, as, past her first youth, with only the eyes and the smile unchanged, she lies on a bear-skin before the fire on a chilly evening in late spring, and goes over a recent experience. A half humorous smile with a tinge of mockery in it plays round her lips as she says—

"Twenty years ago. Queer how it should fit in after all that time!"

✻ ✻ ✻

"Tell you how it was? That is not very easy, pathos may become bathos in the telling. Let me see. Of course it was chance, or is there any such thing as chance? Say fate, instead. The three old ladies who spin our destinies were in want of amusement, so they pitched on me. They sent their messenger to me in the guise of a paper-backed novel with a taking name. I was waiting in a shop for some papers I had ordered when it struck me. I took it up. The author was unknown to me. I opened it at haphazard and a line caught me. I read on. I was roused by the bookseller's suave voice.

"That is a very bad book, Madam. One of the modern realistic school, a *tendenz roman*, I would not advise Madam to read it!"

"A-ah, indeed!"

I laid it down and left the shop, but the words I had read kept dancing before me, I saw them written across the blue of the sky, in the sun streaks on the pavement, and the luminous delicacy of the Norwegian summer nights. They were impressed on my brain in vivid colour, glowing, blushing with ardour as they were. Weeks passed; one afternoon time hung heavily on my hands, and I sent for the book. I read all that afternoon; let the telling words, the passionate pain, the hungry yearning, all the tragedy of a man's soul-strife with evil and destiny, sorrow and sin, bite into my sentient being. When the book was finished I was consumed with a desire to see and know the author. I never reasoned that the whole struggle might only be an extraordinarily clever intuitive analysis of a possible experience. I accepted it as real, and I wanted to help this man. I longed to tell him in his loneness, that one human being, and that one a woman, had courage to help him. The abstract ego of the novel haunted me. I have a will of my own, so I set to work to find him. It was not so easy. None of my acquaintances knew him, or of him. He was a strange meteor, and as the book was condemned by the orthodox I had to feel my way cautiously. Isn't it dreadful to think what slaves we are to custom? I wonder shall we ever be able to tell the truth, ever be able to live fearlessly according to our own light, to believe that what is right for us must be right? It seems as if all the religions, all the advancement, all the culture of the past, has only been a forging of chains to cripple posterity, a laborious building up of moral and legal prisons based on false conceptions of sin and shame, to cramp men's minds and hearts and souls, not to speak of women's. What half creatures we are, we women! Hermaphrodite by force of circumstances.

Deformed results of a fight of centuries between physical suppression and natural impulse to fulfil our destiny. Every social revolution has told hardest on us: when a sacrifice was demanded, let woman make it. And yet there are men, and the best of them, who see all this and would effect a change, if they knew how. Why it came about? Because men manufactured an artificial morality, made sins of things that were as clean in themselves as the pairing of birds on the wing; crushed nature, robbed it of its beauty and meaning, and established a system that means war, and always war, because it is a struggle between instinctive truths and cultivated lies. Yes, I know I speak hotly, but my heart burns in me sometimes, and I hate myself. It's a bad thing when a man or woman has a contempt for himself. There's nothing like a good dose of love fever (in other words, a waking to the fact that one is a higher animal with a destiny to fulfil) to teach one self-knowledge, to give one a glimpse into the contradictory issues of one's individual nature. Study yourself, and what will you find? Just what I did; the weak, the inconsequent, the irresponsible. In one word, the untrue feminine is of man's making, whilst the strong, the natural, the true womanly is of God's making. It is easy to read as a primer; but how change it? Go back to my poet! Well, at length an old bookseller I knew gave me surer information. My intuition was not at fault, the experiences were wrung from the man's soul. As the old superstition has it, a dagger dipped in a man's heart-blood will always strike home, so no wonder they pierced me with their passion, despair, and brave endurance. What the old fellow wrote to him I know not, but I got an unconventional pretty letter from him, and it ended in our writing to one another.

As my time to leave drew near, the desire to see him became overpowering. I could afford it; he could not. It ended in our arranging to meet at a little town on the coast. It is strange how the idea of a person one has never seen can possess one as completely as this did me. I, who, as you know, think as little of starting alone for say, Mexico, as another woman of going to afternoon tea, who have trotted the globe without male assistance, felt as tremulously stirred as at confirmation day. There are days that stand out in the gallery of one's remembrances clean painted as a Van de Hooge, with a sharp clearness. I slept on board, and early the next morning, it was Sunday, I stood on deck watching the coast as we glided through the water that danced in delicious September sunshine. I was happily expectant. At dinner hour we passed a fjord, a lovely deep blue fjord winding to our right as we passed, with the spire of a church just visible amongst the fir trees round the bend. Boats of all kinds, from a smart cutter to a pram were coming out after the service. The white sails swelled as they caught the breeze, flapped as they tacked, hung listlessly a second, and then dashed with a swerve, like swift snowy-winged birds, through the water. I had not troubled with church-going of late years. Why? oh, speculation—weariness of soul that found no drop of consolation in religious observance, maybe that might be the reason. But all those honest simple folks in their Sunday bravery, fair-haired girls with their psalm-books wrapped up in their only silk kerchief, the ring of laughter echoing across the water, the magic of sun and sky, mountain and fjord, made me feel that I, too, was church-going, and I felt strangely happy. It is the off-moments that we do not count as playing any part in our lives that are, after all, the best we have. I am afraid it would be impossible to make you see things as I felt them. I went up to the hotel when I landed; I had the reputation of riches, the hotel was at my service. I inquire for him, go down to my sitting-room, send him my card, and wait. I wait with an odd feeling that I am outside myself, watching myself as it were. I can see the very childishness of my figure, the too slight hips and bust, the flash of rings on my fingers; they are pressed against my heart, for it is beating hatefully; ay, the very expectant side-poise of head is visible to me somehow. It flashes across me as I stand that so might a slave wait for the coming of a new master, and I laugh at myself for my want-wit agitation. A knock... "Come in!"...The door opens, and I am satisfied. In the space of a second's gaze I meet what my soul has been waiting for,—ah, how long? I think always: Have I lived before in some other life, that no surprise touches me? That it is just as if I am only meeting the embodiment of a disintegrated floating image that has often flashed before my consciousness, and flown before I could fix it? Has this man or some psychical part of this man been in touch with me before, or how is it? I stand still and stretch out my hand. I check an impulse to put out both. I feel so tremulously happy. I know before he speaks how his voice will sound, what his touch will be like before he clasps my hand. It is odd how the most important crisis of our lives often comes upon us in the most commonplace way. It is the fashion to decry love, yet the vehemence of the denials, the keenness of the weapons of satire and scepticism that are turned against it, only prove its existence. As long as man is man and woman is woman, it will be to them at some time the sweetest, and possibly the most fatal interest in life. Thrust it aside for ambition or gain, slight it as you will, sooner or later it will have its revenge. I had felt no breath of it as maid, wife, or widow, my heart had been a free, wild, shy thing, jessed by my will. Sometimes, by way of experiment, I let it fly to some one for an hour, but always to call it back again to my own safe keeping. Now it left me. We sat and talked, rather I talked, I think, and he listened. He said my going to see him even on literary grounds was eccentric, but then it seemed I had a way of doing as I pleased without exciting much comment. How did he know that? Oh, he had heard it! Was I really going away? How tiresome it was, really awfully tiresome! What was he like? Well, an American bison or a lion. You might put his head amongst the rarest and handsomest heads in the world. Prejudiced in his favour! No, not a bit. His hands, for instance, are great labourer's hands, freckled too; I don't like his gait either, indeed a dozen things. What we talked about? well, as I said, he listened mostly, laughed

with a great joyous boyish laugh with a deep musical note in it. He has a deferential manner and a very caressing smile; a trick, too, of throwing back his
head and tossing his crest of hair. Why he laughed? well, I suppose I made
him. I told him all about myself, turned myself inside out, good and bad
alike, as one might the pocket of an old gown, laughed at my own expense,
hid nothing. An extraordinary thing to do, was it? I suppose it was—but the
whole thing was rather unusual. He got up and walked about. Sometimes he
thrust his hands in his pockets and exclaimed "The Deuce," etc. I fancy he
learnt a good deal about me in a few hours. You see it was not as if one were
talking to a stranger, it was as if one had met part of one's self one had lost
for a long time and was filling up the gaps made during the absence. You
can't understand. I think we were both very happy. He admired—no, that is
not the word—he was taken with me, that is better. He said my hands were
"as small as a child's," the tablecloth was dark red plush that made a good
background. He pointed timidly, as a great shy boy might, to one of my
rings. You see they don't as a rule wear many rings up there. I suppose they
gave an impression of wealth. "That one is very beautiful!" I laughed, I was
so glad my hands were pretty; pretty hands last so much longer than a pretty face. I laughed too at his finger, it had such a deferential expression about
it, and I called him a great child. I think we were both like two great children, we had found a common interest to rejoice in—we had found ourselves. Every moment was delightful, we were making discoveries, finding we
had had like experiences, had both hungered, both known want, were both
of an age. We were both unconventional, and were shaking hands mentally
all the time. I don't remember now what it was he said, but I remember I
was obliged to drop my head, and I felt I was smiling from sheer delicious
pleasure. He cried laughingly: "You say I am a great child, you are a child
yourself when you smile!" He was to have supper with me, and he went away
for an hour. After he left I walked over to a long mirror and looked at
myself. Tried to fancy how *he* saw me; that might be different, you know. I
had colour, life, eyes like stars, trembling, smiling lips. There was something
quivering, alert about me. I scarce knew myself. Of course the same hips, figure, features were reflected there—it was something shining through that
struck me as foreign. Do you know what I did? I danced all round the room.
Shows what an idiot an old woman can be. By the way, he denied that I was
old. I was like a little girl—but a remarkable little girl. No wonder people
always noticed me, as if I were a somebody. How did he know that? oh, he
had heard it, for that matter seen it too, at the pier. He knew the moment I
stepped off the boat that it was I. Yes, people always stared at me, but how
could he know? Ah! presentiment perhaps. So he was on the pier? why did
he not come and meet me? No audible answer, but a slow reddening up to
the roots of his fair hair. I do not know quite how he conveyed it, but I had
the sensation, a charming one, of being treated as a queen. But to go back.

I sat or rather lay in an arm-chair at the window and watched the water and the ships. It was getting dusk, the luminous dusk of the north, as if a soft transparent purple veil is being dropped gently over the world. The fjord was full of lights from the different crafts at anchor, and the heaven full of stars, and the longer one looked up there, the more one saw myriads of glimmering eyes of light, until one's brain seemed full of their brightness, and one forgot one's body in gazing. Long silvery streaks glistened through the heaving water, like the flash of feeding trout, and lads and lasses in boats rowed to and fro, and human vibration seemed to thrill from them, filling the atmosphere with man and woman. And the silken air caressed my face at the touch of cool soft fingers. I had a feeling of perfect well-being; one does not get many such moments in one's life, does one? I think I just was happy, rehearsing the hours that flew too quickly, recalling every look, tone, gesture, and smile. The *jomfru* came in to lay the table. She knew me from a previous visit and began to talk, but I wanted to be alone with my thoughts. So I went up stairs, washed my hands and puffed them with sweet-smelling powder, and then when I went down again and sat and waited, I clasped them up over my head to make them white. He came back, flung his hat on the sofa out of sheer boyish delight at being back, came over and stood and looked down at me and I laughed up to him. If I were to talk until Dooms-day, I could not make you understand what I cannot yet understand myself. After supper, at which I just sipped my tea and watched him, we sat at the window and looked out at the purple world. I had told him he might smoke... Well? well, we talked, and we talked when we were both silent, and he, I mean his thinking self came to me, and I, well, I believe, from the moment he came into the room, all the best of me went straight to him. The lights out in the harbour twinkled, a star fell, and I wished—well, wishes are foolish. I think he must have been watching my face, for when our eyes met, he smiled as if he understood. Sometimes he jumped up and stood rocking a chair backwards and forwards. He was sorry I was going away! Yes? oh, we might meet again! That might be difficult! Indeed? I should have thought *he* would be the last person in the world to say it was difficult to meet. He laughed at that, with a quick sidelong look he has, like a Finn dog; and said I was sharp, awfully sharp, as if he liked being caught. By the way, he occasionally used strong language, said I must forgive him, he wasn't very used to ladies' society.

At ten I said I would say good-night for conventionality's sake. He begged, humbly it struck me, for a little longer. I was to leave by the steamer at eight in the morning—would be down at seven—he might come to me. Would I give him a portrait of myself? Yes, I would get one specially done. As much in profile as possible, he thought that would be happier.—Yes.—He came to the top of the stairs with me, and when we bade good-night he took my hand and held it curiously as if it were something fearfully fragile, and stood and watched me down the corridor. And will you credit it? I said prayers that night, thanked God—I don't quite know what for—I suppose I did then—perhaps for being happy. I looked at my foreign self in the glass too—and when the light was out...Yes?... I did what you and every other woman might do, I cuddled my face to an imaginary face, rubbed my cheek to an imaginary cheek, whispered a God bless you! and fell asleep.

I was down before seven, paid my bill, and sat waiting, with the little tray, with its thick white cups and lumpy yellow cream before me. He came. Such a glad man, with glad eyes, glad smile, and outstretched hands. And I, I was so glad, too, that I could have shouted out for very joy of living. I might have been drinking some magic elixir instead of coffee.

"It is tiresome!" he said impatiently.

"What is tiresome? You have said that so often."

"It is tiresome when a person one wants so badly to keep in the country is going out of it."

"Supposing I were to stay in it, you would probably be in one place and I in another. It is only a question of a little dearer postage!"

We both laughed at that. It takes such a little thing to make one laugh when one is happy. Then the steamer came in sight, and we walked down through the bright morning to the pier, and went on board. He stood silently. We only looked at one another. It did not then strike me as odd—it does now. The first bell rang! I felt a chill steal over me. "It is tiresome, it is hateful!" His smile had flown; and old deep lines and traces of past suffering I had not noticed before showed plainly....

"I will come back," I said, "when the winter is over!"

"Ah, but winter is long, or it used to be!"

"No matter, I will come with the spring!"

The second bell rang.... Ah, why can't we do as our hearts bid us? We have one short life, and it is spoiled by chains of our own forging, in deference to narrow custom. I shivered. There was after all an autumn chill in the air. I hate the sound of a steamer bell now.... The third bell.... We turn, and I tighten my small fingers in his great hand, and I say good-bye and God bless you! Not from a purely religious conception of God. Unless it be that God, and I think it does, means all that is good and beautiful, tender and best. I might have said "The best I can think of befall you!" A second later and the steamer rail separates us. I look into his soul through his eyes, and see it is sorry, regretful; as sorry as I am glad it is so—he is sorry I am going from him, and in that short concentrated gaze his soul comes to me as I would have it come to me.

"When spring comes!" I whisper as I lean over to him, whilst the steamer glides out. He follows it to the end of the pier, and stands there as long as we are in sight. If he had held out his arms and said: "Woman, stay with me!" I would, I fear, have jumped down and stayed. Didn't know anything about him! No, that is true, only that I had been waiting for something ever since I was old enough to have a want, and that he was that something, that I was nearly thirty when I found him, and…life is short!

I was so glad, in spite of leaving him, that I believe I thought the sun shone differently—I almost asked some people on deck if they did not think that the day was quite the loveliest day that ever dawned since the world was a world; if there was not something peculiarly and singularly delicious in the very air? I found a quiet sofa, and lay with closed eyes and lived it over again.

The rest is more difficult to tell you…. I was insanely happy, then I was intensely miserable. I sent him my portrait and a letter, and counted the days and the hours to a reply. It came. I stole away to read all the warm meaning ill concealed under the words of it. Slept with it under my pillow, carried it in my bosom, and answered it straight from my heart. Why try and tell you of the aftertime? I would not go through that winter again for anything in the world. Hope, fear, suspense, joy, despondency, all the strongest feelings that can torture or wear out a heart, were mine. I longed to be up on a high mountain alone with my dream. I wonder does a man ever realise the beauty there is in a woman's thought of him. What kind were the letters? Warm, passionate, yet with a *reservatio mentalis* that hurt me, but always with a "When spring comes!" in them. It is amazing to what depths of folly a human being can descend. I had his photograph on my table. I greeted it as a Russian peasant his household saint…. It would be hard to find my match in idiocy. I felt a letter coming, and waited with strained ears and fever-racked nerves for the postman's knock. Do you know there is something touchingly pitiful in the way one finds out all the tender bits in a letter and re-reads them. I have kissed a thumb-mark on the paper. Heavens, how the days dragged! I was ill with yearning thought. Night brought no rest but the comfort of being alone. All the years of my life were not as long as that weary winter. Sleep fled, and nervous pain took its place… It was foolish, exceedingly foolish, because it was fatal to my looks. At the rare times I looked at myself I got a glimpse of a thin waxen yellow face with dark ringed eyes, and I was certainly older-looking. Thinking of it all dispassionately, I am inclined to believe I was hysterical. How many of the follies and frailties of women are really due to hysterical rather than moral irresponsibility, is a question. You see there is no time of sowing wild oats for women; we repress, and repress, and then some day we stumble on the man who just satisfies our sexual and emotional nature, and then there is shipwreck of some sort. When we shall live larger and freer lives, we shall be better balanced than we are now. If what I suffered is love, all I can say is I would not ask a better sample of the conventional hell's pain. Hus-sh! Very well, I won't say those things!

It is bad enough to be a fool and not to know it, but to be a fool and feel with every fibre of your being, every shred of our understanding that you are one, and that there is no help for it; that all your philosophy won't aid you;

that you are one great want, stilled a little by a letter, only to be haunted afresh by the personality of another creature tortured with doubts and hurt by your loss of self-respect.... A-ah! it was a long winter! Then the New Year came and went, and time dragged slowly but surely. At length the Almanacs said it was spring-time, and the girls at the street corners called: "vilets, sweet vilets!"; and the milliners marked down guinea bonnets to 12s. 11d., and I watched each token of its coming with a fearsome joyous expectation... "Go on," ah yes, I'll go on, where was I? Oh, Spring was coming, wasn't it? I do not laugh as I used to, eh? How used I laugh? I forget. Well, I won't laugh if it hurts you, dear, not even at myself.

Well, once again, I was standing at a table in a hotel room waiting. It is the simple things that are so hard to describe, and that are most complicated in their effects. I said again "Come in!" held fast to the table with my left hand and smiled—to be accurate, began a smile. Spring is later up there, perhaps some of the winter's frost was still in the atmosphere, for something froze it on my lips. I felt a curious stiffening in my face, and the touch of his hand did not thaw me. Feel happy? No, I was numb in one way and yet keenly alive to impressions. I felt as if my nerve-net was outside my skin, not under it, and that the exposure to the air and surrounding influences made it intensely, acutely sensitive. I seemed to see with my sense of feeling as well as my sight. You know how in great cold you seem to burn your hand with an icy heat if you suddenly grasp a piece of iron; well, I felt as though I was touched by glowing shivers; that sounds nonsense, but it expresses the feeling. Why? I don't know why. I was analysing, being analysed, criticising, being criticised. It was all so different, you see. Supposing you had just sipped a beaker of exhilarating, life-giving, rich wine with an exquisite bouquet, and a glow that steals through you and witches and warms you; and suddenly, without your knowing how it happens, the draught is transformed into lukewarm water, or "Polly" without the "dash" in it. What did he say? Let me think. Oh yes, I was wretchedly thin. Odd how things strike one. I once saw a representation of Holberg's Stundeslöse in Copenhagen. One of the characters is an ancient housekeeper, with a long money-bag, who is, as they term it, "marriage-sick." A match is arranged between her and a young spark in the village. The scene is this:—whilst the monetary part of the affair is being arranged by the notary, etc., he says to her:—"Permit me to pass my hand over your bosom, mistress?" She simpers, and I shall never forget the comical expression of dismay with which the suitor rolls his eyes and drops his jaw as he turns aside. I felt rather than saw the comprehensive look which accompanied his comment on my thinness, and that scene flashed across my inner vision. Odd, was it not? A sort of sympathetic after-comprehension. It was as if I, too, were having a hand passed across the flatness of my figure.

"Yes, I have got thin"—silence—had I been very ill? Yes, very! Was that why I was so pale? It was fearful, not a tinge of warm colour in my face. One would be afraid to touch me. I felt as if I were being totted up. Item, so much colour, item, so much flesh.... Had I been worried? I had lost that buoyant childishness that was so attractive. Ah, yes, I had dwelt too much on a trouble I had. Did I sleep? not much! That was foolish! I ought to eat plenty too. I looked as if I didn't eat enough, my eyes and cheeks were hollowed out. Ah, yes, no doubt I did look older than in Autumn! I was not contradicted. I would have told a little lie to spare a man's feelings. Men are perhaps more conscientious. What else? I am rehearsing it all as best I can. Oh, my hands were altered, he thought they were not so small, eh?... Might be my wrists were less round, that made a difference! Did it? They certainly were larger, and not so white.... Did he kiss me? Oh, yes. You see I wanted to sift this thing thoroughly to get clear into my head what ground I was standing on. So I let him. They were merely lip kisses; his spirit did not come to mine, and I was simply analysing them all the time. Did I not feel anything? Yes, I did, deeply hurt. Ah, I can't say how they hurt me; they lacked everything a kiss, as the expression of the strongest, best feeling of a man and woman, *can* hold. How do I know? My dear woman, have you never dreamt, felt, had *intuitive experiences?* I have. I am not sure that I had not a keen sense of the ludicrous side of the whole affair, that one portion of my soul was not having a laugh at the other's expense. I do not quite know what I had been expecting. 'Tis true he had written me beautiful letters. You see he is too much of a word-artist to write anything else. Treated me badly?... No, I am not prepared to say that he did. I am glad he was too honest to hide his startled realisation of the fact that Autumn and Spring are different seasons, and that one's feelings may undergo a change in a winter. I do not see why I should resent that. Why, it would be punishing him for having cared for me. To put it in his words: "I came as a strangely lovely dream into his life." Probably the whole mistake lay in that. He thought of me as a dream lady with dainty hands, idealised me—and wrote to the dream creature. When I came back in the flesh, he realised that I was a prosaic fact, with less charming hands, a tendency to leanness, and coming crow's feet. His look of dismayed awakening was simply delicious. I wish I could catch and fasten the fleeting images that flit across my memory, you would grasp my mental attitude better. In the midst of all my pain, I was sitting next him, and he was stroking my hand mechanically, I noticed a glass case on the wall containing an Italian landscape with ball-blue sky and pink lakes. Pasteboard figures of Dutch-peasant build, with Zouave jackets, Tyrolese hats, and bandaged legs, figured in the foreground. You wound it up, and the figures danced to a *varsoviana.* I was listening to him, and yet at the same time I caught myself imagining how he and I would look dressed like that, bobbing about to the old-fashioned tune. I could hardly keep from shrieking with laughter. He had a turn-down collar on; he ought always to wear unstarched linen—it and his throat didn't fit. You cannot understand me? Dearest woman, I do not pretend to understand the thing myself.

Did we not talk about anything? Of course we did. Tolstoi and his doctrine of celibacy. Ibsen's Hedda. Strindberg's view of the female animal. And we agreed that Friedrich Nietzche appealed to us immensely. You must make allowances. Here was a man passionately attached to his art. His art that he had been treating churlishly for months, for the sake of a dream. The dream was out, and he feared her revenge. That is the one potent element of consolation for me. If one has made an idiot of one's-self, it is at least self-consoling to have done so for a genius. He chose the better part, if you come to think of it. The man or woman who jeopardises a great talent, be it of writing, painting, or acting for marriage's sake, is bartering a precious birthright for a mess of pottage—mostly indifferent pottage. And even if it were excellent, it is bound to pall, when one has it every day. There never was a marriage yet in which one was not a loser; and it is generally the more gifted half who has to pay the heavier toll... I believe he was intensely sorry for me; I asked him once you know, half playfully, half maliciously, if he had meant something; something deliciously tender which I quoted out of one of his letters. He paled to his lips, closed his eyes for a second, and I saw drops of sweat break out on his forehead. I sprang up and turned aside his answer. I remember when I was a little child I never would pick a flower. I always fancied they felt it and bled to death. I used to sneak behind and gather up all those my playmates threw down on the road or fields, and put them, stalks down, into the water in the ditch or brook—even now I can't wear them. I did not wish to hurt him either, he could not help his passion-flower withering. I suppose it was written that my love should turn, like fairy gold, into withered leaves in my grasp... What, dear? a white hair! oh, I saw several lately. How did it end? Oh, he said that he was going away to glean material for a new book; that he would burn my letters; it was safer and wiser to burn letters. No, I did not ask him, he volunteered it. He asked me, did I not think so? I said Yes. But is it not marvellous how dazzlingly swift our thoughts can travel; like light. Whilst I was saying "yes," one often regretted not having burned letters; receipts, receipts for bills were really the only things of importance to keep. I was thinking and crying inwardly over my letters. Such letters. One only writes once like that, I think. All the perfume of the flowers I ever smelt, all the sun-glints on hill and sea, all the strains of music and light and love I had garnered from the glad fresh young years, when I tossed cowslip balls in the meadows, were crystallised into love-words in those letters of mine. It seemed to me often that the words burnt with a white flame as I wrote them, and I was shy when I saw them written. And he said: "I shall burn them!" much as you might say: "I shall take the trimming off that last summer hat of mine." I did not like to think of his burning them, perhaps with his old washing bills. Do you know, if I had a finger or toe cut off, I wouldn't like them to take it away, I'd like to bury it. A sort of feel, I suppose.... Well, we said good-bye! I felt as if I had a sponge with a lot of holes in it, instead of a heart, and that all the feeling had oozed away through them. He was glad to go, I think; he felt a brute, I daresay, yet how could he help it?

※ ※ ※

Were you ever at the Scandinavian church in the Docks? I went one Sunday after I came back. I like those blue-eyed, seafaring folk; and the priest wears a black gown and stiff ruff like Luther of mixed renown. An apple-tree outside the open door was struggling to open its delicate pink blossoms; each petal had a tinge of soot; it reminded me of the pretty cheeks of a grimy maid-of-all-work. I sat still. A sunbeam came in and pierced Judas's heart, as he sat at his section of the Last Supper table, and it wrapped me up in a sun haze, so that all was misty around me. The sermon only struck my ear with a soothing, drowsy roll, something like the wave-note of the in-curling sea in the Mediterranean, a *legato* accompaniment to my thoughts; and I had a grand burial all by myself. I dug a deep grave and laid all my dreams and foolish wishes and sweet hopes in it. A puff of wind rustled through the riggings of the ships and set the flags with their yellow cross fluttering, and scattered a few of the tender blooms over it…and, ah well…it seems hard to realize now Spring has gone!

Do you really think that crinolines will be worn?

SARAH GRAND
(FRANCES ELIZABETH CLARKE MCFALL, 1854-1943)

Sarah Grand (Frances Elizabeth Clarke McFall) was born in Ireland to Margaret Bell Sherwood Clarke and Edward John Bellenden Clarke, a naval officer. Her father died when she was seven, and her family moved to Yorkshire. At age sixteen Grand married David Chambers McFall, an army surgeon who was thirty-nine years old and a widower with two sons. The Beth Book (1897), a Bildungsroman, is a fictional account of a girl's early years which closely resemble those of Grand.

Grand traveled widely with her husband until he retired from the military; they had one son. She had begun writing early in her marriage and published several short stories in magazines before the publication of her first novel, Ideala (1888), gave her the financial security necessary to leave her husband. This novel, as well as her later fiction, depicts what Grand felt to be wrong with marriage in her time and, like The Heavenly Twins, is partially based on her own marriage experience. Ideala was published anonymously.

Grand's best-known novel, The Heavenly Twins (1893), was her first book to be published with the pseudonym Sarah Grand, the name by which she then became known. It deals with the marriage issue through the experiences of three heroines whose different fates demonstrate the various wrongs committed against women. Grand believed that society's acceptance of the sexual double standard allowed promiscuous men "with a past" to marry innocent and unsuspecting women who were then infected with venereal disease. She was the first writer to deal openly with the subject of sexually transmitted diseases in fiction. One of the heroines of The Heavenly Twins gives birth to a syphilitic child, then goes mad herself from the disease and dies. Another of the novel's heroines, Evadne, refuses to consummate her marriage after learning on her wedding day that her husband has a promiscuous past. Grand believed that men should be held to the same sexual standard as women and her essays, like her novels, demand purity for men, not sexual license for women. Despite her criticism of marriage in both fiction and essays, Grand believed that women's ultimate happiness lay in marriage, although she never again married.

In the twentieth century Grand became involved in the suffrage movement and was a member of the Women Writers' Suffrage League. She continued to publish but her novels did not get the same attention from critics as did those from the 1890s. She visited the United States where she lectured around the country for four months. In 1920 she moved to Bath where she served as "mayoress" of the city, assisting the mayor who was a widower. She died fifty years after the publication of The Heavenly Twins.

THE UNDEFINABLE

[*Cosmopolitan* 17 (October 1894): 745-57]

"That certain something."—Ruskin

A Story of an Artist's Model

I.

It was a hot summer evening, and I had gone into the studio after dinner to sit opposite my last accomplished work, and smoke a cigarette to add to my joy in the contemplation thereof. It is a great moment, even for a great artist, when he can sit and sigh in solitary satisfaction before a finished picture. I had looked in at it while I was waiting for dinner, and even in that empty hour it had seemed most masterly, so that now, when I may, perhaps,—if I apologize in advance for the unacademical vulgarism of the idea,—be allowed to say that I was comfortably replete, I expected to feel in it that which passes the merely masterly of talent (to which degree of excellence ordinary painters, undowered by the divine afflatus, may attain by eminent industry), and approaches the superb—ecstatic—well, in a word, "the undefinable of genius," if (with all becoming diffidence, and only, it will be understood, for the good-natured purpose of making myself intelligible to the general reader,) I may venture to quote a remarkable critic of mine, a most far-seeing fellow, who, in recognizing the early promise of my work in the days when I was still struggling to scale those heights to which I afterwards successfully attained, thus aptly described whatever of merit I had then displayed. This was what I had come to recognize on the great canvas before me, to feel, to revel in, to *know*, in the utmost significance of the term, as something all-comprehensive enough to be evident to the meanest man's capacity in its power to make him feel, while yet remaining beyond the range of language to convey.

I had sat some time, however, my cigarette was half finished, the enjoyable sensation of having dined was uninterrupted by any feeling of regret on the subject of what I had eaten. I had, in fact, forgotten what I had eaten, and this, when the doctor has put us under stoppages, as the military phrase is, and we have, nevertheless, ventured upon forbidden fruit, I take to be a proof that we have done so with impunity. The balmy summer air blew in upon me freshly from the garden through the south lattice of the studio; blackbird and thrush no longer lifted their love-songs—it was late; but a nightingale from the top of a tall tree, unseen, filled the innermost recesses of audition with inimitable sound. The hour, the scene—and the man, I may say—were all that is best calculated to induce the proper appreciation of a noble work of art; but, although I had reclined in a deep, easy chair long enough to finish a cigarette, not a single fiber of feeling had responded to the call of the canvas upon it. I felt the freshness, the nightingale's note in the stillness, that luxurious something of kinship which comes from the near neighborhood of a great city, with companionable effect, when one is well disposed; but the work of art before me moved me no more than a fresh canvas, standing ready stretched upon an easel, with paints and palette lying ready for use beside it, would have done—not so much, in fact, for such preparations were only made when a new idea was burning in my being to be expressed. I should have been feeling it then; but now I was conscious of nothing more entrancing than the cold ashes of this old one. Yes, cold ashes, quite extinct they were, and I found myself forced to acknowledge it, although, of course, I assured myself at the same time that the fault was in my mood of the moment, not in the picture.

If I went out into the streets and brought in a varied multitude to gaze, I never doubted but that I should hear them shout again those pæans of praise to which I had been accustomed—accustomed, that is, as we are to the daily bread which we eat without much thought or appetite, but cannot do without.

On this particular evening, while I gazed, however, persistent thoughts obtruded themselves instead of refined sensations. As I rounded that exquisite arm, I remembered now that I had had in my mind the pleasurable certainty that the smiles of the Lady Catherine Claridge, her little invitations to "come when you have nothing better to do,—but not on my regular day, you know,—*you* will always find me at home;" and her careless seeming hint of a convenient hour, meant as much as I cared to claim. There had been in her blush, I knew, the material for my little romance of that season, and then, as I flecked in those floating clouds, I had been calculating the cost of these little romances, and deciding the sum it would be necessary to set upon this picture in order to cover the more than usually extravagant outlay which would be entailed by her gentle ladyship's idea of my princely habits.

When I was engaged upon those love-limpid eyes it had occurred to me to calculate how much a year I should lose by spending the price of this picture, instead of reserving it as capital to be invested; and here I had asked myself, was it wise to lavish so much on one caprice? Then, suddenly my mind had glanced off to the last levée. I had certainly been slighted on that occasion,— obviously neglected,—allowed to pass with the kind of nod of recognition which does for a faithful lackey. At the recollection of it my forehead contracted with anger, the pride of performance forsook me, my effect had not come to those eyes, and I threw down my brush in disgust. I had gone over all that ground afterwards, for it is well known that I am nothing if not painstaking; but now, again, as I gazed, the effect that I had tried for was absent; the work answered not at all to my expectations; and there gradually took possession of me a great amazement, not to say alarm, as I forced myself to acknowledge that there must be some blunting of my faculties to account for the powerlessness of the picture to move me as it ought. What could be the matter with me? Loss of nerve power? Visions of delicate artistic suscepti-bilities injured when not actually wiped out by the coarse influences of indi-gestion, horrid possibilities, had begun to assail me rudely, when the ringing of the studio bell suddenly startled me back to my normal state of mind. It rang once sharply, and although it is not my habit to answer bells for myself, I arose on some unaccountable impulse, and, going to the outer door of the studio, which opened on a flight of steps leading down into the road, did so on this occasion.

A young woman was waiting without. The electric light from behind me fell full upon her face. I did not think her particularly attractive in appear-ance, and the direct look of her eyes into mine was positively distasteful. It was the kind of glance which either fascinates or creates a feeling of repulsion. Coming from a creature whose exterior does not please, such a glance repels inevitably, especially if there is anything commanding in it; and more partic-ularly the command of a strong nature in an inferior position, when it is like-ly to cause a degree of irritation which would, amongst unrefined people, result in an outburst of rough hostility, but with us, of course, only expresses itself in a courtly coldness.

"Do you want a model?" the young woman asked, speaking without a par-ticle of respect or apology, as if to an equal.

I would have answered in the negative shortly, and shut the door, but for— I had it just now, the reason—but it has escaped me. However, I shall remem-ber it by and by; and, for the present, it is only necessary to state that I did not say no, or shut the door. I hesitated.

"You can't tell, of course, until you see me," the applicant pursued in a con-fident tone. "I had better come in and show myself."

And involuntarily I stood aside to let her pass, conscious at the same time, that I was bending my body from the waist, although I certainly never meant to bow to a model. My position necessitates so many bows, however, that it has really become more natural to me to acknowledge the approach of a fellow-creature so than in any other position.

Ah! now I recall what it was that had made me hesitate—her voice. It was not the voice of a common model. And as she passed me now, she struck me as not being a common person of any kind. Some one in distress, I thought, driven to earn an honest penny. All sorts of people come in this way to us artists, and we do what we can for them without asking questions. Sometimes we get an invaluable model with distinct marks of superior breeding, in this way, a king's daughter, displaying in every lineament the glory of race, which inspires. Oftener it is a pretty "young lady" out of a situation. The latter appears in every academy by the name of some classical celebrity. But, then again, we have applicants like the present, not attractive, whom it would be folly to engage to sit, however willing we may be to oblige them by employing them. In such cases a sovereign or so is gratefully accepted as a rule, and there the matter ends; and I had put my hand in my pocket as I followed my visitor in, thinking that I could satisfy her with such substantial proof of sympathy, and so get rid of her; but the moment she stopped and turned to me, I felt an unaccountable delicacy about doing so. "This is no beggar, no ordinary object of charity," I thought; "it would be an insult to offer her anything that she has not earned."

She had placed herself full in the light for my inspection, with her back to my picture, and I looked at her attentively, gauging the possibility of making anything out of such a face, and the rather tall bundle of loose, light wraps which was the figure she presented. "Hopeless!" was my first impression. "I'm not so sure," the second; and the third, "Skin delicate, features regular, eyes"—but there the fault was, I discovered,—not in the shape or color, but in the expression of them. They were the mocking eyes of that creature most abhorrent to the soul of man, a woman who claims to rule, and does not care to please; eyes out of which an imperious spirit shone independently—not looking up, but meeting mine on the same level. Now, a really attractive, *womanly* woman looks up, clings, depends, so that a man can never forget his own superiority in her presence.

"Well?" she broke in upon my reflections, prolonging the word melodiously.

And instantly it occurred to me that, as I had not yet begun another serious work, I might as well do a good deed, and keep my hand in at the same time, by making a study of her. Certainly the type was uncommon.

"Yes," I replied, speaking, to my own surprise, in a satisfied tone, as if I were receiving, instead of conferring, a favor, although I cannot understand why I should have done so. "You may come to-morrow and give me some sittings. Be here at ten."

She was turning away without a word, and she had not ventured to look at the picture; but this I thought was natural diffidence, so I called her back, feeling that a man in my position might, without loss of dignity, give the poor creature a treat.

"You may look at the picture if you like," I said, speaking involuntarily, very much as I should have done to—well, to the Lady Catherine Claridge herself! Without returning, she glanced at the picture over her shoulder: "Pooh!" she said. "Do you call that a picture?" and then she looked up in my face and laughed.

When next I found myself thinking coherently, it was about her teeth. "What wonderfully white ones she has," I was saying to myself. But the studio

door was shut, and all echo of her departing footsteps had died away long
before I arrived at that reflection.

II

The next morning I was in the studio before ten o'clock, and the first thing I
did was to cover my new work with a curtain, and then I set my palette. But a
quarter past ten arrived and no model. Half past—this was hardly respectful.
Eleven, twelve, luncheon, light literature, a drive, the whole day—what could
the woman mean? I had intended to take tea with Lady Catherine; but just as
I approached the house I was suddenly seized with a curious dislike of the
visit, an unaccountable distaste for herself and everything about her, which
impelled me to drive on past the place without casting a glance in that direction. I wondered afterward if she had seen me, but I did not care in the least
whether she had or not.

After dinner, as on the previous evening, I retired to the studio to enjoy a
cigarette, but this time I sat with my back to the picture, before which the
curtain remained undrawn, and looked out of the lattice at the lights which
leaves take when fluttering in the moonlight; and listened to the nightingale,
until there stole upon my senses something—that something which did not
come to me out of my picture the night before. I found myself in a moment
drinking in the beauty of the night with long, deep sighs, and thinking
thoughts. I had even felt the first thrill of a great aspiration, when I was disturbed again by the ringing of the studio bell. Again, involuntarily, I hastened to open the door, and there she stood in exactly the same position at
the foot of the steps, looking up at me with her eyes that repelled—but no!
I was mistaken. How could I have thought her eyes repellant? They were
merrily dancing, mischievous eyes that made you smile in spite of yourself.
"Well, I didn't come, you see," she said in a casual way. "I knew you wouldn't
be ready for me."

"Not ready for you!" I exclaimed, without thinking whether I ought to condescend to parley with a model. "Why, I waited for you the whole morning!"

"Oh, that is nothing," she answered cheerfully; "nothing, at least, if nothing comes of it. You *must* wait, you know, to recover yourself. You've lost such
a lot. What is the use of having paint on your palette, if the rage to apply it is
not *here!*" She looked up at me with big, bright, earnest eyes as she spoke, and
clasped her hands over her chest. Then she stooped and peeped unceremo-
niously under my arm into the studio. "Ah!" she said, "you have covered that
thing up!" (meaning my picture.) "That's right. And you've been sitting by
the lattice—there's your chair! Last night it was in front of the easel. Well! I
will look in to-morrow, just to see how you are getting on. No trouble, I assure
you. Now you can shut the door. If you stand there when I am gone (staring

at the spot where I stood), as you did last night, you'll be in a draft, and catch cold, which is risky for a middle-aged man, just now especially, with so much influenza about. Good-night!"

She turned to walk away as she spoke, and her gait was like music in motion, she moved so rhythmically.

"What an extraordinary person!" I exclaimed, when she was out of sight. While she was with me, however, she had not seemed so; and it was only after she had gone that I ever recognized the utter incongruity of my own attitude towards her, when under the immediate influence of her singular personality.

But what was it that had set me thinking of Martha troubled about many things, when she mentioned the draft and influenza?

Now, somehow, next morning I knew better than to expect her at ten o'clock; I noticed that the paint had dried on my palette, and ordered my man to clean it; but I did not set it afresh, "for what," I asked myself, "is the use of paint on a palette if one has nothing to express?"

The day was devoted to social duties: I went in and out several times, asking always, on my return, if any one had been, to which my man, an old and faithful servant, invariably replied, as if he understood me: "Not even a model, sir."

I had had to attend a levée in the afternoon, and when it was over, one of the dukes, a noted connoisseur, asked me if I would "be so good" as to show him my new picture,—the exact expression was: "Your last great work." Other gentlemen came up while he was speaking to me, and it ended in several of them returning with me forthwith to view the picture.

I had not looked at it myself since I had covered it up, and, now that I was forced to draw the curtain from before it, I felt it to be a distasteful duty.

"Well, that *is* a picture!" the duke exclaimed, and all the other gentlemen praised the work in a choice variety of elegantly-selected phrases. They even looked as if they liked it, a fact which clearly proved to me that they had not, one of them got further than I had myself, before dinner on the eventful evening when she first appeared.

I was to have dined out that day, but just as I was about to step into my carriage, I saw a figure, in loose, light draperies, charmingly disposed, approaching. What was it made me think of Lot's wife? I turned back into the house on the instant, and retired to the studio, the outer door of which I opened at once for her convenience.

She walked straight in without ceremony.

"You were going to some feeding-function to-night, I suppose," she observed. Then she looked around, chose a chair, and sat herself down deliberately.

I remained standing myself, with my hands folded, regarding her with an expression in which I hoped she would see good-natured tolerance of one of the whimsical sex struggling with a certain amount of impatience carefully controlled. And she did study my face and attitude critically for some seconds, but then she shook her head.

"Don't like it!" she exclaimed. "No native dignity in it, because anybody could see that you are posing."

Involuntarily I altered my position, planting myself more firmly on my feet.

"That's better," she said, and then she looked at me again, frowning intently, and shook her head. "You live too well, you know," she admonished me. "There is a certain largeness in your very utterance which bespeaks high feeding, and an oleosaccharine quality in the courtly urbanity even of your every-day manner which comes of constant repletion. One is obliged to fall into it one's self to express it properly," she added, apologetically. "But you are a prince now, you know; you're not an artist. You've eaten all that out of yourself."

"I am not a great eater," I protested, in a tone which should have showed her that I was gravely offended by the liberty of language she allowed herself.

"Well, don't be huffy," she said. "It is not so much in the matter of meat and drink that your appetite is gross, I allow; it was the Tree of Life to which I alluded. You cannot pretend that you only nibble at that! You know you deny yourself none of it, so long as what you can reach is sufficiently refined to please you. You have fed your senses to such monstrous girth that they have crowded the soul out of you. What you put into your pictures now is knowledge, not inspiration. But that is the way with all of you artist-princes at present. Inspiration is extinct at Hampstead and in St. John's Wood, and even here on the heights there is scarcely ever a flicker." She slowly removed her outer wrap, and as she put the long pin with a black glass head which held it together carefully back in it, she added emphatically: "People may look at your pictures to their head's content, but their hearts you never touch."

She sat still, looking gravely at the ground for a few seconds after this last utterance, and then she rose in her deliberate, languid way, and went, with her long wraps depending from her left arm and gracefully trailing after her, up to the picture, and drew aside the curtain that concealed it. "Now, look at that!" she exclaimed. "Your flesh is flesh, and your form is form; likewise your color is color, and your draperies are drapery; but there isn't a scrap of human interest in the whole composition, and the consequence is a notable flatness and insipidity, as of soup without salt." She looked close into the picture, then drew back and contemplated it from a little distance with her head on one side, and then she carefully covered it up with the curtain, remarking as she did so, contemptuously: "There is not a scrap of 'that certain something' in it, you know; it is merely a clever contrivance in paint upon canvas."

"But there is pleasure in the contemplation of a coat of color laid on with a master's hand," I modestly observed, changing my balance from one leg to the other, and crisping the fingers of my left hand as they lay upon the right.

"For some people," she replied. "There is an order of mind, mind in its infancy, which can be so diverted. You never know, however, what people are looking at in a picture. We have a pet frame-maker at home (Who can she be?) and, one day, when he brought back a new picture, we thought we would give him a treat, so we took him into the picture-gallery (A picture-gallery argues a mansion!), and invited him to look at the pictures, and then we watched him walking down the long length of the gallery slowly, passing in review a whole sequence of art, ancient and modern (She must belong to considerable people, there are not many such private collections!); but not a muscle of his face moved until he came to one exquisite little modern gem,— it was not one of yours," she hastened to assure me. I made a deprecatory gesture to show her I had not had the egotism to suppose it might be. "Gems by you are exceedingly difficult to procure," she proceeded, in a tone which suggested something sarcastic, but I failed to comprehend. "Well," she pursued, "our good frame-maker stopped opposite to that gem. His countenance, which had been somber as that of one who patiently accomplishes a task, now cleared, his eyes brightened intelligently, his cheeks flushed, his lips parted to exclaim, and I thought to myself, 'Now for a genuine glimpse of the soul of a working man!' He looked again, as if to make sure, before he committed himself, then, turning to me, he exclaimed triumphantly: '*I* made that frame!'"

"Ah,—yes," I was conscious of murmuring politely. "Extremely good. But we were talking about paints."

"Oh, well, of course, if you can't see the point!" She shrugged her shoulders and turned the palms of her hands outward. Then she sat down again, and looked at my feet. I shifted them uneasily. "I was going out to dinner," I ventured at last, breaking in upon her meditations, tentatively.

"I know," she responded, with a sigh, as if she were wearied in mind. "It would be just as well to send the carriage back. There is no use keeping the coachman and horses at the door. I dare say the cook has some cutlets that will do for us."

"I am sure I shall be delighted if you will do me the honor,—" I was beginning, when again she laughed in my face, showing much of her magnificent set of strong, white teeth. Why did I never dream of opposing her?

"O come, now!" she exclaimed, apparently much amused, "you are not at court, you know. Here in the studio you should be artistic, not artificial; and what you don't feel you shouldn't pretend to feel. Shall we dine here? Put that thing back" (pointing to the picture), "pull out the throne, it will make a capital low table, and order in two easy couches for us to recline upon opposite to each other. You are nothing if not classical in appearance. Fancy you in a frock-coat, with spats on your boots! and you in modern evening dress! it is absurd! You should wear a toga."

I was going to say something about the incongruity of such a costume, but she would not let me speak. "Just wait a moment," she said, "it is my innings.

And nobody knows better than I do that London would be more amazed than edified by the apparition of yourself in a toga, or, better still, for I take you to be more Greek than Roman, 'clad in the majestic folds of the himation, and without a cravat'—admirably as either would set off your attractive personal appearance. Here on the hill, however, it is different. I tell you you are nothing if not classical, both in your person and your work; but a modern man must add of the enlightenment of to-day that which was wanting to the glory of the Greeks. Your work at present is purely Greek,—form without character, passionless perfection, imperfectly perfect, wanting the spirit part, which was not in Greece, but is, or ought to be, in you; without which the choicest masterpiece of old was merely 'icily regular, splendidly null;' with which the veriest street Arab, put upon canvas is 'equal to the god!' I tell you you are a true Greek; but you must be something more, for this is not Athens in Greece, but London,—coming from whence we will accept nothing but positive perfection, which is form and character, flesh and blood, body and soul, the divine in the human,—But there!" she broke off. "That is as much as you must have at present. And I am fatigued. Do get the room arranged, and order in dinner, while I retire to refresh myself by removing my wraps." She walked with easy grace out of the studio into the house when she had spoken, leaving me gravely perplexed. And again I wonder why, at the time, it never occurred to me to oppose her; but certainly it never did.

My difficulty now was how to make the arrangements she required without taking the whole establishment into my confidence; but, while I still stood in the attitude in which she had left me,—an attitude, I believe, of considerable dignity, the right foot being a little advanced, at right angles to the left, and the left elbow supported on the back of the right hand, so that the fingers caressed the left cheek,—my faithful, old, confidential servant entered.

"Beg pardon, sir," he began,—and I observed that he seemed perturbed and anxious, like one in dread, lest he shall not perform the duty exacted of him satisfactorily,—"but the lady said you wanted me to arrange the scene for the new picture."

Instantly I understood her delicate manner of getting me out of my difficulty, and, having given my man full directions, I stood looking on while the necessary arrangements were being completed, making a suggestion now and then as to the disposition of table decorations, and myself choosing the draperies that were to decorate the lounges upon which we were to recline. While so engaged, I, as it were—if I may venture to use such an expression,—warmed to the work. At first I had looked on, as a grown-up person might, when viewing, with pleased toleration, the preparations for some childish frolic; but, as the arrangements neared completion, and I gradually beheld one end of my studio transformed, with the help of rare, ancient vessels, statues, and furniture of the most antique design, which I had collected for the purpose of my art, into such a scene as Apelles himself might have countenanced, I felt an unwonted glow of enthusiasm, and fell to adjusting hangings and dragging lounges about myself. It was a close evening, and the unwonted exertion made me so hot that, without a thought of my dignity, I dashed my coat and vest on the floor, and worked in my shirt-sleeves.

"That's right!" said a tuneful voice, at last, and, upon looking around, I saw my model; or, guest of the evening shall I say? She was standing between two heavy curtains which screened off one side of the studio from an outer apartment. Her right hand was raised high in the act of holding one of the curtains back, and her bare, round arm shone ivory white against the dark folds of the curtains. It was a striking attitude, instinct with a singular grace and charm, both of which, on looking back, I now recognize as having been eminently characteristic. Their immediate effect upon me was to get her not to move for a moment until I had caught the pose in a rapid sketch. She signified her assent by standing quiescent as a statue while I hastily got out my materials, choosing charcoal for my medium, and set to work; and so great was my eagerness that I actually remained in my shirt-sleeves without being aware of the fact, a statement which will, I know, astonish my friends, and appear to them to be incredible, even upon my own authority; but, that there must have been something powerfully—what shall I say, about this extraordinary woman—demoralizing? And yet it was not at all that, but elevating rather. Even my model man-servant, to judge by his countenance, felt her effect. Under the strange, benign influence of her appearance, as she stood there, I could see that he had suddenly ceased to be an impassive serving machine, and had become an emotional human being. There was interest in his eyes, and admiration, besides an all-devouring anxiety to be equal to the occasion—a disinterested trepidation on my account, too, as well as his own. He was fearful lest I should not answer to expectation, as was evident from the way that he, hitherto the most respectful of fellows, forgot himself, and ventured upon the liberty of looking on, first at the model and then at my sketch as it progressed. He came and peeped over my shoulder, went up to the model for a nearer view, then stepped off again to see her from another point, as we do when studying a fascinating object; and so natural did it seem even for a man-servant to think and feel in her presence, that I allowed his demonstrations to pass unreproved, as though it were part of the natural order of things for a lackey to comport himself so.

But, in the meantime, the attention to my subject which the making of the sketch necessitated, brought about a revelation. As I rapidly read each lineament for the purpose of fixing it on my paper, I asked myself involuntarily, how I could possibly have supposed for a moment that this magnificent creature was unattractive! Why, from the crown of her head to the sole of her foot—what expression! There was a volume of verse in her glance,—O Sappho! a bounteous vitality in her whole person,—O Ceres! an atmosphere of life, of love, surrounded her,—O Venus! a modest reserve of womanhood,—Diana! a—

"Get on; do!" she broke in upon my fervid analysis.

An aplomb, I concluded, a confidence of intellect; decision, intelligence, and force of fine feeling combined in her which brought her down to the present day.

"Yes," she observed, dropping the curtain and coming forward when I had finished my sketch, in which, by the way, she took not the slightest interest, for she did not cast so much as a glance at it. "Yes," she repeated, as if in answer to my thoughts,—I wonder if, perchance, I had uttered them aloud? "Yes, you are right. I commanded you. I *am* a woman with all the latest improvements. The creature the world wants. Nothing can now be done without me." She silently surveyed me after this with critical eyes. "But, hop out of that ridiculous dress, *do!*" she said at last, "and get into something suitable for summer, for a man of your type, and for the occasion."

I instantly unbuttoned a brace.

"Hold on a moment," she said, rather hastily. "Where is your classical wardrobe?"

My man, who had stood waiting on her words, as it were, ran to a huge carved chest at the further end of the studio, and threw up the lid, for answer.

"Johnson, as he appears in St. Paul's cathedral, may be all very well for people at church to contemplate, but that isn't my idea of a dinner dress," she proceeded.

She was walking toward the chest as she spoke, and I noticed that her own dress, which had struck me, at first, as being purely classical, was not really of any form with which I was acquainted, ancient or modern; but was of a design which I believe to be perfectly new, or, at all events, a most original variation upon already-known designs. It was made of several exquisitely-harmonized tints of soft silks.

When she reached the great chest, she stood a moment looking into it, and then began to pull the things out, and throw them on the floor behind her, diving down deeper and deeper into the chest, till she had to stand on tip-toe to reach at all, and the upper part of her body disappeared at every plunge. Near the bottom she found what she wanted. This proved to be a short-sleeved tunic reaching to the knees, with a handsome Greek border embroidered upon it; some massive gold bracelets, a pair of sandals, and a small harp, such as we associate with Homer.

She gathered all these things up in her arms, brought them to me, and threw them down at my feet. "There!" she exclaimed, "be quick! I want my dinner." With which, she delicately withdrew until my toilet was complete.

When she returned, she held in her hand a laurel wreath, tied at the back with a bow of ribbon, and with the leaves lying symmetrically towards the front, where they met in a point. It was the form which appears in ancient portraits crowning the heads of distinguished men.

I had placed myself near a pedestal, with the harp in my hand, and felt conscious of nothing but my bare legs as she approached. My man, who had helped to attire me, also stood by, bespeaking her approval with deprecating glances entreatingly.

Having crowned me, she stepped back to consider the effect, and instantly she became convulsed with laughter. My servant assumed a dejected attitude upon this, and silently slunk away.

"Oh dear! O dear!" she exclaimed, "if society could only see you now! It isn't that you don't look well," she hastened to reassure me, "and I trust you will kindly excuse my inopportune mirth. It is a disease of the mind which I inherit from an ancestor of mine, who was a funny man. He worked for a comic paper, and was expected to make new jokes every week; a consequence of which strain upon his mind was the setting up of the deplorable disease of inopportune mirth, which has, unfortunately, been transmitted to me. But I am altogether an outcome of the age, you will perceive. But, as I was going to say, those ambrosial locks and that classic jowl of yours, not to mention your manly arms embraceleted, and—" But here she hesitated, apparently not liking to mention my legs, although she looked at them. "Well!" she hurriedly summed up, "I always said you would look lovely in a toga, and the short tunic is also artistic in its own way. But now let us dine. I am mortal hungry."

I was about to hasten, harp in hand, across the studio to ring for dinner, but the moment I moved she went off again into convulsions of laughter.

"Excuse me," she implored, drying her eyes, "but it *is* so classical I can't help it, really! just to see you go gives me little electric shocks all over! But don't be huffy. You never looked nicer, I declare. And you can put on a toga, you know, if the tunic isn't enough. It *is* somewhat skimpy, I confess, for a man of your girth."

When she had spoken she went to the chest, and obligingly looked me out some yards of stuff which, she said, when properly draped, would do for a toga; and, having arranged it upon my shoulders to please herself, she conducted me to one of the couches, remarking that dinner would be sure to come all in good time, and recommending me to employ the interval in cultivating a cheerful frame of mind: one, two, three, four, five, six, seven,—a copy-book precept, good for the digestion when practiced, she insisted, as she thoughtfully adjusted my harp, after which she begged me to assume a classical attitude, and then proceeded to dispose herself, in like manner, on the other couch opposite.

"This is delicious," she said, sighing luxuriously as she sank upon it. "I guess the Greeks and Romans never really knew what comfort was. Imagine an age without springs!"

Dinner was now served by my man, who was, I could see, shaking in his shoes with anxiety lest everything should not be to her mind. He had donned a red gown in her honour, similar to that worn by attendants at the Royal Academy on state occasions, and was suffering a good deal from the heat in consequence. But the dinner was all that could be desired, as my guest herself observed. And she should have known, too, for she ate with a will. "I must tell you," she explained, "Æsculapius prescribed a tonic for me on one occasion, and I have been taking it, off and on, ever since, so that now I am almost all appetite."

What was it made me think, at that moment, of Venus' visit to Æsculapius?

We were now at dessert, nibbling fruit and sipping wine, and my face was suffused with smiles, but my companion looked grave, and I thought that her mood was resolving itself into something serious, by the sober way she studied my face.

"Excuse me, but your wreath is all on one side," she remarked at last,— quite by the way, however.

I rose hastily to readjust the wreath at a mirror, and then returned and leisurely resumed my seat. I had been about to speak, but something new in the demeanor of the lady opposite caused me to forget my intention. There was an indescribable grace in her attitude, a perfect abandon to the repose of the moment which was in itself an evidence of strength in reserve, and fascinating to a degree. But the curious thing about the impression which she was now making upon me is that she had not moved. She had been reclining in an easy manner since the servant left the room, with her arm resting on the back of her couch, twirling a flower in her fingers, and had not swerved from the pose a fraction; but a certain quietude had settled upon her, and was emanating from her forcibly as I felt; and with this quietude there came to me quite suddenly a new and solemn sense of responsibility, something grave and glad which I cannot explain, something which caused me an exquisite sense of pleasurable emotion, and made me feel the richer for the experience. My first thought was of England and America, of the glorious womanhood of this age of enlightenment compared with the creature as she existed merely for man's use and pleasure of old, the toy-woman, drudge, degraded domestic animal, beast of intolerable burdens. How could the sons of slaves ever be anything but slaves themselves? slaves of various vices, the most execrable form of bondage. To paint,—to paint this woman as she is! In her youth, in her strength, in her beauty,—in her insolence even! in the fearless candor of her perfect virtue; the trifler of an idle hour, the strong, true spirit of an arduous day: to paint her so that every man might feel her divinity and worship that truly!

I had covered my eyes with my hand so as the better to control my emotions, and collect my thoughts; but now a current of cold air playing upon my limbs, and the faint sith of silk aroused me. I looked up. The couch was empty.

III

The next morning she arrived by ten o'clock, in a very ugly, old, gray cloak. I was engaged at the moment in reading the report in a morning paper of the dinner at which I ought to have appeared on the previous evening, and the letter of apology for my unavoidable absence which, I forgot to mention, my guest had induced me to send. She came and read the report over my shoulder.

"That is graceful," was her comment upon my letter. "You are a charming phrase-maker. Such neatness of expression is not common. But," she added severely, "it is also disgraceful, because you didn't mean a word of it. And an artist should be an honest, earnest man, incapable of petty subterfuge, otherwise, however great he may be, he falls short of the glory, just as you do. But there!" she added plaintively, "you know all that; or, at all events, you used to know it."

"He is the greatest artist who has the greatest number—" I was beginning, when she interrupted me abruptly.

"Oh, I know! you have it all off by heart so pat!" she exclaimed. "But what good do precepts do you? Why, if maxims could make an artist I should be one myself, for I know them all; yet I am no artist!"

"I don't know that," slipped from me unawares.

"That is because you have become a mere appraiser of words," she declared. "You as an artist would have divined that if I could paint myself I should not be here. I should be doing what I want for myself, instead of using my peculiar power to raise you to the necessary altitude."

"Oh, of course?" I hastened to agree, apologetically, feeling myself on familiar ground at last. "The delicate, subtly inspiring presence is the woman's part; the rough work is for the man, the interpreter. No woman has ever truly distinguished herself except in her own sphere.

"Now no cant, *please*," she exclaimed. "You are not a pauper priest, afraid that the offertory will fall off if he doesn't keep the upper hand of all the women in the parish."

"But," I protested, "few women have ever—"

"Now just reflect," she interrupted, "and you will remember that in the days of our slavery there were more great women than there have ever been great men who were also slaves, so that now that our full emancipation is imminent, why, you shall see what you shall see."

"Then, why don't you paint?" I asked her blandly.

"All in good time," she answered suavely. "But I have not come to bandy words with you, nor to be irritated by hearing nonsensical questions asked by a man of your age and standing. I am here to be painted. Just set your palette while I see to my attire. You seem to have forgotten lately that a woman is a creature of clothes in these days, and there never were more delightful days, by the way, since the world began."

When she returned she ascended the throne, but before falling into a set attitude, she addressed me from thence: "The great stories of the world are deathless and ageless because of the human nature that is in them, and you know that in your head, but your heart does not feel it a bit. Your sentiments are irreproachable, but they have survived the vivifying flush of feeling, parent of sympathetic insight, upon which you formed them, and the mere dry knowledge that remains is no use for creative purposes. All through nature strong emotion is the motive of creation, and in art also the power to create is invariably the outcome of an ardent impulse. But there you stand in full conceit before your canvas with your palette and brushes in your hand, a mere cool, calculating workman, without an atom of love or reverence, not to mention inspiration, to warm your higher faculties into life and action; and in that mood you have the assurance to believe that you have only to choose to paint me as I am and you will be able to do so—able to paint not merely a creature of a certain shape, but a creature of boundless possibilities, instinct with soul—no! though I wrong you!" she broke off scornfully. "The soul of me, the only part that an artist should specially crave to render through the medium of this outer shell, which of itself alone is hardly worth the trouble of copying on to the canvas, has never cost you a thought. Rounded form, healthy flesh, and lively glances are all that appeal to you now."

I bent my head, considering if this were true; but even while I asked myself the question I was conscious of a curious shock—a shock of awakening, as it were, a thrill that traversed my body in warm, swift currents, making me tingle. I knew what it was in a moment. Her enthusiasm. She had communicated it to me occultly, a mere spark of it at first, but even that was animating to a degree that was delicious.

"Don't put anything on canvas that you cannot glorify," she resumed. "The mere outer husk of me is nothing, I repeat; you must interpret, you must reveal the beyond of that, the grace, I mean, all resplendent within." She clasped her hands upon her breast, and looked into my eyes. "You remember your first impression when I offered myself as a model?" she pursued. I felt ashamed of my own lack of insight, and hung my head. "Compare your present idea of my attractions with that, and see for yourself how far you have lapsed. You have descended from art to artificiality, I tell you. You have ceased to see and render like a sentient being; you are nothing now but a painting machine. But there!" she exclaimed, clapping her hands together, "stand straight, and look at me!"

Like one electrified, I obeyed.

"I am the woman who stood at the outer door of your studio and summoned you to judge me; the same whom in your spiritual obscurity you then found wanting. Rend now that veil of flesh, and look! Who was at fault?"

"I was!" burst from me involuntarily.

When I had spoken, I clasped my palette, and hastily selected a brush. Her exaltation had rapidly gained upon me. I was consumed with the rage to paint her; or, rather to paint that in her which I suddenly saw and could reproduce upon canvas, but could not otherwise express.

Slowly, without another word, she lapsed into an easy attitude, fixing her wonderful eyes upon mine. For a moment my vision was clouded; I saw nothing but mist. As that cleared, however, there penetrated to the innermost recesses of my being, there was revealed to me—but the tone-poets must find the audible expression of it. My limit is to make it visible.

But never again, I said to myself as I painted, shall mortal stand before a work of mine unmoved; never again shall it be said: "Well, it may be my ignorance, which it would be bad taste for me to display in the presence of a picture by so great a man, but, all the same, I must say I can't see anything in it!" No, never again! If I have to sacrifice every delight of the body to keep my spiritual vision unobscured, for there is no joy like this joy, nothing else that is human which so nearly approaches the divine as the exercise of this power.

"For heaven's sake, don't move!" I implored.

She had not moved, but the whole expression of her face had changed with an even more disastrous effect. The glorious light which had illuminated such rapturous enthusiasm in me passed out of her eyes, giving place to the cold, critical expression which repelled, and she smiled enigmatically.

"I can't stand here all day," she said, stepping down from the throne. "You know now what you want."

She was at the outer door as she pronounced those words, and instantly after she had uttered them she was gone, absolutely gone, before I could remonstrate.

I had thrown myself on my knees to beg for another hour, and now, when I realized the cruelty of her callous desertion of me at such a juncture, I sank beside the easel utterly overcome, and remained, for I cannot tell how long, in a kind of stupor, from which, however, I was at length aroused by a deep-drawn sigh. I looked up, and then I rose to my feet. It was my faithful servant who had sighed. He stood gazing before the all unfinished work. I looked at it myself.

"It is wonderful, sir," he said, speaking in an undertone, as if in the presence of something sacred.

Yes, it was wonderful even then and what would it be when it was finished? Finished! How could I finish it without a model? Without that model in particular? I recognized her now—a free woman, a new creature, a source of inspiration the like of which no man hitherto has ever imagined in art or literature. Why had she deserted me? For she had, and I knew it at once. I felt she would not return, and she never did, nor have I ever been able to find her, although I have been searching for her ever since. You may see me frequently in the corner of an open carriage, with my man seated on the box beside the coachman; and as we drive through the streets we gaze up at the windows, and into the faces of the people we pass, in the hope that some day we shall see her; but never a glimpse, as yet, have we obtained.

My man says that such capricious conduct is just what you might expect of a woman, old fashioned or new; but I cannot help thinking myself that both in her coming and in her going, her insolence and her ideality, her gravity and her levity, there was a kind of allegory. "With all my faults nothing uncommonly great can be done without my countenance," this was what she seemed to have said to me; "but my countenance you shall not have to perfection until the conceit of you is conquered, and you acknowledge all you owe me. Give me my due. When *you* help *me,* I will help *you!*"

NETTA SYRETT (1865-1943)

Netta Syrett was born Janet Syrett, the daughter of Ernest Syrett, a silk merchant. She was the niece of the writer Grant Allen. Syrett attended Cambridge Training College to become a teacher and then taught for two years at a school in Swansea. She then moved to London, living with her four sisters and teaching at the London Polytechnic School for Girls. Two of her sisters, Mabel and Nellie, studied art; Nellie illustrated Netta's book for children, The Garden of Delight: Fairy Tales *(1898), and also* The Dream Garden *(1905). Netta eventually published twenty children's books which include fairies, fantastic creatures, and supernatural elements.*

Through her friend Mabel Beardsley, Netta met Aubrey Beardsley, Mabel's brother, and through him she was introduced to Henry Harland and then to writers associated with the Yellow Book, *including Evelyn Sharp and Ella D'Arcy. Syrett's story, "Thy Heart's Desire," appeared in the* Yellow Book *in July 1894; she had two other stories published in the quarterly. Her first novel,* Nobody's Fault *(1896), was then published by John Lane in the Keynotes Series. The novel's protagonist, Bridget, suffers in an unhappy marriage and has few opportunities for employment. However, she begins to write, eventually publishing a novel. The female protagonists in two other novels by Syrett,* The Day's Journey *(1905) and* The Victorians: The Development of a Modern Woman *(1915), also write novels. Much of Syrett's fiction, as is characteristic of other New Woman writers, deals with the marriage question and with occupations for women. During her long career as a writer Syrett published thirty-eight novels, eighteen short stories, which appeared in various periodicals, and four plays, as well as her many children's books. She never married.*

THY HEART'S DESIRE

[*Yellow Book* II (July 1894): 228-55]

I

The tents were pitched in a little plain surrounded by hills. Right and left there were stretches of tender vivid green where the young corn was springing; further still, on either hand, the plain was yellow with mustard-flower; but in the immediate foreground it was bare and stony. A few thorny bushes pushed their straggling way through the dry soil, ineffectively as far as the grace of the landscape was concerned, for they merely served to emphasise the barren aridness of the land that stretched before the tents, sloping gradually to the distant hills.

The hills were uninteresting enough in themselves; they had no grandeur of outline, no picturesqueness even, though at morning and evening the sun, like a great magician, clothed them with beauty at a touch.

They had begun to change, to soften, to blush rose-red in the evening light, when a woman came to the entrance of the largest of the tents and looked towards them. She leant against the support on one side of the canvas flap, and putting back her head, rested that too against it, while her eyes wandered over the plain and over the distant hills.

She was bareheaded, for the covering of the tent projected a few feet to form an awning overhead. The gentle breeze which had risen with sundown, stirred the soft brown tendrils of hair on her temples, and fluttered her pink cotton gown a little. She stood very still, with her arms hanging and her hands clasped loosely in front of her. There was about her whole attitude an air of studied quiet which in some vague fashion the slight clasp of her hands accentuated. Her face, with its tightly, almost rigidly closed lips, would have been quite in keeping with the impression of conscious calm which her entire presence suggested, had it not been that when she raised her eyes a strange contradiction to this idea was afforded. They were large grey eyes, unusually bright and rather startling in effect, for they seemed the only live thing about her. Gleaming from her still set face, there was something almost alarming in their brilliancy. They softened with a sudden glow of pleasure as they rested on the translucent green of the wheat fields under the broad generous sunlight, and then wandered to where the pure vivid yellow of the mustard-flower spread in waves to the base of the hills, now mystically veiled in radiance. She stood motionless watching their melting elusive changes from palpitating rose to the transparent purple of amethyst. The stillness of evening was broken by the monotonous, not unmusical creaking of a Persian wheel at some little distance to the left of the tent. The well stood in a little grove of trees: between their branches she could see, when she turned her head, the coloured *saris* of the village women, where they stood in groups chattering as they drew the water, and the little naked brown babies that toddled beside them or sprawled on the hard ground beneath the trees. From the village of flat-roofed mud-houses under the low hill at the back of the tents, other women were crossing the plain towards the well, their terra-cotta water-jugs poised easily on their heads, casting long shadows on the sun-baked ground as they came.

Presently, in the distance, from the direction of the sunlit hills opposite, a little group of men came into sight. Far off, the mustard-coloured jackets and the red turbans of the orderlies made vivid splashes of colour on the dull plain. As they came nearer, the guns slung across their shoulders, the cases of mathematical instruments, the hammers and other heavy baggage they carried for the Sahib, became visible. A little in front, at walking pace, rode the Sahib himself, making notes as he came in a book he held before him. The girl at the tent-entrance watched the advance of the little company indifferently, it seemed; except for a slight tightening of the muscles about her mouth, her face remained unchanged. While he was still some little distance away, the man with the note-book raised his head and smiled awkwardly as he saw her standing there. Awkwardness, perhaps, best describes the whole man. He was badly put together, loose-jointed, ungainly. The fact that he was tall profited him nothing, for it merely emphasised the extreme ungracefulness of his figure. His long pale face was made paler by a shock of coarse, tow-coloured hair; his eyes even looked colourless, though they were certainly the least uninteresting feature of his face, for they were not devoid of expression. He had a way of slouching when he moved that singularly intensified the general uncouthness of his appearance. "Are you very tired?" asked his wife gently when he had dismounted close to the tent. The question would have been an unnecessary one had it been put to her instead of to her husband, for her voice had that peculiar flat toneless sound for which extreme weariness is answerable.

"Well, no, my dear, not very," he replied, drawling out the words with an exasperating air of delivering a final verdict, after deep reflection on the subject.

The girl glanced once more at the fading colours on the hills. "Come in and rest," she said, moving aside a little to let him pass.

She stood lingering a moment after he had entered the tent, as though unwilling to leave the outer air; and before she turned to follow him she drew a deep breath, and her hand went for one swift second to her throat as though she felt stifled.

Later on that evening she sat in her tent sewing by the light of the lamp that stood on her little table.

Opposite to her, her husband stretched his ungainly length in a deck-chair, and turned over a pile of official notes. Every now and then her eyes wandered from the gay silks of the table-cover she was embroidering to the canvas walls which bounded the narrow space into which their few household goods were crowded. Outside there was a deep hush. The silence of the vast empty plain seemed to work its way slowly, steadily in, towards the little patch of light set in its midst. The girl felt it in every nerve; it was as though some soft-footed, noiseless, shapeless creature, whose presence she only dimly divined, was approaching nearer—*nearer*. The heavy outer stillness was in some way made more terrifying by the rustle of the papers her husband was reading, by the creaking of his chair as he moved, and by the little fidgeting grunts and half exclamations which from time to time broke from him. His wife's hand shook at every unintelligible mutter from him, and the slight habitual contraction between her eyes deepened.

All at once she threw her work down on to the table. "For Heaven's sake— *please,* John, *talk!*" she cried. Her eyes, for the moment's space in which they met the startled ones of her husband, had a wild hunted look, but it was gone almost before his slow brain had time to note that it had been there—and was vaguely disturbing. She laughed a little, unsteadily.

"Did I startle you? I'm sorry. I—" she laughed again. "I believe I'm a little nervous. When one is all day alone—" She paused without finishing the sentence. The man's face changed suddenly. A wave of tenderness swept over it, and at the same time an expression of half-incredulous delight shone in his pale eyes.

"Poor little girl, are you really lonely?" he said. Even the real feeling in his tone failed to rob his voice of its peculiarly irritating grating quality. He rose awkwardly and moved to his wife's side.

Involuntarily she shrank a little, and the hand which he had stretched out to touch her hair sank to his side. She recovered herself immediately and turned her face up to his, though she did not raise her eyes; but he did not kiss her. Instead, he stood in an embarrassed fashion a moment by her side, and then went back to his seat.

There was silence again for some time. The man lay back in his chair, gazing at his big clumsy shoes, as though he hoped for some inspiration from that quarter, while his wife worked with nervous haste.

"Don't let me keep you from reading, John," she said, and her voice had regained its usual gentle tone.

"No, my dear; I'm just thinking of something to say to you, but I don't seem—"

She smiled a little. In spite of herself, her lip curled faintly. "Don't worry about it—it was stupid of me to expect it. I mean—" she added hastily, immediately repenting the sarcasm. She glanced furtively at him, but his face was quite unmoved. Evidently he had not noticed it, and she smiled faintly again.

"Oh, Kathie, I knew there was *something* I'd forgotten to tell you, my dear; there's a man coming down here. I don't know whether—"

She looked up sharply. "A man coming *here?* What for?" she interrupted breathlessly.

"Sent to help me about this oil-boring business, my dear."

He had lighted his pipe, and was smoking placidly, taking long whiffs between his words.

"Well?" impatiently questioned his wife, fixing her bright eyes on his face.

"Well—that's all, my dear."

She checked an exclamation. "But don't you know anything about him— his name? where he comes from? what he is like?" She was leaning forward against the table, her needle with a long end of yellow silk drawn halfway through her work, held in her upraised hand, her whole attitude one of quivering excitement and expectancy.

The man took his pipe from his mouth deliberately, with a look of slow wonder.

"Why Kathie, you seem quite anxious. I didn't know you'd be so interested, my dear. Well,"—another long pull at his pipe—"his name's Brook—*Brookfield*, I think." He paused again. "This pipe don't draw well a bit; there's something wrong with it, I shouldn't wonder," he added, taking it out and examining the bowl as though struck with the brilliance of the idea.

The woman opposite put down her work and clenched her hands under the table.

"Go on, John," she said presently in a tense vibrating voice——"his name is Brookfield. Well, where does he come from?"

"Straight from home, my dear, I believe." He fumbled in his pocket, and after some time extricated a pencil with which he began to poke the tobacco in the bowl in an ineffectual aimless fashion, becoming completely engrossed in the occupation apparently. There was another long pause. The woman went on working, or feigning to work, for her hands were trembling a good deal.

After some moments she raised her head again. "John, will you mind attending to me one moment, and answering these questions as quickly as you can?" The emphasis on the last word was so faint as to be almost as imperceptible as the touch of exasperated contempt which she could not absolutely banish from her tone.

Her husband, looking up, met her clear bright gaze and reddened like a schoolboy.

"Whereabouts *'from home'* does he come?" she asked in a studiedly gentle fashion.

"Well, from London, I think," he replied, almost briskly for him, though he stammered and tripped over the words. "He's a University chap; I used to hear he was clever—I don't know about that, I'm sure; he used to chaff me, I remember, but—"

"Chaff *you?* You have met him then?"

"Yes, my dear"—he was fast relapsing into his slow drawl again—"that is, I went to school with him, but it's a long time ago. Brookfield—yes, that must be his name."

She waited a moment, then "When is he coming?" she inquired abruptly.

"Let me see—to-day's—"

"*Monday*," the word came swiftly between her set teeth.

"Ah, yes,—Monday—well," reflectively, "*next* Monday, my dear."

Mrs. Drayton rose, and began to pace softly the narrow passage between the table and the tent-wall, her hands clasped loosely behind her.

"How long have you known this?" she said, stopping abruptly. "Oh, John, you *needn't* consider; it's quite a simple question. To-day? Yesterday?" Her foot moved restlessly on the ground as she waited.

"I think it was the day before yesterday," he replied.

"Then why in Heaven's name didn't you tell me before?" she broke out fiercely.

"My dear, it slipped my memory. If I'd thought you would be interested—"

"Interested?" She laughed shortly. It *is* rather interesting to hear that after six months of this"—she made a quick comprehensive gesture with her hand—"one will have some one to speak to—some one. It is the hand of Providence; it comes just in time to save me from—" She checked herself abruptly.

He sat staring up at her stupidly, without a word.

"It's all right, John," she said, with a quick change of tone, gathering up her work quietly as she spoke. "I'm not mad—yet. You—you must get used to these little outbreaks," she added after a moment, smiling faintly, "and to do me justice, I don't *often* trouble you with them, do I? I'm just a little tired, or it's the heat or—something. No—don't touch me," she cried, shrinking back, for he had risen slowly and was coming towards her.

She has lost command over her voice, and the shrill note or horror in it was unmistakable. The man heard it, and shrank in his turn.

"I'm so sorry, John," she murmured, raising her great bright eyes to his face. They had not lost their goaded expression, though they were full of tears. "I'm awfully sorry, but I'm just nervous and stupid, and I can't bear *any one* to touch me when I'm nervous."

II

"Here's Broomhurst, my dear! I made a mistake in his name after all, I find. I told you Brookfield, I believe, didn't I? Well, it isn't Brookfield, he says; it's Broomhurst."

Mrs. Drayton had walked some little distance across the plain to meet and welcome the expected guest. She stood quietly waiting while her husband stammered over his incoherent sentences, and then put out her hand.

"We are very glad to see you," she said with a quick glance at the newcomer's face as she spoke.

As they walked together towards the tent, after the first greetings, she felt his keen eyes upon her before he turned to her husband.

"I'm afraid Mrs. Drayton finds the climate trying?" he asked. "Perhaps she ought not to have come so far in this heat?"

"Kathie is often pale. You *do* look white to-day, my dear," he observed, turning anxiously towards his wife.

"Do I?" she replied. The unsteadiness of her tone was hardly appreciable, but it was not lost on Broomhurst's quick ears. "Oh, I don't think so. I *feel* very well."

"I'll come and see if they've fixed you up all right," said Drayton, following his companion towards the new tent that had been pitched at some little distance from the large one.

"We shall see you at dinner then?" Mrs. Drayton observed in reply to Broomhurst's smile as they parted.

She entered the tent slowly, and moving up to the table, already laid for dinner, began to rearrange the things upon it in a purposeless mechanical fashion.

After a moment she sat down upon a seat opposite the open entrance, and put her hand to her head.

"What is the matter with me?" she thought wearily. "All the week I've been looking forward to seeing this man—*any* man, *any one* to take off the edge of this." She shuddered. Even in thought she hesitated to analyse the feeling that possessed her. "Well, he's here, and I think I feel *worse.*" Her eyes travelled towards the hills she had been used to watch at this hour, and rested on them with a vague unseeing gaze.

"Tired, Kathie? A penny for your thoughts, my dear," said her husband, coming in presently to find her still sitting there.

"I'm thinking what a curious world this is, and what an ironical vein of humour the gods who look after it must possess," she replied with a mirthless laugh, rising as she spoke.

John looked puzzled.

"Funny my having known Broomhurst before, you mean?" he said doubtfully.

"I was fishing down at Lynmouth this time last year," Broomhurst said at dinner. "You know Lynmouth, Mrs Drayton? Do you never imagine you hear the gurgling of the stream? I am tantalised already by the sound of it rushing through the beautiful green gloom of those woods—*aren't* they lovely? And *I* haven't been in this burnt-up spot as many hours as you've had months of it."

She smiled a little.

"You must learn to possess your soul in patience," she said, and glanced inconsequently from Broomhurst to her husband, and then dropped her eyes and was silent a moment.

John was obviously, and a little audibly, enjoying his dinner. He sat with his chair pushed close to the table, and his elbows awkwardly raised, swallowing his soup in gulps. He grasped his spoon tightly in his bony hand so that its swollen joints stood out larger and uglier than ever, his wife thought.

Her eyes wandered to Broomhurst's hands. They were well shaped, and though not small, there was a look of refinement about them; he had a way of touching things delicately, a little lingeringly, she noticed. There was an air of distinction about his clear-cut, clean-shaven face, possibly intensified by contrast with Drayton's blurred features; and it was, perhaps, also by contrast with the grey cuffs that showed beneath John's ill-cut drab suit that the linen Broomhurst wore seemed to her particularly spotless.

Broomhurst's thoughts, for his part, were a good deal occupied with his hostess.

She was pretty, he thought, or perhaps it was that, with the wide dry lonely plain as a setting, her fragile delicacy of appearance was invested with a certain flower-like charm.

"The silence here seems rather strange, rather appalling at first, when one is fresh from a town," he pursued, after a moment's pause, "but I suppose you're used to it; eh, Drayton? How do *you* find life here, Mrs. Drayton?" he asked a little curiously, turning to her as he spoke.

She hesitated a second. "Oh, much the same as I should find it anywhere else, I expect," she replied; "after all, one carries the possibilities of a happy life about with one—don't you think so? The Garden of Eden wouldn't necessarily make my life any happier, or less happy, than a howling wilderness like this. It depends on oneself entirely."

"Given the right Adam and Eve, the desert blossoms like the rose, in fact," Broomhurst answered lightly, with a smiling glance inclusive of husband and wife; "you two don't feel as though you'd been driven out of Paradise evidently."

Drayton raised his eyes from his plate with a smile of total incomprehension.

"Great Heavens! What an Adam to select!" thought Broomhurst involuntarily, as Mrs. Drayton rose rather suddenly from the table.

"I'll come and help with that packing-case," John said, rising, in his turn, lumbering from his place; "then we can have a smoke—eh? Kathie don't mind, if we sit near the entrance."

The two men went out together, Broomhurst holding the lantern, for the moon had not yet risen. Mrs. Drayton followed them to the doorway, and, pushing the looped-up hanging further aside, stepped out into the cool darkness.

Her heart was beating quickly, and there was a great lump in her throat that frightened her as though she were choking.

"And I am his *wife*—I *belong* to him!" she cried, almost aloud.

She pressed both her hands tightly against her breast, and set her teeth, fighting to keep down the rising flood that threatened to sweep away her composure. "Oh, what a fool I am! What an hysterical fool of a woman I am!" she whispered below her breath. She began to walk slowly up and down outside the tent, in the space illumined by the lamplight, as though striving to make her outwardly quiet movements react upon the inward tumult. In a little while she had conquered; she quietly entered the tent, drew a low chair to the entrance, and took up a book, just as footsteps became audible. A moment afterwards Broomhurst emerged from the darkness into the circle of light outside, and Mrs. Drayton raised her eyes from the pages she was turning to greet him with a smile.

"Are your things all right?"

"Oh yes, more or less, thank you. I was a little concerned about a case of books, but it isn't much damaged fortunately. Perhaps I've some you would care to look at?"

"The books will be a godsend," she returned with a sudden brightening of the eyes; "I was getting *desperate*—for books."

"What are you reading now?" he asked, glancing at the volume that lay in her lap.

"It's a Browning. I carry it about a good deal. I think I like to have it with me, but I don't seem to read it much."

"Are you waiting for a suitable optimistic moment?" Broomhurst inquired smiling.

"Yes, now you mention it, I think that must be why I am waiting," she replied slowly.

"And it doesn't come—even in the Garden of Eden? Surely the serpent, pessimism, hasn't been insolent enough to draw you into conversation with him?" he said lightly.

"There has been no one to converse with at all—when John is away, I mean. I think I should have liked a little chat with the serpent immensely by way of a change," she replied in the same tone.

"Ah, yes," Broomhurst said with sudden seriousness, "it must be unbearably dull for you alone here, with Drayton away all day."

Mrs. Drayton's hand shook a little as she fluttered a page of her open book.

"I should think it quite natural you would be irritated beyond endurance to hear that all's right with the world, for instance, when you were sighing for the long day to pass," he continued.

"I don't mind the day so much—it's the evenings." She abruptly checked the swift words and flushed painfully. "I mean—I've grown stupidly nervous, I think—even when John is here. Oh, you have no idea of the awful silence of this place at night," she added, rising hurriedly from her low seat, and moving closer to the doorway. "It is so close, isn't it?" she said, almost apologetically. There was silence for quite a minute.

Broomhurst's quick eyes noted the silent momentary clenching of the hands that hung at her side as she stood leaning against the support at the entrance.

"But how stupid of me to give you such a bad impression of the camp—the first evening, too," Mrs. Drayton exclaimed presently, and her companion mentally commended the admirable composure of her voice.

"Probably you will never notice that it *is* lonely at all," she continued, "John likes it here. He is immensely interested in his work, you know. I hope *you* are too. If you are interested it is all quite right. I think the climate tries me a little. I never used to be stupid—and nervous. Ah, here's John; he's been round to the kitchen-tent, I suppose."

"Been looking after that fellow cleanin' my gun, my dear," John explained, shambling towards the deck-chair.

Later, Broomhurst stood at his own tent-door. He looked up at the star-sown sky, and the heavy silence seemed to press upon him like an actual, physical burden.

He took his cigar from between his lips presently and looked at the glowing end reflectively before throwing it away.

"Considering that she has been alone with him here for six months, she has herself very well in hand—*very* well in hand," he repeated.

III

It was Sunday morning. John Drayton sat just inside the tent, presumably enjoying his pipe before the heat of the day. His eyes furtively followed his wife as she moved about near him, sometimes passing close to his chair in search of something she had mislaid. There was colour in her cheeks; her eyes, though preoccupied, were bright; there was a lightness and buoyancy in her step which she set to a little dancing air she was humming under her breath.

After a moment or two the song ceased, she began to move slowly, sedately; and as if chilled by a raw breath of air, the light faded from her eyes, which she presently turned towards her husband.

"Why do you look at me?" she asked suddenly.

"I don't know, my dear," he began, slowly and laboriously as was his wont. "I was thinkin' how nice you looked—jest now—much better you know—but somehow"—he was taking long whiffs at his pipe, as usual, between each word, while she stood patiently waiting for him to finish—"somehow, you alter so, my dear—you're quite pale again all of a minute."

She stood listening to him, noticing against her will the more than suspicion of cockney accent and the thick drawl with which the words were uttered.

His eyes sought her face piteously. She noticed that too, and stood before him torn by conflicting emotions, pity and disgust struggling in a hand-to-hand fight within her.

"Mr. Broomhurst and I are going down by the well to sit; it's cooler there. Won't you come?" she said at last gently.

He did not reply for a moment, then he turned his head aside sharply for him.

"No, my dear, thank you; I'm comfortable enough here," he returned huskily.

She stood over him, hesitating a second, then moved abruptly to the table, from which she took a book.

He had risen from his seat by the time she turned to go out, and he intercepted her timorously.

"Kathie, give me a kiss before you go," he whispered hoarsely. "I—I don't often bother you."

She drew her breath in deeply as he put his arms clumsily about her, but she stood still, and he kissed her on the forehead, and touched the little wavy curls that strayed across it gently with his big trembling fingers.

When he released her she moved at once impetuously to the open doorway. On the threshold she hesitated, paused a moment irresolutely, and then turned back.

"Shall I—Does your pipe want filling, John?" she asked softly.

"No, thank you, my dear."

"Would you like me to stay, read to you, or anything?"

He looked up at her wistfully. "N-no, thank you, I'm not much of a reader, you know, my dear—somehow."

She hated herself for knowing that there would be a "my dear," probably a "somehow" in his reply, and despised herself for the sense of irritated impatience she felt by anticipation, even before the words were uttered.

There was a moment's hesitating silence, broken by the sound of quick firm footsteps without. Broomhurst paused at the entrance, and looked into the tent.

"Aren't you coming, Drayton?" he asked, looking first at Drayton's wife and then swiftly putting in his name with a scarcely perceptible pause. "Too lazy? But you, Mrs. Drayton?"

"Yes, I'm coming," she said.

They left the tent together, and walked some few steps in silence.

Broomhurst shot a quick glance at his companion's face.

"Anything wrong?" he asked presently.

Though the words were ordinary enough, the voice in which they were spoken was in some subtle fashion a different voice from that in which he had talked to her nearly two months ago, though it would have required a keen sense of nice shades in sound to have detected the change.

Mrs. Drayton's sense of niceties in sound was particularly keen, but she answered quietly, "Nothing, thank you."

They did not speak again till the trees round the stone-well were reached.

Broomhurst arranged their seats comfortably beside it.

"Are we going to read or talk?" he asked, looking up at her from his lower place.

"Well, we generally talk most when we arrange to read, so shall we agree to talk to-day for a change, by way of getting some reading done?" she rejoined, smiling. "*You* begin."

Broomhurst seemed in no hurry to avail himself of the permission, he was apparently engrossed in watching the flecks of sunshine on Mrs. Drayton's white dress. The whirring of insects, and the creaking of a Persian wheel somewhere in the neighbourhood, filtered through the hot silence.

Mrs. Drayton laughed after a few minutes; there was a touch of embarrassment in the sound.

"The new plan doesn't answer. Suppose you read as usual, and let me interrupt, also as usual, after the first two lines."

He opened the book obediently, but turned the pages at random.

She watched him for a moment, and then bent a little forward towards him.

"It is my turn now," she said suddenly. "Is anything wrong?"

He raised his head, and their eyes met. There was a pause. "I will be more honest than you," he returned. "Yes, there is."

"What?"

"I've had orders to move on."

She drew back, and her lips whitened, though she kept them steady.

"When do you go?"

"On Wednesday."

There was silence again; the man still kept his eyes on her face.

The whirring of the insects and the creaking of the wheel had suddenly grown so strangely loud and insistent, that it was in a half-dazed fashion she at length heard her name—*"Kathleen!"*

"Kathleen!" he whispered again hoarsely.

She looked him full in the face, and once more their eyes met in a long grave gaze.

The man's face flushed, and he half rose from his seat with an impetuous movement, but Kathleen stopped him with a glance.

"Will you go and fetch my work? I left it in the tent," she said, speaking very clearly and distinctly; "and then will you go on reading? I will find the place while you are gone."

She took the book from his hand, and he rose and stood before her.

There was a mute appeal in his silence, and she raised her head slowly.

Her face was white to the lips, but she looked at him unflinchingly; and without a word he turned and left her.

IV

Mrs. Drayton was resting in the tent on Tuesday afternoon. With the help of cushions and some low chairs she had improvised a couch, on which she lay quietly with her eyes closed. There was a tenseness, however, in her attitude which indicated that sleep was far from her.

Her features seemed to have sharpened during the last few days, and there were hollows in her cheeks. She had been very still for a long time, but all at once with a sudden movement she turned her head and buried her face in the cushions with a groan. Slipping from her place she fell on her knees beside the couch, and put both hands before her mouth to force back the cry that she felt struggling to her lips.

For some moments the wild effort she was making for outward calm, which even when she was all alone was her first instinct, strained every nerve and blotted out sight and hearing, and it was not till the sound was very near that she was conscious of the ring of horse's hoofs on the plain.

She raised her head sharply with a thrill of fear, still kneeling, and listened.

There was no mistake. The horseman was riding in hot haste, for the thud of the hoofs followed one another swiftly.

As Mrs. Drayton listened her white face grew whiter, and she began to tremble. Putting out shaking hands, she raised herself by the arms of the folding-chair and stood upright.

Nearer and nearer came the thunder of the approaching sound, mingled with startled exclamations and the noise of trampling feet from the direction of the kitchen tent.

Slowly, mechanically almost, she dragged herself to the entrance, and stood clinging to the canvas there. By the time she had reached it, Broomhurst had flung himself from the saddle, and had thrown the reins to one of the new men.

Mrs. Drayton stared at him with wide bright eyes as he hastened towards her.

"I thought you—you are not—" she began, and then her teeth began to chatter. "I am so cold!" she said, in a little weak voice.

Broomhurst took her hand, and led her over the threshold back into the tent.

"Don't be so frightened," he implored; "I came to tell you first. I thought it wouldn't frighten you so much as—Your—Drayton is—very ill. They are bringing him. I—"

He paused. She gazed at him a moment with parted lips, then she broke into a horrible discordant laugh, and stood clinging to the back of a chair.

Broomhurst started back.

"Do you understand what I mean?" he whispered. "Kathleen, for God's sake—*don't*—he is *dead.*"

He looked over his shoulder as he spoke, her shrill laughter ringing in his ears. The white glare and dazzle of the plain stretched before him, framed by the entrance to the tent; far off, against the horizon, there were moving black specks, which he knew to be the returning servants with their still burden.

They were bringing John Drayton home.

V

One afternoon, some months later, Broomhurst climbed the steep lane leading to the cliffs of a little English village by the sea. He had already been to the inn, and had been shown by the proprietress the house where Mrs. Drayton lodged.

"The lady was out, but the gentleman would likely find her if he went to the cliffs—down by the bay, or thereabouts," her landlady explained, and, obeying her directions, Broomhurst presently emerged from the shady woodland path on to the hillside overhanging the sea.

He glanced eagerly round him, and then with a sudden quickening of the heart, walked on over the springy heather to where she sat. She turned when the rustling his footsteps made through the bracken was near enough to arrest her attention, and looked up at him as he came. Then she rose slowly and stood waiting for him. He came up to her without a word and seized both her hands, devouring her face with his eyes. Something he saw there repelled him. Slowly he let her hands fall, still looking at her silently. "You are not glad to see me, and I have counted the hours," he said at last in a dull toneless voice.

Her lips quivered. "Don't be angry with me—I can't help it—I'm not glad or sorry for anything now," she answered, and her voice matched his for greyness.

They sat down together on a long flat stone half embedded in a wiry clump of whortleberries. Behind them the lonely hillsides rose, brilliant with yellow bracken and the purple of heather. Before them stretched the wide sea. It was a soft grey day. Streaks of pale sunlight trembled at moments far out on the water. The tide was rising in the little bay above which they sat, and Broomhurst watched the lazy foam-edged waves slipping over the uncovered rocks towards the shore, then sliding back as though for very weariness they despaired of reaching it. The muffled pulsing sound of the sea filled the silence. Broomhurst thought suddenly of hot Eastern sunshine, of the whirr of insect wings on the still air, and the creaking of a wheel in the distance. He turned and looked at his companion.

"I have come thousands of miles to see you," he said; "aren't you going to speak to me now I am here?"

"Why did you come? I told you not to come," she answered, falteringly. "I—" she paused.

"And I replied that I should follow you—if you remember," he answered, still quietly. "I came because I would not listen to what you said then, at that awful time. You didn't know *yourself* what you said. No wonder! I have given you some months, and now I have come."

There was silence between them. Broomhurst saw that she was crying; her tears fell fast on to her hands, that were clasped in her lap. Her face, he noticed, was thin and drawn.

Very gently he put his arm round her shoulder and drew her nearer to him. She made no resistance—it seemed that she did not notice the movement; and his arm dropped at his side.

"You asked me why I had come? You think it possible that three months can change one, very thoroughly, then?" he said in a cold voice.

"I not only think it possible, I have proved it," she replied wearily.

He turned round and faced her.

"You *did* love me, Kathleen!" he asserted; "you never said so in words, but I know it," he added fiercely.

"Yes, I did."

"And—You mean that you don't now?"

Her voice was very tired. "Yes—I can't help it," she answered, "it has gone—utterly."

The grey sea slowly lapped the rocks. Overhead the sharp scream of a gull cut through the stillness. It was broken again, a moment afterwards, by a short hard laugh from the man.

"Don't!" she whispered, and laid a hand swiftly on his arm. "Do you think it isn't worse for me? I wish to God I *did* love you," she cried passionately. "Perhaps it would make me forget that to all intents and purposes I am a murderess."

Broomhurst met her wide despairing eyes with an amazement which yielded to sudden pitying comprehension.

"So that is it, my darling? You are worrying about *that?* You who were as loyal, as—"

She stopped him with a frantic gesture.

"Don't! *don't!*" she wailed. "If you only knew; let me try to tell you—will you?" she urged pitifully. "It may be better if I tell some one—if I don't keep it all to myself, and think, and *think.*"

She clasped her hands tight, with the old gesture he remembered when she was struggling for self-control, and waited a moment.

Presently she began to speak in a low hurried tone: "It began before you came. I know now what the feeling was that I was afraid to acknowledge to myself. I used to try and smother it, I used to repeat things to myself all day—poems, stupid rhymes—*anything* to keep my thoughts quite underneath—but I—*hated* John before you came! We had been married nearly a year then. I never loved him. Of course you are going to say: 'Why did you marry him?'" She looked drearily over the placid sea. "Why *did* I marry him? I don't know; for the reason that hundreds of ignorant inexperienced girls marry, I suppose. My home wasn't a happy one. I was miserable, and oh,—*restless.* I wonder if men know what it feels like to be restless? Sometimes I think they can't even guess. John wanted me very badly—nobody wanted me at home particularly. There didn't seem to be any point in my life. Do you understand?.... Of course being alone with him in that little camp in that silent plain"—she shuddered—"made things worse. My nerves went all to pieces. Everything he said—his voice—his accent—his walk—the way he ate—irritated me so that I longed to rush out sometimes and shriek—and go *mad*. Does it sound ridiculous to you to be driven mad by such trifles? I only know I used to get up from the table sometimes and walk up and down outside, with both hands over my mouth to keep myself quiet. And all the time I *hated* myself—how I hated myself! I never had a word from him that wasn't gentle and tender. I believe he loved the ground I walked on. Oh, it is *awful* to be loved like that, when you—" She drew in her breath with a sob. "I—I—it made me sick for him to come near me—to touch me." She stopped a moment.

Broomhurst gently laid his hand on her quivering one. "Poor little girl!" he murmured.

"Then *you* came," she said, "and before long I had another feeling to fight against. At first I thought it couldn't be true that I loved you—it would die down. I think I was *frightened* at the feeling; I didn't know it hurt so to love any one."

Broomhurst stirred a little. "Go on," he said tersely.

"But it didn't die," she continued in a trembling whisper, "and the other *awful* feeling grew stronger and stronger—hatred; no, that is not the word—*loathing* for—for—John. I fought against it. Yes," she cried feverishly, clasping and unclasping her hands, "Heaven knows I fought it with all my strength, and reasoned with myself, and—oh, I did *everything*, but—" Her quick-falling tears made speech difficult.

"Kathleen!" Broomhurst urged desperately, "you couldn't help it, you poor child. You say yourself you struggled against your feelings—you were always gentle. Perhaps he didn't know."

"But he did—he *did*," she wailed, "it is just that. I hurt him a hundred times a day; he never said so, but I knew it; and yet I *couldn't* be kind to him—except in words—and he understood. And after you came it was worse in one way, for he knew. I *felt* he knew that I loved you. His eyes used to follow me like a dog's, and I was stabbed with remorse, and I tried to be good to him, and I couldn't."

"But—he didn't suspect—he trusted you," began Broomhurst. "He had every reason. No woman was ever so loyal, so—"

"Hush," she almost screamed. "Loyal! it was the least I could do—to stop you, I mean—when you—After all, I knew it without your telling me. I had deliberately married him without loving him. It was my own fault. I felt it. Even if I couldn't prevent his knowing that I hated him, I could prevent *that*. It was my punishment. I deserved it for *daring* to marry without love. But I didn't spare John one pang, after all," she added bitterly. "He knew what I felt towards him—I don't think he cared about anything else. You say I mustn't reproach myself? When I went back to the tent that morning—when you—when I stopped you from saying you loved me, he was sitting at the table with his head buried in his hands; he was crying—bitterly: I saw him—it is terrible to see a man cry—and I stole away gently, but he saw me. I was torn to pieces, but I *couldn't* go to him. I knew he would kiss me, and I shuddered to think of it. It seemed more than ever not to be borne that he should do that—when I knew *you* loved me."

"Kathleen" cried her lover again, "don't dwell on* it all so terribly— don't—"

"How can I forget?" she answered despairingly, "and then"—she lowered her voice—"oh, I can't tell you—all the time, at the back of my mind somewhere, there was a burning wish that he might *die*. I used to lie awake at night, and do what I would to stifle it, that thought used to *scorch* me, I wished it so intensely. Do you believe that by willing one can bring such things to pass?" she asked, looking at Broomhurst with feverishly bright eyes. "No?—well, I don't know—I tried to smother it. I *really* tried, but it was there, whatever other thoughts I heaped on the top. Then, when I heard the horse galloping across the plain that morning, I had a sick fear that it was *you*. I knew something had happened, and my first thought when I saw you alive and well, and knew that it was *John*, was, *that it was too good to be true.* I believe I laughed like a maniac, didn't I?.... Not to blame? Why, if it hadn't been for me he wouldn't have died. The men say they saw him sitting with his head uncovered in the burning sun, his face buried in his hands—just as I had seen him the day before. He didn't trouble to be careful—he was too wretched."

She paused, and Broomhurst rose and began to pace the little hillside path at the edge of which they were seated.

Presently he came back to her.

"Kathleen, let me take care of you," he implored, stooping towards her. "We have only ourselves to consider in this matter. Will you come to me at once?"

She shook her head sadly.

Broomhurst set his teeth, and the lines round his mouth deepened. He threw himself down beside her on the heather.

"Dear," he urged still gently, though his voice showed he was controlling himself with an effort. "You are morbid about this. You have been alone too much—you are ill. Let me take care of you: I *can*, Kathleen—and I love you. Nothing but morbid fancy makes you imagine you are in any way responsible for—Drayton's death. You can't bring him back to life, and—"

"No," she sighed drearily, "and if I could, nothing would be altered. Though I am mad with self-reproach, I feel *that*—it was all so inevitable. If he were alive and well before me this instant my feeling towards him wouldn't have changed. If he spoke to me, he would say 'My dear'—and I should *loathe* him. Oh, I know! It is *that* that makes it so awful."

"But if you acknowledge it," Broomhurst struck in eagerly, "will you wreck both of our lives for the sake of vain regrets? Kathleen, you never will."

He waited breathlessly for her answer.

"I won't wreck both our lives by marrying again without love on my side," she replied firmly.

"I will take the risk," he said. "You *have* loved me—you will love me again. You are crushed and dazed now with brooding over this—this trouble, but—"

"But I will not allow you to take the risk," Kathleen answered. "What sort of woman should I be to be willing again to live with a man I don't love? I have come to know that there are things one owes to *oneself.* Self-respect is one of them. I don't know how it has come to be so, but all my old feeling for you has *gone.* It is as though it had burnt itself out. I will not offer grey ashes to any man."

Broomhurst looking up at her pale, set face, knew that her words were final, and turned his own aside with a groan.

"Ah!" cried Kathleen with a little break in her voice, *"don't.* Go away and be happy and strong, and all that I loved in you. I am so sorry—so sorry to hurt you. I—" her voice faltered miserably. "I—I only bring trouble to people."

There was a long pause.

"Did you never think that there is a terrible vein of irony running through the ordering of this world?" she said presently. "It is a mistake to think our prayers are not answered—they are. In due time we get our heart's desire— when we have ceased to care for it."

"I haven't yet got mine," Broomhurst answered doggedly, "and I shall never cease to care for it."

She smiled a little with infinite sadness.

"Listen, Kathleen," he said. They had both risen and he stood before her, looking down at her. "I will go now, but in a year's time I shall come back. I will not give you up. You shall love me yet."

"Perhaps—I don't think so," she answered wearily.

Broomhurst looked at her trembling lips a moment in silence, then he stooped and kissed both her hands instead.

"I will wait till you tell me you love me," he said.

She stood watching him out of sight. He did not look back, and she turned with swimming eyes to the grey sea and the transient gleams of sunlight that swept like tender smiles across its face.

VICTORIA CROSS
(ANNIE SOPHIE CORY, 1868-1952)

Victoria Cross (Annie Sophie Cory) was born in the Punjab, India (today Pakistan), to Arthur and Elizabeth Fanny Griffin Cory. Her father was in the military. After an education in England, Cross began her literary career with the publication of "Theodora: A Fragment," in the Yellow Book *in January 1895. Her first novel,* The Woman Who Didn't *(1895) was published by John Lane in the Keynotes Series. It was marketed as a response to Grant Allen's* The Woman Who Did, *also published in 1895 in the same series, which tells the story of a woman who rejects marriage but lives with her lover in a free union. The* Woman Who Didn't *is narrated by a man, Evelyn, whose offers of love are rejected by Eurydice, a married woman.*

In a later novel, Six Chapter of a Man's Life *(1903), Cross revisits her earlier story "Theodora" and frames the fragment by providing earlier and later events of the plot. In the novel, Theodora dresses and passes as a man to accompany Cecil to Egypt as the companion he desired in the story. She finally commits suicide, believing that Cecil is unable to accept her and live with her in an equal relationship.*

Cross published three collections of short stories and twenty-three novels, among them Anna Lombard *(1901),* Life's Shop Window *(1907), and* Five Nights *(1908). Her fiction, characterized by extravagant plots and passionate struggles, was advanced in its depiction of interracial relationships and androgynous women who wear men's clothes and adopt their mannerisms.*

THEODORA. A FRAGMENT.

[*Yellow Book* IV (January 1895): 156-88]

I did not turn out of bed till ten o'clock the next morning, and I was still in dressing-gown and slippers, sitting by the fire looking over a map, when Digby came in upon me.

"Hullo, Ray, only just up, eh? as usual?" was his first exclamation as he entered, his ulster buttoned to his chin, and the snow thick upon his boots. "What a fellow you are! I can't understand anybody lying in bed till ten o'clock in the morning."

"And I can't understand anybody driving up at seven," I said, smiling, and stirring my coffee idly. I had laid down the map with resignation. I knew Digby had come round to jaw for the next hour at least. "Can I offer you some breakfast?"

"Breakfast!" returned Digby contemptuously. "No, thanks. I had mine hours ago. Well, what do you think of her?"

"Of whom?—this Theodora?"

"Oh, it's Theodora already, is it?" said Digby, looking at me. "Well, never mind: go on. Yes, what do you think of her?"

"She seems rather clever, I think."

"Do you?" returned Digby, with a distinct accent of regret, as if I had told him I thought she squinted. "I never noticed it. But her looks, I mean?"

"She is very peculiar," I said, merely.

"But you like everything extraordinary. I should have thought her very peculiarity was just what would have attracted you."

"So it does," I admitted; "so much so, that I am going to take the trouble of calling this afternoon expressly to see her again."

Digby stared hard at me for a minute, and then burst out laughing. "By Jove! You've made good use of your time. Did she ask you?"

"She did," I said.

"This looks as if it would be a case," remarked Digby lightly, and then added, "I'd have given anything to have had her myself. But if it's not to be for me, I'd rather you should be the lucky man than any one else."

"Don't you think all that is a little 'previous'?" I asked satirically, looking at him over the coffee, which stood on the map of Mesopotamia.

"Well, I don't know. You must marry some time, Cecil."

"Really!" I said, raising my eyebrows and regarding him with increased amusement. "I think I have heard of men remaining celibates before now, especially men with my tastes."

"Yes," said Digby, becoming suddenly as serious and thoughtful as if he were being called upon to consider some weighty problem, and of which the solution must be found in the next ten minutes. "I don't know how you would agree. She is an awfully religious girl."

"Indeed?" I said with a laugh. "How do you know?"

Digby thought hard.

"She is," he said with conviction, at last. "I see her at church every Sunday."

"Oh then, of course she must be—proof conclusive," I answered.

Digby looked at me and then grumbled, "Confounded sneering fellow you are. Has she been telling you she is not?"

I remembered suddenly that I had promised Theodora not to repeat her opinions, so I only said, "I really don't know what she is; she may be most devout for all I know—or care."

"Of course you can profess to be quite indifferent," said Digby ungraciously. "But all I can say is, it doesn't look like it—your going there this afternoon; and anyway, she is not indifferent to you. She said all sorts of flattering things about you."

"Very kind, I am sure," I murmured derisively.

"And she sent round to my rooms this morning a thundering box of Havannahs in recognition of my having won the bet about your looks."

I laughed outright. "That's rather good biz for you! The least you can do is to let me help in the smoking of them, I think."

"Of course I will. But it shows what she thinks of you, doesn't it?"

"Oh, most convincingly," I said with mock earnestness. "Havannahs are expensive things."

"But you know how awfully rich she is, don't you?" asked Digby, looking at me as if he wanted to find out whether I were really ignorant or affecting to be so.

"My dear Charlie, you know I know nothing whatever about her except what you tell me—or do you suppose she showed me her banking account between the dances?"

"Don't know, I am sure," Digby grumbled back. "You sat in that passage long enough to be going through a banking account, and balancing it too, for that matter! However, the point is, she is rich—tons of money, over six thousand a year."

"Really?" I said, to say something.

"Yes, but she loses every penny on her marriage. Seems such a funny way to leave money to a girl, doesn't it? Some old pig of a maiden aunt tied it up in that way. Nasty thing to do, I think; don't you?"

"Very immoral of the old lady, it seems. A girl like that, if she can't marry, will probably forego nothing but the ceremony."

"She runs the risk of losing her money, though, if anything were known. She only has it *dum casta manet*, just like a separation allowance."

"Hard lines," I murmured sympathetically.

"And so of course her people are anxious she should make a good match—take some man, I mean, with an income equal to what she has now of her own, so that she would not feel any loss. Otherwise, you see, if she married a poor man, it would be rather a severe drop for her."

"Conditions calculated to prevent any fellow but a millionaire proposing to her, I should think," I said.

"Yes, except that she is a girl who does not care about money. She has been out now three seasons, and had one or two good chances and not taken them. Now myself, for instance, if she wanted money and position and so on, she could hardly do better, could she? And my family and the rest of it are all right; but she couldn't get over my red hair—I know it was that. She's mad upon looks—I know she is; she let it out to me once, and I bet you anything, she'd take you and chuck over her money and everything else, if you gave her the chance."

"I am certainly not likely to," I answered. "All this you've just told me alone would be enough to choke me off. I have always thought I could never love a decent woman unselfishly enough, even if she gave up nothing for me; and, great heavens! I should be sorry to value myself, at—what do you say she has?—six thousand a year?"

"Leave the woman who falls in love with the cut of your nose to do the valuation. You'll be surprised at the figure!" said Digby with a touch of resentful bitterness, and getting up abruptly. "I'll look round in the evening," he added, buttoning up his overcoat. "Going to be in?"

"As far as I know," I answered, and he left.

I got up and dressed leisurely, thinking over what he had said, and those words "six thousand" repeating themselves unpleasantly in my brain.

The time was in accordance with strict formality when I found myself on her steps. The room I was shown into was large, much too large to be comfortable on such a day; and I had to thread my way through a perfect maze of gilt-legged tables and statuette-bearing tripods before I reached the hearth. Here burnt a small, quiet, chaste-looking fire, a sort of Vestal flame, whose heat was lost upon the tesselated tiles, white marble, and polished brass about it. I stood looking down at it absently for a few minutes, and then Theodora came in.

She was very simply dressed in some dark stuff that fitted closely to her, and let me see the harmonious lines of her figure as she came up to me. The plain, small collar of the dress opened at the neck, and a delicious, solid, white throat rose from the dull stuff like an almond bursting from its husk. On the pale, well-cut face and small head great care had evidently been bestowed. The eyes were darkened, as last night, and the hair arranged with infinite pains on the forehead and rolled into one massive coil at the back of her neck.

She shook hands with a smile—a smile that failed to dispel the air of fatigue and fashionable dissipation that seemed to cling to her; and then wheeled a chair as near to the fender as she could get it.

As she sat down, I thought I had never seen such splendid shoulders combined with so slight a hip before.

"Now I hope no one else will come to interrupt us," she said simply. "And don't let's bother to exchange comments on the weather or last night's dance. I have done that six times over this morning with other callers. Don't let's talk for the sake of getting through a certain number of words. Let us talk because we are interested in what we are saying."

"I should be interested in anything if you said it," I answered.

Theodora laughed. "Tell me something about the East, will you? That is a nice warm subject, and I feel so cold."

And she shot out towards the blaze two well-made feet and ankles.

"Yes, in three weeks' time I shall be in a considerably warmer climate than this," I answered, drawing my chair as close to hers as fashion permits.

Theodora looked at me with a perceptibly startled expression as I spoke.

"Are you really going out so soon?" she said.

"I am really," I said with a smile.

"Oh I am so sorry!"

"Why?" I asked merely.

"Because I was thinking I should have the pleasure of meeting you lots more times at different functions."

"And would that be a pleasure?"

"Yes, very great," said Theodora, with a smile lighting her eyes and parting faintly the soft scarlet lips.

She looked at me, a seducing softness melting all her face and swimming in the liquid darkness of the eyes she raised to mine. A delicious intimacy seemed established between us by that smile. We seemed nearer to each other after it than before, by many degrees. A month or two of time and ordinary intercourse may be balanced against the seconds of such a smile as this.

A faint feeling of surprise mingled with my thoughts, that she should show her own attitude of mind so clearly, but I believe she felt instinctively my attraction towards her, and also undoubtedly she belonged, and had always been accustomed, to a fast set. I was not the sort of man to find fault with her for that, and probably she had already been conscious of this, and felt all the more at ease with me. The opening-primrose type of woman, the girl who does or wishes to suggest the modest violet unfolding beneath the rural hedge, had never had a charm for me. I do not profess to admire the simple violet; I infinitely prefer a well-trained hothouse gardenia. And this girl, about whom there was nothing of the humble, crooked-neck violet—in whom there was a dash of virility, a hint at dissipation, a suggestion of a certain decorous looseness of morals and fastness of manners—could stimulate me with a keen sense of pleasure, as our eyes or hands met.

"Why would it be a pleasure to meet me?" I asked, holding her eyes with mine, and wondering whether things would so turn out that I should ever kiss those parting lips before me.

Theodora laughed gently.

"For a good many reasons that it would make you too conceited to hear," she answered. "But one is because you are more interesting to talk to than the majority of people I meet every day. The castor of your chair has come upon my dress. Will you move it back a little, please?"

I pushed my chair back immediately and apologised.

"Are you going alone?" resumed Theodora.

"Quite alone."

"Is that nice?"

"No. I should have been very glad to find some fellow to go with me, but it's rather difficult. It is not everybody that one meets whom one would care to make such an exclusive companion of, as a life like that out there necessitates. Still, there's no doubt I shall be dull unless I can find some chum there."

"Some Englishman, I suppose?"

"Possibly; but they are mostly snobs who are out there."

Theodora made a faint sign of assent, and we both sat silent, staring into the fire.

"Does the heat suit you?" Theodora asked, after a pause.

"Yes, I like it."

"So do I."

"I don't think any woman would like the climate I am going to now, or could stand it," I said.

Theodora said nothing, but I had my eyes on her face, which was turned towards the light of the fire, and I saw a tinge of mockery come over it.

We had neither said anything further, when the sound of a knock reached us, muffled, owing to the distance the sound had to travel to reach us by the drawing-room fire at all, but distinct in the silence between us.

Theodora looked at me sharply.

"There is somebody else. Do you want to leave yet?" she asked, and then added in a persuasive tone, "Come into my own study, where we shan't be disturbed, and stay and have tea with me, will you?"

She got up as she spoke.

The room had darkened considerably while we had been sitting there, and only a dull light came from the leaden, snow-laden sky beyond the panes, but the firelight fell strongly across her figure as she stood, glancing and playing up it towards the slight waist, and throwing scarlet upon the white throat and under-part of the full chin. In the strong shadow on her face I could see merely the two seducing eyes. Easily excitable where once a usually hypercritical or rather hyperfanciful eye has been attracted, I felt a keen sense of pleasure stir me as I watched her rise and stand, that sense of pleasure which is nothing more than an assurance to the roused and unquiet instincts within one, of future satisfaction or gratification, with, from, or at the expense of the object creating the sensation. Unconsciously a certainty of possession of Theodora to-day, to-morrow, or next year, filled me for the moment as completely as if I had just made her my wife. The instinct that demanded her was immediately answered by a mechanical process of the brain, not with doubt or fear, but simple confidence. "This is a pleasant and delightful object to you—as others have been. Later it will be a source of enjoyment to you—as others have been." And the lulling of this painful instinct is what we know as pleasure. And this instinct and its answer are exactly that which we should not feel within us for any beloved object. It is this that tends inevitably to degrade the loved one, and to debase our own passion. If the object is worthy and lovely in any sense, we should be ready to love it as being such, for itself, as moralists preach to us of Virtue, as theologians preach to us of the Deity. To love or at least to strive to love an object for the object's sake, and not our own sake, to love it in its relation to *its* pleasure and not in its relation to our own pleasure, is to feel the only love which is worthy of offering to a fellow human being, the one which elevates—and the only one—both giver and receiver. If we ever learn this lesson, we learn it late. I had not learnt it yet.

I murmured a prescribed "I shall be delighted," and followed Theodora behind a huge red tapestry screen that reached half-way up to the ceiling.

We were then face to face with a door which she opened, and we both passed over the threshold together.

She had called the room her own, so I glanced round it with a certain curiosity. A room is always some faint index to the character of its occupier, and as I looked a smile came to my face. This room suggested everywhere, as I should have expected, an intellectual but careless and independent spirit. There were two or three tables, in the window, heaped up with books and strewn over with papers. The centre-table had been pushed away, to leave a clearer space by the grate, and an armchair, seemingly of unfathomable depths, and a sofa, dragged forward in its place. Within the grate roared a tremendous fire, banked up half-way to the chimney, and a short poker was thrust into it between the bars. The red light leapt over the whole room and made it brilliant, and glanced over a rug, and some tumbled cushions on the floor in front of the fender, evidently where she had been lying. Now, however, she picked up the cushions, and tossed them into the corner of the couch, and sat down herself in the other corner.

"Do you prefer the floor generally?" I asked, taking the armchair as she indicated it to me.

"Yes, one feels quite free and at ease lying on the floor, whereas on a couch its limits are narrow, and one has the constraint and bother of taking care one does not go to sleep and roll off."

"But suppose you did, you would then but be upon the floor."

"Quite so; but I should have the pain of falling."

Our eyes met across the red flare of the firelight.

Theodora went on jestingly: "Now, these are the ethics of the couch and the floor. I lay myself voluntarily on the floor, knowing it thoroughly as a trifle low, but undeceptive and favourable to the condition of sleep which will probably arise, and suitable to my requirements of ease and space. I avoid the restricted and uncertain couch, recognising that if I fall to sleep on that raised level, and the desire to stretch myself should come, I shall awake with pain and shock to feel the ground, and see above me the couch from which I fell—do you see?"

She spoke lightly, and with a smile, and I listened with one. But her eyes told me that these ethics of the couch and floor covered the ethics of life.

"No, you must accept the necessity of the floor, I think, unless you like to forego your sleep and have the trouble of taking care to stick upon your couch; and for me the difference of level between the two is not worth the additional bother."

She laughed, and I joined her.

"What do you think?" she asked.

I looked at her as she sat opposite me, the firelight playing all over her, from the turn of her knee just marked beneath her skirt to her splendid shoulders, and the smooth soft hand and wrist supporting the distinguished little head. I did not tell her what I was thinking; what I said was: "You are very logical. I am quite convinced there's no place like the ground for a siesta."

Theodora laughed, and laid her hand on the bell.

A second or two after, a door, other than the one we had entered by, opened, and a maid appeared.

"Bring tea and pegs," said Theodora, and the door shut again.

"I ordered pegs for you because I know men hate tea," she said. "That's my own maid. I never let any of the servants answer this bell except her; she has my confidence, as far as one ever gives confidence to a servant. I think she likes me. I like making myself loved," she added impulsively.

"You've never found the least difficulty in it, I should think," I answered, perhaps a shade more warmly than I ought, for the colour came into her cheek and a slight confusion into her eyes.

The servant's re-entry saved her from replying.

"Now tell me how you like your peg made, and I'll make it," said Theodora, getting up and crossing to the table when the servant had gone.

I got up, too, and protested against this arrangement.

Theodora turned round and looked up at me, leaning one hand on the table.

"Now, how ridiculous and conventional you are!" she said. "You would think nothing of letting me make you a cup of tea, and yet I must by no means mix you a peg!"

She looked so like a young fellow of nineteen as she spoke that half the sense of informality between us was lost, and there was a keen, subtle pleasure in the superficial familiarity with her that I had never felt with far prettier women. The half of nearly every desire is curiosity, a vague, undefined curiosity, of which we are hardly conscious; and it was this that Theodora so violently stimulated, while her beauty was sufficient to nurse the other half. This feeling of curiosity arises, of course, for any woman who may be new to us, and who has the power to move us at all. But generally, if it cannot be gratified for the particular one, it is more or less satisfied by the general knowledge applying to them all; but here, as Theodora differed so much from the ordinary feminine type, even this instinctive sort of consolation was denied me. I looked down at her with a smile.

"We shan't be able to reconcile Fashion and Logic, so it's no use," I said. "Make the peg, then, and I'll try and remain in the fashion by assuming it's tea."

"Great Scott! I hope you wont fancy it's tea while you are drinking it!" returned Theodora laughing.

She handed me the glass, and I declared nectar wasn't in it with that peg, and then she made her own tea and came and sat down to drink it, in not at all an indecorous, but still informal proximity.

"Did you collect anything in the East?" she asked me, after a minute or two.

"Yes; a good many idols and relics and curiosities of sorts," I answered. "Would you like to see them?"

"Very much," Theodora answered. "Where are they?"

"Well, not in my pocket," I said smiling. "At my chambers. Could you and Mrs. Long spare an afternoon and honour me with a visit there?"

"I should like it immensely. I know Helen will come if I ask her."

"When you have seen them I must pack them up, and send them to my agents. One can't travel about with those things."

A sort of tremor passed over Theodora's face as I spoke, and her glance met mine, full of demands and questionings, and a very distinct assertion of distress. It said distinctly, "I am so sorry you are going." The sorrow in her eyes touched my vanity deeply, which is the most responsive quality we have. It is difficult to reach our hearts or our sympathies, but our vanity is always available. I felt inclined to throw my arm round that supple-looking waist—and it was close to me—and say, "Don't be sorry; come too." I don't know whether my looks were as plain as hers, but Theodora rose carelessly, apparently to set her teacup down, and then did not resume her seat by me, but went back to the sofa on the other side of the rug. This, in the state of feeling into which I had drifted, produced an irritated sensation, and I was rather pleased than not when a gong sounded somewhere in the house and gave me a graceful opening to rise.

"May I hope to hear from you, then, which day you will like to come?" I asked, as I held out my hand.

Now this was the moment I had been expecting, practically, ever since her hand had left mine last night, the moment when it should touch it again. I do not mean consciously, but there are a million slight, vague physical experiences and sensations within us of which the mind remains unconscious. Theodora's white right hand rested on her hip, the light from above struck upon it, and I noted that all the rings had been stripped from it; her left was crowded with them, so that the hand sparkled at each movement, but not one remained on her right. I coloured violently for the minute as I recollected my last night's pressure, and the idea flashed upon me at once that she had removed them expressly to avoid the pain of having them ground into her flesh.

The next second Theodora had laid her hand confidently in mine. My mind, annoyed at the thought that had just shot through it, bade me take her hand loosely and let it go, but Theodora raised her eyes to me, full of a soft disappointment which seemed to say, "Are you not going to press it, then, after all, when I have taken off all the rings entirely that you may?" That look seemed to push away, walk over, ignore my reason, and appeal directly to the eager physical nerves and muscles. Spontaneously, whether I would or not, they responded to it, and my fingers laced themselves tightly round this morsel of velvet-covered fire.

We forgot in those few seconds to say the orthodox good-byes; she forgot to answer my question. That which we were both saying to each other, though our lips did not open, was, "So I should like to hold and embrace you;" and she, "So I should like to be held and embraced."

Then she withdrew her hand, and I went out by the way of the drawing-room where we had entered.

In the hall her footman showed me out with extra obsequiousness. My three-hours' stay raised me, I suppose, to the rank of more than an ordinary caller.

It was dark now in the streets, and the temperature must have been somewhere about zero. I turned my collar up and started to walk sharply in the direction of my chambers. Walking always induces in me a tendency to reflection and retrospection, and now, removed from the excitement of Theodora's actual presence, my thoughts lapped quietly over the whole interview, going through it backwards, like the calming waves of a receding tide, leaving lingeringly the sand. There was no doubt that this girl attracted me very strongly, that the passion born yesterday was nearing adolescence; and there was no doubt, either, that I ought to strangle it now before it reached maturity. My thoughts, however, turned impatiently from this question, and kept closing and centring round the object itself, with maddening persistency. I laughed to myself as Schopenhauer's theory shot across me that all impulse to love is merely the impulse of the genius of the genus to select a fitting object which will help in producing a Third Life. Certainly the genius of the genus in me was weaker than the genius of my own individuality, in this instance, for Theodora was as unfitted, according to the philosopher's views, to become a co-worker with me in carrying out Nature's aim, as she was fitted to give me as an individual the strongest personal pleasure.

I remember Schopenhauer does admit that this instinct in man to choose some object which will best fulfil the duty of the race, is apt to be led astray, and it is fortunate he did not forget to make this admission, if his theory is to be generally applied, considering how very particularly often we are led astray, and that our strongest, fiercest passions and keenest pleasures are constantly not those suitable to, nor in accordance with, the ends of Nature. The sharpest, most violent stimulus, we may say, the true essence of pleasure, lies in some gratification which has no claim whatever, in any sense, to be beneficial or useful, or to have any ulterior motive, conscious or instinctive, or any lasting result, or any fulfilment of any object, but which is simple gratification and dies naturally in its own excess.

As we admit of works of pure genius that they cannot claim utility, or motive, or purpose, but simply that they exist as joy-giving and beautiful objects of delight, so must we have done with utility, motive, purpose, and the aims of Nature, before we can reach the most absolute degree of positive pleasure. To choose an admissible instance, a naturally hungry man, given a slice of bread, will he or will he not devour it with as great a pleasure as the craving drunkard feels in swallowing a draught of raw brandy?

In the first case a simple natural desire is gratified, and the aim of Nature satisfied; but the individual's longing and subsequent pleasure cannot be said to equal the furious craving of the drunkard, and his delirious sense of gratification as the brandy burns his throat.

My inclination towards Theodora could hardly be the simple, natural instinct, guided by natural selection, for then surely I should have been swayed towards some more womanly individual, some more vigorous and at the same time more feminine physique. In me, it was the mind that had first suggested to the senses, and the senses that had answered in a dizzy pleasure, that this passionate, sensitive frame, with its tensely-strung nerves and excitable pulses, promised the height of satisfaction to a lover. Surely to Nature it promised a poor if possible mother, and a still poorer nurse. And these desires and passions that spring from that border-land between mind and sense, and are nourished by the suggestions of the one and the stimulus of the other, have a stronger grip upon our organisation, because they offer an acuter pleasure, than those simple and purely physical ones in which Nature is striving after her own ends and using us simply as her instruments.

I thought on in a desultory sort of way, more or less about Theodora, and mostly about the state of my own feelings, until I reached my chambers. There I found Digby, and in his society, with his chaff and gabble in my ears, all reflection and philosophy fled, without leaving me any definite decision made.

The next afternoon but one found myself and Digby standing at the windows of my chambers awaiting Theodora's arrival. I had invited him to help me entertain the two women, and also to help me to unearth and dust my store of idols and curiosities, and range them on the tables for inspection. There were crowds of knick-knacks picked up in the crooked streets and odd corners of Benares, presents made to me, trifles bought in the Cairo bazaars, and vases and coins discovered below the soil in the regions of the Tigris. Concerning several of the most typical objects Digby and I had had considerable difference of opinion. One highly interesting bronze model of the monkey-god at Benares he had declared I could not exhibit on account of its too pronounced realism and insufficient attention to the sartorial art. I had insisted that the god's deficiencies in this respect were not more striking than the objects in flesh-tints, hung at the Academy, that Theodora viewed every season.

"Perhaps not," he answered. "But this is *not* in pink and white, and hung on the Academy walls for the public to stare at, and therefore you can't let her see it."

This was unanswerable. I yielded, and the monkey-god was wheeled under a side-table out of view.

Every shelf and stand and table had been pressed into the service, and my rooms had the appearance of a corner in an Egyptian bazaar, now when we had finished our preparations.

"There they are," said Digby, as Mrs. Long's victoria came in sight.

Theodora was leaning back beside her sister, and it struck me then how representative she looked, as it were, of herself and her position. From where we stood we could see down into the victoria, as it drew up at our door. Her knees were crossed under the blue carriage-rug, on the edge of which rested her two small pale-gloved hands. A velvet jacket, that fitted her as its skin fits the grape, showed us her magnificent shoulders, and the long easy slope of her figure to the small waist. On her head in the least turn of which lay the acme of distinction, amongst the black glossy masses of her hair, sat a small hat in vermilion velvet, made to resemble the Turkish fez. As the carriage stopped, she glanced up; and a brilliant smile swept over her face, as she bowed slightly to us at the window. The handsome painted eye, the naturally scarlet lips, the pallor of the oval face, and each well-trained movement of the distinguished figure, as she rose and stepped from the carriage, were noted and watched by our four critical eyes.

"A typical product of our nineteenth-century civilisation," I said, with a faint smile, as Theodora let her fur-edged skirt draw over the snowy pavement, and we heard her clear cultivated tones, with the fashionable drag in them, ordering the coachman not to let the horses get cold.

"But she's a splendid sort of creature, don't you think?" asked Digby. "Happy the man who—eh?"

I nodded. "Yes," I assented. "But how much that man should have to offer, old chap, that's the point; that six thousand of hers seems an invulnerable protection."

"I suppose so," said Digby with a nervous yawn. "And to think I have more than double that and yet—It's a pity. Funny it will be if my looks and your poverty prevent either of us having her."

"My own case is settled," I said decisively. "My position and hers decide it for me."

"I'd change places with you this minute if I could," muttered Digby moodily, as steps came down to our door, and we went forward to meet the women as they entered.

It seemed to arrange itself naturally that Digby should be occupied in the first few seconds with Mrs. Long, and that I should be free to receive Theodora.

Of all the lesser emotions, there is hardly any one greater than that subtle sense of pleasure felt when a woman we love crosses for the first time our own threshold. We may have met her a hundred times in her house, or on public ground, but the sensation her presence then creates is altogether different from that instinctive, involuntary, momentary and delightful sense of ownership that rises when she enters any room essentially our own.

It is the very illusion of possession.

With this hatefully egoistic satisfaction infused through me, I drew forward for her my own favourite chair, and Theodora sank into it, and her tiny, exquisitely-formed feet sought my fender-rail. At the murmured invitation from me, she unfastened and laid aside her jacket. Beneath, she revealed some purplish, silk-like material, that seemed shot with different colours as the firelight fell upon it. It was strained tight and smooth upon her, and the swell of a low bosom was distinctly defined below it. There was no excessive development, quite the contrary, but in the very slightness there was an indescribably sensuous curve, and a depression, rising and falling, that seemed as if it might be the very home itself of passion. It was a breast with little suggestion of the duties or powers of Nature, but with infinite seduction for a lover.

"What a marvellous collection you have here," she said throwing her glance round the room. "What made you bring home all these things?"

"The majority were gifts to me—presents made by the different natives whom I visited or came into connection with in various ways. A native is never happy, if he likes you at all, until he has made you some valuable present."

"You must be very popular with them indeed," returned Theodora, glancing from a brilliant Persian carpet, suspended on the wall, to the gold and ivory model of a temple, on the console by her side.

"Well, when one stays with a fellow as his guest, as I have done with some of these small rajahs and people, of course one tries to make oneself amiable."

"The fact is, Miss Dudley," interrupted Digby, "Ray admires these fellows, and that is why they like him. Just look at this sketch-book of his—what trouble he has taken to make portraits of them."

And he stretched out a limp-covered pocket album of mine.

I reddened slightly and tried to intercept his hand.

"Nonsense, Digby. Give the book to me," I said; but Theodora had already taken it, and she looked at me as I spoke with one of those delicious looks of hers that could speak so clearly. Now it seemed to say, "If you are going to love me, you must have no secrets from me." She opened the book and I was subdued and let her. I did not much care, except that it was some time now since I had looked at it, and I did not know what she might find in it. However, Theodora was so different from girls generally, that it did not greatly matter.

"Perhaps these are portraits of your different conquests amongst the Ranees, are they?" she said. "I don't see 'my victims,' though, written across the outside as the Frenchmen write on their albums."

"No," I said, with a smile, "I think these are only portraits of men whose appearance struck me. The great difficulty is to persuade any Mohammedan to let you draw him."

The very first leaf she turned seemed to give the lie to my words. Against a background of yellow sand and blue sky, stood out a slight figure in white, bending a little backward, and holding in its hands, extended on either side, the masses of its black hair that fell through them till they touched the sand by its feet. Theodora threw a side glance full of derision on me, as she raised her eyes from the page.

"I swear it isn't," I said hastily, colouring, for I saw she thought it was a woman. "It's a young Sikh I bribed to let me paint him."

"Oh, a young Sikh, is it?" said Theodora, bending over the book again. "Well it's a lovely face; and what beautiful hair!"

"Yes, almost as beautiful as yours," I murmured, in safety, for the others were wholly occupied in testing the limits of the flexibility of the soapstone.

Not for any consideration in this world could I have restrained the irresistible desire to say the words, looking at her sitting sideways to me, noting that shining weight of hair lying on the white neck, and that curious masculine shade upon the upper lip. A faint liquid smile came to her face.

"Mine is not so long as that when you see it undone," she said, looking at me.

"How long is it?" I asked mechanically, turning over the leaves of the sketch-book, and thinking in a crazy sort of way what I would not give to see her with that hair unloosed, and have the right to lift a single strand of it.

"It would not touch the ground," she answered, "it must be about eight inches off it, I think."

"A marvellous length for a European," I answered in a conventional tone, though it was a difficulty to summon it.

Within my brain all the dizzy thoughts seemed reeling together till they left me hardly conscious of anything but an acute painful sense of her proximity.

"Find me the head of a Persian, will you?" came her voice next.

"A Persian?" I repeated mechanically.

Theodora looked at me wonderingly and I recalled myself.

"Oh, yes," I answered, "I'll find you one. Give me the book."

I took the book and turned over the leaves towards the end. As I did so, some of the intermediate pages caught her eye, and she tried to arrest the turning leaves.

"What is that? Let me see."

"It is nothing," I said, passing them over. "Allow me to find you the one you want."

Theodora did not insist, but her glance said: "I will be revenged for this resistance to my wishes!"

When I had found her the portrait, I laid the open book back upon her knees. Theodora bent over it with an unaffected exclamation of delight. "How exquisite! and how well you have done it! What a talent you must have!"

"Oh no, no talent," I said hastily. "It's easy to do a thing like that when your heart is in it."

Theodora looked up at me and said simply, "This is a woman."

And I looked back in her eyes and said as simply, "Yes, it is a woman."

Theodora was silent, gazing at the open leaf, absorbed. And half-unconsciously my eyes followed hers and rested with hers on the page.

Many months had gone by since I had opened the book; and many, many cigars, that according to Tolstoi deaden every mental feeling, and many, many pints of brandy that do the same thing, only more so, had been consumed, since I had last looked upon that face. And now I saw it over the shoulder of this woman. And the old pain revived and surged through me, and it was dull—dull as every emotion must be in the near neighbourhood of a new object of desire—every emotion except one.

"Really it is a very beautiful face, isn't it?" she said at last, with a tender and sympathetic accent, and as she raised her head our eyes met.

I looked at her and answered, "I should say yes, if we were not looking at it together, but you know beauty is entirely a question of comparison."

Her face was really not one-tenth so handsome as the mere shadowed, inanimate representation of the Persian girl, beneath our hands. I knew it and so did she. Theodora herself would have been the first to admit it. But nevertheless the words were ethically true. True in the sense that underlay the society compliment, for no beauty of the dead can compare with that of the living. Such are we, that as we love all objects in their relation to our own pleasure from them, so even in our admiration, the greatest beauty, when absolutely useless to us, cannot move us as a far lesser degree has power to do, from which it is possible to hope, however vaguely, for some personal gratification. And to this my words would come if translated. And I think Theodora understood the translation rather than the conventional form of them, for she did not take the trouble to deprecate the flattery.

I got up, and, to change the subject, said, "Let me wheel up that little table of idols. Some of them are rather curious."

I moved the tripod up to the arm of her chair.

Theodora closed the sketch-book and put it beside her, and looked over the miniature bronze gods with interest. Then she stretched out her arm to lift and move several of them, and her soft fingers seemed to lie caressingly—as they did on everything they touched—on the heads and shoulders of the images. I watched her, envying those senseless little blocks of brass.

"This is the Hindu equivalent of the Greek Aphrodite," I said, lifting forward a small, unutterably hideous, squat female figure, with the face of a monkey, and two closed wings of a dragon on its shoulders.

"Oh, Venus," said Theodora. "We must certainly crown her amongst them, though hardly, I think, in this particular case, for her beauty!"

And she laughingly slipped off a diamond half-hoop from her middle finger, and slipped the ring on to the model's head. It fitted exactly round the repulsive brows of the deformed and stunted image, and the goddess stood crowned in the centre of the table, amongst the other figures, with the circlet of brilliants, flashing brightly in the firelight, on her head. As Theodora passed the ring from her own warm white finger on to the forehead of the misshapen idol, she looked at me. The look, coupled with the action, in my state, went home to those very inner cells of the brain where are the springs themselves of passion. At the same instant the laughter and irresponsible gaiety and light pleasure on the face before me, the contrast between the delicate hand and the repellent monstrosity it had crowned—the sinister, allegorical significance—struck me like a blow. An unexplained feeling of rage filled me. Was it against her, myself, her action, or my own desires? It seemed for the moment to burn against them all. On the spur of it, I dragged forward to myself another of the images from behind the Astarte, slipped off my own signet-ring, and put it on the head of the idol.

"This is the only one for me to crown," I said bitterly, with a laugh, feeling myself whiten with the stress and strain of a host of inexplicable sensations that crowded in upon me, as I met Theodora's lovely inquiring glance.

There was a shade of apprehensiveness in her voice she said, "What is that one?"

"Shiva," I said curtly, looking her straight in the eyes. "The god of self-denial."

I saw the colour die suddenly out of her face, and I knew I had hurt her. But I could not help it. With her glance she had summoned me to approve or second her jesting act. It was a challenge I could not pass over. I must in some correspondingly joking way either accept or reject her coronation. And to reject it was all I could do, since this woman must be nothing to me. There was a second's blank pause of strained silence. But, superficially, we had not strayed off the legitimate ground of mere society nothings, whatever we might feel lay beneath them. And Theodora was trained thoroughly in the ways of fashion.

The next second she leant back in her chair, saying lightly, "A false, absurd, and unnatural god; it is the greatest error to strive after the impossible; it merely prevents you accomplishing the possible. Gods like these," and she indicated the abominable squint-eyed Venus, "are merely natural instincts personified, and one may well call them gods since they are invincible. Don't you remember the fearful punishments that the Greeks represented as over-

taking mortals who dared to resist nature's laws, that they chose to individu-
alise as their gods? You remember the fate of Hippolytus who tried to disdain
Venus, of Pentheus who tried to subdue Bacchus? These two plays teach the
immortal lesson that if you have the presumption to try to be greater than
nature she will in the end take a terrible revenge. The most we can do is to
guide her. You can never be her conqueror. Consider yourself fortunate if she
allows you to be her charioteer."

It was all said very lightly and jestingly, but at the last phrase there was a
flash in her eye, directed upon me—yes, me—as if she read down into my
inner soul, and it sent the blood to my face.

As the last word left her lips, she stretched out her hand and deliberately
took my ring from the head of Shiva, put it above her own diamonds on the
other idol, and laid the god I had chosen, the god of austerity and mortifica-
tion, prostrate on its face, at the feet of the leering Venus.

Then, without troubling to find a transition phrase, she got up and said, "I
am going to look at that Persian carpet."

It had all taken but a few seconds; the next minute we were over by the carpet, standing in front of it and admiring its hues in the most orthodox terms.
The images were left as she had placed them. I could do nothing less, of course,
than yield to a woman and my guest. The jest had not gone towards calming my
feelings, nor had those two glances of hers—the first so tender and appealing
as she had crowned the Venus, the second so virile and mocking as she had dis-
crowned the Shiva. There was a strange mingling of extremes in her. At one
moment she seemed will-less, deliciously weak, a thing only made to be taken
in one's arms and kissed. The next, she was full of independent uncontrollable
determination and opinion. Most men would have found it hard to be indifferent to her. When beside her you must either have been attracted or repelled.
For me, she was the very worst woman that could have crossed my path.

As I stood beside her now, her shoulder only a little below my own, her
neck and the line of her breast just visible to the side vision of my eye, and
heard her talking of the carpet, I felt there was no price I would not have paid
to have stood for one half-hour in intimate confidence with her, and been
able to tear the veils from this irritating character.

From the carpet we passed on to a table of Cashmere work and next to a
pile of Mohammedan garments. These had been packed with my own personal luggage, and I should not have thought of bringing them forth for
inspection. It was Digby who, having seen them by chance in my portman-
teau, had insisted that they would add interest to the general collection of
Eastern trifles. "Clothes, my dear fellow, clothes; why, they will probably
please her more than anything else."

Theodora advanced to the heap of stuffs and lifted them.

"What is the history of these?" she said laughing. "These were not presents
to you!"

"No," I murmured. "Bought in the native bazaars."

"Some perhaps," returned Theodora, throwing her glance over them. "But a great many are not new."

It struck me that she would not be a woman very easy to deceive. Some men value a woman in proportion to the ease with which they can impose upon her, but to me it is too much trouble to deceive at all, so that the absence of that amiable quality did not disquiet me. On the contrary, the comprehensive, cynical, and at the same time indulgent smile that came so readily to Theodora's lips charmed me more, because it was the promise of even less trouble than a real or professed obtuseness.

"No," I assented merely.

"Well, then?" asked Theodora, but without troubling to seek a reply. "How pretty they are and how curious! this one, for instance." And she took up a blue silk zouave, covered with gold embroidery, and worth perhaps about thirty pounds. "This has been a good deal worn. It is a souvenir, I suppose?"

I nodded. With any other woman I was similarly anxious to please I should have denied it, but with her I felt it did not matter.

"Too sacred perhaps, then, for me to put on?" she asked with her hand in the collar, and smiling derisively.

"Oh dear no!" I said, "not at all. Put it on by all means."

"Nothing is sacred to you, eh; I see. Hold it then."

She gave me the zouave and turned for me to put it on her. A glimpse of the back of her white neck, as she bent her head forward, a convulsion of her adorable shoulders as she drew on the jacket, and the zouave was fitted on. Two seconds perhaps, but my self-control wrapped round me had lost one of its skins.

"Now I must find a turban or fez," she said, turning over gently, but without any ceremony, the pile. "Oh, here's one!" She drew out a white fez, also embroidered in gold, and, removing her hat, put it on very much to one side, amongst her black hair, with evident care lest one of those silken inflected waves should be disturbed; and then affecting an undulating gait, she walked over to the fire.

"How do you like me in Eastern dress, Helen?" she said, addressing her sister, for whom Digby was deciphering some old coins. Digby and I confessed afterwards to each other the impulse that moved us both to suggest it was not at all complete without the trousers. I did offer her a cigarette, to enhance the effect.

"Quite passable, really," said Mrs. Long, leaning back and surveying her languidly.

Theodora took the cigarette with a laugh, lighted and smoked it, and it was then, as she leant against the mantel-piece with her eyes full of laughter, a glow on her pale skin, and an indolent relaxation in the long, supple figure, that I first said, or rather an involuntary, unrecognised voice within me said, "It is no good; whatever happens I must have you."

"Do you know that it is past six, Theo?" said Mrs. Long.

"You will let me give you a cup of tea before you go?" I said.

"Tea!" repeated Theodora. "I thought you were going to say haschisch or opium, at the least, after such an Indian afternoon."

"I have both," I answered, "would you like some?" thinking, "By Jove, I should like to see you after the haschisch."

"No," replied Theodora, "I make it a rule not to get intoxicated in public."

When the women rose to go, Theodora, to my regret, divested herself of the zouave without my aid, and declined it also for putting on her own cloak. As they stood drawing on their gloves I asked if they thought there was anything worthy of their acceptance amongst these curiosities. Mrs. Long chose from the table near her an ivory model of the Taj, and Digby took it up to carry for her to the door. As he did so his eye caught the table of images.

"This is your ring, Miss Dudley, I believe," he said.

I saw him grin horridly as he noted the arrangement of the figures. Doubtless he thought it was mine.

I took up my signet-ring again, and Theodora said carelessly, without the faintest tinge of colour rising in her cheek, "Oh, yes, I had forgotten it. Thanks."

She took it from him and replaced it.

I asked her if she would honour me as her sister had done.

"There is one thing in this room that I covet immensely," she said, meeting my gaze.

"It is yours, of course, then," I answered. "What is it?"

Theodora stretched out her open hand. "Your sketch-book."

For a second I felt the blood dye suddenly all my face. The request took me by surprise, for one thing; and immediately after the surprise followed the vexatious and embarrassing thought that she had asked for the one thing in the room that I certainly did not wish her to have. The book contained a hundred thousand memories, embodied in writing, sketching, and painting, of those years in the East. There was not a page in it that did not reflect the emotions of the time when it had been filled in, and give a chronicle of the life lived at the date inscribed on it. It was a sort of diary in cipher, and to turn over its leaves was to relive the hours they represented. For my own personal pleasure I liked the book and wanted to keep it, but there were other reasons too why I disliked the idea of surrendering it. It flashed through me, the question as to what her object was in possessing herself of it. Was it jealousy of the faces or any face within it that prompted her and would she amuse herself, when she had it, by tearing out the leaves or burning it? To give over these portraits merely to be sacrificed to a petty feminine spite and malice, jarred upon me. Involuntarily I looked hard into her eyes to try and read her intentions, and I felt I had wronged her. The eyes were full of the softest, tenderest light. It was impossible to imagine them vindictive. She had seen my hesitation and she smiled faintly.

"Poor Herod with your daughter of Herodias," she said, softly. "Never mind, I will not take it."

The others who had been standing with her saw there was some embarrassment that they did not understand, and Mrs. Long turned to go slowly down the corridor. Digby had to follow. Theodora was left standing alone before me, her seductive figure framed in the open doorway. Of course she was irresistible. Was she not the new object of my desires?

I seized the sketch-book from the chair. What did anything matter?

"Yes," I said hastily, putting it into that soft, small hand before it could draw back. "Forgive me the hesitation. You know I would give you anything."

If she answered or thanked me, I forget it. I was sensible of nothing at the moment but that the blood seemed flowing to my brain, and thundering through it, in ponderous waves. Then I knew we were walking down the passage, and in a few minutes more we should have said good-bye, and she would be gone.

An acute and yet vague realisation came upon me that the corridor was dark, and that the others had gone on in front, a confused recollection of the way she had lauded Nature and its domination a short time back, and then all these were lost again in the eddying torrent of an overwhelming desire to take her in my arms and hold her, control her, assert my will over hers, this exasperating object who had been pleasing and seducing every sense for the last three hours, and now was leaving them all unsatisfied. That impulse towards some physical demonstration, that craving for physical contact, which attacks us suddenly with its terrific impetus, and chokes and stifles us, ourselves, beneath it, blinding us to all except itself, rushed upon me then, walking beside her in the dark passage; and at that instant Theodora sighed.

"I am tired," she said languidly. "May I take your arm?" and her hand touched me.

I did not offer her my arm, I flung it round her neck, bending back her head upon it, so that her lips were just beneath my own as I leant over her, and I pressed mine on them in a delirium of passion.

Everything that should have been remembered I forgot.

Knowledge was lost of all, except those passive, burning lips under my own. As I touched them, a current of madness seemed to mingle with my blood, and pass flaming through all my veins.

I heard her moan, but for that instant I was beyond the reach of pity or reason, I only leant harder on her lips in a wild, unheeding, unsparing frenzy. It was a moment of ecstasy that I would have bought with years of my life. One moment, the next I released her, and so suddenly, that she reeled against the wall of the passage. I caught her wrist to steady her. We dared neither of us speak, for the others were but little ahead of us; but I sought her eyes in the dark.

They met mine, and rested on them, gleaming through the darkness. There was no confusion nor embarrassment in them, they were full of the hot clear, blinding light of passion; and I knew there would be no need to crave forgiveness.

The next moment had brought us up to the others, and to the end of the passage.

Mrs. Long turned round, and held out her hand to me.

"Good-bye," she said. "We have had a most interesting afternoon."

It was with an effort that I made some conventional remark.

Theodora, with perfect outward calm, shook hands with myself and Digby, with her sweetest smile, and passed out.

I lingered some few minutes with Digby, talking; and then he went off to his own diggings, and I returned slowly down the passage to my rooms.

My blood and pulses seemed beating as they do in fever, my ears seemed full of sounds, and that kiss burnt like the brand of hot iron on my lips. When I reached my rooms, I locked the door and flung both the windows open to the snowy night. The white powder on the ledge crumbled and drifted in.

Ada Radford (1859-1934)

Ada Radford was the sister of Ernest Radford, a poet and member of the Rhymers' Club; she collaborated with her brother on his book Songs in the Whirlwind *(1918). Ada was educated at Girton, became assistant mistress of a High School and then a secretary to a Working Women's College. She published two stories in the* Yellow Book, *in October 1896 and April 1897. In 1897 she married Graham Wallas, an economist and a leader of the Fabian Society; they had a daughter. In the twentieth century she published primarily nonfiction, including* Before the Bluestockings *(1929) and* Daguerreotypes *(1929), a book of early reminiscences. Both books were published under her married name, Ada Radford Wallas.*

Lot 99

[*Yellow Book* XI (October 1896): 267-82]

The library in the house where I was born was a well aired and well dusted room, but the things we kept in it were so connected in the mind with dust and fustiness that it was difficult to feel happy there.

There were preserved fish of various kinds hanging from the walls, there was a large glass case of sea birds, one of many varieties of inland birds, cases of minerals, and, all over the mantelpiece, and on the shelves, there were little Hindoo gods, models of Keltic crosses, models of every imaginable thing from Cleopatra's needle to the Eddystone lighthouse.

As a child I hated this room. Although it was called the library there were few books in it. The writing-desk, where I was often sent to do my lessons, was horribly uncomfortable and in a bad light.

My lessons always took me a long time in this room, for although I hated being there, and longed to be away, and off with Lionel, the evil-looking gods, and the fishes glaring at me with their glass eyes, chained me to the spot. I never felt at home, and yet I remember that Aunt Lizzie had been all round the room with me, and had told me the history of every object, where father had bought it, and how much it had cost, and I could hear my voice, as a sound outside me, saying: "Yes, Auntie, did he really?" and hers, like a nearer sound in answer, to my surprise: "My dear child, that's a trifle for a genuine antique."

How I hated those birds and fishes! Not only were they dead, but the life had been dried, inflated, and stuffed out of them, and horror of horrors, glass eyes had been forced into their senseless heads.

And yet one day I heard Aunt Lizzie tell a lady she was calling on, that I was wonderfully intelligent. "It's the kind of mind I like," she said. "She's like our side of the family, she takes interest in external objects."

I can see Aunt Lizzie's bonnet now as she said it. The mauve that blondes used to wear, and on one side, a daring arrangement in imitation coral and sea-weed. Even in her bonnets Aunt Lizzie's personality shone out, and very marked were the personalities of what I now learnt was *my* side of the family.

It did not improve the library to my mind that Aunt Lizzie chose it as the place in which to hang large photographs of her brothers and sisters. They were striking people; I felt it as a child when I met them, and now I am sure of it. Amiable, strong willed and capable, they indeed were always interested in external objects. They were a great contrast to the other side of the family, my mother's side, "your poor dear mother" as Aunt Lizzie always called her, although my father who was also dead was always referred to simply as John. Of my mother and her people I knew little, our grandparents were dead and my mother's only sister was married and had a large family of her own in Australia.

"I think your poor dear mother did wonderfully considering her people," I remember Aunt Lizzie once said to me. "They never got on. No common sense. Fortunately your mother married young, and altered a good deal. At first she had the most unpractical ideas. She would have no nurse for you children. She would tell her housemaid not to hurry home in the evening if she were enjoying herself. She thought of every one before herself; that's very pretty in a young girl, but it may be carried too far. John's influence steadied her. But I used to think that John was just the least little bit foolish about her, although I like to see a happy marriage; but really John gave one the idea that there was no one but Mary in the world. He sometimes neglected his own people. It was not your mother's fault, my dear; no one could have been more anxious to have us. John got an idea that she ought to have quiet, and insisted on it, and poor Mary died when you were six; and we might have brightened her last days much more than we did, but for John's obstinacy. Your mother was a most lovable woman. I was almost glad John never noticed her lack of common sense."

I had very little to remind me of my mother. I had been given a little packet of letters, of father's to her and hers to father, but I burnt them unread; besides those I had nothing but a few little trinkets. Dainty old-fashioned things; beautiful, although bought in the days of the worst taste. Little things that his sisters would not have looked at. I liked them. They strengthened a feeling I had that my mother had made her impression on one member of the family of dominant personalities, at any rate he had cared to know her mind and tastes, and I felt more gently towards the ladies and gentlemen who hung in the library with their marked features and heavy ornaments. To one of them the family qualities had not been everything, and a member of the family doomed as regards success had been made a close study of. Still I was oppressed in the library, the features of the uncles and aunts, the want of view from the window, the glass eyes of innumerable birds, the height of the room, or the combination of all these things, made my heart feel solid lead and my head a disused machine. And it seems to me now in looking back that whenever anything painful has happened to me it has happened in that room; if I have a nightmare I am there and every object is in its place; although last time I saw the most hated of them, they were together in a heap (lot 99), at the sale.

In that room I fought my first important battle and lost. I think I was too anxious to be calm and logical. I knew my brother's opinion of girls. I knew that he had had a legal training, and I knew that I had had no training. I wanted him to tell me whether it would be possible for my trustees to advance me some capital.

It would not have surprised him more if I had asked whether he thought it well that I should keep a tame tiger, but he only raised his eyebrows slightly. It was a possibility under the will, he said, if the trustees were prepared to take a certain amount of responsibility in the matter.

He sat at the desk, and I having put my tennis hat on one stiff backed chair took the other, as near as the window as I could get. I told him that I wanted it for educational purposes, and he asked me what had been wrong with my education.

I told him that it had not left me in a position to maintain myself.

"Let us be practical," Lionel said, assuming the expression of one of his uncles on the wall; and he made a few notes on a bit of paper.

"When you are thirty," he told me next, "you will be independent, because that little property of mother's falls to you then."

I was nineteen.

"Thirty?" I said quietly. "I might as well be dead."

Lionel did not argue that point. He looked at me critically. I felt him notice my disordered hair and blue flannel blouse.

"You are pretty," he said judicially.

I was annoyed that I blushed, but I said in a sufficiently matter-of-fact tone: "But not very."

He acquiesced, and said, "It's difficult not to be pretty in this climate at nineteen. I don't think it will last."

"No," I broke in eagerly. "It's only complexion. Aunt Lizzie said so a few days ago."

Lionel looked a little surprised at my eagerness to go off, but I knew well that my looks were being weighed against the probability of my doing anything. His next words confirmed my suspicions.

"You'll marry," he remarked.

"Lionel," I said in a tone so emphatic that again he raised his eyebrows slightly, "I shall not marry," and I meant it.

Lionel smiled the smile of a man who has lived five years longer than the person he is speaking to, and that person his sister.

It was true that sometimes on our country walks I had wished that I were engaged, for Jack and Lionel would not stop long in beautiful places, and they would not let me pick things; if I said I wanted to, they would stuff my hands full of flowers and hurry me along. If I saw something pretty across a stream and waded for it, Jack would say: "Do come on, stupid! you're getting your feet wet!" and yet the bogs he'd have brought me through that very day! And I had thought vaguely, that the person I was engaged to would not mind waiting for me, or be bored at loitering. But I never had these ideas indoors, and the knowledge that Lionel was weighing my chances drove all lingering romance from my head.

"I have never had an offer," I said, hoping that this statement would have due weight with him in his final decision.

Lionel's smile this time made me flush indignantly. I saw that he was laughing at me.

"Aunt Lizzie had had more than one before she was my age," I said coolly, "but I do not see what this has to do with the question."

"It has this," said Lionel, "whether we boys marry or not, we have our livings to get; you have not to, you have a home with Aunt Lizzie until you marry, and in any case just enough money of your own when you are thirty. It would be simple madness to touch your capital."

I felt completely crushed. I did not in reality know enough about our affairs to ask an intelligent question, and Lionel's last emphatic statement had made its impression. He saw that he had won.

"What had you thought of doing?" he asked now not unkindly.

"I thought I'd prepare myself to be a teacher," I said apologetically.

"Oh, don't," he said. "You'd find it an awful grind, you wouldn't be half so jolly, and when we came home there'd only be Aunt Lizzie, or if you were here at all, you'd be half asleep and talking shop." I suppose I did not look convinced, for Lionel grew really distressed and his legal manner disappeared completely, and he said with what for him was a show of feeling, "We always said we'd stick together, Grace."

None the less that this was the first I had heard of it I was moved, my plans melted away. I held out my hand and renewed the compact, although vaguely I realised that it meant Lionel would go and I should stick.

If in my little bedroom there were no objects of interest, it was not Aunt Lizzie's fault, but my own.

Lionel had won and I had given up the idea of going away from home for the time being, but from that day I spent some hours every day in my bedroom studying, preparing, working for examinations, so that I should be ready—for what I hardly knew.

Aunt Lizzie expressed disappointment that I did not choose to do my work in the library, but on that point I was firm. I could hardly tell her that I disliked the birds and fishes; if I had, the statement would have been met with the same pained surprise as if I had told her I disliked the portrait of my uncle, the Rev. Samuel Bayley, that hung under the most surprising swordfish in the room. So I did not go into the matter. I simply told her that I preferred my own room, and every morning I found the maid had lighted the fire there and made it ready for me. I think no girl ever had an easier aunt to live with.

For more than a year I worked very hard; but I said nothing to Lionel about it, from a feeling I had that he might think it unfair of me.

Aunt Lizzie stood by me in this effort at doing some solid work. For I remember once, that an old friend of my mother's who took an interest in me, pointed out to us that it was a pity for a girl to be too clever, and to lose her opportunities.

Once I came into the drawing-room when she and Aunt Lizzie were engaged in eager conversation. I was going away again, but Aunt Lizzie kept me, saying, "We were saying nothing unsuitable for you to hear, my dear."

I guessed as I turned over a book on the table that this was hardly her visitor's opinion.

"The women of my family have never been dolls," asserted Aunt Lizzie.

Any one who knew the women of Aunt Lizzie's family would know that when she started from such a fundamental proposition she was ready for a keen argument.

"There is, I hope, something between a doll and a blue-stocking," tittered the other lady, and pointed out that while under proper guidance she thought it quite right that a girl should study, she thought it a great pity she should obtrude her knowledge in conversation. She thought that most unattractive, especially to gentlemen.

"I have never found," said Aunt Lizzie, "that knowledge and intelligence are unappreciated by the other sex. On the contrary—"

She broke off, she was so obviously in a position to judge that it would have been indelicate on her part to pursue the point she had made.

"I know they appreciate it," said Mrs. Merrit, with a curious stress on the word appreciate, "but down here in the country, at any rate, I don't think they like it in their wives;" and then we were told, with the little nervous giggle that I knew Aunt Lizzie thought detestable, that the girls Mrs. Merrit knew who got engaged first were not clever, not even pretty, but gentle and anxious to please.

"I have no wish for my niece to become engaged while her judgment is immature," said Aunt Lizzie. Mrs. Merrit would have liked to point out that by the time the judgment is matured the complexion has gone off, but Aunt Lizzie with her handsome face, her few words, and the manner of her family, was frightening this eminently feminine little person.

I was amused at the conversation, but I turned rather wearily away. I wandered round the library, and finding no rest there, went out into the garden. Lionel had been at home so little lately. My time when I had done my work hung very heavily on my hands. I wanted to get away from home, where, I did not know or care. I was amused at Aunt Lizzie and the family. Of course I thought, of course I studied. Of course we weren't dolls, the women of our family.

What a curious emphatic way Aunt Lizzie had with her.

I was in the library with Lionel one evening. He was a full-fledged lawyer now, living at home with us in the old house. Latterly I had not seen much of him. He was out a great deal. I had fancied he seemed worried. But it was not our way to sympathise with each other. My standard of manners and expression of feeling had been learnt from my brothers. Lionel and I had even left off our good-night kiss. "It's rather a senseless form," I had said, and that settled it.

It has been a very hot day. Lionel sat at the desk writing, and I at the open window. I was oppressed and pining for air, but I had an unusual feeling that I must wait for Lionel to go into the garden with me.

"Grace, I want to tell you something."

My heart seemed to stop, for into our even lives something was coming. I knew it, for Lionel's usually matter-of-fact voice was charged with feeling.

"Will you tell me in the garden?" I asked.

But no, he would rather tell me where we were. I cannot remember the words he used. I remember that I tried not to show how much I felt, and encouraged him quietly to talk. It was this: it seemed that Lionel was going to marry a girl I had never seen, a girl not in our social position, and I remember now in what a relieved tone he said:

"But I knew that you would not mind about that," and I only gathered gradually that there was something more than this. He did not think she was a girl Aunt Lizzie would receive; it was a marriage that would hurt his practice—perhaps a little separate him from his friends.

Suddenly I had kissed Lionel, the first time for years. I do not know what I said; I had only one thought in the midst of my feelings—that he should feel that there was some one who would love her, some one who did not care what people said.

He stroked my hair and seemed touched and surprised at my warmth. In my heart was a great joy that a subtle barrier I had felt between us was gone. I asked no questions and had hardly any fears. He must love her, that was enough. He must be right. Only one thing would have broken my heart—if Lionel had not depended on me to love her too.

A few days later, although I had never seen her I fought Nelly's battle with Aunt Lizzie. And it seemed that I won, for in the evening I was able to tell

Lionel that Aunt Lizzie had written to ask Nelly to stay with us, before their wedding which was to take place soon.

I see now that Aunt Lizzie did all in her power to save Lionel from this step, and I used all my strength and inexperience to hurry him.

"He loves her," I said, as if that settled the matter.

And there in her favourite room Aunt Lizzie enlightened me about the world I lived in.

Fierce indignation woke in my heart, and unreasoningly it was directed against Aunt Lizzie, none the less that I knew she was telling me facts. One moment I hated her for telling me, and the next I was hating her for not having told me before; and then myself for the way I took it.

Aunt Lizzie did not guess how much she was stirring me. I sat very quiet while she talked. I can remember her saying that many people, even the clergy, thought it right to chain a young man to his folly, to make him bear the consequences. In that she saw a lack of common sense. She would never be one to drive Lionel.

The only light I could stretch out into all this darkness was my love for Lionel. For better or worse, I had given him my hand over this marriage, and Aunt Lizzie, although she did her best to make me use my influence with him, might just as well have talked to one of the stuffed birds in the cases.

When she found it was useless, as regards Nelly's visit she gave in completely and graciously, and I knew her well enough to know that she would do her best to make it pleasant for her.

I have often thought how well Aunt Lizzie bore with us both, with Lionel and me. For she was proud of Lionel, of his brains and his common sense, and in both of us up to this time she had seen the qualities of her own family, and now Lionel was on the brink of a piece of quixotic folly, and I was backing him up.

In all that talk Aunt Lizzie did not once remind me of my youth and inexperience. She told me facts and she appealed to my common sense. However often she thought of her, she did not once mention my poor dear mother.

But I had only one clear idea in my head: the world was a hard cruel unjust place; Lionel chose to defy it. No one I cared for should defy it alone.

I have often thought that Aunt Lizzie was not unjustly proud of the common sense of her family, but I have wondered if she ever knew how much I appreciated a quality she had that was not common sense.

It was some weeks after that scene in the library in which nominally I had come off victorious. Lionel's Nelly had been with us a week. Aunt Lizzie and I had never spoken of her since she came. Lionel and I had tried to once, but we never tried again and never shall.

I was alone in the library, the gloomy room. I tried to look forward. What was there in my life? How I had wound it round Lionel and his happiness, and how it took all my strength to hide my bitter disappointment! Lionel was entrapped—be-fooled. I had given him my word that I would stand by him and her. But what lifeless support!

I could not save him. The less I was with them the better. My heart grew heavier and heavier. Could Lionel with his keen sense mistake the tawdry little thing? More painful was the thought that was beginning to take possession of me that he had not mistaken her; he saw, and seeing had made up his mind.

Looking forward I could see nothing in my own life. Of what use was my love to Lionel? Life and health were strong within me; outside—nothing, nothing. I burst into tears; unconscious that I could be seen from the garden, unconscious of everything but my own misery. All the objects in the room were blurred, Nelly's face was everywhere, and Lionel's voice when he first told me about her.

I became aware that some one was in the room and close to me. I started up in terror. It might be Lionel. Not only would he see me crying but he would know why, and then what use—

It was Aunt Lizzie, who had seen me from the garden and had come in quickly.

"Lionel and Nelly, dear, are coming down the path," she said, in a matter-of-fact, but rather hurried voice.

I rose quickly and stood out of sight. Aunt Lizzie had done me a great kindness. A week or two ago I had told her that I at any rate should love Nelly, that I was not chained by conventional ideas, that Lionel was and must be the best judge where his own feelings were concerned.

She must have seen my struggles to keep up for days. Now she had her enemy down she would not say a word, I knew. What humiliation she could she had saved me. I wanted her to know that I appreciated her generosity; and as I stood at the door on my way upstairs, I made an effort to speak. Apparently she did not hear me, for she said in a vexed tone as she too left the room:

"In spite of all this education it will be a long time before we get any really nice feeling into the working classes. That new girl has taken a piece of old lace I left on my dressing-table—a piece that belonged to your grandmother, my dear—and she's actually starched and ironed it!"

The vivid light that any sudden change throws on the past may not be a true light, but I know that when Aunt Lizzie died, for a long time I saw our early life at home as one sees the scenes on the brightly lighted stage; the present as the dim faces around one, and the future not at all. My later friends, the ties I had formed, such joys and troubles as I had, claimed for a time a small share in my thoughts.

They were busied with scraps of Aunt Lizzie's talk; all I should ever hear now of my mother and father. Lionel, Jack, and I, children walking, learning, living together, and Aunt Lizzie in our midst, always treating us as rational, almost as grown-up, beings; the house, the garden, in which parts were always kept "as John left them, my dear," the seat he had put for "your poor dear mother," so sheltered, that in that western country, the year she died, she had sat out of doors in November.

I had had a happy childhood, except for vague depressions which I had never tried to account for. My lacks were too great for any child to grasp. Looking back, there are some things in my bringing-up for which I am most grateful.

It was with my brothers that I learnt to love Nature, so that it was not as a series of pictures one turns tired eyes on in the hope of finding rest and refreshment, but as some people love their homes. I learnt to live out of doors; we walked, we swam, we ate and slept, as it pleased us, in the open air. We did not go into the country in the July and August glare, and sit shivering by our fires in the other months. We watched the spring come in, and we tramped the winter through. Better than a cloudless summer day we loved a storm, and to be swept dry after it by the northwest wind.

There were bad times ahead of me, for I had made the mistake Aunt Lizzie made, in thinking that I had the stable qualities of her family. I am glad that she never knew how completely they failed me. But I would give, if I could, to any one else, who had painful surprises in store for them, the part of my life that I spent in the open air with my brothers.

And one other thing I am grateful for—that Aunt Lizzie treated me, long before I deserved it, as a rational being. I feel no compunction when I realise that I got this treatment entirely under false pretences. The features of her family—a boy's standard of outspokenness and endurance in external things—have taken in other people besides Aunt Lizzie. But this much she gave me of what she expected from me: that when I saw my failure, though there were many names by which it might have been called, I put them away and gave it the ugliest and the truest.

One of Aunt Lizzie's brothers was at the funeral. I had never seen much of Uncle Willie. We walked, after it was over, around the desolate garden, more desolate, I thought, because down there flowers linger into November that should be over and done with long before.

Uncle Willie took comfort in what seemed to me the strangest things; in the number of persons present at the burial, and in the fact that the mourning of some very distant cousins was as deep as our own.

One thing he regretted—that the house must be sold. "Neither of your brothers is in a position to buy it," he said regretfully, and then touched on their careers: Lionel's unfortunate marriage; Jack's absurd scheme, which had been broached to him to-day, and which he was glad, indeed, dear Lizzie had not lived to hear, of giving up the bar, where he promised to do well for writing, if you please, using the little capital Aunt Lizzie had left him in the meantime.

I heard Uncle Willie's voice rather distantly as our feet sounded on the gravel, and felt a certain gratitude to him that, although his position might have justified it, he did not touch on my life or affairs. He simply told me that my new black was most becoming, and that I had managed to make every one as comfortable as possible on this sad occasion. I was relieved when he was gone, and mechanically I turned into the library, which I knew now would soon be dismantled, and although it was not from affection as of old, once there, my feet seemed rooted.

After a time, Lionel and Jack came in, and we stayed there, talking in our old quiet, undemonstrative way about the sale and the arrangements we had to make. I remember my relief when Lionel told me that if I did not want them, he and Jack would like the photographs of our uncles and aunts; and he told me, too, that Aunt Lizzie had said she thought I should like to have some of the things that father had bought.

"I don't want any of them," I said. "Wouldn't some museum be glad of these things!" and I pointed to the birds and the fishes and many other objects in the room.

I think Jack was a little shocked at my want of sentiment, but Lionel's smile, as he said: "You never cared for relics," took me back to our childhood, the time when we were such great friends.

MABEL E. WOTTON (1863-1927)

Mabel Emily Wotton was born in London to Frances Emily and John Stirling Wilmot Wotton. Little is known about her life. She published a novel, A Girl Diplomatist, *in 1892, followed by* Day-Books *in 1896.* Day-Books *was a collection of four stories, published in John Lane's Keynotes Series. In 1889 she published another collection of stories,* A Pretty Radical and Other Stories. *Her other publications include* Word Portraits of Famous Writers *(1887) and* H.B. Irving: An Appreciation *(1912). She never married and died in London.*

THE HOUR OF HER LIFE

[*Day-Books.* London: John Lane, 1896; Boston: Roberts Bros., 1896]

It was at the beginning of last season that a flower-shop was started in the heart of Clubland, which, had it continued open, would have been town-famed long ere this. Instead of holding the orthodox stiff-backed chairs and counter, the interior was as prettily arranged a little nook as could be found in all London. Bits of old brocades and trailing plants covered the walls, and the stock-in-trade, which consisted exclusively of men's buttonholes, was dispensed by so beautiful a woman that she was able to make it a rule from the very first, that whatever might be the price of the flowers when sold by her two assistants, they doubled in value when touched by her own fair hands. Annette was the name over the window, and it very soon became "the thing" with a certain section of society to lounge into the flower-shop on spring afternoons, and to waste a fair amount of time and money over the excellent tea (which was given gratis), and the purchase of flowers, whose perfection and cost put a certain *cachet* upon the customers. A favoured few were occasionally admitted into an inner sanctum, and this, though it was merely divided from the outer room by a curtain, it became the fashion to desire to enter. The place was fitted in Liberty's best style, the lounges were luxurious, and the object was flirtation.

The piquancy of it, such as it was, lay in Annette herself. A small, impudent-toned, rosy-faced girl would have vulgarised the affair at once; it was so exactly what would have been expected. But Annette was a graceful, loose-limbed woman, whose complete indifference stood her in lieu of dignity, and whose absolutely colourless face, crowned by a mass of dyed auburn hair, to which only one man was so fastidious as to object, brought into greater prominence a pair of big changeful eyes, which were long-lashed, and of a perfect forget-me-not blue. Her manner was usually grave to sombreness, and, as Freddy Calvin averred, it was not altogether unlike making love to an iceberg. It being pointed out to him that this could scarcely be deemed a satisfactory occupation, he shifted both his ground and his simile, and vowed it more resembled wooing an angel, and made him feel kind of churchy and good. And, besides, he never knew when she would snub him, and when fall in with radiant delight with his own plans; and this perhaps held the case in a nutshell.

One morning early in May, Mr. Freddy Calvin—heart-whole, strictly inoffensive, and heir to Lord Sydthorpe, he was registered in the matchmakers' books that season—came strolling along Piccadilly in the glossiest of new hats, and the broadest of smiles. He was a young gentleman who was invariably on excellent terms both with himself and the world at large, and he thought the universe at that moment held no greater bliss than the knowledge he was going to Annette, and felt tolerably assured of his welcome.

"I shall marry that woman if she will have me," he had said to Luke Felstead the night before, and it had left him totally unruffled that his friend had rudely replied: "Then, my dear Freddy, the more fool you."

Felstead was the one man who objected to Annette's dyed hair, and was also the mentor who occasionally took Freddy to task. Farthermore, although this is a detail, he was the one man for whom Annette cared a rush.

Freddy reached his destination, and finding the shop empty but for the two little blue-gowned white-capped maids, begged one of them to find out if mademoiselle would admit him to the inner room. To brush past the curtain uninvited was more than the most courageous of the men would have dared.

"Mam'selle says 'Please come in,'" was the message brought back, and Freddy, with sufficient delicacy to feel he should sink the trade in the courtship, left on the table the rose he had just purchased, and went in with alacrity.

Annette was doing some needlework, some lacey sort of stuff, but put it down at once to stretch a greeting hand towards him.

"I am so glad to see you!" and there was enough music in her soft tones to make the words sound not commonplace.

"It is downright good of you to let me come in," responded Freddy heartily; he was barely of age, and his diction was still boyish. "Is that a thing that wants holding, Annette? My cousin Mary is always doing work that wants another fellow holding, and I'll do it for you at once. Uncle Sydthorpe is in town again."

"Is he?" asked his hostess. Freddy's chatter bored her, because she knew there was so much of it she should have to sit through before he could be helped on to the one subject which interested her keenly, and of which only he could tell her.

To-day, however, her patience was less severely taxed than usual, for when he had continued discussing his relations for some minutes, he broke off abruptly to remark he had seen Felstead last night, and to quote his opinions about his cousin Mary.

Annette's indifference vanished.

"What did you say he said of Miss Calvin?" she asked breathlessly.

"Oh, he admires her."

"She is pretty?"

"Pretty?" Freddy whistled. "No, she is plain, but Felstead cares nothing for looks. He like a Vere de Vere individual, who would rather die than send you in to dinner with the wrong girl."

Annette's laugh sounded forced.

"And I was studying up the Peerage last night to understand the carriage panels," she said. "Ah, well! it takes all sorts to make a world, doesn't it?"

"As if you weren't a whole century better than she in every way," Freddy cried out indignantly. "I only wish you cared half as much for yourself as I care for you, and then you'd die of self-love."

"A pleasing ending," replied Annette.

She spoke listlessly, for what was the use of it all, when everything she could learn of Luke Felstead tended to show the sharp line of demarcation he drew between women of his own class, and others? What was the use of enduring the society of this talkative lad, if it never brought her nearer his friend?

Freddy was going on in a more ardent strain now, not quite venturing on the intended proposal, but making as hot love as his honest heart and limited vocabulary would allow. Annette thought her own thoughts the while, and when they grew too bitter, dismissed him almost curtly.

Five minutes after his departure she caught the tones of another voice enquiring for her, a pleasant, full-toned voice this one, and as courteous in its manner of addressing the white-capped maids as if they had been royal. Annette passed swiftly through the curtain, and confronted a grave-looking middle-aged man, with a pale pink flush rising slowly in her cheeks.

"Yes, Mr. Felstead?"

The newcomer raised his hat. "I am an early visitor, but I thought I should find Freddy here," he explained, and his listener chose to construe his sentence into; "Otherwise I should not have come."

So she answered defiantly that he had been, and had stayed a long time, and all the while had a miserable knowledge that she would regret the words as soon as Felstead had left her.

"I saw you last night," she continued.

"And I you," he responded, "though I did not go in myself. I hope you liked the play?"

"No. I was with Roger Bryant, and he always palls on me after a bit. You will ask me why I go with him then?"

"Certainly not," said Felstead swavely. "I should not be so impertinent as to question your movements."

Adding a good day, he went off, and Annette retreated into the inner room. Had she done anything wrong? she asked herself, in a white heat of rage. No, she knew she had not, for ladies—real ladies—went out in the evening with men who were not their husbands: the society papers said so; so how dared he say in that distant polished voice: "Certainly not."

The days went on. May came to an end, and June dawned amid all the sunny-houred fashion and fuss which inaugurates so much enjoyment, and disguises so much of tragedy. Annette had disposed of the amorous Bryant by snubbing him so effectually that that hero went flowerless for a week and then, in the natural reaction from misery to annoyance, took to buying his buttonholes at another shop.

"We were talking away in quite a friendly fashion," he informed his brother some months later, "when she told me suddenly I had gone too far, and must stop. I declare to you I was trying to be as agreeable as possible. As I didn't at once well, what do you imagine this extraordinary woman did? She just rang the bell, and told one of her maids to stay in the room with us; and then she turned to me with the most beaming of smiles. 'You were saying—' she said sweetly."

Bryant deposed, left Freddy Calvin an undisputed first, and a rare round of delight he had, in which the river and many theatres played prominent parts, and which were as innocent, and undoubtedly as enjoyable, as if they had been shared by the most lynx-eyed of chaperons.

At length came the day when Luke Felstead saw that if ever he intended to win Freddy from a not over-desirable influence, now was the time to do it. Why he interested himself in the young man, with whom he had but little in common, is not to be related here. It took its rise from a memory associated with his mother, and was an unwritten chapter of Felstead's lonely life. Enough that Freddy, left to himself, would inevitably drift downwards, and accordingly must be taken in hand at once.

So his mentor, with a vast amount of self-pity, for he hated interfering with other people's affairs, betook himself to Charing Cross in order to meet the train which brought up the two from a half day at Richmond, and there asked Annette, as simply as if it were not thoroughly alien to his ordinary line of conduct, if she would accord him an interview the following morning. It hardly required the demure "Yes, I shall be very pleased," for her eyes shone for the moment, and the quick breath parted her lips.

"It is a sad waste of expression," thought Felstead, half-contemptuously, as he watched her companion put her into a cab. "What a flirt she is!"

Next morning Annette was up betimes. She wanted both herself and her room to look their prettiest, and he had not said at what hour he would call. But as the time dragged leadenly by, she was seized with a great nervousness, and was fit for nothing more than to sit trembling, with her ears strained to catch the first sound of his approach. He was coming to her of his own free will! The thought rang like a jubilant note of victory. She knew she was beautiful; she had but little vanity, but she could not help knowing that; had he grown to think so too?

Was he coming to her because her tactics of patient waiting had been crowned with success at last? Was her double endeavour never to force their possible friendship, but to learn of his desires through Freddy, and then be swayed by them, while at the same time she trusted he might be piqued by her apparent preference for another man,—was it to yield her happiness to-day? She pushed up the hair which was growing damp with anxiety upon her forehead, and rubbed her hands to bring some warmth into them. Then—

"Can I see your mistress? She is expecting me."

"Yes, sir, if you will go in to her, please," and Luke Felstead entered the room. The hour of her life had come.

"Will you—will you sit down?" she said, when the maid had pulled to an inner door behind the curtain, for he had not relinquished her fingers, but was looking at her gravely. "What is it?" she added involuntarily.

"I think it is good of you to see me," he told her, seating himself at some little distance, and scanning her as she stood before him, a straight motionless figure in her dark blue gown. "You do not know me at all well, and I have no right to ask it."

She murmured something inaudible, and he continued—

"Will you promise not to turn me out of the room, for I am going to be impertinent, and shall deserve it?"

Even had Annette been a novice in the hearing of love vows, which she certainly was not, she would have taken heart from the direct personal tone of his words; but she controlled herself, and answered him very quietly.

"You have always been scrupulously careful, Mr. Felstead. Even if you were, as you say, 'impertinent,' I would forgive you, now."

She had dropped on to a couch with loosely-clasped hands and half-averted head. It made no impression on him, but having her here to himself, Felstead began dimly to comprehend somewhat of the fascination she might possess for younger men.

"You are too young and too beautiful to be here by yourself," he said abruptly. "Haven't you people of your own to live with?"

She shook her head.

"My father was an officer—Lion Browning of the Guards; perhaps you have heard of him—Mad Lion, they called him. He cut the service when he married my mother, and I was born in France. She sold oranges in Drury Lane; and I have been told he was tipsy at the time. But I won't think that. He was my father, and I like to think he was a gentleman, and be proud of him."

Watching her kindling eyes, and the eloquent little gesture with which she flung back her head, Felstead thought so too.

"I see," he said kindly. "And being your father's child, you did not care much about your other relations."

"That was just it," she answered. "I went to my grandfather—his father, you know—once, and he turned me from the house. A low-looking man, I think he said he was a coster, found me out another time, and insisted he was my uncle, so I did the same friendly office by him. I am a sort of Mahomet's coffin, Mr. Felstead, and hang between the two worlds without belonging to either."

Felstead was silent. This explained much which had hitherto puzzled him.

"I came to ask you a big kindness," he said at last. "I came to you yourself, direct, because if I can read faces at all, yours proves you are good-hearted. Are you fond of Freddy Calvin, Miss Browning?"

Annette hesitated.

"Why?" she asked.

"Because I want you to give up the boy, and let him go."

The woman's heart beat almost to suffocation. Was this tantamount to saying, "that I may take his place?"

"Why?" she said again, and stopped short.

Then he told her. What he said was as delicately veiled as was compatible with absolute clearness; not by one expression or inflexion of his voice would he wantonly wound her; but the naked truth was unmistakable. A woman in her position, who had been fêted by a vast number of the fastest men in town; whose beauty had enabled her to sell flowers at fancy prices, and whose life generally since the opening of the shop had proved she was answerable to no one for her actions, was assuredly not the sort of woman to become the future Lady Sydthorpe. He did not fancy her affection could really have been caught by the errant fancy of a boy some year or two her junior. Would she not show herself capable of a great goodness, and break the chains which held him?

Annette heard him steadily to the end. A dull brickdust red had suffused her pale cheeks, and her eyes had darkened.

"I may not know the ways of your world, Mr. Felstead," she said when he had finished, "but I am not a bad woman."

The man flushed in his turn.

"You and I may not much like each other," he told her, "but if any man in my presence dared to say that you were, I would knock him down for a liar."

Annette had set her teeth so hard, that it was with physical effort she unclenched them to answer him.

"Then why can't I marry him?" she demanded. "Understand that I do not say I would, I do not say I care two straws about him. I only say, why shouldn't I?"

Her companion murmured something about an impressionable lad like Calvin wanting a wife who would hold him up, and not pull him down in the social scale; but Annette had risen to her feet, and broke in upon his words with a sudden passion and energy that made them fail upon his lips.

"Why should you try to spare your friend?" she cried. "What have I done? My father's birth was as good as his own; you yourself admit that whatever I may do, it is in the open daylight; I am well favoured enough to have won his love, and I have wit enough to keep it. I have got my own living, it is true, but is that a shame to me? When the men I know overstep the bounds of friendship, I send them away. I don't keep my discarded lovers dangling about me. Is that so much lower than the fine ladies of your own set? When the—"

What Luke Felstead might have answered had her impetuous ringing speech continued to its end, remained unspoken, for as the words came pouring forth as she stood fronting the man who, perfectly unmoved, perfectly courteous, listened to her, a chance remark of his which Freddy had repeated flashed through her brain. Felstead could only care for a woman who would "rather die," as the boy had phrased it, than commit the slightest social solecism, and this sudden remembrance tolled the death-knell to her hopes. She stood silent, and looked at him piteously.

"Could a woman of my class never make a man of yours happy?"

"Never," said Felstead, firmly. "There would be the same difficulty, Miss Browning, if you were a princess. To be happy the boy should marry in his own swim."

"Couldn't my love for my husband do anything?" Her voice was dangerously sweet, her blue eyes were liquid with tears she was too proud to shed. "It should teach me to sink my old life utterly; I would have no will nor aim but his."

The face she was watching did not soften, and Annette drew back a step, as though the quiet figure had struck her.

"I see. I am a fool," she said, and the pleading had died from her voice. Then: "You want me to send him away, Mr. Felstead? If I do, it will be to please you." She turned from him abruptly, and walking over to the mantel-shelf rested her elbow on its ledge, her chin on her hand. "I wonder if I shall do it."

"To please me?"

Felstead rose from his seat, startled, bewildered. What did she mean?

"Yes," said Annette, slowly, "you. I—I am whimsical, Mr. Felstead, and just because, as you say, we two don't much like each other, I've a fancy—to be well thought of—by you." She spoke unsteadily, almost jerkily. "Come back to-morrow morning, will you, and bring Freddy with you? I," her fingers stole over her quivering mouth, and hid it from him, "I will do what you want. Will you shake hands with me—now?"

That day the flower-shop was closed, and a neat placard affixed to its shutters, which the friends read next morning with a conviction on at least the elder man's part that the announcement meant for always. "Gone away" was what it said.

ELLA D'ARCY (1857?-1937?)

Ella D'Arcy was born in London and spent some time during her childhood in the Channel Islands, the setting for several of her stories. D'Arcy was a realistic writer whose stories reveal an interest in psychology and the influence of such writers as Honoré de Balzac, Emile Zola, and Henry James. She was most successful as a writer of short fiction and is best known for her association with the Yellow Book *at which she functioned as an unofficial subeditor to Henry Harland, the literary editor. Her story "Irremediable" was included in the first volume (April 1894) of the* Yellow Book; *her stories appeared in ten of the thirteen volumes of the quarterly. John Lane published a collection of six of her short stories, four of which had earlier appeared in the* Yellow Book, *in 1895 in a volume called* Monochromes, *as part of the Keynotes Series. "The Pleasure Pilgrim," included in this collection, is perhaps D'Arcy's best known and most frequently anthologized story. Another collection of her stories, all of which had previously appeared in the* Yellow Book, *was published by Lane in 1898 as* Modern Instances. *That same year D'Arcy published her one novel,* The Bishop's Dilemma. *After the nineteenth century D'Arcy rarely published and spent her later years in Paris, never marrying.*

The women in D'Arcy's stories are often represented as ignorant and destructive; they tyrannize over men, and men rather than women become the victims in relationships. Such portrayals of women have caused readers to find D'Arcy's stories to be antifeminist. But most of her stories are told from a male point of view and can be seen as an indictment of men's attitudes towards women and of a society that drives women to such unpleasant behavior. Her stories reveal what men think about women, not necessarily what women, including the writer, believe to be true about women.

WHITE MAGIC

[*Monochromes.* London: John Lane, 1895; Boston: Roberts Bros., 1895]

I spent one evening last summer with my friend Mauger, *pharmacien* in the little town of Jacques-le-Port. He pronounces his name Major, by the by, it being a quaint custom of the Islands to write proper names one way and speak them another, thus serving to bolster up that old, old story of the German savant's account of the difficulties of the English language,—"where you spell a man's name Verulam," says he reproachfully, "and pronounce it Bacon."

Mauger and I sat in the pleasant wood-panelled parlor behind the shop, from whence all sorts of aromatic odors found their way in through the closed door to mingle with the fragrance of figs, Ceylon tea, and hot *gôches-à-beurre*, constituting the excellent meal spread before us. The large old-fashioned windows were wide open, and I looked straight out upon the harbor, filled with holiday yachts, and the wonderful azure sea.

Over against the other islands, opposite, a gleam of white streaked the water, white clouds hung motionless in the blue sky, and a tiny boat with white sails passed out round Falla Point. A white butterfly entered the room to flicker in gay uncertain curves above the cloth, and a warm reflected light played over the slender rat-tailed forks and spoons, and raised by a tone or two the color of Mauger's tanned face and yellow beard. For, in spite of a sedentary profession, his preferences lie with an out-of-door life, and he takes an afternoon off whenever practicable, as he had done that day, to follow his favorite pursuit over the golf-links at Les Landes.

While he had been deep in the mysteries of teeing and putting, with no subtler problem to be solved than the judicious selection of mashie and cleek, I had explored some of the curious cromlechs or *pouquelayes* scattered over this part of the island, and my thoughts and speech harked back irresistibly to the strange old religions and usages of the past.

"Science is all very well in its way," said I; "and of course it's an inestimable advantage to inhabit this so-called nineteenth century; but the mediæval want of science was far more picturesque. The once universal belief in charms and portents, in wandering saints and fighting fairies, must have lent an interest to life which these prosaic days sadly lack. Madelon then would steal from her bed on moonlight nights in May, and slip across the dewy grass with naked feet, to seek the reflection of her future husband's face in the first running stream she passed; now, Miss Mary Jones puts on her bonnet and steps round the corner, on no more romantic errand than the investment of her month's wages in the savings bank at two and a half per cent."

Mauger laughed. "I wish she did anything half so prudent! That has not been my experience of the Mary Joneses."

"Well, anyhow," I insisted, "the Board School has rationalized them. It has pulled up the innate poetry of their nature to replace it by decimal fractions."

To which Mauger answered, "Rot!" and offered me his cigarette-case. After the first few silent whiffs, he went on as follows: "The innate poetry of Woman! Confess now, there is no more unpoetic creature under the sun. Offer her the sublimest poetry ever written and the 'Daily Telegraph's' latest article on fashions, or a good sound murder or reliable divorce, and there's no betting on her choice, for it's a dead certainty. Many men have a love of poetry, but I'm inclined to think that a hundred women out of ninety-nine positively dislike it."

Which struck me as true. "We'll drop the poetry, then," I answered; "but my point remains, that if the girl of to-day has no superstitions, the girl of to-morrow will have no beliefs. Teach her to sit down thirteen to table, to spill the salt, and walk under a ladder with equanimity, and you open the door for Spencer and Huxley, and,—and all the rest of it," said I, coming to an impotent conclusion.

"Oh, if superstition were the salvation of woman,—but you are thinking of young ladies in London, I suppose? Here, in the Islands, I can show you as much superstition as you please. I'm not sure that the country-people in their heart of hearts don't still worship the old gods of the *pouquelayes*. You would not, of course, find any one to own up to it, or to betray the least glimmer of an idea as to your meaning, were you to question him, for ours is a shrewd folk, wearing their orthodoxy bravely; but possibly the old beliefs are cherished with the more ardor for not being openly avowed. Now you like bits of actuality. I'll give you one, and a proof, too, that the modern maiden is still separated by many a fathom of salt seawater from these fortunate isles.

"Some time ago, on a market morning, a girl came into the shop, and asked for some blood from a dragon. 'Some what?' said I, not catching her words. 'Well, just a little blood from a dragon,' she answered very tremulously, and blushing. She meant, of course, 'dragon's blood,' a resinous powder formerly much used in medicine, though out of fashion now.

"She was a pretty young creature, with pink cheeks and dark eyes, and a forlorn expression of countenance which didn't seem at all to fit in with her blooming health. Not from the town, or I should have known her face; evidently come from one of the country parishes to sell her butter and eggs. I was interested to discover what she wanted the 'dragon's blood' for, and after a certain amount of hesitation she told me. 'They do say it's good, sir, if anything should have happened betwixt you an' your young man.' 'Then you have a young man?' said I. 'Yes, sir.' 'And you've fallen out with him?' 'Yes, sir.' And tears rose to her eyes at the admission, while her mouth rounded with awe at my amazing perspicacity. 'And you mean to send him some dragon's blood as a love potion?' 'No, sir; you've got to mix it with water you've fetched from the Three Sisters' Well, and drink it yourself in nine sips on nine nights running, and get into bed without once looking in the glass; and then if you've done anything properly, and haven't made any mistake, he'll come back to you, an' love you twice as much as before.' 'And la Mère Todevinn (Tostevin) gave you that precious recipe, and made you cross her hand with silver into the bargain?' said I severely; on which the tears began to flow outright.

"You know," said Mauger, breaking off his narration, "the old lady who lives in the curious stone house at the corner of the market-place? A reputed witch who learned both black and white magic from her mother, who was a daughter of Hélier Mouton, the famous sorcerer of Cakeuro. I could tell you some funny stories relating to la Mère Todevinn, who numbers more clients among the officers and fine ladies here than in any other class; and very curious, too, is the history of that stone house, with the Brancourt arms still sculptured on the side. You can see them, if you turn down by the Water-gate. This old sinister-looking building, or rather portion of a building, for more modern houses have been built over the greater portion of the site, and now press upon it from either hand, once belonged to one of the finest mansions in the Islands, but through a curse and a crime has been brought down to its present condition; while the Brancourt family has long since been utterly extinct. But all this isn't the story of Elsie Mahy, which turned out to be the name of my little customer.

"The Mahys are of the Vauvert parish, and Pierre Jean, the father of this girl, began life as a day laborer, took to tomato-growing on borrowed capital, and now owns a dozen glasshouses of his own. Mrs. Mahy does some dairy-farming on a minute scale, the profits of which she and Miss Elsie share as pin-money. The young man who is courting Elsie is a son of Toumes the builder. He probably had something to do with the putting up of Mahy's greenhouses, but anyhow, he has been constantly over at Vauvert during the last six months, superintending the alterations at de Câterelle's place.

"Toumes, it would seem, is a devoted but imperious lover, and the Persian and Median laws are as butter compared with the inflexibility of his decisions. The little rift within the lute, which has lately turned all the music to discord, occurred last Monday week,—bank-holiday, as you may remember. The Sunday-school to which Elsie belongs—and it's a strange anomaly, isn't it, that a girl going to Sunday-school should still have a rooted belief in white magic?—the school was to go for an outing to Prawn Bay, and Toumes had arranged to join his sweetheart at the starting-point. But he had made her promise that if by any chance he should be delayed, she would not go with the others, but would wait until he came to fetch her.

"Of course, it so happened that he *was* detained, and, equally of course, Elsie, like a true woman, went off without him. She did all she knew to make me believe she went quite against her own wishes, that her companions forced her to go. The beautifully yielding nature of a woman never comes out so conspicuously as when she is being coerced into following her own secret desires. Anyhow, Toumes, arriving some time later, found her gone. He followed on, and under ordinary circumstances, I suppose, a sharp reprimand would have considered sufficient. Unfortunately, the young man arrived on the scene to find his truant love deep in the frolics of kiss-in-the-ring. After tea in the Câterelle Arms, the whole party had adjourned to a neighboring meadow, and were thus whiling away the time to the exhilarating strains of a French horn and a concertina. Elsie was led into the centre of the ring by various country bumpkins, and kissed beneath the eyes of heaven, of her neighbors, and of her embittered swain.

"You may have been amongst us long enough to know that the Toumes family are of a higher social grade than the Mahys, and I suppose the Misses Toumes never in their lives stooped to anything so ungenteel as public kiss-in-the-ring. It was not surprising, therefore, to hear that after this incident 'me an' my young man had words,' as Elsie put it.

"Note," said Mauger, "the descriptive truth of this expression 'having words.' Among the unlettered, lovers only do have words when vexed. At other times they will sit holding hands throughout a long summer's afternoon, and not exchange two remarks an hour. Love seals their tongue; anger alone unlooses it, and naturally, when unloosed, it runs on, from sheer want of practice, a great deal faster and further than they desire.

"So, life being thorny and youth being vain, they parted late that same evening, with the understanding that they would meet no more; and to be wroth with one we love worked its usual harrowing effects. Toumes took to billiards and brandy, Elsie to tears and invocations of Beelzebub; then came Mère Todevinn's recipe, my own more powerful potion, and now once more all is silence and balmy peace."

"Do you mean to tell me you sold the child a charm, and didn't enlighten her as to its futility?"

"I sold her some bicarbonate of soda worth a couple of *doubles*, and charged her five shillings for it into the bargain," said Mauger, unblushingly. "A wrinkle I learned from once overhearing an old lady I had treated for nothing expatiating to a crony, 'Eh, but, my good, my good! dat Mr. Major, I don't t'ink much of him. He give away his add-vice an' his meddecines for nuddin'. Dey not wurt nuddin' neider for sure.' So I made Elsie hand me over five British shillings, and I gave her the powder, and told her to drink it with her meals. But I threw in another prescription, which, if less important, must nevertheless be punctiliously carried out, if the charm was to have any effect. 'The very next time,' I told her, 'that you meet your young man in the street, walk straight up to him without looking to the right or to the left, and hold out your hand, saying these words: "Please, I so want to be friends again!" Then if you've been a good girl, have taken the powder regularly, and not forgotten one of my directions, you'll find that all will come right.'"

"Now, little as you may credit it," said Mauger, smiling, "the charm worked, for all that we live in the so-called nineteenth century. Elsie came into the shop only yesterday to tell me the results, and to thank me very prettily. 'I shall always come to you now, sir,' she was good enough to say, 'I mean, if anything was to go wrong again. You know a great deal more than Mère Todevinn, I'm sure.' 'Yes, I'm a famous sorcerer,' said I, 'but you had better not speak about the powder. You are wise enough to see that it was just your own conduct in meeting your young man rather more than halfway, that did the trick—eh?' She looked at me with eyes brimming over with wisdom. 'You needn't be afraid, sir, I'll not speak of it. Mère Todevinn always made me promise to keep silence too. But of course I know it was the powder that worked the charm.'"

"And to that belief the dear creature will stick to the last day of her life. Women are wonderful enigmas. Explain to them that tight-lacing displaces all the internal organs, and show them diagrams to illustrate your point, they smile sweetly, say, 'Oh, how funny!' and go out to buy their new stays half an inch smaller than their old ones. But tell them they must never pass a pin in the street for luck's sake, if it lies with its point towards them, and they will sedulously look for and pick up every such confounded pin they see. Talk to a woman of the marvels of science, and she turns a deaf ear, or refuses point-blank to believe you; yet she is absolutely all ear for any old wife's tale, drinks it greedily in, and never loses hold of it for the rest of her days."

"But does she?" said I; "that's the point in dispute; and though your story shows there's still a commendable amount of superstition in the Islands, I'm afraid if you were to come to London, you would not find sufficient to cover a threepenny-piece."

"Woman is woman all the world over," said Mauger, sententiously, "no matter what mental garb happens to be in fashion at the time. *Grattez la femme, et vous trouvez la folle.* For see here: if I had said to Mademoiselle Elsie, 'Well, you were in the wrong; it's your place to take the first step towards reconciliation,' she would have laughed in my face, or flung out of the shop in a rage. But because I sold her a little humbugging powder under the guise of a charm, she submitted herself with the docility of a pet lambkin. No; one need never hope to prevail through wisdom with a woman, and if I could have realized that ten years ago, it would have been better for me."

He fell silent, thinking of his past, which to me, who knew it, seemed almost an excuse for his cynicism. I sought a change of idea. The splendor of the pageant outside supplied me with one.

The sun had set; and all the eastern world of sky and water, stretching before us, was steeped in the glories of the after-glow. The ripples seemed painted in dabs of ruddy gold upon a surface of polished blue-gray steel. Over the islands opposite hung a far-reaching golden cloud, with faint-drawn, up-curled edges, as though thinned out upon the sky by some monster brush; and while I watched it, this cloud changed from gold to rose-color, and instantly the steel mirror of the sea glowed rosy too, and was streaked and shaded with a wonderful rosy-brown. As the color grew momentarily more intense in the sky above, so did the sea appear to pulse to a more vivid cop-perish-rose, until at last it was like nothing so much as a sea of flowing fire. And the cloud flamed fiery too, yet all the while its up-curled edges rested in exquisite contrast upon a background of most cool cerulean blue.

The little sailing-boat, which I had noticed an hour previously, reappeared from behind the Point. The sail was lowered as it entered the harbor, and the boatman took to his oars. I watched it creep over the glittering water until it vanished beneath the window-sill. I got up and went over to the window to hold it still in sight. It was sculled by a young man in rosy shirt-sleeves, and opposite to him, in the stern, sat a girl in a rosy gown.

So long as I had observed them, not one word had either spoken. In silence they had crossed the harbor, in silence the sculler had brought his craft alongside the landing-stage, and secured her to a ring in the stones. Still silent, he helped his companion to step out upon the quay.

"Here," said I to Mauger, "is a couple confirming your 'silent' theory with a vengeance. We must suppose that much love has rendered them absolutely dumb."

He came and leaned from the window too.

"It's not *a* couple, but *the* couple," said he; "and after all, in spite of cheap jesting, there are some things more eloquent than speech." For at this instant, finding themselves alone upon the jetty, the young man had taken the girl into his arms, and she had lifted a frank responsive mouth to return his kiss.

Five minutes later the sea had faded into dull grays and sober browns, starved white clouds moved dispiritedly over a vacant sky, and by cricking the back of my neck I was able to follow Toumes' black coat and the white frock of Miss Elsie until they reached Poidevin's wine-vaults, and, turning up the Water-gate, were lost to view.

PART TWO

ARTICLES

THE DEBATE OVER WOMEN'S SUFFRAGE

During the 1890s, the New Woman writers' primary focus was on social, economic, and educational reforms rather than on political issues. However, women's suffrage was a subtext for many of the arguments made for the emancipation of women, and some New Women, notably Sarah Grand, did discuss women's suffrage in their essays. Many of the questions raised by the New Woman writers in the 1890s were integral to the suffrage debate during the late nineteenth and early twentieth centuries: What is woman's sphere? Do men and women have different and competing interests? Would women use the vote to penalize male vice? Do unmarried women have different interests from married women?

In 1918 the Representation of the People Act gave the vote to women of Great Britain aged 30 and over who were householders, wives of householders, occupiers of property with an annual rent of £5, or university graduates. All women who were 21 and over were not granted the vote until 1928. However, the campaign for women's suffrage began long before, in the mid-nineteenth century, with the formation of local suffrage associations. In 1866 John Stuart Mill introduced to Parliament the first suffrage petition that sought to extend the franchise to all male and female householders; it was the same year that the National Society for Women's Suffrage was formed. During the 1870s six Women's Suffrage Bills lost in the House of Commons as did the attempt to attach a women's suffrage amendment to the Third Reform Bill of 1884 that entitled about two-thirds of the male population to vote.

Men were not the only ones to oppose the enfranchisement of women; many wealthy and titled women also opposed it. In June 1889 Mrs. Humphry Ward (Mary Ward, 1851-1920), a well-known novelist, along with many other prominent or well-connected women, such as Mrs. Leslie Stephen, Virginia Woolf's mother, published "An Appeal Against Female Suffrage" in the *Nineteenth Century*. The first signatory of the "Appeal" was Lady Stanley of Alderley. Lady Stanley (1807-95) was a well-known public figure; she was a friend of the writer Thomas Carlyle and Frederick Denison Maurice, a professor at Cambridge, and was married to Edward John Stanley, the second Baron Stanley, a Whig Member of Parliament. She was herself active in politics for the Liberal party and a promoter of women's education. In the July issue of the same journal, Millicent Garrett Fawcett and Margaret Mary Dilke (d. 1914) responded, each with a separate "Reply." Millicent Fawcett (1847-1929) was a significant figure in the women's suffrage movement. In 1897 she became president of the National Union of Women's Suffrage Societies (NUWSS), which united all the earlier suffrage organizations. The NUWSS supported franchise for women on the same terms as men, although Fawcett's "Reply" did not take this position in 1889 when she distinguished between married and unmarried women. The NUWSS remained non-militant in its approach, in contrast to the Women's Social and Political Union (WSPU), founded by Emmeline Pankhurst and her family in 1903, which used increasingly violent tactics to gain suffrage for women.

Several New Woman writers later became actively involved in the suffrage movement. The Women Writers' Suffrage League, formed in 1908 to promote the suffrage cause through publications and book sales, included such New Woman writers as Sarah Grand and Olive Schreiner, together with the later well-known suffrage writers Elizabeth Robins and Cicely Hamilton.

"An Appeal Against Female Suffrage"

[*Nineteenth Century* 25 (June 1889): 781-88]

We, the undersigned, wish to appeal to the common sense and the educated thought of the men and women of England against the proposed extension of the Parliamentary suffrage to women.

1. While desiring the fullest possible development of the powers, energies, and education of women, we believe that their work for the State, and their responsibilities towards it, must always differ essentially from those of men, and that therefore their share in the working of the State machinery should be different from that assigned to men. Certain large departments of the national life are of necessity worked exclusively by men. To men belong the struggle of debate and legislation in Parliament; the hard and exhausting labour implied in the administration of the national resources and powers; the conduct of England's relations towards the external world; the working of the army and navy; all the heavy, laborious, fundamental industries of the State, such as those of mines, metals, and railways; the lead and supervision of English commerce, the management of our vast English finance, the service of that merchant fleet on which our food supply depends. In all these spheres women's direct participation is made impossible either by the disabilities of sex, or by strong formations of custom and habit resting ultimately upon physical difference, against which it is useless to contend. They are affected indeed, in some degree, by all these national activities; therefore they ought in some degree to have an influence on them all. This influence they already have, and will have more and more as the education of women advances. But their direct interest in these matters can never equal that of men, whose whole energy of mind and body is daily and hourly risked in them. Therefore it is not just to give

to women direct power of deciding questions of Parliamentary policy, of war, of foreign or colonial affairs, of commerce and finance equal to that possessed by men. We hold that they already possess an influence on political matters fully proportioned to the possible share of women in the political activities of England.

At the same time we are heartily in sympathy with all the recent efforts which have been made to give women a more important part in those affairs of the community where their interests and those of men are equally concerned; where it is possible for them not only to decide but to help in carrying out, and where, therefore, judgment is weighted by a true responsibility, and can be guided by experience and the practical information which comes from it. As voters for or members of School Boards, Boards of Guardians, and other important public bodies, women have now opportunities for public usefulness which must promote the growth of character, and at the same time strengthen among them the social sense and habit. All these changes of recent years, together with the great improvements in women's education which have accompanied them, we cordially welcome. But we believe that the emancipating process has now reached the limits fixed by the physical constitution of women, and by the fundamental difference which must always exist between their main occupations and those of men. The care of the sick and the insane; the treatment of the poor; the education of children: in all these matters, and others besides, they have made good their claim to larger and more extended powers. We rejoice in it. But when it comes to questions of foreign or colonial policy, or of grave constitutional change, then we maintain that the necessary and normal experience of women—speaking generally and in the mass—does not and can never provide them with such materials for sound judgment as are open to men.

To sum up: we would give them their full share in the State of social effort and social mechanism; we look for their increasing activity in that higher State which rests on thought, conscience, and moral influence; but we protest against their admission to direct power in that State which *does* rest upon force—the State in its administrative, military, and financial aspects—where the physical capacity, the accumulated experience and inherited training of men ought to prevail without the harassing interference of those who, though they may be partners with men in debate, can in these matters never be partners with them in action.

2. If we turn from the *right* of women to the suffrage—a right which on the grounds just given we deny—to the effect which the possession of the suffrage may be expected to have on their character and position and on family life, we find ourselves no less in doubt. It is urged that the influence of women in politics would tell upon the side of morality. We believe that it does so tell already, and will do so with greater force as women by improved education fit themselves to exert it more widely and efficiently. But it may

be asked, On what does this moral influence depend? We believe that it depends largely on qualities which the natural position and functions of women as they are at present tend to develop, and which might be seriously impaired by their admission to the turmoil of active political life. These qualities are, above all, sympathy and disinterestedness. Any disposition of things which threatens to lessen the national reserve of such forces as these we hold to be a misfortune. It is notoriously difficult to maintain them in the presence of party necessities and in the heat of party struggle. Were women admitted to this struggle, their natural eagerness and quickness of temper would probably make them hotter partisans than men. As their political relations stand at present, they tend to check in them the disposition to partisanship, and to strengthen in them the qualities of sympathy and disinterestedness. We believe that their admission to the suffrage would precisely reverse this condition of things, and that the whole nation would suffer in consequence. For whatever may be the duty and privilege of the parliamentary vote for men, we hold that citizenship is not dependent upon or identical with the possession of the suffrage. Citizenship lies in the participation of each individual in effort for the good of the community. And we believe that women will be more valuable citizens, will contribute more precious elements to the national life without the vote than with it. The quickness to feel, the willingness to lay aside prudential considerations in a right cause, which are amongst the peculiar excellencies of women, are in their right place when they are used to influence the more highly trained and developed judgment of men. But if this quickness of feeling could be immediately and directly translated into public action, in matters of vast and complicated political import, the risks of politics would be enormously increased, and what is now a national blessing might easily become a national calamity. On the one hand, then, we believe that to admit women to the ordinary machinery of political life would inflame the partisanship and increase the evils, already so conspicuous, of that life, would tend to blunt the special moral qualities of women, and so to lessen the national reserves of moral force; and, on the other hand, we dread the political and practical effects which, in our belief, would follow on such a transformation as is proposed, of an influence which is now beneficent largely because it is indirect and gradual.

3. Proposals for the extension of the suffrage to women are beset with grave practical difficulties. If votes be given to unmarried women on the same terms as they are given to men, large numbers of women leading immoral lives will be enfranchised on the one hand, while married women, who, as a rule, have passed through more of the practical experiences of life than the unmarried, will be excluded. To remedy part of this difficulty it is proposed by a large section of those who advocate the extension of the suffrage to women, to admit married women with the requisite property qualification.

This proposal—an obviously just one if the suffrage is to be extended to women at all—introduces changes in family life, and in the English conception of the household, of enormous importance, which have never been adequately considered. We are practically invited to embark upon them because a few women of property possessing already all the influence which belongs to property, and a full share of that public protection and safety which is the fruit of taxation, feel themselves aggrieved by the denial of the parliamentary vote. The grievance put forward seems to us wholly disproportionate to the claim based upon it.

4. A survey of the manner in which this proposal has won its way into practical politics leads us to think that it is by no means ripe for legislative solution. A social change of momentous gravity has been proposed; the mass of those immediately concerned in it are notoriously indifferent; there has been no serious and general demand for it, as is always the case if a grievance is real and reform necessary; the amount of information collected is quite inadequate to the importance of the issue; and the public has gone through no sufficient discipline of discussion on the subject. Meanwhile pledges to support female suffrage have been hastily given in the hopes of strengthening existing political parties by the female vote. No doubt there are many conscientious supporters of female suffrage amongst members of Parliament; but it is hard to deny that the present prominence of the question is due to party considerations of a temporary nature. It is, we submit, altogether unworthy of the intrinsic gravity of the question that it should be determined by reference to the passing needs of party organisation. Meanwhile we remember that great electoral changes have been carried out during recent years. Masses of new electors have been added to the constituency. These new elements have still to be assimilated; these new electors have still to be trained to take their part in the national work; and while such changes are still fresh, and their issues uncertain, we protest against any further alteration in our main political machinery, especially when it is an alteration which involves a new principle of extraordinary range and significance, closely connected with the complicated problems of sex and family life.

5. It is often urged that certain injustices of the law towards women would be easily and quickly remedied were the political power of the vote conceded to them; and that there are many wants, especially among working women, which are now neglected, but which the suffrage would enable them to press on public attention. We reply that during the past half century all the principal injustices of the law towards women have been amended by means of the existing constitutional machinery; and with regard to those that remain, we see no signs of any unwillingness on the part of Parliament to deal with them. On the contrary, we remark a growing sensitiveness to the claims of women, and the rise of a new spirit of justice and sympathy among men, answering to

those advances made by women in education, and the best kind of social influence, which we have already noticed and welcomed. With regard to the business or trade interests of women,—here, again, we think it safer and wiser to trust to organisation and self-help on their own part, and to the growth of a better public opinion among the men workers, than to the exercise of a political right which may easily bring women into direct and hasty conflict with men.

In conclusion: nothing can be further from our minds than to seek to depreciate the position or importance of women. It is because we are keenly alive to the enormous value of their special contribution to the community, that we oppose what seems to us likely to endanger that contribution. We are convinced that the pursuit of a mere outward equality with men is for women not only vain but demoralising. It leads to a total misconception of woman's true dignity and special mission. It tends to personal struggle and rivalry, where the only effort of both the great divisions of the human family should be to contribute the characteristic labour and the best gifts of each to the common stock. [The names of 104 women are listed.]

Female Suffrage: A Women's Protest

The undersigned protest strongly against the proposed Extension of the Parliamentary Franchise to Women, which they believe would be a measure distasteful to the great majority of the women of the country—unnecessary—and mischievous both to themselves and to the State.

"THE APPEAL AGAINST FEMALE SUFFRAGE: A REPLY. I"

MILLICENT GARRETT FAWCETT

[*Nineteenth Century* 26 (July 1889): 86-96]

... The ladies who sign the *Nineteenth Century* Protest against the enfranchisement of women ... do not wish it to be supposed that they are opposed to the recent improvements that have taken place in the education of women, or to their increased activity in various kinds of public work. "All these changes," they say, "together with the great improvements in women's education which have accompanied them, we cordially welcome. But we believe that the emancipating process has now reached the limits fixed by the physical constitution of women." In other passages they attribute the greatest value to the influence of women in politics, recognising it as a moral force, which is likely to grow stronger as the results of the improved education of women make themselves felt. In the concluding paragraph they, with some want of humour, I think, asseverate that nothing is further from their minds, "than to seek to depreciate the position and importance of women." To acknowledge the importance of women conveys a height and depth and breadth of condescension which is difficult to measure. A lady last year at Lucerne, admiring the view of lake and mountains, said in a similar spirit, "It is lovely: my daughter says, if she had made it herself she could not have done better." And we may take it as a grain of comfort that the writer of the Protest gives her sanction and approval to the scheme of creation. She "acknowledges the importance" of half the human family; if she had made it herself she could hardly, perhaps, have done better. Mr. Disraeli[1] once said in the House of Commons, referring to a speech which had just been delivered by Mr. W.E. Forster: "The right honourable gentleman has acknowledged in the handsomest manner that the agricultural labourer is a human being." The hundred and four ladies have acknowledged in the handsomest way "the importance of women." Let us inquire a little in detail into the line of argument adopted, in the Protest, and also analyse somewhat the list of names by which the arguments are supported.

The Protest speaks in congratulatory words of all recent changes which have given extended opportunities of usefulness to women. Special reference is made to improvements in education, and among other subjects mentioned are "the care of the sick and the insane, the treatment of the poor, the education of children: in all these matters, and in others besides, they [women] have made good their claim to larger and more extended powers. We rejoice in it." But, on reading the names appended to the Protest, the most striking fact about them is that hardly any out of the hundred and four ladies who now rejoice in these changes have helped them while their issue was in any way doubtful. They hardly deserve even to be called the patrons of any effort to improve the social, legal, or educational position of women—unless, indeed, we adopt Dr. Johnson's[2] famous definition of the word "patron": "Is not a patron, my lord, one who looks with unconcern on a man struggling for life in the water, and, when he has reached the ground, encumbers him with help?" A good many of the hundred and four hardly preserved an attitude of neutrality whilst the changes they now rejoice in were "struggling for life in the water;" while success was still uncertain, many a backhander has been dealt at them by the same ladies who now announce themselves as rejoicing in their success. Very few are there, among the hundred and four, who moved purse, tongue, or pen in support of these changes before they became accomplished facts. This is the general character of the list of names. But let it be at once acknowledged that there are exceptions, chief of whom is the lady whose name heads the list—the Dowager Lady Stanley of Alderley. She has been a constant, a generous, and an outspoken friend of better education for women of all classes. There are other exceptions, but they are less striking, and I think they could easily be counted on the fingers of one hand. The women to whose initiative we owe the improvements which the hundred and four rejoice in, are not to be found in the *Nineteenth Century* list. Work for others is one of the most educating influences either man or woman can have. Professor Marshall recently said in his presidential address at the Co-operative Congress: "He who lived and worked only for himself, or even only for himself and his family, led an incomplete life. To complete it he needed to work with others for some broad and high aim." The women who have worked with others for the object of lifting the lives of women to a higher level educationally, socially, and industrially, are not in the *Nineteenth Century* list. The names of the women to whose unselfish and untiring labours we owe what has been done for women during the last twenty-five years in education, in social and philanthropic work, in proprietary rights, in some approach towards justice as regards the guardianship of children, in opening the means of medical education, are conspicuous by their absence, and for an excellent reason: they support the extension of the suffrage to duly qualified women. At the head of the educational movement for women are Miss Emily Davies, Miss Clough, Mrs. Henry Sidgwick, Miss Dorothea Beale of Cheltenham, Mrs. William Grey, Miss Shirreff, Miss Buss, and Miss Eleanor Smith of Oxford. They, and many others too numerous to mention, to whom the girls and women of England owe a revival of learning hardly less remarkable than that of the sixteenth century, are with us in the matter of the franchise; so are the Misses Davenport Hill, Miss Florence Nightingale, Miss Cons, Mrs. Josephine Butler, Mrs. Bright Lucas, Mrs. Barnett, and Miss Irby, as representing the best women's work in philanthropy of various kinds; so are Dr. Elizabeth Blackwell, Mrs. Garrett Anderson, M.D., Dr. Sophia Jex Blake, Miss Edith Pechey, M.D., and, I believe, all the women who have helped to open the medical profession to women.

A further consideration of the *Nineteenth Century* list of names shows that it contains a very large preponderance of ladies to whom the lines of life have fallen in pleasant places. There are very few among them of the women who have had to face the battle of life alone, to earn their living by daily hard work. Women of this class generally feel the injustice of their want of representation. The weight of taxation falls upon them just as if they were men, and they do not see why representation should not go with taxation in their case, simply because their physical strength is less than that of men. No one proposes to relieve them of fiscal burdens because of "the limits fixed by the physical constitution of women."...

A large part of the Protest is directed against women taking an active part in the turmoil of political life. This has nothing to do with voting or not voting. For instance, women vote in school board elections; but they can please themselves about taking part in the turmoil of a school board contest.

Thousands of women vote who keep completely clear of meetings, canvassing, committees, and all the rest of the electioneering machinery. On the other hand, women do not vote in Parliamentary elections, but they are invited and pressed by all parties to take an active part in the turmoil of political life. Among other inconsistencies of the protesting ladies, it should not be forgotten that many of them, as presidents and vice-presidents of women's political associations, encourage the admission of women to the ordinary machinery of political life, although they say in this Protest that this admission would be dangerous to the best interests of society. If women are fit to advise, convince, and persuade voters how to vote, they are surely also fit to vote themselves. On the other hand, if it is true, as the *Nineteenth Century* ladies state, that women on the whole "are without the materials for forming a sound judgment" on matters of constitutional change, why are we invited by those same ladies to form our unsound judgments, and do all in our power to induce others to share them? If we have no materials, or insufficient materials, for forming a sound judgment in politics, we should not be invited to enrol ourselves in Primrose Leagues, or in the Women's Liberal Federation,[3] or in the Women's Liberal Unionist Association. To say simultaneously to women, "The materials for forming a sound judgment are not open to you," and "We beg you to influence electors to whom is entrusted the fate of the empire," is to run with the hare and hunt with the hounds. One position or the other must be abandoned, unless these ladies have cultivated with unusual skill the art of believing two contradictory things at the same time....

The "party, nothing but party" politician in England, as well as in America, looks with distrust on women's suffrage. Women would be an unknown quantity, less amenable to party discipline, less expectant of party loaves and fishes, and consequently less obedient to the party whip than the present electorate. They might take the bit in their mouth and insist on voting in a way inconvenient to their party on temperance, and on matters of religion and morals. These fears tell against us very heavily, and we cannot allay them; because the fear that women will be independent and will dare to vote for what they think is right, whether the professional politician likes it or not, is, in our minds, not a fear but a hope, and a hope which is at the root of all we are working for. If women's suffrage should tend to strengthen the group, which exists in every constituency, of the voters whose political views are not dictated to them from a central office in Parliament Street or Victoria Street, but are the result of independent thought, study of facts, and conscientious obedience to moral considerations, it is a matter of very small importance which party will gain or lose by the female vote; all parties will be the better for it....

It was natural that the subscribers to the Protest should make the most of a subject on which the supporters of women's suffrage are not at one: viz.[4] the admission or the exclusion of married women. The party in favour of an extension of the suffrage is seldom in absolute harmony upon the extent of the change which they demand. Some of the supporters of the Reform Bills of 1832, 1867, and 1884 would have liked, far better than these gradual extensions, to have leapt at once to universal suffrage. But our national habit in these things is to go slowly, one step at a time, and be sure of a firm foothold in one place before we go on to another. Both the Bills for women's suffrage that were introduced this session were drawn in this spirit: they would have enfranchised those women who have already received the municipal, county council, and school board suffrages; *i.e.* single women and widows who are householders, property owners, and otherwise fulfil the conditions by law on male electors.

The *Nineteenth Century* ladies think that these Bills would "enfranchise large numbers of women leading immoral lives," and on the other hand, by excluding wives, would shut out those women "who, as a rule, have passed through more of the practical experiences of life than the unmarried." Both these statements invite comment. By the words "large numbers of women leading immoral lives," it may be presumed that the ladies refer to some women who might become qualified to vote under the lodger franchise. Among "the materials for forming a sound judgment" in this matter are the following facts, which are not beyond the grasp of the female intellect. Two consecutive years' residence in the same apartments, and also personal application to be placed upon the Parliamentary register are required of any one claiming the lodger franchise. These conditions have, as regards the male sex, made this franchise almost a dead letter: for example, in the borough of Blackburn, with 13,000 electors, only fifteen men vote under the lodger franchise. In most constituencies the lodgers are an absolutely insignificant fraction of the whole body of electors. The conditions which prevent men lodgers from becoming electors would be even more effective in preventing women lodgers, of the unhappy class referred to, from getting upon the register. On the other hand, the large class of most respectable and worthy women who live in lodgings, such as teachers and others engaged in education, would have no difficulty in fulfilling the conditions demanded, and would form a valuable addition to the electorate.

Foreigners often talk of English hypocrisy; and this bugbear about women's suffrage rendering it possible for an immoral woman to vote for a member of Parliament, appears an excellent example of it. How long has a stainless moral character been one of the conditions for exercising the Parliamentary suffrage? When it is remembered that no moral iniquity disqualifies a man from voting, that men of known bad character not only vote but are voted for, it is hardly possible to accept as genuine the objection to women's suffrage based on the possibility of an immoral woman voting. In times gone by women of this character had more political power than any other women. The mistresses of kings and of their ministers have often been centres of political power. But the modern democratic movement of society has modified this state of things; there is a transfer of political power from the Perrerses and the Du Barrys[5] to the humbler but more self-respecting women who worthily represent the true womanhood of the country. Who can say, if women's suffrage were carried, that the new electors would not be of a character calculated to raise, rather than depress, the moral level of the constituencies to which they belong?

The next objection of the hundred and four is that, if wives are excluded, those who would be shut out are women "who have, as a rule, passed through more of the practical experiences of life than the unmarried;" whilst if they are included, "changes of enormous importance, which have never been adequately considered, would be introduced into home life.". . . The ladies . . . mention the undoubted fact that married women must either be included or excluded in any women's suffrage Bill: if they are excluded, many of the best women will be shut out; if they are included, changes will be introduced into home life which have not been adequately considered. For my own part, it has always seemed for many reasons right to recognise this, and therefore to support the measures which would enfranchise single women and widows, and not wives during the lifetime of their husbands. The case for the enfranchisement of women who are standing alone and bearing the burden of citizenship as ratepayers and taxpayers, seems unanswerable. If we have household suffrage, let the head of the house vote, whether that head be a man or a woman. The enfranchisement of wives is an altogether different question. The enfranchisement of single women and widows gives electoral power to a class who are in a position of social and financial independence. To give these women votes would be a change in their political condition, bringing it into harmony with their social, industrial, and pecuniary position. This would not be the case with wives. If they were enfranchised, the effect, in ninety-nine cases out of a hundred, would be to give two votes to the husband. Wives are bound by law to obey their husbands. No other class in the community is in this position, and it seems inexpedient to allow political independence (which would only be nominal) to precede actual independence. The legal position of a married woman has changed considerably in the direction of independence, but the change is, after all, only partial (it is not argued here whether or not it is desirable to make it complete); and, in my opinion, a change in political status should always be attendant on a corresponding and preceding change in the social and legal status. The limitation of female suffrage to those women not under coverture[6] would no doubt exclude from representation many women of high character and capacity. A similar objection can be made to every limitation of the suffrage. It must also be remembered that if the Bill lately before Parliament were carried, no set of women would be definitely and permanently excluded, as at present all women are. Marriage is to nearly all women a state either of experience or of expectation. There would be a constant passing to and fro, from the ranks of the represented and the unrepresented, and consequently the closest identity of interest would exist between them. In this way the direct representation of some women would become the indirect representation of all women. Many valued friends of the Women's Suffrage movement take a different view, and urge that we should seek to remove the disability of coverture simultaneously with the disability of sex; and that to exclude married women is to place a slight upon marriage. Others, with whom I sympathise, believe this to be a mistaken view; as regards the alleged slight on marriage, married women never discovered that they were insulted when their single or widowed sisters were entrusted with the school board, municipal, and county council suffrages. It is on the lines laid down by our previous experiences of women's suffrage that it will probably be found best to proceed in the future.

In conclusion, the ladies of the *Nineteenth Century* Protest may be reminded that the friends of women's suffrage value the womanliness of women as much as themselves. True womanliness grows and thrives on whatever strengthens the spontaneity and independence of the character of women. Women, for instance, are more womanly in England, where Florence Nightingale and Mary Carpenter[7] have taught them how women's work ought to be done, than they are in Spain, where they accept the masculine standard in matters of amusement and go in crowds to see a bull-fight. The most unfeminine of English women are to be found in those classes which are either so high or so low in the social scale as to have been comparatively little influenced by the emancipating process of the last fifty years. They set their ideas of pleasure and amusement by the masculine, not by the feminine standard. At the top of the social scale, these women (who are bad imitations of men) go on the turf, practice various kinds of sport, or if they do not kill with their own hands, stand by and see others kill pheasants in a battue, or pigeons at Hurlingham. At the other end of the social scale there are women whose feminine instincts are so little developed that betting and drinking are their chief enjoyments. These are the really unfeminine women. We do not want women to be bad imitations of men; we neither deny nor minimise the differences between men and women. The claim of women to representation depends to a large extent on those differences. Women bring something to the service of the state different from that which can be brought by men. Let this fact be frankly recognised and let due weight be given to it in the representative system of the country.

"The Appeal Against Female Suffrage: A Reply. II"

M.M. Dilke

[*Nineteenth Century* 26 (July 1889): 97-103]

It has been no secret to the supporters of woman suffrage that a section of prominent women in London society have remained unconvinced by the arguments for the enfranchisement of women; but their opposition long remained of so indefinite and nebulous a character, that it was obviously difficult to grapple with it. Now that they have written an appeal and stated their objections in clear, straightforward language, and signed their names to the number of a hundred and more; now that they have entered the lists to fight, not for, but against the extension of political rights to their own sex, it is possible to gauge their strength, to test their reasoning powers, to place, indeed, once more before the public the reasons *pro* and *con* the most absorbing and important movement of the century. Those who have spoken and written repeatedly on this subject for the last dozen years have a feeling of hesitation and shyness at being obliged to use the same arguments again and again, and to bring but little fresh fuel to feed the furnace of public opinion; but it is only necessary to read through the appeal with care to find that the opponents of further progress have simply burnished up the old weapons and sharpened the time-worn steel. No new artillery of novel design makes necessary the reconstruction of fortress or line of defence; the only real difference, and it is of importance in politics as in war, is that the sharp-shooters and freelances who for long carried on a war of chance encounters and night surprises now find themselves in possession of an important fortress, and instead of devising a telling attack, they have to maintain their hard-won position and repulse an apparently formidable assault.

We have to thank these ladies for their approval of the reforms that have been already carried, to be grateful to them for their acceptance of accomplished facts. And yet with the honourable exception of Lady Stanley of Alderley, whose name, with a consciousness of its exceptional weight, they have placed at the head of the list, it is not in this list that we find the names of the women who have given time and energy and money to carry these reforms. It is notorious that those women who have the best right to speak for their sex, as they have already made many and great sacrifices for it, have again and again signed memorials and petitions in favour of woman suffrage, pleading that their just work was made difficult, and even in the end was but inefficiently accomplished, because they had no vote to legalise their proceedings and facilitate its accomplishment. These ladies take upon themselves to say the time has come to arrest all further progress; ignoring the fact that as the old bonds and fetters fall away from women's limbs new requirements arise, new possibilities open out before them, and careers that but a short quarter of a century ago would have seemed far out of their reach now open before them and seem to call able and well-educated women to fill posts for which their training has fitted them.

While men have been considering the danger to society of allowing women to take the first step that is said to cost so much, that step and many others have been quietly taken, and women have already half climbed the ladder. But can any position be more useless and illogical than that of a person who having half climbed a ladder is told to pause, to remain 'twixt heaven and earth, and to forego the object with which the climb was undertaken? Ladies of intellect and social standing can always make their voices heard, can always write to the papers and magazines, can command the sympathy and attention of public men whenever they feel they receive less than justice. But the supporters of woman suffrage aspire to help those other women whose lives are spent in humble toil, whose work is ill paid, whose education has been defective or entirely neglected. They wish to see women's power and influence more evenly divided, more fairly distributed. They wish women to vote because they are different from men, and because no alteration of laws, or customs, or social habits will make them the same as men.

The supporters of woman suffrage do not believe in indirect representation under any circumstances, but least of all when the influx of women into the labour market brings them, whether they will it or no, into competition with those whose interests and capacities are different; it is not the Woman Suffrage Societies that have brought about this great social change. A man is no longer expected, even in well-to-do middle-class society, to support his adult sisters and daughters as well as his wife and infant children. The societies, accepting the new state of things, wish to protect the earning of these women, to teach them self-reliance, to help them in the only way human beings can be efficiently helped—shown how to help themselves.

It is strange that the vote should have come to be looked on as necessarily a masculine adjunct. It was certainly originally intended to give effect to the opinions of the quiet, orderly citizen, instead of leaving power in the hands of the strong and warlike. The citizen may be ill or crippled, immoral or sentimental, illiterate or drunken, without risking his right to vote; and women will always resent having their claim to vote denied because individuals among them may suffer from any or all of these disadvantages. No reliable substitute for a vote has ever been invented, or is likely to be discovered in the future. A vote is not an end in itself, it is only a means to an end. It is as useful as a lever to lift a weight, or as a key to open a door, but has in itself no intrinsic value. Women do not imagine that the Millennium will have been attained when some or indeed all of them have votes; but as long as they have no votes they risk the loss of all those improvements in the position of their sex for which they have toiled so unremittingly. People without votes who deliberately say they do not want them are like a crowd standing outside a concert-hall, eager to hear every note of the music, refusing to take the key and unlock the door so that they may enter, and yet triumphantly pointing out to those who advise the use of that simple implement that, the windows being partly open, faint echoes of the melody reach them now and again if they listen with sufficient attention.

We are told again and again that society rests ultimately on force, and women, in the willing tribute they pay to brave, strong, and courageous men, are the first to acknowledge it; but more than half the men of every European country, even in these days of compulsory military service, have to stand aside and relegate the actual defence of their country to those who can most efficiently perform it. Women will always have to stand aside, and while battle wages give, like every other citizen, money to supply the sinews of war; and for their own special contribution, that care of the sick and wounded that has become so much more efficient and valuable since science and hospital experience and technical training of the best kind have developed their finest faculties. If the men had not some special sphere—that of war—in which nature has intended that they shall specially excel, they would not be the equals but the inferiors of women, who have other spheres equally necessary, for which they and they alone are indispensable.

But there are other great facts of life besides force which are of equally paramount importance. One of these great facts is, that every mother who brings a child into the world risks her life in that most necessary beginning of all existence; and surely, if men take so much credit for endangering their lives in war, this should not be forgotten or ignored in calculating the services the two sexes severally give to society. Again, while we say that society rests ultimately on force, we also say with equal truth and cogency that society rests on work. The problems connected with the labour question are most urgent and pressing, and it is impossible to attempt to solve them without taking woman into account. Women's home work has always been unpaid, whether well or ill-performed, but, taken as a whole, has in the past times been quite as often well done, and been quite as fundamental a part of civilised life, as the paid labour of men. But every census shows that more women enter the paid labour market year by year.

The main causes are, the preponderance of female compared to male population owing to emigration, the invention of labour-saving household implements that lighten indoor work, the co-operative tendencies of city life that cause baking, washing, dressmaking, and upholstering to be done outside; and more especially the increased orderliness and propriety of English life that enables women to go and come in the streets and public conveyances without fear of insult or assault. The rapidly increasing wealth of the middle classes has deprived thousands of women of the necessity for household toil; but education and increased opportunities for intellectual and public work draw these same women, if not in the first, then in the second generation, into busy useful lives, giving satisfaction to themselves and benefit to the community at large. If, then, society rests on labour, and women contribute more and more to that labour, it becomes absolutely necessary for them to have a voice in all labour laws and regulations, and in all social questions.

It is quite possible that the most crying injustices from which women suffer may be removed by a Parliament of men, elected only by men; but women have had to complain in the past more of the ignorance and prejudice of men in regard to labour legislation than of their unfairness or injustice. They have repeatedly attempted by legislation to prevent women from working in the most difficult and exhausting fields of labour. The result has been merely to reduce their wages and increase their hours of work in the unrestricted employments; whereas, had men invited the co-operation of women in trades unions as well as in legislation, it is probable their efforts would have been better directed, and have borne good fruit for men and women alike. Moreover, all trade legislation undertaken by men alone is open to the accusation, often, unfortunately, too well founded, of restricting women's labour, not in the most irksome, but in the best-paid posts.

Were men of their own free will to remove all the unjust laws of which women complain, they would find they had removed all the barriers to feminine emancipation invented in the past to shut women out from wage-earning and public life. They would find women placed immediately in such a position of social and economic equality with men, that to withhold merely the vote would be illogical and inconvenient. We have one great proof in England that legislation in this direction has not gone faster than public wants and opinions. When the law allowed women to become guardians of the poor, excellent women of character were ready at once to occupy the posts. When the law allowed women to become members of School Boards, no difficulty was found in securing suitable candidates. When women can vote, they do vote, in ever-increasing numbers. They have never yet shirked the responsibility once it has been imposed, and, though Mr. Labouchere[8] may say not one women in a thousand wants a vote, we have only to turn to well-ascertained facts to point to a very different conclusion.

One of the grave disadvantages about substituting feminine influence for feminine votes is the extremely demoralising effect it has always had on men's characters to find the female part of the community entirely dependent on them for their rights and privileges. Men are but human, and while they never fail to taunt lady canvassers with working most heartily for the best-looking candidate, they must be aware that the personal charms of the women who ask them for help and protection have much more to do with securing their attention and devotion than such an abstract consideration as justice.

We are anxious to relieve men of this responsibility, and provide members of Parliament, through the ballot-box, with a means of impartially carrying out the ascertained wishes of their feminine constituents, whether old or young, ill-favoured or fair to look upon.

It is really an interesting study to notice how every argument used to delay the enfranchisement of working men and farm labourers reappears to do duty against women. How often has the question been asked, "What does Hodge know about finance and foreign policy, colonial affairs and commercial interests?"

The fact is, we have made up our minds in England that to insure every class obtaining justice every class must be directly represented; and that, while we pay large salaries to specialists to look after these great questions, we cannot have too wide an opinion from the people as a whole on the main principles that are to guide our life as a nation. Woman may never be intellectually fitted for the position of minister of the Crown or ambassador, though with her present rate of progress he would be a rash man who would attempt to predict exactly how far she will go; but that does not affect one way or the other her right to vote, or the right of the nation to have her recorded opinion on every question with which she is familiar. Why should she sit on a School Board, and in that capacity make recommendations to the Government on the Education Code, and yet when that same Code is before Parliament have no power to support its provisions or secure its rejection? Why should she sit on boards of guardians, and after visiting pauper schools, and planning perhaps some new scheme that will turn our most hopeless and wretched population into valuable bread-winners, yet have no influence with Parliament to get that scheme carried into effect?

We cannot afford as a nation to allow such a potent moral influence as that of women to lie fallow. It is very well to call it a reserve force, but a reserve force that is never to be put into action is of small practical value. We think the time has come when that moral influence must be both organised and put in action. In old times, when population was scattered and manners were patriarchal, individual charity and personal influence could work wonders. With our vast cities and ever-increasing complication of interests and industries, combination of influence and co-operation in good works have become absolutely necessary, unless the feminine element is to be entirely eliminated. Men are going forward so fast, that the rift between the sexes will become wider if women are to continue working on the old lines and never take a step in advance. The choice is not between going on and standing still, it is between advancing and retreating.

The practical difficulties that beset the question of dividing women into electors and non-electors are precisely similar to the same division among men. It is equally objectionable to base the suffrage on marriage or no marriage, as it is on property or no property. But this molehill that seems such a mountain can easily be swept aside by practical persons. The nation, we believe, would like to make an experiment in woman suffrage by enfranchising a limited number and then judging of the result before going further. We believe the experiment will be successful, and will prove a precedent for future legislation whatever the section of women selected in the first instance; and that there should be a difference of opinion among women themselves on this point only proves how keen they are to take a responsible part in the national life, and directly contradicts the supposed apathy that is said to exist.

The appeal is superior to the ordinary male attack on woman suffrage, in so far that it does not condescend to discuss which political party will momentarily benefit by the passing of a Suffrage Bill into law. For this we are duly thankful. These ladies seem to consider that the question has not been sufficiently discussed, and they take the best possible means for remedying the want by raising afresh this controversy, in a way that has called forth an echo in almost every periodical in the United Kingdom.

It is not controversy that we fear. We passed successfully through the storm of ridicule and contempt, and we have languished through years of indifference and neglect; and, just when we thought the public tired with our innumerable meetings and bored with signing our petitions—when we were beginning to think that every one had made up his mind, and that the kindest and most judicious course for us to pursue would be to take every opportunity in Parliament of getting the matter settled once and for all—we are refreshed and invigorated by being told that more information is wanted, and that the public has gone through no sufficient discipline of discussion on the subject. We should be the last to shrink from this test. We have always found that every discussion, every large audience, every newspaper controversy, has added to our numbers and increased our organisations. Converts among our opponents have not been rare of late years, but undoubtedly our greatest victories have been won in the past (and are possibly awaiting us in the near future) among those men and women who have never thought about the subject at all.

"A JINGLE OF THE FRANCHISE"

[*Shafts* 1, (31 December 1892). This periodical, issued from 3 November 1892 to April 1900, contained articles for women and the working classes. The initials S.S. are the only clue to the identity of the author of this satirical poem.]

Gladstone,[9] leader of the nation,
    Says he deems it wise to pause
Ere sanctioning emancipation
    Of the women, lest it cause

Them to trespass, all unwitting,
On those gentle charms befitting
Woman's nature, thus committing
   Violence 'gainst nature's laws.

Chorus of Advocates:—For a difference he can see,
   Though not quite plain to you and me,
   'Twixt tweedledum and tweedledee.

"So, to grant this woman suffrage
   I am greatly disinclined;
For I fear 'twould sadly outrage"
   [Says the man of LIBERAL mind]
"Woman's pure and lofty nature,
As described by poet, preacher,
Politician, sage and teacher,
   And by Providence designed."

Chorus:—There's a difference that we,
   Lacking logic, cannot see,
   'Twixt tweedledum and tweedledee.

Feminine participation,
   When 'tis benefiting them,
In the "Liberal Federation,"
   Truly he does not condemn;
For this sort of influence is
Not opposed to Providence's
Great and wise decrees, and hence is
   Quite permissible.—Ahem!

Chorus:—For 'tis different, says he.
   It's just the difference, don't you see,
   'Twixt tweedledum and tweedledee?

By consensus of opinion,
   Women may participate,
Thus throughout the Queen's dominion,
   Working for male candidate,
Canvassing, electioneering,
In such cases is appearing
(Truly is the subject clearing!)
   Perfectly legitimate.

Chorus:—O, 'tis different, don't you see?
   What wide distinction there must be
   'Twixt tweedledum and tweedledee!

Why direct participation
   Gladstone's moral sense so shocks;
Wherefore this slight innovation—
   Placing papers in a box—
Should result in our unsexing,
Is a question most perplexing,
Which our souls is greatly vexing,
   And our keenest wisdom mocks.

Chorus:—For this difference we can't see,
   So illogical are we,
   'Twixt tweedledum and tweedledee.

O wise parliamentary leader
   Of a nation great and free,
It is clear to every reader
   Of this singular decree,
That the jewel that your name is
Symbol of, sure, not the same is
As the one of old whose fame is,—
   That bright gem, Consistency!

Chorus:—None are so blind as who won't see
   That no distinction there can be
   'Twixt tweedledum and tweedledee.

NOTES

1. Benjamin Disraeli (1804-81) was the British Conservative Prime Minister in 1868 and again from 1874-80.
2. Dr. Samuel Johnson (1709-84) was a poet, essayist, and compiler of the first standard English dictionary.
3. The Primrose League and the Women's Liberal Federation were official organizations for women in the Conservative (or Tory) Party and the Liberal Party. Women within these organizations worked for the election of male party candidates within their respective parties.
4. viz., namely (Latin).

5. Alice Perrers (d. 1400) was the mistress of Edward III of England. She had great influence over him and was later banished from the royal household by Parliament. However, she returned to the court of Richard II in 1377. Madame Marie Jeanne Du Barry (1743-93) was the mistress of Louis XV of France.

6. Coverture was the legal status of a woman after she married: her legal existence as an individual was suspended and she and her husband were considered a single entity. A married woman could not own property, make a contract or a will, or sue or be sued.

7. Florence Nightingale (1820-1910) is considered the founder of the modern nursing profession. She was known as the "Lady with the Lamp" for her work as a nurse during the Crimean War (1854-56). Mary Carpenter (1807-77) was a philanthropist, social reformer, and founder of free schools for poor children, the "ragged schools." She supported the movement for higher education for women.

8. Henry Labouchere was a Member of Parliament. (When Parliament passed the Criminal Law Amendment Act in 1885, Labouchere introduced a clause making it a crime punishable by two years in prison for any male person to commit an act of gross indecency with another male person, thus criminalizing homosexual behavior. This was the law under which Oscar Wilde was convicted in 1895.)

9. William Gladstone (1809-97) was Liberal Prime Minister four times: 1868-74, 1880-85, 1886, and 1892-94. Emmeline Pankhurst, in *My Own Story* (1914), called Gladstone "an implacable foe of woman suffrage" who "so arranged Parliamentary business that the bill [for suffrage] never even came up for discussion."

SARAH GRAND ON THE NEW WOMAN:
HER CRITICS RESPOND

Sarah Grand is credited with coining the term "New Woman," which she introduced in "The New Aspect of the Woman Question," an essay published in March 1894. With the publication of her novel *The Heavenly Twins* (1893), one of the first of the New Woman novels, Grand became a public figure. Many of her subsequent articles, such as the two below, identified her as "Author of *The Heavenly Twins*." This novel was one of the first works of fiction to deal openly with the subject of venereal disease, which Grand saw as evidence of the immoral behavior of many men. Grand believed women were morally superior to men, and in her fiction and essays she is highly critical of men's sexual behavior, demanding that they live up to the same moral code they imposed on women. Her so-called purity campaign was endorsed by other women, such as H.E. Harvey, who also condemns the sexual double standard in her essay "Science and the Rights of Women."

In 1868 Eliza Lynn Linton (1822-98) had anonymously published an essay called "The Girl of the Period" in the *Saturday Review*. It created a sensation for its attack on women's emancipation and its lament over the demise of the pure English girl. By the 1890s Linton with her reactionary views on women had become a target of satire. Grand's "The Man of the Moment" satirizes Linton's earlier essay; it attacks as well the men of Grand's time.

The essays by Grand and the interview with her reveal the variety of reforms she included as part of the New Woman's agenda: everything from education to bicycling to suffrage to rational dress. While not all New Woman writers took the same position as Grand on these issues, particularly on those relating to sexual purity, they did agree that reform in many areas of life was necessary for women's emancipation.

Naturally Grand's statements, as well as the New Woman, her ideas, and her behavior, provoked a response, sometimes angry but occasionally humorous. Two satirical responses to Sarah Grand's essays were published in *Punch, or the London Charivari* in 1894. The New Woman or a caricature of her was satirized in cartoons, poems, and essays in *Punch*, as well as other periodicals, during the 1890s.

Ouida, author of "The New Woman," was the nom de plume of Marie Louise de la Ramée (1839-1908) who was born in England to a French father and English mother. She was a popular romantic novelist during the latter half of the nineteenth century; her best-known novel, *Under Two Flags* (1867), sold millions of copies. She eventually wrote 44 novels and collections of stories. When her popularity as a novelist faded during the 1880s, Ouida turned to writing critical commentary; though the targets of her attack were many, they included female suffrage and cruelty to animals. Ouida's criticism of the New Woman, particularly Grand's characterization of her and her agenda, appeared in the same volume of the *North American Review* as Sarah Grand's essay, "The Man of the Moment."

Boyd Winchester (1836-1923), an American and author of the final essay, "The Eternal Feminine," praises the New Woman at the beginning of the twentieth century. However, as his description of the New Woman demonstrates, there was not one single definition of the New Woman but many competing definitions, each revealing the writer's own political and social agenda. Winchester practised law in Louisville, Kentucky. From 1869 to 1873 he served as a representative from Kentucky to the United States Congress and was appointed Minister Resident and Consul General to Switzerland from 1885 to 1889.

"The New Aspect of the Woman Question"

Sarah Grand

[*North American Review* 158 (March 1894): 270-76]

It is amusing as well as interesting to note the pause which the new aspect of the woman question has given to the Bawling Brothers who have hitherto tried to howl down every attempt on the part of our sex to make the world a pleasanter place to live in. That woman should ape man and desire to change places with him was conceivable to him as he stood on the hearth-rug in his lord-and-master-monarch-of-all-I-survey attitude, well inflated with his own conceit; but that she should be content to develop the good material which she finds in herself and be only dissatisfied with the poor quality of that which is being offered to her in man, her mate, must appear to him to be a thing as monstrous as it is unaccountable. "If women don't want to be men, what do they want?" asked the Bawling Brotherhood when the first misgiving of the truth flashed upon them; and then, to reassure themselves, they pointed to a certain sort of woman in proof of the contention that we were all unsexing ourselves.

It would be as rational for us now to declare that men generally are Bawling Brothers or to adopt the hasty conclusion which makes all men out to be fiends on the one hand and all women fools on the other. We have our Shrieking Sisterhood, as the counterpart of the Bawling Brotherhood. The latter consists of two sorts of men. First of all is he who is satisfied with the cow-kind of woman as being most convenient; it is the threat of any strike among his domestic cattle for more consideration that irritates him into loud and angry protests. The other sort of Bawling Brother is he who is under the influence of the scum of our sex, who knows nothing better than women of that class in and out of society, preys upon them or ruins himself for them, takes his whole tone from them, and judges us all by them. Both the cowwoman and the scum-woman are well within the range of the comprehension of the Bawling Brotherhood, but the new woman is a little above him, and he never even thought of looking up to where she has been sitting apart in silent contemplation all these years, thinking and thinking, until at last she solved the problem and proclaimed for herself what was wrong with Home-is-the-Woman's-Sphere, and prescribed the remedy.

What she perceived at the outset was the sudden and violent upheaval of the suffering sex in all parts of the world. Women were awaking from their long apathy, and, as they awoke, like healthy hungry children unable to articulate, they began to whimper for they knew not what. They might have been easily satisfied at that time had not society, like an ill-conditioned and ignorant nurse, instead of finding out what they lacked, shaken them and beaten them and stormed at them until what was once a little wail became convulsive shrieks and roused up the whole human household. Then man, disturbed by the uproar, came upstairs all anger and irritation, and, without waiting to learn what was the matter, added his own old theories to the din, but, finding they did not act rapidly, formed new ones, and made an intolerable nuisance of himself with his opinions and advice. He was in the state of one who cannot comprehend because he has no faculty to perceive the thing in question, and that is why he was so positive. The dimmest perception that you may be mistaken will save you from making an ass of yourself.

We must look upon man's mistakes, however, with some leniency, because we are not blameless in the matter ourselves. We have allowed him to arrange the whole social system and manage or mismanage it all these ages without ever seriously examining his work with a view to considering whether his abilities and his motives were sufficiently good to qualify him for the task. We have listened without a smile to his preachments, about our place in life and all we are good for, on the text that "there is no understanding a woman." We have endured most poignant misery for his sins, and screened him when we should have exposed him and had him punished. We have allowed him to exact all things of us, and have been content to accept the little he grudgingly gave us in return. We have meekly bowed our heads when he called us bad names instead of demanding proofs of the superiority which alone would give him a right to do so. We have listened much edified to man's sermons on the subject of virtue, and have acquiesced uncomplainingly in the convenient arrangement by which this quality has come to be altogether practised for him by us vicariously. We have seen him set up Christ as an example for all men to follow, which argues his belief in the possibility of doing so, and have not only allowed his weakness and hypocrisy in the matter to pass without comment, but, until lately, have not even seen the humor of his pretensions when contrasted with his practices nor held him up to that wholesome ridicule which is a stimulating corrective. Man deprived us of all proper education, and then jeered at us because we had no knowledge. He narrowed our outlook on life so that our view of it should be all distorted, and then declared that our mistaken impression of it proved us to be senseless creatures. He cramped our minds so that there was no room for reason in them, and then made merry at our want of logic. Our divine intuition was not to be controlled by him, but he did his best to damage it by sneering at it as an inferior feminine method of arriving at conclusions; and finally, after having had his own way until he lost his head completely, he set himself up as a sort of a god and required us to worship him, and to our eternal shame be it said, we did so. The truth has all along been in us, but we have cared more for man than for truth, and so the whole human race has suffered. We have failed of our effect by neglecting our duty here, and have deserved much of the obloquy that was cast upon us. All that is over now, however, and while on the one hand man has shrunk to his true proportions in our estimation, we, on the other, have been expanding to our own; and now we come confidently forward to maintain, not that this or that was "intended," but that there are in ourselves, in both sexes, possibilities hitherto suppressed or abused, which, when properly developed, will supply to either what is lacking in the other.

The man of the future will be better, while the woman will be stronger and wiser. To bring this about is the whole aim and object of the present struggle, and with the discovery of the means lies the solution of the Woman Question. Man, having no conception of himself as imperfect from the woman's point of view, will find this difficult to understand, but we know his weakness, and will be patient with him, and help him with his lesson. It is the woman's place and pride and pleasure to teach the child, and man morally is in his infancy. There have been times when there was a doubt as to whether he was to be raised or woman was to be lowered, but we have turned that corner at last; and now woman holds out a strong hand to the child-man, and insists, but with infinite tenderness and pity, upon helping him up.

He must be taught consistency. There are ideals for him which it is to be presumed that he tacitly agrees to accept when he keeps up an expensive establishment to teach them: let him live up to them. Man's faculty for shirking his own responsibilities has been carried to such an extent in the past that, rather than be blamed himself when it did not answer to accuse woman, he imputed the whole consequence of his own misery-making peculiarities to God.

But with all his assumption man does not make the most of himself. He has had every advantage of training to increase his insight, for instance, but yet we find him, even at this time of day, unable to perceive that woman has a certain amount of self-respect and practical good sense—enough at all events to enable her to use the proverb about the bird in the hand to her own advantage. She does not in the least intend to sacrifice the privileges she enjoys on the chance of obtaining others, especially of the kind which man seems to think she must aspire to as so much more desirable. Woman may be foolish, but her folly has never been greater than man's conceit, and the one is not more disastrous to the understanding than the other. When a man talks about knowing the world and having lived and that sort of thing, he means something objectionable; in seeing life he generally includes doing wrong; and it is in these respects he is apt to accuse us of wishing to ape him. Of old if a woman ventured to be at all unconventional, man was allowed to slander her with the imputation that she must be abandoned, and he really believed it because with him liberty meant license. He has never accused us of trying to emulate him in any noble, manly quality, because the cultivation of noble qualities has not hitherto been a favorite pursuit of his, not to the extent at least of entering into his calculations and making any perceptible impression on public opinion; and he never, therefore, thought of considering whether it might have attractions for us. The cultivation of noble qualities has been individual rather than general, and the person who practised it is held to be one apart, if not actually eccentric. Man acknowledges that the business of life carried on according to his methods corrodes, and the state of corrosion is a state of decay; and yet he is fatuous enough to imagine that our ambition must be to lie like him for our own benefit in every public capacity. Heaven help the child to perceive with what travail and sorrow we submit to the heavy obligation, when it is forced upon us by our sense of right, of showing him how things ought to be done.

We have been reproached by Ruskin for shutting ourselves up behind park palings and garden walls,[1] regardless of the waste world that moans in misery without, and that has been too much our attitude; but the day of our acquiescence is over. There is that in ourselves which forces us out of our apathy; we have no choice in the matter. When we hear the "Help! help! help!" of the desolate and the oppressed, and still more when we see the awful dumb despair of those who have lost even the hope of help, we must respond. This is often inconvenient to man, especially when he has seized upon a defenceless victim whom he would have destroyed had we not come to the rescue; and so, because it is inconvenient to be exposed and thwarted, he snarls about the end of all true womanliness, cants on the subject of the Sphere,[2] and threatens that if we do not sit still at home with cotton-wool in our ears so that we cannot be stirred into having our sympathies aroused by his victims when they shriek, and with shades over our eyes that we may not see him in his degradation, we shall be afflicted with short hair, coarse skins, unsymmetrical figures, loud voices, tastelessness in dress, and an unattractive appearance and character generally, and then he will not love us any more or marry us. And this is one of the most amusing of his threats, because he has said and proved on so many occasions that he cannot live without us whatever we are. O man! man! You are a very funny fellow now we know you! But take care. The standard of your pleasure and convenience has already ceased to be our conscience. On one point, however, you may reassure yourself. True womanliness is not in danger, and the sacred duties of wife and mother will be all the more honorably performed when women have a reasonable hope of becoming wives and mothers of *men*. But there is the difficulty. The trouble is not because women are mannish, but because men grow ever more effeminate. Manliness is at a premium now because there is so little of it, and we are accused of aping men in order to conceal the side from which the contrast should evidently be drawn. Man in his manners becomes more and more wanting until we seem to be near the time when there will be nothing left of him but the old Adam, who said, "It wasn't me."

Of course it will be retorted that the past has been improved upon in our day; but that is not a fair comparison. We walk by the electric light: our ancestors had only oil-lamps. We can see what we are doing and where we are going, and should be as much better as we know how to be. But where are our men? Where is the chivalry, the truth, and affection, the earnest purpose, the plain living, high thinking, and noble self-sacrifice that make a man? We look in vain among the bulk of our writers even for appreciation of these qualities. With the younger men all that is usually cultivated is that flippant smartness which is synonymous with cheapness. There is such a want of wit amongst them, too, such a lack of variety, such monotony of threadbare subjects worked to death! Their "comic" papers subsist upon repetitions of those three venerable jests, the mother-in-law, somebody drunk, and an edifying deception successfully practised by an unfaithful husband or wife. As they have nothing true so they have nothing new to give us, nothing either to expand the heart or move us to happy mirth. Their ideas of beauty threaten always to be satisfied with the ballet dancer's legs, pretty things enough in their way, but not worth mentioning as an aid to the moral, intellectual, and physical strength that make a man. They are sadly deficient in imagination, too; that old fallacy to which they cling, that because an evil thing has always been, therefore it must always continue, is as much the result of want of imagination as of the man's trick of evading the responsibility of seeing right done in any matter that does not immediately affect his personal comfort. But there is one thing the younger men are specially good at, and that is giving their opinion; this they do to each other's admiration until they verily believe it to be worth something. Yet they do not even know where we are in the history of the world....

There are upwards of a hundred thousand women in London doomed to damnation by the written law of man if they dare to die, and to infamy for a livelihood if they must live; yet the man at the head of affairs wonders what it is that we with the power are protesting against in the name of our sex. But *is* there any wonder we women wail for the dearth of manliness when we find men from end to end of their rotten social system forever doing the most cowardly deed in their own code, striking at the defenceless woman, especially when she is down?

The Bawling Brotherhood have been seeing reflections of themselves lately which did not flatter them, but their conceit survives, and they cling confidently to the delusion that they are truly all that is admirable, and it is the mirror that is in fault. Mirrors may be either a distorting or a flattering medium, but women do not care to see life any longer in a glass darkly. Let there be light. We suffer in the first shock of it. We shriek in horror at what we discover when it is turned on that which was hidden away in dark corners; but the first principle of good housekeeping is to have no dark corners, and as we recover ourselves we go to work with a will to sweep them out. It is for us to set the human household in order, to see to it that all is clean and sweet and comfortable for the men who are fit to help us to make home in it. We are bound to raise the dust while we are at work, but only those who are in it will suffer any inconvenience from it, and the self-sufficing and self-supporting are not afraid. For the rest it will be all benefits. The Woman Question is the Marriage Question, as shall be shown hereafter.

"THE MAN OF THE MOMENT"

SARAH GRAND

[*North American Review* 158 (May 1894): 620-25]

Man is an exceedingly difficult and delicate subject to approach. If a woman have anything to say about him that is not altogether flattering, it is necessary to begin by an emphatic qualification of each assertion separately,—such as that it never did and never could apply to men generally, only to individuals; otherwise the greater number will take it to themselves and be irritated—a curious fact. The dear-old-lady-men of all ages are up in epithets directly if a type is presented without the saving clause, which, in order to prevent heartburning and bitterness, must be as cautiously worded as a legal document.

We do not think of accusing men of supposing that all women are Becky Sharps, but men think it necessary to warn us repeatedly that all men are not Roderick Randoms.[3] When man is put out his sense of humor is suspended, and then he becomes exceedingly amusing. Many a man who read *The Heavenly Twins* would have shot the book if he had a pistol in his hand at the moment. And there is one threatening old gentleman just now who turns purple at his club, shakes his stick at the whole sex through the window, and bawls that "Women had better let men alone!" It has never occurred to this old gentleman that woman would be only too glad to let man alone if he would return the compliment.

When woman ceases to suffer degradation at the hands of man, she will be satisfied, and let him alone. But there will be no peace from now on in the human household until that happy day arrives. We are bound to defend our own sex, especially when we find them suffering injustice, injury, poverty, and disgrace, until men are manly and chivalrous enough to relieve us of the horrid necessity. There is happily nowadays an ever-increasing number of men on whom we can rely; but there are more who are not to be relied upon in this matter; and if you happen to have the wrong one to deal with, of what avail is it that the right one exists? Laws are not made because we are all criminals. But nevertheless, be careful of the saving clause; and if you are dealing with man's morals, do not be surprised if there are complaints because you have not also mentioned his taste in dress.

The man of the moment, so called because he cannot continue unchanged on into the brighter and the better day which we are approaching, is he against whom woman has a just cause of complaint. If the modern maiden in her transition stage is an interesting person in view of the Woman Question, so also, and for the same reason, is the man of the moment. As a candidate for marriage he is the more interesting of the two perhaps, because he is not so well known. Woman is always being exhibited as maid, wife, widow, and mother-in-law; but man for the most part is taken for granted. If there is anything to be gained by it he puffs himself out, but he comes quietly as a candidate for marriage. Least said, soonest mended. When there is any question of altering the position of women, or educating them better, the dear-old-lady-men of all ages are full of fears. They write reams to prove to each other's satisfaction that motherhood is incompatible with mathematics, and the higher education of women would lead to the physical impoverishment and final extinction of the human race. And, having relieved their minds on the subject, they devote themselves to the establishment of the schoolboard system for the teaching to death of half-starved growing children; and the competitive examination test which is warranted to sap the nerve-power at a critical age of all who go in for it. The brains of the dear-old-lady-men appear to be divided into separate little compartments which have no communication with each other. When they come out from one of these compartments the door shuts with a spring, and then they forget what is in it until they go back again: which convenient arrangement enables them to air the most opposite theories without being conscious of any inconsistency. So we see them in terror one day because some few women are entering the professions and making an income for themselves; this means empty nurseries, they maintain, which is something too disastrous to anticipate. They play in this compartment so long as the interest lasts, then bang goes the door, another is opened, and they find themselves out of the region of theory into the region of fact; and now what to do with the superfluous population is the difficulty. In the midst of this a cry is heard that the physique of the race is deteriorating. Bang goes the population-difficulty door, and now there is some really beautiful talk about health and virtue. The care of the constitution is a duty which parents owe to their children, therefore women must really be made to order their lives on the most approved method. We have learnt to understand why men bawl at preaching women, and to sympathize with their exasperation when they are preached at, for do they not preach us into preaching in self-defence? We feel ourselves entitled to some little pleasure in life, so we preach back, for the preacher at least enjoys himself. It is a wise provision of nature, however, which sets man talking while woman is putting her own ideas to the test of practical experiment. She does not talk much when she means business; and he does not meddle once she settles him to cackle comfortably over his cigar about her, "don't you know, and all she is fit for, by Jove, I tell you, sir!"

During one of these phases, when the girl is being sermonized to distraction, little or nothing is said about the growing boy: his training in the matter of responsibility towards his possible children, and duty to the nation generally. Nothing used to be expected of him in the way of virtue and self-denial. It is shameful to think how he was neglected and allowed to act on his own worst impulses until the new woman came to correct him. If his education had been carefully planned to make him morally a weak-willed, inconsistent creature, and lower him altogether in our estimation, it could not have succeeded better. And that is what the modern woman complains of when the man of the moment comes as a candidate for marriage. Her ideal of a husband is a man whom she can reverence and respect from end to end of his career, especially in regard to his relations with her own sex.

Philosophers show that the stability of nations depends practically upon ethics. When they do not aspire to be as perfect as they know how to be, they collapse. As a low tone about women is a sign of a degenerated gentleman, so is it also the sign of a decaying nation. The man of the moment does anything but aspire, and it is the low moral tone which he cultivates that threatens to enervate the race. In fact, were it not for the hard fight women will make to prevent it, there would be small hope of saving us from flickering out like all the older peoples. Woman, however, by being dissatisfied with the inferior moral qualities of her suitors, is coming to the rescue. The unerring sex-instinct informed her that a man's whole system deteriorates for want of moral principle. Feeling was her guide at first. Something about the man repelled her, and she would not have him; that was all. Now she knows. But all along there have been indications which confirmed the conclusions of her senses. One finds wise men in all ages and in many unexpected places holding as an opinion what we now accept as knowledge of the subject. Count von Moltke[4] drew his conclusions with regard to the strength of the French army, not from its numbers, but from its condition morally. When asked, after a visit to France before the Franco-German war, what he thought Germany would have to fear in the event of an encounter with France, he answered contemptuously, "Nothing!" Because there was scarcely an officer in the French army who hadn't an indecent picture of women in his room. And something analogous has been noticed in the British service. The regiments which turn out the finest men, and do the best service on occasion, are those in which a low tone about women is voted bad form. When invitations were being sent out the other day for a great public function, there was a question as to which regiments should be asked in order to secure the best set of officers, and it was found afterwards that in every instance the regiment chosen was distinguished for the chivalrous loyalty of its tone in regard to women. In some regiments there is a by-law still in force forbidding the mention of a lady's name in mess. This is doubtless a survival of the day when a man who spoke disrespectfully of a woman was liable to be called upon to answer for the insult with his life. And, perhaps, considering the kind of conversation rife in clubs and messes of to-day, it would be well to introduce some such regulation, if it were only to save the members from making themselves ridiculous.... Physical courage is mere brute force; to make it a manly quality it must have moral courage to complete it. The latter argues intellectual capacity also, without which courage is an edged tool in the clumsy hands of a child. Man's own undisputed assertion used to be sufficient for himself as to the kind of conduct which would make him agreeable to women. It was he who described her as adoring "a regular dog, don't you know." Women had not asked at that time what being "a regular dog" implied. But when they became acquainted with the qualifications and improving details of the career of the creature, and found the most rascally degradation of their own sex involved in his habits, they expressed their opinion of him. "A regular dog" is not at all to the taste of the modern woman, and when he comes upon the stage expecting to find that he has wiped out the misdeeds of a life by facing the enemy for a week, and will be acknowledged as rehabilitated, she laughs at him. He has to face the enemy, of course. War is the dirty work of a nation, and he cannot expect her to do it; but even when he does it well, it is only one of the necessary qualifications that go to the making of man. What is he like when not fighting—at home, for instance? Many a man would face a cannon who cannot deny himself a dish at dinner that disagrees with him. The dish is a daily occurrence, and women do well to remember that it is with the unreasonableness which results from it that they have to deal, waging unedifying war with it to guard their children if possible from the evil and misery of an exasperating example, long after the heroism of the cannon exploit is over.

Mere brute courage will not do at the present time. It is not peculiar to either sex. Every woman that marries risks her life, and does not expect a medal for it, either. Physical courage is a physical condition proper to healthy people, and too common to be of any account at this period of our progress without moral courage to dignify it. Without moral courage, there is no such thing as manliness. And nowadays it is difficult to read a paper without wondering where the men are. In this mismanaged world it looks as if we should soon be obliged to do their work as well as our own, or nothing will be done. We are forced forward at a cost of suffering to ourselves which probably only we ourselves can appreciate, because there are not men enough to defend the women of any class. "Where are the gentlemen?" a lady asked on her way through the hall to mount her horse the other morning. "Please, my lady," the footman answered, "the gentlemen are in bed." It was a country house, and only the middle-aged men were ever down at a reasonable hour in the morning. They had twice the stamina as well as twice the wit of the men-of-the-moment kind; and if a lady wanted a companion who would be up and fresh to accompany her, and would not be a bore, it was a middle-aged man she chose.

If "Where are the men?" is asked in the boudoir, the contemptuous answer is, "In mischief—or else in bed," and it sounds like a note of national deterioration. Girls can be busy from morning till night, in doors and out. They attend to their duties and their pleasures, too; work, walk, ride, drive, and dance to-day, and come down as fresh as ever to work, walk, ride, drive, and dance to-morrow without support from any stimulant but their own good spirits, good appetites, and unimpaired digestions. But with regard to the young men, after any extra exertion, it is always the same story: "Please, my lady, the gentlemen are in bed." And not only after extraordinary exertion. In hundreds of households, wherever it is possible, it is the rule. The girls are up and doing in the morning, while the young men, indolent and nerveless, lie long in bed.

Idleness and luxury are making men flabby, and the man at the head of affairs is beginning to ask seriously if a great war might not help them to pull themselves together. It shows the unfitness of his unaided intellect for the office when he has to go back to that clumsy old method for a remedy. He would make certain to clear off the strongest men of the nation in the hope of getting rid of the weakly ones as well—an effectual arrangement on a par with the Chinese principle of roasting the pig by burning down the house. The best thing to cure men of their effeminacy would be to deprive all the idle and luxurious ones of their incomes. Give them the choice of starvation or work; either would answer the purpose.

From the modern girl's point of view, the man of the moment is not of much account. The instinct of natural selection which inclined her first of all to set him aside, for his flabbiness, is strengthened now by her knowledge of his character. She knows him much better than her parents do, and in proportion as she knows him she finds less and less reason to respect him. The girls discuss him with each other and with the younger married women, and out of their discussions is arising a strong distaste for him. "I'm not going to marry a man I can't respect," "I shan't marry unless I find a man of honor with no horrid past," and "Don't offer me the mutilated remains of a man," coupled with the names of Tom Jones[5] and Roderick Random, are the commonest expressions of it. And it is in vain for the man of the moment when he marries to hope to conceal the consequences of the past from his wife by assuming a highly refined objection to "allowing" her to read any book that would open her eyes. The manners of the new woman are perfect. She is never aggressive, never argumentative; but she understands the art of self-defence, and reads what she pleases.

The men with whom a girl is brought up have the habit of respecting her, but it is impossible to be sure of polite consideration from any she does not know, and this sets them both at a disadvantage. The girl dare not be natural for fear of being misunderstood, and, worse still, misrepresented. She can never be sure that the apparently chivalrous gentleman with whom she has been talking unguardedly, drawn out by his seemingly sympathetic interest, will not repeat and ridicule every ill-chosen word she has blundered upon in her efforts to express herself. The first principle of honor in social intercourse is never to repeat a private conversation; but this is so little observed one would think it was scarcely known. To the modern girl the man of the moment, when she begins to know his habits of mind, appears as a common creature, of no ideals, deficient in breadth and depth, and only of a boundless assurance. She makes merry over him, and thinks him a subject both for contempt and pity. We are now at the swing of the pendulum in the Woman Question. Ideas are all at extremes. And it is not ideas only that are at extremes. Where woman have been unjustly treated they are inclined to retaliate, as if an eye for an eye ever mended matters! In the nursery the little boy used to have it all his own way. He was the first to be considered, the others were "only little girls." To this tune his life was set at the outset, and he sang it himself to the end. Now, however, the pendulum swings back. In many nurseries Master Bob is no longer allowed to lord it over the little ladies. He must be taught to wait on them, and behave like a gentleman; but, still, equality, the true ideal, is not reached. It is oftenest only the opposite of the old extreme. He is made to do the fetching and carrying and to understand also that he is altogether an inferior sort of person: "Bob's such a brute," "If you don't look after Bob, he'll over-eat himself," "You'll have to thump him if you want to make him understand," and so on from the little girls in a strain that is not good for anybody. Until he goes to school he may be loved as of old, but also ridiculed; and when he grows up the position is unaltered. Women may like him, but they will neither fear nor respect him just because he tells them they must. When he deserves respect, the balance between the sexes will be properly adjusted. He is not yet sufficiently aware of his own imperfections to do much for himself; but women need not be disheartened. Now is the time to cultivate a cheerful frame of mind, and remember that if there is little hope for the present generation, they can spank proper principles into the next in the nursery.

"A Ballade of the New Manhood"

[*Punch* 106 (26 May 1894): 249]

By an Unregenerate Male

["Madame Grand is going to take *Caliban*[6] in hand, and make a new man of him. But the present generation is past praying for. Man has been allowed to act on his own 'worst impulses.' 'His education has been carefully planned to make him morally a weak-willed, inconsistent creature.' ... It is the next generation which is to have 'proper principles spanked into it in the nursery.'" *Pall Mall Gazette*, May 16.]

Yes, it pains me indeed to relate
    To the rising male genus the news—
At the terrible thought of their fate
    They may shiver and shake in their shoes!
    For from one of the monthly reviews
It appears they'll be taken in hand
    By the New Womanhood, that pursues
The programme of grim Madame Grand!

Poor youths! At an imminent date
    All the foibles of man they're to lose;
If one ventures to lie in bed late,
Or latchkeys and "language" to use,
    Or play penny nap, or amuse
His weak wits with aught else that is banned,
    He'll be spanked till for pardon he sues—
'Tis the fiat of firm Madame Grand!

Still, there's *one* fact, I'm happy to state,
  That some consolation endues!
To reform each grown-up reprobate
Is too hard—'tis enough to abuse!
  So we men will go on as we choose,
And unlimited *Caudle*[7] we'll stand,
  And with chastened, amusement peruse
The attacks of irate Madame Grand.

Envoi

Mr. Punch, pray do not refuse
To spread through the length of the land
  Your decided dissent from the views,
And the plans of severe Sarah Grand!

"THE NEW WOMAN"

[*Punch* 106 (26 May 1894): 252]

(A New Nursery Rhyme. For Child-men.)

["Ouida" says "the New Woman" is an unmitigated bore. "Sarah Grand" declares that Man, morally, "is in his infancy," and that "now Woman holds out a strong hand to the Child-man, and insists upon helping him up" by spanking proper principles into him in the nursery."]

There is a New Woman, and what do you think?
She lives upon nothing but Foolscap and Ink!
But, though Foolscap and Ink form the whole of her diet,
This nagging New Woman can never be quiet!

"THE NEW WOMAN"

OUIDA

[*North American Review* 158 (May 1894): 610-19]

It can scarcely be disputed, I think, that in the English language there are conspicuous at the present moment two words which designate two unmitigated bores: The Workingman and the Woman. The Workingman and the Woman, the New Woman, be it remembered, meet us at every page of literature written in the English tongue; and each is convinced that on its own especial W hangs the future of the world. Both he and she want to have their values artificially raised and rated, and a status given to them by a favor in lieu of desert. In an age in which persistent clamor is generally crowned by success they have both obtained considerable attention; is it offensive to say much more of it than either deserves? Your contributor avers that the Cow-Woman and the Scum-Woman, man understands; but that the New Woman is above him. The elegance of these appellatives is not calculated to recommend them to readers of either sex; and as a specimen of style forces one to hint that the New Woman who, we are told, "has been sitting apart in silent contemplation all these years" might in all these years have studied better models of literary composition. We are farther on told "that the dimmest perception that you may be mistaken, will save you from making an ass of yourself." It appears that even this dimmest perception has never dawned upon the New Woman.

We are farther told that "thinking and thinking" in her solitary sphynx-like contemplation she solved the problem and prescribed the remedy (the remedy to a problem!); but what this remedy was we are not told, nor did the New Woman apparently disclose it to the rest of womankind, since she still hears them in "sudden and violent upheaval" like "children unable to articulate whimpering for they know not what." It is sad to reflect that they might have been "easily satisfied at that time" (at what time?), "but society stormed at them until what was a little wail became convulsive shrieks"; and we are not told why the New Woman who had "the remedy for the problem," did not immediately produce it. We are not told either in what country or at what epoch this startling upheaval of volcanic womanhood took place in which "man merely made himself a nuisance with his opinion and advice," but apparently did quell this wailing and gnashing of teeth since it would seem that he has managed still to remain more masterful than he ought to be.

We are further informed that women "have allowed him to arrange the whole social system and manage or mismanage it all these ages without ever seriously examining his work with a view to considering whether his abilities and his methods were sufficiently good to qualify him for the task."

There is something deliciously comical in the idea, thus suggested, that man has only been allowed to "manage or mismanage" the world because woman has graciously refrained from preventing his doing so. But the comic side of this pompous and solemn assertion does not for a moment offer itself to the New Woman sitting aloof and aloft in her solitary meditation on the superiority of her sex. For the New Woman there is no such thing as a joke. She has listened without a smile to her enemy's "preachments"; she has "endured poignant misery for his sins," she has "meekly bowed her head when he called her bad names"; and she has never asked for "any proof of the superiority" which could alone have given him a right to use such naughty expressions. The truth has all along been in the possession of woman; but strange and sad perversity of taste! she has "cared more for man than for truth, and so the whole human race has suffered!"

"All that is over, however," we are told, and "while on the one hand man has shrunk to his true proportions" she has, all the time of this shrinkage, been herself expanding, and has in a word come to "fancy herself" extremely. So that he has no longer the slightest chance of imposing upon her by his game-cock airs.

Man, "having no conception of himself as imperfect," will find this difficult to understand at first; but the New Woman "knows his weakness," and will "help him with his lesson." *"Man morally is in his infancy."* There have been times when there was a doubt as to whether he was to be raised to her level, or woman to be lowered to his, but we "have turned that corner at last and now woman holds out a strong hand to the child-man and insists upon helping him up." The child-man (Bismarck? Herbert Spencer? Edison? Gladstone? Alexander III? Lord Dufferin? The Duc d'Aumale?)[8] the child-man must have his tottering baby steps guided by the New Woman, and he must be taught to live up to his ideals. To live up to an ideal, whether our own or somebody else's, is a painful process; but man must be made to do it. For, oddly enough, we are assured that despite "all his assumption he does not make the best of himself," which is not wonderful if he be still only in his infancy; and he has the incredible stupidity to be blind to the fact that "woman has self-respect and good sense," and that "she does not in the least intend to sacrifice the privileges she enjoys on the chance of obtaining others."...

The whole kernel of the question lies in this. Your contributor says that the New Woman will not surrender her present privileges; *i.e.*, she will still expect the man to stand that she may sit; the man to get wet through that she may use his umbrella. But if she retain these privileges she can only do so by an appeal to his chivalry, *i.e.*, by a confession that she is weaker than he. But she does not want to do this: she wants to get the comforts and concessions due to feebleness, at the same time as she demands the lion's share of power due to superior force alone. It is this overweening and unreasonable grasping at both positions which will end in making her odious to man and in her being probably kicked back roughly by him into the seclusion of a harem.

Before me lies an engraving in an illustrated journal of a woman's meeting; whereat a woman is demanding in the name of her sovereign sex the right to vote at political elections. The speaker is middle-aged and plain of feature; she wears an inverted plate on her head tied on with strings under her double-chin; she has balloon-sleeves, a bodice tight to bursting, a waist of ludicrous dimensions in proportion to her portly person; she is gesticulating with one hand, of which all the fingers are stuck out in ungraceful defiance of all artistic laws of gesture. Now, why cannot this orator learn to gesticulate and learn to dress, instead of clamoring for a franchise? She violates in her own person every law, alike of common-sense and artistic fitness, and yet comes forward as a fit and proper person to make laws for others. She is an exact representative of her sex.

Woman, whether new or old, has immense fields of culture untilled, immense areas of influence wholly neglected. She does almost nothing with the resources she possesses, because her whole energy is concentrated on desiring and demanding those she has not. She can write and print anything she chooses; and she scarcely ever takes the pains to acquire correct grammar or elegance of style before wasting ink and paper. She can paint and model any subjects she chooses, but she imprisons herself in men's *ateliers* to endeavor to steal their technique and their methods, and thus loses any originality she might possess. Her influence on children might be so great that through them she would practically rule the future of the world; but she delegates her influence to the vile school boards if she be poor, and if she be rich to governesses and tutors; nor does she in ninety-nine cases out a hundred ever attempt to educate or control herself into fitness for the personal exercise of such influence. Her precept and example in the treatment of the animal creation might be of infinite use in mitigating the hideous tyranny of humanity over them, but she does little or nothing to this effect; she wears dead birds and the skins of dead creatures; she hunts the hare and shoots the pheasant, she drives and rides with more brutal recklessness than men; she watches with delight the struggles of the dying salmon, of the gralloched deer; she keeps her horses standing in snow and fog for hours with the muscles of their heads and necks tied up in the torture of the bearing rein; when asked to do anything for a stray dog, a lame horse, a poor man's donkey, she is very sorry, but she has so many claims on her already; she never attempts by orders to her household, to her *fournisseurs*,[9] to her dependents, to obtain some degree of money in the treatments of sentient creatures and in the methods of their slaughter.

The immense area which lies open to her in private life is almost entirely uncultivated, yet she wants to be admitted into public life. Public life is already overcrowded, verbose, incompetent, fussy, and foolish enough without the addition of her in her sealskin coat with the dead humming bird on her hat. Woman in public life would exaggerate the failings of men, and would not have even their few excellencies. Their legislation would be, as that of men is too often, the offspring of panic or prejudice; and she would not put on the drag of common-sense as man frequently does in public assemblies. There would be little to hope from her humanity, nothing from her liberality; for when she is frightened she is more ferocious than he, and when she has power more merciless.

"Men," says your contributor, "deprived us of all proper education and then jeered at us because we had no knowledge." How far is this based on facts? Could not Lady Jane Grey learn Greek and Latin as she chose? Could not Hypatia lecture? Were George Sand or Mrs. Somerville withheld from study? Could not in every age every woman choose a Corinna or Cordelia as her type? become either Helen or Penelope? If the vast majority have not either the mental or physical gifts to become either, that was Nature's fault, not man's. Aspasia and Adelina Patti[10] were born, not made. In all eras and all climes a woman of great genius or of great beauty has done what she chose; and if the majority of women have led obscure lives, so have the majority of men. The chief part of humanity is insignificant, whether it be male or female. In most people there is very little character indeed, and as little mind. Those who have much never fail to make their marks, be they of which sex they may.

The unfortunate idea that there is no good education without a college curriculum is as injurious as it is erroneous. The college education may have excellencies for men in its *frottement*,[11] its preparation for the world, its rough destruction of personal conceit; but for women it can only be hardening and deforming. If study be delightful to a woman, she will find her way to it as the hart to water brooks. The author of *Aurora Leigh*[12] was not only always at home, but she was an invalid; yet she became a fine classic, and found her path to fame. A college curriculum would have done nothing to improve her rich and beautiful mind; it might have done much to debase it.

The perpetual contact of men with other men may be good for them, but the perpetual contact of women with other women is very far from good. The publicity of a college must be odious to a young girl of refined and delicate feeling.

The "Scum-woman" and the "Cow-woman," to quote the elegant phraseology of your contributor, are both of them less of a menace to humankind than the New Woman with her fierce vanity, her undigested knowledge, her over-weening estimate of her own value and her fatal want of all sense of the ridiculous.

When scum comes to the surface it renders a great service to the substance which it leaves behind it; when the cow yields pure nourishment to the young and the suffering, her place is blessed in the realm of nature; but when the New Woman splutters blistering wrath on mankind she is merely odious and baneful.

The error of the New Woman (as of many an old one) lies in speaking of women as the victims of men, and entirely ignoring the frequency with which men are the victims of women. In nine cases out of ten the first to corrupt the youth is the woman. In nine cases out of ten also she becomes corrupt herself because she likes it.

It is all very well to say that prostitutes were at the beginning of their career victims of seduction; but it is not probable and it is not provable. Love of drink and of finery, and a dislike to work, are the more likely motives and origin. It never seems to occur to the accusers of man that women are just as vicious and as lazy as he is in nine cases out of ten, and need no invitation from him to become so.

A worse prostitution than that of the streets, *i.e.*, that of loveless marriages of convenience, are brought about by women, not by men. In such unions the man always gives much more than he gains, and the woman in almost every instance is persuaded or driven into it by women—her mother, her sisters, her acquaintances. It is rarely that the father interferes to bring about such a marriage.

In even what is called a well-assorted marriage, the man is frequently sacrificed to the woman. As I wrote long ago, Andrea del Sarte's wife has many sisters. Correggio dying of the burden of the family, has many brothers.[13] Men of genius are often dragged to earth by their wives. In our own day a famous statesman is made very ridiculous by his wife; frequently the female influences brought to bear on him render a man of great and original powers and disinterested character, a time-server, a conventionalist, a mere seeker of place. Woman may help man sometimes, but she certainly more often hinders him. Her self-esteem is immense, and her self-knowledge very small. I view with dread for the future of the world the power which modern inventions place in the hands of woman. Hitherto her physical weakness has restrained her in a great measure from violent action; but a woman can make a bomb and throw it, can fling vitriol, and fire a repeating revolver as well as any man can. These are precisely the deadly, secret, easily handled modes of warfare and revenge, which will commend themselves to her ferocious feebleness....

In the pages of this *Review* a physician has lamented the continually increasing unwillingness of women of the world to bear children, and the consequent increase of ill-health, whilst to avoid child-bearing is being continually preached to the working classes by those who call themselves their friends.

The elegant epithet of Cow-woman implies the contempt with which maternity is viewed by the New Woman who thinks it something fine to vote at vestries, and shout at meetings, and lay bare the spines of living animals, and haul the gasping salmon from the river pool, and hustle male students off the benches of amphitheatres.

Modesty is no doubt a thing of education or prejudice, a conventionality artificially stimulated; but it is an exquisite grace, and womanhood without it loses its most subtle charm. Nothing tends so to destroy modesty as the publicity and promiscuity of schools, of hotels, of railway trains and sea voyages. True modesty shrinks from the curious gaze of other women as from the coarser gaze of man.

Men, moreover, are in all except the very lowest classes more careful of their talk before young girls than women are. It is very rarely that a man does not respect real innocence; but women frequently do not. The jest, the allusion, the story which sullies her mind and awakes her inquisitiveness, will much oftener be spoken by women than men. It is not from her brothers, nor her brother's friends, but from her female companions that she will understand what the grosser laugh of those around her suggests. The biological and pathological curricula complete the loveless disflowering of her maiden soul.

Everything which tends to obliterate the contrast of the sexes, like your mixture of boys and girls in your American common schools, tends also to destroy the charm of intercourse, the savor and sweetness of life. Seclusion lends an infinite seduction to the girl, as the rude and bustling publicity of modern life robs woman of her grace. Packed like herrings in a railway carriage, sleeping in odious vicinity to strangers on a shelf, going days and nights without a bath, exchanging decency and privacy for publicity and observation; the women who travel, save those rich enough to still purchase seclusion, are forced to cast aside all refinement and delicacy.

It is said that travel enlarges the mind. There are many minds which can no more be enlarged, by any means whatever, than a nut or a stone. The fool remains a fool, though you carry him or her about over the whole surface of the globe, and it is certain that the promiscuous contact and incessant publicity of travel, which may not hurt the man, do injure the woman.

Neither men nor women of genius are, I repeat, any criterion for the rest of their sex; nay, they belong, as Plato placed them, to a third sex which is above the laws of the multitude. But even whilst they do so they are always the foremost to recognize that it is the difference, not the likeness, of sex which makes the charm of human life. Barry Cornwall wrote long ago:

"As the man beholds the woman,
    As the woman sees the man;
Curiously they note each other,
    As each other only can.

"Never can the man divest her
    Of that mystic charm of sex;
Ever must she, gazing on him,
    That same mystic charm annex."

That mystic charm will long endure despite the efforts to destroy it of orators in tight stays and balloon sleeves, who scream from platforms, and the beings so justly abhorred of Mrs. Lynn Lynton, who smoke in public carriages and from the waist upward are indistinguishable from the men they profess to despise.

But every word, whether written or spoken, which urges the woman to antagonism against the man, every word which is written or spoken to try and make of her a hybrid, self-contained, opponent of men, makes a rift in the lute to which the world looks for its sweetest music.

The New Woman reminds me of an agriculturist who, discarding a fine farm of his own, and leaving it to nettles, stones, thistles, and wire-worms, should spend his whole time in demanding neighboring fields which are not his. The New Woman will not even look at the extent of ground indisputably her own, which she leaves unweeded and untilled.

Not to speak of the entire guidance of childhood, which is certainly already chiefly in the hands of woman (and of which her use does not do her much honor), so long as she goes to see one of her own sex dancing in a lion's den, the lions being meanwhile terrorized by a male brute; so long as she wears dead birds as millinery and dead seals as coats; so long as she goes to races, steeplechases, coursing and pigeon matches; so long as she "walks with the guns"; so long as she goes to see an American lashing horses to death in idiotic contest with velocipedes; so long as she courtesies before princes and emperors who reward the winners of distance-rides; so long as she receives physiologists in her drawing-rooms, and trusts to them in her maladies; so long as she invades literature without culture and art without talent; so long as she orders her court-dress in a hurry; so long as she makes no attempt to interest herself in her servants, in her animals, in the poor slaves of her tradespeople; so long as she shows herself as she does at present without scruple at every brutal and debasing spectacle which is considered fashionable; so long as she understands nothing of the beauty of meditation, of solitude, of Nature; so long as she is utterly incapable of keeping her sons out of the shambles of modern sport, and lifting her daughters above the pestilent miasma of modern society—so long as she does not, can not, or will not either do, or cause to do, any of these things, she has no possible title or capacity to demand the place or the privilege of man.

"THE WOMAN'S QUESTION.
AN INTERVIEW WITH MADAME SARAH GRAND"

[This interview was conducted by Sarah A. Tooley and published in the *Humanitarian* 8.3 (March 1896): 161-69]

When writing her first story, *Ideala*, Madame Grand found that social questions would get into it. The story was a study from life, and in drawing the characters she simply reproduced people with whose lives she was intimately acquainted. "I do not," she said, "like to see puppets in a book who are placed there for the purpose of saying certain things, and to give expression to a writer's theory. To be true to life should be the first aim of an author, and if one deals with social questions one must study them in the people who hold them, not invent a puppet to give forth one's views. One thing has struck me as being very significant, and that is that literal facts are so often received by the critics with incredulity. The story of Evangeline in *Our Manifold Nature*, is a case in point; it has been attacked as 'melodramatic' and 'impossible,' yet it is a true story from beginning to end, ungarnished by fictional embellishments."

After the publication of *Ideala*, a long interval elapsed before Madame Grand brought out the notable book which has done so much to rouse men and women to a thoughtful consideration of the evil which it seeks to expose. The *Heavenly Twins* took two years to write and three years to find a publisher. One publisher to whom it was offered replied that is was a neurotic novel, and could not be expected to succeed, adding that "it was calculated to give great pain to the majority of novel readers, who were ladies." Another was known to have said that it was a book which no respectable house would publish, but, after it had achieved success, this same publisher was most anxious to publish her next book. "Success makes such a difference, don't you know?" said Madame Grand with a smile, as she referred to these little incidents. The criticism evoked by the *Heavenly Twins* was, as most people know, almost wholly adverse. Nearly all the reviews were against it, but from private correspondents the author received many sympathetic and encouraging communications, and even still the letters continue to come as the book penetrates into the remoter regions of civilization.

"Who were your most sympathetic correspondents, men or women?" I asked, as we sat talking over these things in the twilight of a February afternoon.

"Men, decidedly," replied Madame Grand. "I had a large number of letters from Anglican clergymen, Roman Catholic priests, and doctors. Men knew so much better than women the need there was for the book, and that I rather under-estimated than over-estimated the evil. The letters which I received showed that I had not come forward upon a trivial pretext, and that the evil was far greater than I had imagined. Men endeavour to protect themselves from disease by restrictive laws bearing on women, but nothing has yet been done to protect the married women from contagion. I hope that we shall soon see the marriage of certain men made a criminal offence. This is one of the things which, as women, we must press forward. Men are very nice creatures in a general way," continued Madame Grand, with a smile. "I value my men friends exceedingly, and have always the feeling that one should not seek to interfere with men's private lives—never interfere except where women are to be degraded. When the weaker of our sex are subjected to great wrongs we, as women, are bound to look after them, and if that brings us into opposition to some men we cannot help ourselves, but I always feel very sorry when it occurs. I entirely deprecate rivalry and the spirit of war between the sexes; what we want is to work together for the good of each. And after all it is very cheering to find so many good men willing to aid in the uplifting of women and in the dethronement of vice, and their number is steadily increasing."

"Do you consider, Madame Grand, that legislation may safely be left in the hands of men; they have been instrumental during the last twenty years in passing laws which have greatly improved the position of women, and they will doubtless proceed on the same lines in the future. In view of this, do you feel that there is any urgent need for the extension of the Parliamentary Franchise to women?"

"I certainly think that it is most important that women should have the right to vote in Parliamentary elections. We shall do no good until we get the Franchise, for however well-intentioned men may be, they cannot understand our wants as well as we do ourselves. Then too, those men who will not listen to argument, will listen to force, and having a vote is an immense lever to wield against them. It is said, I know, that women are not ripe for the vote yet, but surely they are quite as ripe for it as the agricultural labourer, and indeed as the majority of men. Surely no one can suppose that all the wisdom and discretion has been given to one half of the human race and none to the other. There are silly men just as there are thoughtless women, but that is never held to be a reason for disfranchising the whole of the male sex. That women are acknowledged to be able to form a judgment on political questions is tacitly admitted by the organisations which employ women to canvas for parliamentary elections. We have there the absurd position of women being sent to educate the voters, while, when the polling day comes, they are declared to be unfit to give a vote themselves. And not only are women using their influence in this semi-private way, but they come on to the public platform at political meetings and speak for their party, and often plead the claims of a parliamentary candidate better probably than he can do it himself. Whichever way one looks at the question it seems to me that a great injustice is being done to women by withholding the vote from them. Apart from their mental qualification they have the property-owner's right, and the taxpayer's right to representation, for have we not been taught as a tenet of constitutional law that taxation without representation is tyranny?

"There is a further side to the question," continued Madame Grand, "and that is the good effect which responsibility will have upon women themselves. I believe that it is good for us to have a feeling of responsibility engendered; it strengthens character and develops ideas, which is exactly what women need. The influence of politics would be educative, and therefore desirable. On the other hand one may offer a grain of comfort to opponents by assuring them that from their standpoint it will be a good thing for women to come into political life, for many will be so disgusted at the rivalry, jobbery, and self-seeking which exist in both great parties that they will become speedily nauseated and leave the field in disgust. For myself, I look forward to the influence of women to raise the tone of political life, just as they have already, I am told, improved the political meetings by their presence in the audiences and on the platforms; there is not so much of the coarse element as there formerly was."

"Do you favour the admission of women to Parliament?"

"It is perhaps a little early in the day to discuss that question; we must get the Franchise first and then consider the further step, but I tell you what I should like, and that is to do away with the House of Lords and establish a House of Ladies."

"How would you accomplish that; on the elective principle, the same as we have in the House of Commons?"

"The method of doing it I leave to the wiseacres, but it has often occurred to me that a chamber composed of women qualified to watch legislation as it affects their own sex, and to report their ideas to the House of Commons, would be doing more useful work on behalf of the general community than the present House of Lords is doing. Having a separate chamber for women would meet the objection of those who dislike the idea of mixing the sexes in Parliament, although these objectors seem to forget that women serve along with men on all our local governing bodies, and the arrangement appears to answer very well. However, a House of Ladies would be able to discuss many questions which call for reform with greater freedom than women could in a mixed assembly. Our influence would be chiefly felt upon questions of morality, and would, I believe, tend to purify the political atmosphere."

"How would you meet the oft-repeated objection that women suffer degradation by close contact with public life, and that taking an interest in politics and in some of the social questions of the day has a tendency to unsex them?"

"I do not think that the best specimens of advanced women are those whom any thoughtful person would call 'unsexed.' Take one of those splendid workers of the past, Elizabeth Fry.[14] She had a family of eight children, whom she looked after in a most exemplary manner, as she did after everything connected with her home; yet fully occupied as she was with a busy domestic life, Elizabeth Fry found time to do a great work in the world. Today everyone reveres her name, but those of her own time thought it a very unwomanly thing for a woman to visit the prisons and to talk with the degraded ones of her sex, and there was quite a storm of opposition when she modestly asked to be permitted to listen to a debate in the House of Commons arising out of the prison reforms, of which she was the initiator."

"Yes, I remember, and as a last resort she asked to be allowed to listen outside one of the ventilators of the House, and the country squires were up in arms, and said that it would crush the fabric of domestic life if it came to the ears of their wives and daughters that a woman had listened to a Parliamentary debate, even through a ventilator."

"How amusing and childish all that seems to-day," replied Madame Sarah Grand, with a laugh, "and so will the arguments to which we are now treated seem fifty years hence. Has it not often struck you that people are always ready to carp at a woman when she tries to do some useful work in the world? Our critics have not a word to say against the society woman who neglects her home and her children for gaieties. The frivolous women are rarely found fault with; the great crime is to have a serious purpose in life. I believe that men do not like women to be clever, because they think that they will be found out."

"Do you think that is the cause of the opposition to the higher education of women, and to the granting to them of University degrees?"

"Yes, largely. Then again, men do not seem willing to give merited honour to women, or there would not be so much opposition to giving them degrees. People seem to forget that women cannot take University degrees unless they win them by the same tests to which men are subjected, and if a woman earns the honour on what fair ground can it be denied to her? The same thing is seen in the scanty recognition of a great woman like Florence Nightingale. Had it been a man who had originated and demonstrated a scheme for training nurses for service in time of war, he would have been given a title by the Government and otherwise publicly honoured, but as it was only a woman who did it, fitting gratitude has not been shown. I always admire the Quakers for the fair treatment they give to women; there is no undervaluing of intellect because it chances to be found in the head of a woman, and the good result is seen in the splendid work accomplished by Quaker ladies in the social and philanthropic movements of the day. It affords an excellent example of the wisdom of giving women freedom to do the best that is in them. A Quaker woman is taught self-respect, while we are taught self-depreciation. I cannot understand how anyone can think that the graces of life are to be lost by educating and elevating women. I am afraid that some people do not mind them being unsexed, but object to their being improved; that is why the costumes of the ballet girl are not severely handled, while the rational costume for women who ride the bicycle is."

"Do you cycle yourself, Madame?"

"Yes, I am devoted to cycling, and you cannot think how much better I am in health since I took to it."

"And you wear the rational costume?"[15]

"I always do in Paris, where I first began to ride. There the *culotte* is the usual costume for lady cyclists and causes little remark. But I must frankly admit that our rational costume is exceedingly ugly; I wish we could invent something more graceful and so here I always ride in a skirt, which looks better and attracts less attention. It is necessary for a New Woman to be very careful about her appearance."

"But what about the comfort and utility?"

"There is no comparison; it takes ten years off your age to wear rational dress. There is nothing to catch the wind and impede your progress. I found a most astonishing difference when riding *en culotte* in Paris, indeed I never could have believed the difference it made to the ease and pleasure of riding. But the dress is so unsightly. The French women do not mind because they are more inclined to study utility in their dress than we are; they consider it the best taste to be suitably attired for what you are doing."

"You referred a few minutes ago, Madame Grand, to the necessity for a New Woman to be particular about her dress; do you not think that the movement has suffered by advanced women being a little careless in this matter?"

"Most certainly I do. Want of taste in dress on the part of many women, who advocate what are called advanced views, has thrown back the woman's cause fifty years. Everyone who takes part in the movement ought to be particularly careful in dress and manners; and I am sorry to say that the manners of some are simply disgraceful; so utterly wanting in tact and ordinary politeness. It seems to me also that any attempt to disparage the home duties is such a mistake. While being fully in favour of women entering the professions, speaking on public platforms, and taking their part in the movements of the time, I think that they should always consider their homes and families first of all. The average middle-class woman with a home and a young family to look after cannot have time for much else. There is no more delicate or beautiful work than training and developing the minds of little children, and I have no respect for women who do not feel this to be important work. The influence of a mother is paramount, and I do not think that a woman can be better engaged anywhere than in her own nursery, for if we wish to teach men justice to women it is with the small boy that we must start. It has been the custom in the past to encourage a boy to regard his little sister as, 'only a girl,' and it is small wonder that he ends by assuming that women are his inferiors. The nursery is the proper place to teach the equality of the sexes, and a system of co-education would greatly help in this direction."

"There has been so much discussion recently with regard to the marriage question, and the position of married women under the law that I should be glad to hear what view you take, Madame Grand?"

"Women have nothing to gain from any laxity in the marriage laws. Marriage was certainly instituted in the interests of women; men are not likely to be specially anxious about the legal bonds, and the majority submit to it, in the first instance, as the only condition upon which they can expect a woman to take them. Laws pressed hardly upon married women in the past undoubtedly, but the passing of the Married Woman's Property Act, and the Married Women's Protection Act have materially altered their position for the better. There has also been a great advance made in the position of the married mother by the passing of the Custody of Children's Act.[16] The law of divorce still calls for reform."

"Do you advocate greater facility for divorce, or simply equality?"

"I am against making divorce easier, it would do a great deal of harm. We should have people separating over every little quarrel, and then repenting when they had cooled down and thought things over. Divorce should be granted only on the ground of adultery, and the law applied equally to the husband and the wife. It ought not to be necessary for the wife to have to prove cruelty as well as unfaithfulness, as is now the case, although the husband can divorce her for unfaithfulness alone."

"You would consider, I gather, that a woman who enters upon a matrimonial relationship without the protection of a legal ceremony is, to put it on the lowest grounds, foolish?"

"Yes, she is acting against her own interests, and doing a great wrong to her possible children. I should be sorry to say anything which would give pain, but the Lanchester case naturally suggests itself as an example. Doubtless Miss Lanchester[17] in her recent action was acting from a conscientious objection to a legal marriage, and it is well that the subject should be ventilated if she does not mind being the scapegoat, but I think that her position is illogical. By legal marriage we make a binding engagement for life, but she takes her lover on the understanding that if her love ceases she shall be free, and in that way seems to be prophesying an end to her love. If she has implicit faith in her lover, why does she shrink from the tie which makes her union legal, which holds society together and makes her children legitimate? In entering upon such a connection with an implied idea that at some future time they may wish to separate strikes me as showing a want of faith in each other. If the tie can be broken, except for the one reason with which the law deals, then marriage will lose all that is elevating with those whose intentions are good. Laxity in the marriage tie would eventually lead to the younger women constantly changing their lovers and refusing to have children, and when they became old and *passée* men would neglect them. The position of women in middle life and old age would be very sad and desolate, whereas with binding marriage the majority have an honoured position and a fair share of happiness."

"What do you think of *The Woman who Did?*"

"It seems to me that Mr. Grant Allen[18] wants us to return to the customs of the poultry yard."

"But do you think that he means such an inference to be drawn from the book?"

"Yes I do, most seriously. Mr. Grant Allen is a large-minded, liberal man, and he argues that if men are permitted to practise polygamy then women should be equally free to indulge in polyandry. I do not know that he approves of polygamy, only he is liberal enough to say that if men are to claim sexual freedom then it should be accorded to women also. The story answers the question when followed to its logical conclusions, and shows very clearly that women have nothing to gain and everything to lose by renouncing the protection which legal marriage gives. The only difference between us and the beasts of the field is that we can regulate our passions by the exercise of will and principle. It has taken the race long ages to do this and it would be very foolish to come back again into the beast state, as Tennyson says, 'reel back into the beast and be no more.' We want progress, not retrogression. Men could be taught the self-restraint which women have had to learn, and we want the same law for men as for women in these matters. I think too, that women are the proper people to decide on matters of population. Men have not managed to regulate either the population or the social question at all satisfactorily, and it would be well to give us a chance of trying what we can do. We could do much if we had the suffrage; the want of electoral power cripples our efforts. As Harriet Martineau so finely puts it: 'If women were not helpless men would find it far less easy to be vicious.'"

"I need not remind you, Madame Grand, that it is commonly stated by our critics that women are the greatest sinners in respect of the publication of novels which are not quite nice; do you think that is so?"

"Well, I wonder if it is; I am just thinking—perhaps women are bolder because they have suffered more from these sex matters than men. Most of them write with loathing of the subject—I certainly do—but are impelled to it by the hope of remedying the evils which exist. Men do it because these things are in their minds, and they have not the excuse of the object to be attained."

"Surely no woman's novel is written so boldly as *Jude the Obscure?*"

"I have great respect for Mr. Hardy's genius, but I cannot make out whether he intended to teach anything by *Jude the Obscure.* The work is colossal in strength, but ethically, it is amorphous. I perceive no special teaching in it. I have no doubt that there are 'Arabellas,' and it is well that young 'Judes' should be warned against them; Mr. Hardy does that. As for 'Sue,' it would have been a good thing if someone had explained to her that she was not of the right constitution to marry. She was one of 'Nature's Nuns,' a morbid type that is being developed amongst us. The book is a *tour de force.* But as to its doing any harm I do not see how it can, as the whole tendency of the story is to show that these erratic relations between the sexes result in misery."

"What do you think are its teachings on the marriage question? You will remember that 'Sue' marries the old schoolmaster, whom she does not love, in the usual way; but when she takes for a husband 'Jude,' whom she does love, she rebels against going through a legal marriage ceremony. Does Mr. Hardy intend to teach that where love is omnipotent a legal tie is not only unnecessary, but an insult to love?"

"I cannot tell," replied Madame Grand, "but it is a question which I should like to ask Mr. Hardy himself, and I shall do so the next time I see him. But in conclusion, I may say that personally I think marriage is the most sacred institution in the world, and it is better not to interfere with it."

"Science and the Rights of Women"

[Miss] H.E. Harvey.

[*Westminster Review* 148 (August 1897): 205-07]

We live in an age of social revolutions, and, instead of meekly settling down to "do our duty in that station of life to which God has called us," as our forefathers did, we keep asking, "What is Duty?" "What is Right, and what is Wrong?" Finding the Ten Commandments old-fashioned, we formulate systems of ethics, and we talk about right and wrong, purity and justice, as though these things were ends in themselves. But none of the modern reformers have given us any satisfactory reason for doing right rather than wrong, for doing good rather than bad.

I think any one who looks at social questions from a scientific point of view will admit that the only right which we really recognise is the right of the strongest. Those who have had the power in their hands have written books, and set up systems of theology and made laws, to prove that it was right for them to do what they wished to do. If they have not the brains to do it themselves, they can make it worth while for those who have to do it for them. It is only by the right of the strongest that we can have any dominion over the lower animals. It is only by the right of the strongest that one man can live in luxury while others are starving. It is only by the right of the strongest that we can conquer other countries and impose our laws on them. And it is only by the right of the strongest that the male sex has had any ascendency. Men, having always had the means of subsistence in their hands, have been enabled to lay down laws to dictate what women ought to be, to do, to think, and to feel. And women have always found it to their interest to conform to those laws. All the literature of the past tends to prove that women ought to live in subjection to men: because literature has always been in the hands of men. Literature tells us that man was created first, and that woman was made as an afterthought, in order to be a companion to him. But science knows nothing of this tale.

Now, the strength of women lies in the fact that men cannot do without them. If they could have, then women would have become extinct long ago. Neither sex can do without the other. But women, having been rendered timid by centuries of subjection, have never found out where their strength lies. I speak of women in general; for it is a very remarkable fact, that though women in general have always been governed by the laws laid down by men, individual women very often find that they can do just as they please. A woman can nearly always get what she wants if she makes enough fuss about it; and so it happens that in private life it is very often the woman who governs. It is merely a question of which has the stronger will. But, as women have had no literature of their own, and no public life, these individual cases have had no effect at all on the position of women in general. It is a marked characteristic of the dependent condition in which women have always lived, that they have never, till now, combined together to assert their rights; they have always worked individually. This, indeed, was an inevitable result of their position, for they have always been taught that it was their interest to uphold the very laws which kept them in subjection.

But if women could only recognise where their power lies, they might make their own laws for the regulation of their own conduct, instead of submitting to the laws which have been laid down by men. We have seen during the last few years what women can do in the way of revolutionising social laws. A few years ago, it was an unheard-of thing for a woman to go about in knickerbockers on a bicycle; but now we are so accustomed to the sight that we forget to be shocked by it. Women can do what they please if they only knew it; they have only to agree among themselves as to what they wish to do; for, as men cannot do without women, they must take women as they choose to be. The women of the present day are only beginning to find this out. They are beginning to find that they may educate public opinion instead of being educated by it. The next fifty years may perhaps bring about social changes which we have hardly dreamed of yet.

For women are at last beginning to find that they are strong enough to make their own laws to regulate their own conduct. But I think we may do more still. I think we may become strong enough to make laws to regulate the conduct of men, which, as I think most people will admit, stands in need of regulation. And I think that this is the first task which the women of the present day have before them—to educate public opinion to allow more liberty for women and less for men. For these matters lie at the root of all the social questions of the day.

It will not be an easy task. Many of the reformers of the present day, both men and women, have asserted loudly that it is unjust that there should be one law for one sex and another for the other; yet public opinion continues to condemn the slightest offence in women, while it overlooks the habitual misconduct of men. Victor Hugo has written *Les Misérables*, and George Eliot has written *Adam Bede*,[19] and the reading world has been thrilled with pleasurable emotions by the perusal of these tragedies. Yet, only two years ago, a poor girl was turned out of doors to starve, with her baby, only a few weeks old, in her arms, by her own parents; and then condemned to death for childmurder; while her partner escaped without any responsibility. We, as a nation, profess to be guided by the teaching of Christ, and we build stately churches, that His doctrines may be preached in them; yet Christ said, "Let him that is without sin among you cast the first stone at her." Leo Tolstoi has published *The Kreutzer Sonata*,[20] and yet public opinion continues to regard as respectable members of society, and as eligible husbands, men who "have been married a dozen times already!"

These things are tolerated because it has pleased the stronger, and therefore the ruling, sex to exact a much greater degree of purity from women than they care to aspire to themselves. And it is for the women of the future to decide whether these things shall continue to be, or whether they will combine together to make laws for themselves.

"FOIBLES OF THE NEW WOMAN"

ELLA W. WINSTON

[*Forum* 21 (April 1896): 186-92]

When woman revolts against her normal functions and sphere of action, desiring instead to usurp man's prerogatives, she entails upon herself the inevitable penalty of such irregular conduct, and, while losing the womanliness which she apparently scorns, fails to attain the manliness for which she strives. But, unmindful of the frowns of her observers, she is unto herself a perpetual delight, calling herself and her kind by the epithets "new," "awakened," and "superior," and speaking disdainfully of women who differ from her in what, to her judgment, is the all-important question of life— "Shall women vote or not?" To enumerate her foibles is a dangerous task, for what she asserts to-day she will deny to-morrow. She is a stranger to logic, and when consistency was given to mortals the New Woman was conspicuously absent. Her egotism is boundless. She boasts that she has discovered herself, and says it is the greatest discovery of the century. She has christened herself the "new," but when her opponent speaks of her by that name she replies with characteristic contrariety that the New Woman, like the sea-serpent, is largely an imaginary creature. Nevertheless in the next sentence, she will refer to herself by her favorite cognomen. She has made many strange statements, and one question she often asks is, "What has changed woman's outlook so that she now desires that of which her grandmother did not dream?"

Within the past forty years woman has demanded of man much that he has graciously granted her. She wanted equality with him, and it has been given her in all things for which she is fitted and which will not lower the high standard of womanhood that he desires for her. This she accepts without relinquishing any of the chivalrous attentions which man always bestows upon her. The New Woman tells us that "an ounce of justice is of more value to woman than a ton of chivalry." But, when she obtains her "ounce of justice," she apparently still makes rigorous demands that her "ton of chivalry" be not omitted. Woman asked to work by man's side and on his level; and to-day she has the chance of so doing. The fields of knowledge and opportunity have been opened to her; and she still "desires that of which her grandmother did not dream," because, like an over-indulged child, so long as she is denied one privilege, that privilege she desires above all others. She has decided that without the ballot she can do nothing, for, in her vocabulary, ballot is synonymous with power.

The New Woman is oftentimes the victim of strange hallucinations. She persists in calling herself a "slave," despite her high position and great opportunities; and she maintains that, because she cannot vote, she is classed with lunatics and idiots,—until those who are weary of hearing her constant iterations of these themes feel that, if the classification were true, it might not be unjust. Still, it has not been clearly shown that withholding the ballot from woman, in common with lunatics and idiots, necessarily makes her one. Women and cripples are exempt from working on roads; does it follow that all women are cripples? Is a woman a bird because she walks on two legs? This hackneyed cry about lunatics and idiots, which has been uttered by nearly all writers and speakers favoring woman suffrage, appeals to prejudice rather than intelligence. If the would-be female politicians—ignoring woman's great opportunities, especial privileges, and the silent testimony of countless happy wives,—choose to consider themselves "slaves," and to announce whenever they speak that they are classed with lunatics and idiots because they are denied the ballot, they are certainly entitled to all the enjoyment they can get out of the delusion. Sensible people know that such statements are false.

The New Woman says that a "mother's prerogative ends at the garden gate"; but common sense replies that no mother's prerogative ends there. A mother's prerogative is to govern and direct her child; and there is no child that does not carry through life his or her mother's influence. Let that influence be good or bad, it is always present. Any mother can make, if she will, her power over her child "stronger than the seas of earth, and purer than the air of heaven"; and she needs no especial legislative act to accomplish her work. If woman does not make the laws, she trains and educates those who do, and thus is indirectly responsible for all legislation.

The plea which these women make, that they need the ballot for the protection of their homes, is self-contradictory. Has the New Woman never heard that "to teach early is to engrave on marble"? If she would devote some of the time in which she struggles to obtain the ballot to rational reflection on the influence a woman has over the pre-natal life of a child, and would then consider what a mother may do with a plastic human life,—say during the first seven years of its existence and before it goes out to be contaminated by the evil influences of the world,—she would then find that ballots are not what women need for the protection of their homes. But the faculty of logically reasoning from cause to effect has never been characteristic of the New Woman.

She laments because government is deprived, by lack of equal suffrage, of the "keen moral sense that is native to women as a class." Since all the people in the world are born of women and trained by women, it is difficult to see how government, or anything else, lacks woman's "keen moral sense." Can women make no use of their moral sense without the ballot?

It is a chronic grievance with the New Woman that she is taxed without representation. She scorns to be represented by the sons she has reared, or by the men who come under her immediate influence. These she pronounces unworthy and considers incapable of doing her justice. But when she is told that, if women vote, they should also bear the burdens of war in case of necessity, she replies with her usual inconsistency, "She who bears soldiers need not bear arms." She has not the aversion to being represented by men on the field of battle that she has to being represented by them in legislative halls and at the ballot-box. She greatly deprecates man's selfishness and tyranny, as exhibited in human history. But she has come vaunting into the arena with "woman's clubs" and "conventions" and "leagues" and "tribunes" and "signals." If a periodical be not wholly devoted to women, they demand that it must at least have its "woman's column" wherein they may chronicle the most insignificant acts of the sex.

The New Woman tells us that the present century is her own; and, indeed, she approaches the truth in this instance. She has promised us a "Woman's Bible,"[21] and she has shown that even the Infinite Father does not escape her jealousy, for she has discovered that we should pray to a "Heavenly Mother" as well as to a Heavenly Father. She informs us that the Pilgrim Fathers are no more, and adds, "There stepped on Plymouth Rock, on the bleak shores of New England, thirty-two women accompanied by sixty-nine men and children." At expositions she must have a "woman's building," wherein she may glorify the work of her brain and hand. No work done by man can be placed beside hers for examination or competition. Surely she furnishes a noteworthy example of modesty and self-abnegation for the benefit of the tyrant man!

An illustration of the New Woman's fallacious judgment is shown by her belief that all opponents of equal suffrage are controlled by brewers and liquor dealers. "Sold to the liquor interests" is the cry she always utters when she detects a note of opposition. Now, it is entirely probable that some may object to the extension of the franchise to women and, at the same time, lead thoroughly temperate lives and work for the promotion of temperance. The word temperance means more than total abstinence from intoxicating drinks, and the New Woman has not yet proved that a vote by a woman means a vote for temperance principles.

"Woman's vote will purify politics." This is her favorite cry. Not long since a prominent equal-suffrage lecturer, while earnestly setting forth this claim, and enlarging on the shameless manner in which men conduct elections, declared that woman's chaste and refined influence was the only thing that could change the present undesirable condition of affairs. She was not ashamed, however, to relate, before the close of her lecture, that, a short time previous, her sister had induced the family's hired man to vote for a certain measure by presenting him, on the eve of election, with a half-dozen new shirts, made by her own hands. The absurdity of this incident reached a climax when it was noticed that, in a large audience of women, few saw anything wrong in female bribery. The fair speaker omitted to inform her audience whether or not this was to be the prevailing mode of political purification, when one half of the burdens of state rest on female shoulders. But, as women never lack expedients, some purifying process, less laborious than shirt-making, may soon be devised.

The New Woman requests that the opponents of equal suffrage open their "dust-covered histories" and therein read of examples of famous women of the past whose lives forever silence all arguments against granting the ballot to woman. Let it be remembered that the New Woman's greatest grievance, since her earliest advent, is the lack of woman's power. Without the ballot woman can do nothing. "Bricks without straw,—that has been the doom of woman throughout the ages," is her disconsolate wail. An extremely brilliant New Woman rarely makes a speech without saying, "Women will enter every place on the round earth, and they will purify every place they enter." With these statements in mind, by all means let the "dust-covered histories" be opened so that we may see the "bricks without straw" which the women "without power" have made, and the manner in which they have purified every place they have entered.

Catherine de Medici prevailed on Charles IX of France to give the order for the massacre of St. Bartholomew.[22] This crime, which she boasted of to Catholics and excused to Protestants, greatly increased her power, which she used unscrupulously, even conniving at the murder of her own son when she considered him an obstacle to her advancement. She died amid the fierce strife of wars, which she had caused, her use of political power having been only an injury to the world.

Madame de Maintenon, using the power which she so long exercised over Louis XIV, instigated the Revocation of the Edict of Nantes.[23] Its most odious features were her especial work. She had been false to her native creed; and she was determined that her fellow Protestants should be equally false. She drove from the shores of France many of its best and most intelligent people. All the bloody history of that period was the result of one woman's work.

During the reign of Louis XV of France the court was under the absolute dominion of women, yet none of the instances of ancient and modern immorality presents such an astounding display of individual and national corruption as do those of the time when Madame de Pompadour[24] ruled the king of France. She did nothing for the alleviation of human wretchedness during those twenty years of power and splendid opportunity. She was largely to blame for the evils in church and state which caused the revolution and overturned all in one common ruin. It may be urged that no good woman would have been raised to power by such means as she accepted; and consequently no good could be hoped for from her. But she and her successor, Madame Du Barry, furnish proof that there are women whose advancement to high positions would only increase evil influences; and there are many such who would quickly seize the enlarged opportunities of suffrage, while many good women, engrossed with home cares, would be indifferent to the ballot.

Woman's record in the first French revolution was one of cruelty and horror. The "Patriot Knitters," as they were called, could shriek or knit according to the requirements of the case. They could also urge men to deeds of violence; and could themselves do the violent deeds. Carlyle said that these women had exchanged the "distaff for the dagger."[25] If they had kept the distaff and let the dagger alone France would have lost nothing in the way of political advancement, and might have been spared much of her horrifying history. There was an entire absence of any political purification in their influence.

There is no name in history of which women boast more than that of Queen Elizabeth, always quoting her in evidence of what women might do, could they be intrusted with affairs of state. Froude, in summing up his exhaustive work on the time of Queen Elizabeth, wrote:—"The great results of her reign were the fruits of a policy which was not her own, and which she starved and mutilated when energy and completeness were needed. She was remorseless when she ought to have been most forbearing, and lenient when she ought to have been stern. She owned her safety and success to the incapacity and divisions of her enemies, rather than to wisdom and resolution of her own." Humiliating as it may be to those women who clamor for a voice in national affairs, the historical truth is, that the splendors of the Elizabethan age were due to her ministers, Burleigh and Walsingham.[26]

Catherine II of Russia[27] is also a great favorite with the New Woman. One of them has said, "Next to the great Peter, she was the ablest administrator Russia has ever known." In the life and reign of Catherine II, Empress of Russia,—she who became such through the murder of her husband, in which crime she had borne full well her share,—there is but little to admire or emulate. She was unquestionably a woman of great talents and energy, but her morals were no better than Madame de Pompadour's.

These examples and many more may be found in the "dust-covered histories." But, if the New Woman will read history with honest eyes, she can never find that women have ever lacked power; neither can she prove that in the past they have purified all the places they have entered; what authority, then, has she for the statement that they would purify every place they may enter in the future? Woman was endowed by her Creator with marvellous power, and, from the time of our first parents until now, that power has been a "saviour of life unto life, or of death unto death," as has been eminently manifested in the teachings of history and the experience of human life.

The New Woman has a mania for reform movements. No sooner does she descry an evil than she immediately moves against it with some sort of an organized force. This is very noble of her,—if she have no other duties to perform. It would be more gratifying if her organizations met with greater success; but alas! her efforts, mighty as they are, usually represent just so much valuable time wasted. The evils remain, and continue to increase. She disdains to inquire into the cause of her numerous failures, and moves serenely on bent upon reforming everything she imagines to be wrong. When she gets the ballot all will be well with the world, and for that day she works and waits. But if the New Woman or any other woman neglects private duties for public works, her reform efforts are not noble, but extremely unworthy of her; for the "duty which lies nearest" is still the most sacred of duties. Possibly the many *Mrs. Jellybys* of the present day and the undue interest in "Borrioboola-gha"[28] may have something to do with so much being wrong in the average home and with the average individual. When we read of women assembling together, parading streets, and entering saloons to create, as they say, "a public sentiment for temperance," it is but natural to ask, What are the children of such mothers doing in the meantime? And it will not be strange if many of them become drunkards for the coming generation of reformers to struggle with. The New Woman refuses to believe that duty, like charity, begins at home, and cannot see that the most effectual way to keep clean is not to allow dirt to accumulate.

The New Woman professes to believe that all women are good and will use their influence for noble ends,—when they are allowed the right of suffrage. This theory is extremely pleasant, if it were only demonstrable; but here, as elsewhere, it is folly to ignore the incontrovertible facts. Woman cannot shirk her responsibility for the sins of the earth. It is easy for her to say that men are bad; that, as a class, they are worse than women. But who trained these bad men? Was it not woman? Herein lies the inconsistency of women—striving for a chance to do good when the opportunity is inherently theirs. It is only when they have neglected to train the saplings right that the trees are misshapen.

It was the New Woman's earliest, and is her latest, foible that woman is superior to man. Perhaps she is. But the question is not one of superiority or inferiority. There is at bottom of all this talk about women nature's inexorable law. Man is man and woman is woman. That was the order of creation and it must so remain. It is idle to compare the sexes in similar things. It is a question of difference, and the "happiness and perfection of both depend on each asking and receiving from the other what the other only can give."

"For woman is not undevelopt man,
But diverse: could we make her as the man,
Sweet Love were slain: his dearest bond is this,
Not like to like, but like in difference."[29]

Sentimental and slavish as this may sound to many ears, it is as true as any of the unchanging laws governing the universe, and is the Creator's design for the reproduction and maintenance of the race.

"THE ETERNAL FEMININE"

BOYD WINCHESTER

[*Arena* 27 (April 1902): 367-73]

I. The New Woman

In few respects has mankind made a greater advance than in the position of woman—legal, social, and educational. From the darkness of ignorance and servitude woman has passed into the open light of equal freedom. The happiness and progress of society are regarded as depending not more upon the ability of its sons to direct the wheels of prosperous enterprise than upon the intelligence of its daughters to safeguard the very sources of social and household life. By slow but sure and permanent advances has come the recognition of the right of woman to her own development—the right of individuals to know, to learn, to perfect themselves to the utmost of their ability, irrespective of sex.

The energetic, independent woman of culture is frequently caricatured as the "New Woman." The change that has led to the development of this type may be summed up as the improved mental and physical development of the girl, necessarily accompanied by and leading to a different ideal for the woman. There is not a more unmanly cry than that in fashion against "strong-minded women." Either the phrase is an irony which repetition has turned into a serious fallacy—and what is meant is that the so-called "strong-minded women" are *not* strong-minded, and that analogous specimens of men would be regarded as weak-minded—or the phrase is cruel and mean. No woman yet but was better, nobler, and essentially more womanly, in precise proportion as her natural abilities had received all the education of which they were capable. The key-note of her character is self-reliance and power of initiation. She often earns her own living. She aims at being in direct contact with reality and at forming her own judgment upon it. This is an attitude which, of course, is capable of gross exaggeration and misuse, and when carried so far has afforded some justification for the caricature.

Conceding and commending the proper equilibrium of the sexes must not be confused with the doctrine that, with an equal opportunity, woman should prove herself as much of a *man* as anybody. Emancipation from servitude and ignorance does not mean emancipation from womanliness, or what that keen-eyed, patient, steadfast watcher of life, Goethe, calls the "ever woman-ly"—the eternal feminine, as embodying the tender, loving, self-sacrificing, altruistic side of human nature, which is shown in the redeemed soul of *Marguerite*[30] to hold the spiritual power of drawing upward and onward. Every right-minded man will rejoice in woman's attainment of her just rights and opportunities, and will dissent from the utterance of a distinguished Boston minister that "the moment a woman becomes erudite, as she does after the average college course, she becomes a bluestocking and apart from the rest of society, and consequently she does not accomplish the good which she might otherwise."

However, every one who cherishes the slightest regard for the rare virtues and qualities of sweet womanhood must resent and abhor the too manifest tendency of modern social, industrial, and educational innovations to unsex and abase our young women. The passing away of mere amiable weakness and sentimental delicacy, timid gentleness and submissive dependence, need not bring in an impairment of woman's refinement and domesticity. True sweet-ness, true goodness, and true love come not from naïvete or feebleness, but of intelligence and personal force. True learning, like true taste, is modest and unostentatious, and must shed a cheering light over the imaginative sympathy and moral susceptibility which constitute so large a part of woman's genius.

Let woman honor her own distinctive nature, and claim for herself all the culture that will best equip her for her own work—her own sphere. But she must bear in mind that in becoming a sound classicist, a brilliant mathemati-cian, a sharp critic, a faultless grammarian, she may do so at the expense of that ready sympathy, modesty, noble self-control, gentleness, personal tact and temper, so essential for the best type of womanhood and the most exalt-ed standard of female excellence. It would not be for the good of the world were the sentiment and tenderness of woman to be lost in philosophic calm-ness and materialistic indifference.

Thought is masculine; sentiment is feminine. Both must be found, more or less, in every human being. In a manly character the one will prevail—in a womanly character the other. No measure of sentiment that leaves thought sovereign detracts from manliness. No vigor of intellect that does not dispute the empire of sentiment diminishes the grace of woman. All that masculine power accomplishes the feminine resources of the soul render possible. The Muses are feminine, and, in making them so, the subtle imagination of Greece found its way to the fact that the *woman* in humanity is that from which the music of human thought proceeds. A man judges, but it is Themis that inspires the judges. A man philosophizes, but wisdom itself is Athene. Therefore, making sentiment distinctively feminine implies no inferiority in woman. In her it is so quick, so subtle, and so untraceable that we can give it no other name than *feeling*. The eye of her perception is like a divining rod, having its power in the difference of her nature from that of man—the grace of concealment and reserve, a charm that defies analysis, a delicacy that treads untraceable paths and works more finely than explicit thought.

After all, the essential quality of female excellence and charm is *feminineness*. Woman's heart, her mind, her person, to be pleasant, must be feminine. This is, above all else, what we love in woman. It is here that we meet the distinction between what will suffice for such a friendship as we entertain for a man and such a love as we entertain for a woman. "The things we love in a young lady," says Goethe, "are something very different from the understanding. We love in her beauty, youth, playfulness, confidingness—her character, with all her faults and caprices, and God knows what other inexpressible charms. But we do not love her understanding; we respect it when it is brilliant, and it may greatly elevate her in our opinion—nay, worse, it may also serve to fix our attentions where we already love, but it is not that which fires our hearts and inflames our passions."

As in the half-opened rosebud, at once displaying and concealing its beauty, there is a fascination wanting to the full-blown flower, so in a certain undefinable but exalted reserve of woman lurks the finest resource of the race—the inspiration and the reward of our labor. What a beautiful truth is embodied in the Rabbinical application of the Psalmist's words!—"The glory of the king's daughter is within his palace."[31]

Woman's title to power comes not from self-consciousness and mannish assertion. Nature secures it. Authority radiates from her like light from a star. She breathes queenliness, and commands in proportion as she is womanly, and masculine strength bows loyally to her sway. But she bears a veiled scepter, and with every man of fine nature it is indeed rendered irresistible by that subtle and tender concealment. Beautiful in the spirit of self-abandonment, in the strength of her mighty love, acting the highest philosophy of self-renunciation, woman pours the fervent tide of all her trustful nature into the stronger and deeper current of a true and manly heart. Man loves only what pleases him. The heart makes itself heard above the claims of work, above the intellect, demanding for life a recompense, a goal.

Firstly, in a woman, let us have a pure, earnest, loving heart; then, passing over her mind, let her form and features be as graceful as possible. Men want mind and heart—women heart and person. A beautiful person is far from being indifferent at the same time in a man; in the same manner an intelligent and highly cultured mind is an ornament and a treasure of precious worth in a woman. It is only mentioned as subordinate, just as in a piece of music the feelings and senses are perhaps to be more touched than the faculties pertaining to the understanding or the intellect.

With us Americans there is a respect for woman such as is found in no other country and among no other people. In the absence of the ancient caste and throne, womanhood is our pet aristocracy. A deep and religious reverence for woman is infused into the whole system of our institutions and manners; not by artificial and insulting restrictions, but by a manly and voluntary homage, by all the sanctions of opinion and all the obligations of religion. With us the words of Ruskin are fully realized: "She wields the power of the scepter and shield, the power of the royal hand that heals in touching, the throne that is founded on the rock of justice and descended from only by the steps of mercy: *Rex et Regina, Roi et Reine*—queen to your lover, queen to your husband and children, queen you must always be."[32]

The true and full recognition of the dignity and worth of woman is to be found especially in the conjugal relation as it exists in our country—a relation that is essentially the ideal state, the crown of womanhood, and the only sphere that affords adequate competence, happiness, unlimited influence, and unbounded resources for the free exercise and supreme cultivation of her highest and most blessed faculties and attributes. The man of our time and country wants in his wife an intelligent companion, a moral helpmate, an equal "taken from his side," and not a plaything or a slave to follow behind. She takes complete possession of the home life, and, recognizing that she has what we lack, let her excel us, enlighten us, encourage us.

Woman in the United States is what elsewhere she is allowed to be only when she has a coronet upon her brow or scepter of power in her hand. She is not only a supreme power in the silence of the home, but she has come to a degree of knowledge and breadth of intellect, to an influence and grandeur, an authority and eminence, such as the Greeks would have rejected as impracticable and the Romans struggled in vain to obtain. In her progress to this proud eminence the American woman has triumphed and withstood, in all her softer features, that destructive influence of wealth and luxury which corrupted her illustrious prototype, the Roman matron, losing none of her charms and retaining all of her virtues: demonstrating that a woman may be childlike as well as impassioned, tender as well as strong; that she may glow with all love's fire, and yet be delicately obedient to the lightest whisper of honor.

It is not necessary for families of unmarried girls to loiter wearily on into old age, waiting for some one to invite them to take up the duties of life. Our girls are no longer taught that all instincts and ambitions must be crushed that seek outside the seclusion of home life spheres in which their lives may become useful or significant; but they are encouraged to make a life for themselves, that they may become a source of strength and sweetness to their surroundings. And if in this attempt a few mistake their way and fall into mere singularity, it is only a misfortune incident to all pioneers.

Silently, slowly, but irresistibly, an enduring principle has, by Divine ordinance, made its way into man's social and political existence, by the decree that elevated one-half of the human race to its just individual sphere of duty and responsibility and spiritual equality with the other half. When the dignity of her equal birthright was thus divinely proclaimed, woman as the helpmeet and companion of man—no longer the mere toy of passion, or the unequal and degraded victim of polygamy—was assigned to her just and original place in the law of creation: then, and not until then, the names of wife, mother, and daughter began to bear their true significance, and the tie of marriage was placed above all others. Upon this equal union the institution of the family is founded. Home and its relations, the care and education of her children, endowed the wife and mother with powers, duties, and responsibilities but little known before. Increased confidence was followed by increased affection and respect, and the assured legitimacy of offspring induced industry and the acquisition of property, from the sense of reliance upon its transmission and inheritance.

The typical American wife and mother is worthy to have applied to her the old formal term, with all its sweet original significance, "spinster," as it told how the clothing of the entire household came from the active industry and economy of woman; and still more of the Saxon phrase, "Freodowebbe," the weaver of peace, expressing the subtle influence distilled by gentleness and love and trust, which color the web of life with the hues of heaven.

NOTES

1. John Ruskin (1819-1900) was an English critic of art and society. The images mentioned here suggest the writer is referring to Ruskin's "The Mystery of Life and Its Arts," first delivered as a lecture in Dublin in 1868 and then added to *Sesame and Lilies* in 1871.
2. Men and women were assigned separate spheres of activity; women's sphere was supposed to be the home.
3. Becky Sharp is the unscrupulous heroine of William Makepeace Thackeray's novel *Vanity Fair* (1848). Roderick Random is the rakish hero of Tobias Smollett's novel *The Adventures of Roderick Random* (1748).
4. Count von Moltke (1848-1916) was the Prussian Chief of the General Staff from 1858 to 1888. In this position he planned the successful wars of unification against Denmark, Austria, and France.
5. Tom Jones is the hero of Henry Fielding's 1749 novel *Tom Jones*. Despite his love for Sophia Western, he finds it hard to resist sexual temptation.
6. Caliban is the deformed savage slave of Prospero in Shakespeare's *Tempest*.
7. Caudle, a warm drink made of gruel, wine, eggs, sugar, and spices, is given to ailing persons.

8. Prince Otto Eduard Leopold von Bismarck (1815-98) was the first chancellor of the German Empire. Herbert Spencer (1820-1903) was a British social philosopher. Thomas Edison (1847-1931) was an American inventor. William Gladstone (1809-98) was four times the Prime Minister of England. Alexander III (d. 1181) was Pope from 1159-81. Frederick Blackwood (1826-1902), the First Marquess of Dufferin and Ava, was a diplomat and administrator. Henri d'Orleans, the duc d'Aumale (1822-97) and fourth son of King Louis Philippe and Queen Marie Amelie of France, was a military leader and historian.

9. *fournisseurs*, tradesmen (French).

10. Lady Jane Grey (1537-54), nominal Queen of England for 10 days, was deposed and executed. She was versed in Greek, Latin, Italian, and French. Hypatia (370-415), born in Alexandria, was a philosopher and lecturer. George Sand, the pseudonym of Amandine Aurore Lucie Dupin (1804-76), was a French novelist. Mary Somerville (1780-1872) was a scientist; Somerville College (Oxford) is named for her. Corinna is a traditional name for shepherdesses in pastoral poetry. Cordelia is the faithful daughter in Shakespeare's *King Lear*. Helen, in Greek mythology, was the beautiful wife of King Menelaus of Sparta. She eloped to Troy with Paris, thereby causing the Trojan War. Penelope was the faithful wife of Odysseus in Homer's *Odyssey*. Aspasia (470?-410 B.C.) was a hetaira (a paid companion of aristocratic men) and the mistress of Pericles, the leader of Athens. She was skilled in rhetoric and attended symposiums, meeting influential and powerful men. Adelina Patti (1843-1919) was an Italian soprano.

11. *frottement*, friction (French).

12. The English poet Elizabeth Barrett (1806-61), an invalid who lived in semi-seclusion until her elopement with the poet Robert Browning in 1846, wrote *Aurora Leigh*. At home she had studied Latin and Greek, read in history, philosophy, and literature, and written poetry.

13. Andrea del Sarto (1486-1531) was a Florentine painter. After marriage to the beautiful and manipulative Lucrezia in 1513, he became alienated from his family and friends. Antonio Correggio (c.1489-1534) was an Italian painter who, according to Giorgio Vasari in *Lives of the Artists* (1550), was "a slave to his work" for the sake of his family and was burdened by family cares.

14. Elizabeth Fry (1780-1845), a Quaker, was an English prison reformer and philanthropist. She worked to improve conditions for women in Newgate prison.

15. Rational costume was the less restrictive clothing, such as culottes or divided skirts, which women were beginning to adopt at the end of the nineteenth century.

16. The Married Women's Property Acts of 1870 and 1882 allowed married women to keep some of their own earnings. The Infant Custody Act of 1839 allowed the court to award mothers custody of their children under the age of seven and access to those under sixteen.

17. In 1895, when Edith Lanchaster refused to marry her lover, James Sullivan, her

family had her committed to an asylum. She was released in four days and declared sane but "very foolish" for her refusal to marry..

18. Grant Allen's novel of 1895, *The Woman Who Did*, shocked many readers. Its heroine, Herminia Barton, lives with a man while refusing on principle to marry him.

19. Both Victor Hugo's *Les Misérables* (1862) and George Eliot's *Adam Bede* (1859) have a female character who bears a child outside of marriage and whose plight evokes sympathy from the reader.

20. In the *Kreutzer Sonata* (1889), a novel by the Russian Leo Tolstoy (1828-1910), Pózdnyshev recounts his debauched experiences with women before deciding to marry. He states: "Out of the thousands of men who marry (not only among us but unfortunately also among the masses) there is hardly one who has not already been married ten, a hundred, or even, like Don Juan, a thousand times, before his wedding" (Chapter V).

21. In 1895 the American suffrage leader Elizabeth Cady Stanton and a committee of other women published *The Woman's Bible*. Dissatisfied with the Revised Version of the Bible, a new translation put out by the Church of England in 1888, the women wrote commentaries on parts of the Bible that focused on women.

22. Catherine de Medici (1519-89) was the Queen of France, married to King Henry II. She then became regent for her son Charles IX in 1560. At first she adopted a conciliatory position toward the French Protestants, the Huguenots. However, fearing for her own power after the Huguenot leader Gaspard de Coligny gained influence over Charles IX, she took part in planning the massacre of Saint Bartholomew's Day (1572) in which hundreds of Protestants were murdered.

23. Françoise d'Aubigné, Marquise de Maintenon (1635-1719), was first the mistress and then the second wife of the French king Louis XIV. The Edict of Nantes, a decree of 1598 promulgated by King Henry IV, gave many liberties to the Huguenots, the French Protestants. Under Louis XIV these liberties were gradually eroded until the Edict of Nantes was finally revoked in 1685. Madame de Maintenon probably had little to do with the revocation; Louis XIV was persuaded by his Roman Catholic advisers to begin persecution of the Protestants.

24. Madame de Pompadour (1721-64) had great influence over the French king Louis XV; she was his mistress for many years. Madame Jeanne Du Barry (1743-93) was the last mistress of Louis XV.

25. Taken from Thomas Carlyle's *The French Revolution* (1837).

26. James Anthony Froude (1818-94), English historian, writes about Queen Elizabeth in his 12-volume *History of England, from the Fall of Wolsey to the Defeat of the Spanish Armada* (1856-70). William Cecil, Lord Burghley (1520-98) and Sir Francis Walsingham (1530?-90) were ministers during Elizabeth's reign.

27. Catherine II of Russia (1729-96), known as Catherine the Great, was married to Grand Duke Peter of Holstein who came to the throne in 1762. The Imperial Guards overthrew him and replaced him with Catherine.

28. In Charles Dickens' *Bleak House* (1853), Mrs. Jellyby has an obsessive interest in philanthropic work in Africa, "educating the natives of Borrioboola-Gha, on the

left bank of the Niger" (Chapter IV). Meanwhile, she neglects to care for her own children.

29. Lines from Alfred, Lord Tennyson's 1847 narrative poem *The Princess*, Canto VII, 259-62.

30. Johann Wolfgang von Goethe (1749-1832), German poet, dramatist, and novelist. In Goethe's *Faust* (1808), Marguerite is Faust's lover.

31. A version of Psalms 45:13. In the King James' version it reads: "The king's daughter is all glorious within: her clothing is of wrought gold."

32. The quote is a conflation of two separate passages from John Ruskin's "Of Queens' Gardens," published in *Sesame and Lilies* (1865).

THE MARRIAGE QUESTION

When Mona Caird (1854-1932) published her article entitled "Marriage" in the *Westminster Review* in 1888, she provoked a great debate over the marriage question that continued in the periodicals and fiction of the 1890s. The *Daily Telegraph* opened a letters column with the title "Is Marriage a Failure?" Within two months it received 27,000 letters. Obviously Caird's analysis of what was wrong with marriage had struck a response from her readers. (Her marriage articles were later revised and collected as *The Morality of Marriage* [London: George Redway, 1897]). But the marriage question included a debate over many related issues, including the education of girls, the plight of unmarried women, and women's need for economic independence. Caird, whose fiction demonstrated the interrelationship between the marriage question and many other aspects of women's lives, would have agreed with the observation Sarah Grand made in her essay "The New Aspect of the Woman Question": "The Woman Question is the Marriage Question."

In March 1899 the periodical *Lady's Realm* asked several prominent women of the day the question, "Does Marriage hinder a Woman's Self-development?" The responses of Mona Caird and Gertrude Atherton are given below. Atherton (1857-1948) was an American writer, born in San Francisco. After marrying and having two children, she began to write in secret in order to avoid her husband's harassment, publishing her first story anonymously. The sudden death of her husband freed her to pursue a literary career. She moved to New York, lived for a time in London and other European sites, and eventually returned to San Francisco. She wrote 34 novels, many short stories, and journal articles, some of which redefine women and their roles.

Caird's novels explored the marriage question through the experiences of her fictional heroines. *The Daughters of Danaus* (1894), the best known and most successful of her novels on the marriage question, has as its heroine a married woman whose desire to pursue her education as a musician is hindered by her husband and her family. Throughout the 1890s, essays by women relating to the marriage question, such as those by Julia M.A. Hawksley and (Miss) H.E. Harvey which are printed below, were published in a variety of periodicals.

Grant Allen (1848-99) was a scientific writer and a novelist. He wrote 30 works of fiction, including *The Woman Who Did* (1895), which was published by John Lane in his Keynotes Series. It was considered by many to be a New Woman novel. Its heroine, Herminia Barton, is educated at Girton; to demonstrate her desire to free herself from the trappings of marriage, she refuses to marry her lover. However, Herminia's unhappy life after her lover dies, her daughter's rejection of her mother's unconventional ideas on marriage, and Herminia's eventual suicide may indicate that Herminia is a caricature of the New Woman; she is certainly not a woman whose fate makes her brand of liberation attractive. Millicent Fawcett denounced the novel in her essay "The Woman Who Did" published in the *Contemporary Review* 67 (May 1895): 625-31. Fawcett believed that the abolition of marriage, which Allen's novel seemingly advocates, would be disastrous for women. Fawcett stated: "He purports to write in the interests of women, but there will be very few women who do not see that his little book belongs very much more to the unregenerate man than to women at all" (631).

In the spirit of his novel, Allen, in his article, "Plain Words on the Woman Question," ends with no endorsement of marriage, but rather an insistence on women's need to produce children. Nevertheless, in his novel, Herminia has one child, not the obligatory four. Despite the advice Allen gives in his essay, after two marriages he had only one child.

"MARRIAGE"

MONA CAIRD

[*Westminster Review* 130 (August 1888): 186-201]

It is not difficult to find people mild and easy-going about religion, and even politics may be regarded with wide-minded tolerance; but broach social subjects, and English men and women at once become alarmed and talk about the foundations of society and the sacredness of the home! Yet the particular form of social life, or of marriage, to which they are so deeply attached, has by no means existed from time immemorial; in fact, modern marriage with its satellite ideas, only dates as far back as the age of Luther.[1] Of course the institution existed long before, but our particular mode of regarding it can be traced to the era of the Reformation, when commerce, competition, the great *bourgeois* class, and that remarkable thing called "Respectability," also began to arise.

Before entering upon the history of marriage, it is necessary to clear the ground for thought upon this subject by a protest against the careless use of the words "human nature," and especially "woman's nature." History will show us, if anything will, that human nature has an apparently limitless adaptability, and that therefore no conclusion can be built upon special manifestations which may at any time be developed. Such development must be referred to certain conditions, and not be mistaken for the eternal law of being. With regard to "woman's nature," concerning which innumerable contradictory dogmas are held, there is so little really known about it, and its power of development, that all social philosophies are more or less falsified by this universal though sublimely unconscious ignorance.

The difficulties of friendly intercourse between men and women are so great, and the false sentiments induced by our present system so many and so subtle, that it is the hardest thing in the world for either sex to learn the truth concerning the real thoughts and feelings of the other. If they find out what they mutually think about the weather it is as much as can be expected—consistently, that is, with genuine submission to present ordinances. Thinkers, therefore, perforce take no count of the many half-known and less understood ideas and emotions of women, even as these actually exist at the moment, and they make still smaller allowance for potential developments which at the present crisis are almost incalculable. Current phrases of the most shallow kind are taken as if they expressed the whole that is knowable on the subject.

There is in fact no social philosophy, however logical and far-seeing on other points, which does not lapse into incoherence as soon as it touches the subject of women. The thinker abandons the thought-laws which he has obeyed until that fatal moment; he forgets every principle of science previously present to his mind, and he suddenly goes back centuries in knowledge and in the consciousness of possibilities, making schoolboy statements, and "babbling of green fields" in a manner that takes away the breath of those who have listened to his former reasoning, and admired his previous delicacies of thought-distinction. Has he been overtaken by some afflicting mental disease? Or does he merely allow himself to hold one subject apart from the circulating currents of his brain, judging it on different principles from those on which he judges every other subject?

Whatever be the fact, the results appear to be identical. A sudden loss of intellectual power would have exactly this effect upon the opinions which the sufferer might hold on any question afterwards presented to him. Suddenly fallen from his high mental estate, our philosopher takes the same view of women as certain Indian theologians took of the staple food of their country.[2] "The Great Spirit," they said, "made all things, except the wild rice, but the wild rice came by chance." The Muse of History, guided by that of Science, eloquently protests against treating any part of the universe as "wild rice;" she protests against the exclusion of the ideas of evolution, of natural selection, of the well-known influence upon organs and aptitudes of continued use or disuse, influence which every one has exemplified in his own life, which every profession proves, and which is freely acknowledged in the discussion of all questions except those in which woman forms an important element. "As she was in the beginning, is now, and ever shall be—!"[3]

There is a strange irony in this binding of women to the evil results in their own natures of the restrictions and injustice which they have suffered for generations. We chain up a dog to keep watch over our home; we deny him freedom, and in some cases, alas! even sufficient exercise to keep his limbs supple and his body in health. He becomes dull and spiritless, he is miserable and ill-looking, and if by any chance he is let loose, he gets into mischief and runs away. He has not been used to liberty or happiness, and he cannot stand it.

Humane people ask his master: "Why do you keep that dog always chained up?"

"Oh! he is accustomed to it; he is suited for the chain; when we let him loose he runs wild."

So the dog is punished by chaining for the misfortune of having been chained, till death releases him. In the same way we have subjected women for centuries to a restricted life, which called forth one or two forms of domestic activity; we have rigorously excluded (even punished) every other development of power; and we have then insisted that the consequent adaptations of structure, and the violent instincts created by this distorting process are, by a sort of compound interest, to go on adding to the distortions themselves, and at the same time to go on forming a more and more solid ground for upholding the established system of restriction, and the ideas that accompany it. <u>We chain, because we *have chained.*</u> The dog must not be released, because his nature has adapted itself to the misfortune of captivity.

He has no revenge in his power; he must live and die, and no one knows his wretchedness. But the woman takes her unconscious vengeance, for she enters into the inmost life of society. *She* can pay back the injury with interest. And so she does, item by item. Through her, in a great measure, marriage becomes what Milton calls "a drooping and disconsolate household captivity,"[4] and through her influence over children she is able to keep going much physical weakness and disease which might, with a little knowledge, be readily stamped out; she is able to oppose new ideas by the early implanting of prejudice; and, in short, she can hold back the wheels of progress, and send into the world human beings likely to wreck every attempt at social reorganization that may be made, whether it be made by men or by gods.[5]

Seeing, then, that the nature of women is the result of their circumstances, and that they are not a sort of human "wild rice," come by chance or special creation, no protest can be too strong against the unthinking use of the term "woman's nature." An unmanageable host of begged questions, crude assertions, and unsound habits of thought are packed into those two hackneyed words.

Having made this protest, we propose to take a brief glance at the history of marriage, then to consider marriage at the present day, and finally to discuss the marriage of the future. We begin with a time when there was no such thing as monogamy, but it is not necessary for our purpose to dwell upon that age. The first era that bears closely upon our subject is the matriarchal age, to which myths and folk-lore, in almost all countries, definitely point. The mother was the head of the family, priestess, and instructress in the arts of husbandry. She was the first agriculturist, the first herbalist, the initiator (says

Karl Pierson)[6] of all civilization. Of this age many discoveries have lately been made in Germany. The cave in which the mother took shelter and brought up her family was the germ of our "home." The family knew only one parent: the mother; her name was transmitted, and property—when that began to exist—was inherited through her, and her only. A woman's indefeasible right to her own child of course remained unquestioned, and it was not until many centuries later that men resorted to all kinds of curious devices with a view of claiming authority over children, which was finally established by force, entirely irrespective of moral right.

The idea of right always attaches itself in course of time to an established custom which is well backed up by force; and at the present day even persons of high moral feeling see no absurdity in the legal power of a man to dispose of his children contrary to the will of their mother. Not only does the man now claim a right to interfere, but he actually claims sole authority in cases of dispute. This would be incredible were it not a fact.

During the mother-age, some men of the tribe became wandering hunters, while others remained at home to till the soil. The hunters, being unable to procure wives in the woods and solitudes, used to make raids upon the settlements and carry off some of the women. This was the origin of our modern idea of possession in marriage. The woman became the property of the man, his own by right of conquest. Now the wife is his own by right of law.

It is John Stuart Mill, we believe, who says that woman was the first being who was enslaved.[7] A captured wife probably lost her liberty even before animals were pressed into man's service. In Germany, in early times, women were in the habit of dragging the plough. This and many similar facts, we may remark in passing, show that there is no inherent difference in physical strength between the two sexes, and that the present great difference is probably induced by difference of occupation extending backward over many generations.

The transition period from the mother-age to the father-age was long and painful. It took centuries to deprive the woman of her powerful position as head of the family, and of all the superstitious reverence which her knowledge of primitive arts and of certain properties of herbs, besides her influence as priestess, secured her. Of this long struggle we find many traces in old legends, in folk-lore, and in the survival of customs older than history. Much later, in the witch-persecutions of the Middle Ages, we come upon the remnants of belief in the woman's superior power and knowledge, and the determination of man to extinguish it.[8] The awe remained in the form of superstition, but the old reverence was changed to antagonism. We can note in early literature the feeling that women were evil creatures eager to obtain power, and that the man was nothing less than a coward who permitted this low and contemptible influence to make way against him.

During the transition period, capture-marriages, of course, met with strenuous opposition from the mother of the bride, not only as regarded the high-handed act itself, but also in respect to the changes relating to property which the establishment of father-rule brought about. Thus we find a hereditary basis for the (no doubt) divinely instilled and profoundly natural repugnance of a man for his mother-in-law! This sentiment can claim the authority of centuries and almost equal rank as a primitive and sacred impulse of our nature with the maternal instinct itself. Almost might we speak of it tenderly and mellifluously as "beautiful."

On the spread of Christianity and the ascetic doctrines of its later teachers, feminine influence received another check. "Woman!" exclaims Tertullian[9] with startling frankness, "thou art the gate of hell!" This is the key-note of the monastic age. Woman was an ally of Satan, seeking to lead men away from the paths of righteousness. She appears to have succeeded very brilliantly! We have a century of almost universal corruption, ushering in the period of the Minnesingers and the troubadours,[10] or what is called the age of chivalry. In spite of a licentious society, this age has given us the precious germ of a new idea with regard to sex-relationship, for art and poetry now began to soften and beautify the cruder passion, and we have the first hint of a distinction which can be quite clearly felt between love as represented by classical authors and what may be called modern, or romantic, love—as a recent writer named it. This nobler sentiment, when developed and still further inwoven with ideas of modern growth, forms the basis of the ideal marriage, which is founded upon a full attraction and expression of the whole nature.

But this development was checked, though the idea was not destroyed, by the Reformation. It is to Luther and his followers that we can immediately trace nearly all the notions that now govern the world with regard to marriage. Luther was essentially coarse and irreverent towards the oppressed sex; he placed marriage on the lowest possible platform, and, as one need scarcely add, he did not take women into counsel in a matter so deeply concerning them.[11] In the age of chivalry the marriage-tie was not at all strict, and our present ideas of "virtue" and "honour" were practically nonexistent. Society was in what is called a chaotic state; there was extreme licence on all sides and although the standard of morality was far severer for the woman than for the man, still she had more or less liberty to give herself as passion dictated, and society tacitly accorded her a right of choice in matters of love. But Luther ignored all the claims of passion in a woman; in fact, she had no recognized claims whatever; she was not permitted to object to any part in life that might be assigned her; the notion of resistance to his decision never occurred to him—her *rôle* was one of duty and of service; she figured as the legal property of a man, the safeguard against sin, and the victim of that vampire "Respectability" which thenceforth was to fasten upon, and suck the life-blood of all womanhood.

The change from the open licence of the age of chivalry to the decorum of the Philistine *régime*,[12] was merely a change in the *mode* of licentiousness, not a move from evil to good. Hypocrisy became a household god; true passion was dethroned, and with it poetry and romance; the commercial spirit, staid and open-eyed, entered upon its long career, and began to regulate the relations of the sexes. We find a peculiar medley of sensuality and decorum: the mercenary spirit entering into the idea of marriage, women were bought and sold as if they were cattle, and were educated, at the same time, to strict ideas of "purity" and duty, to Griselda-like patience[13] under the severest provocation. Carried off by the highest bidder, they were gravely exhorted to be moral, to be chaste, and faithful and God-fearing, serving their lords in life and in death. To drive a hard bargain, and to sermonize one's victims at the same time, is a feat distinctly of the Philistine order. With the growth of the commercial system, of the rich burgher class, and of all the ideas that thrive under the influence of wealth when divorced from mental cultivation, the status of women gradually established itself upon this degrading basis, and became fixed more and more firmly as the *bourgeois* increased in power and prosperity.

Bebel speaks of Luther as the interpreter of the "healthy sensualism" of the Middle Ages.[14] Any "healthy sensualism," however, which did not make itself legitimate by appeal to the Church and the law was rigorously punished under his system. Women offenders were subject to hideous and awful forms of punishment. Thus we may say that Luther established, in the interests of sensuality and respectability, a strict marriage system. He also preached the devastating doctrine which makes it a duty to have an unlimited number of children. Of course he did not for a moment consider the woman in this matter; why should a thick-skinned, coarse-fibred monk of the sixteenth century consider sufferings which are overlooked by tender-hearted divines of the nineteenth century? The gentle Melanchthon[15] on this subject says as follows: "If a woman becomes weary of bearing children, that matters not; let her only die from bearing, she is there to do it." This doctrine is not obsolete at the present day. It is the rule of life among the mass of our most highly respectable classes, those who hold the scales of public morality in their hands, and whose prerogative appears to be to judge in order that they be not judged.

As an instance of the way in which an exceptionally good man can regard this subject—his goodness notwithstanding—we may turn to the Introduction, by Charles Kingsley, to Brook's *Fool of Quality*, which Kingsley edited.[16] A short account is given of the life of Brook, who flourished (in a very literal sense) in the time of the Restoration, and who was saved, as his biographer points out in joy and thankfulness, from the vices of that corrupt age, by an early marriage. Kingsley goes on to describe the home where all that is commendable and domestic reigned and prospered. He dwells lovingly on that pleasant picture of simple joys and happy cares, upon the swarms of beautiful children who cluster round their father's knee and rescue him from the dangers of a licentious age. Kingsley mentions, just in passing, that the young wife watches the happy scene from a sofa, having become a confirmed invalid from the number of children she has borne during the few years of her married life. But what of that? What of the anguish and weariness, what of the thousand painful disabilities which that young woman has suffered before her nature yielded to the strain—disabilities which she will have to bear to her life's end? Has not the valuable Brook been saved from an immoral life? (Of course Brook could not be expected to save himself!—we are not unreasonable.) Have not Propriety and Respectability been propitiated? And the price of all this? Merely the suffering and life-long injury of one young woman in a thoroughly established and "natural" manner; nothing more. Kingsley feels that it is cheap at the price. *Brook is saved!* Hallelujah!

It is difficult to think without acrimony of the great reformer, conscious though we may be of the untold benefits which he has bestowed upon mankind. It is because of Luther that women are martyred daily in the interests of virtue and propriety! It is to Luther that we owe half the inconsistencies and cruelties of our social laws, to Luther that we owe the extreme importance of the marriage-rite, which is to make the whole difference between terrible sin and absolute duty.

"The Catholic Church had before Luther taught that marriage was a sacrament. We should be the last to defend the truth of such a conception, but we must call attention to the fact that it emphasized something beyond the physical in the conjugal relation, it endowed it with a *spiritual* side. The conception of marriage as a spiritual as well as physical relation seems to us the essential condition of all permanent happiness between man and wife. The intellectual union superposed on the physical is precisely what raises human above brute intercourse.... We believe that the spiritual side must be kept constantly in view if the sanctity of marriage is to be preserved. Here it is that Luther, rejecting the conception of marriage as a sacrament, rushes, with his usual impetuosity, into the opposite and more dangerous extreme."[17]

Luther in destroying the religious sanctity of marriage destroyed also the idea of spiritual union which the religious conception implied;[18] he did his utmost to deprive it of the elements of real affection and sympathy, and to bring it to the very lowest form which it is capable of assuming. It was to be regarded merely as means of avoiding general social chaos; as a "safeguard against sin;" and the wife's position—unless human laws have some supernatural power of sanctification—was the most completely abject and degraded position which it is possible for a human being to hold.

That Luther did not observe the insult to womanhood of such a creed is not to be wondered at, since the nineteenth century has scarcely yet discovered it. Of course from such ideas spring rigid ideas of wifehood. Woman's chastity becomes the watch-dog of man's possession. She has taken the sermon given to her at the time of her purchase deeply to heart, and chastity becomes her chief virtue. If we desire to face the matter honestly, we must not blink at the fact that this virtue has originally no connection with the woman's own nature; it does *not* arise from the feelings which protect individual dignity. The quality, whatever be its intrinsic merits, has attained its present mysterious authority and rank through man's monopolizing jealousy, through the fact that he desired to "have and to hold"[19] one woman as his exclusive property, and that he regarded any other man who would dispute his monopoly as the unforgivable enemy. From this starting-point the idea of a man's "honour" grew up, creating the remarkable paradox of a moral possession or attribute, which could be injured by the action of some other person than the possessor. Thus also arose woman's "honour," which was lost if she did not keep herself solely for her lord, present or to come. Again, we see that *her* honour has reference to some one other than herself, though in course of time the idea was carried further, and has now acquired a relation with the woman's own moral nature, and a still firmer hold upon the conscience. However valuable the quality, it certainly did not take its rise from a sense of self-respect in woman, but from the fact of her subjection to man.

While considering the development of this burgher age, one must not forget to note the concurrence of strict marriage and systematic or legalized prostitution. The social chaos of the age of chivalry was exchanged for comparative order, and there now arose a hard-and-fast line (far more absolute than had existed before in Germany) between two classes of women: those who submitted to the yoke of marriage on Luther's terms, and those who remained on the other side of the great social gulf, subject also to stringent laws, and treated also as the property of men (though not of *one* man). We now see completed our own way of settling the relations of the sexes. The factors of our system are: respectability, prostitution, strict marriage, commercialism, unequal standard for the two sexes, and the subjection of women.

In this brief sketch we have not dwelt upon the terrible sufferings of the subject sex through all the changes of their estate; to do so in a manner to produce realization would lead us too far afield and would involve too many details. Suffice it to say that the cruelties, indignities, and insults to which women were exposed are (as every student of history knows) hideous beyond description. In Mongolia there are large cages in the market-place wherein condemned prisoners are kept and starved to death. The people collect in front of these cages to taunt and insult the victims as they die slowly day by day before their eyes. In reading the history of the past, and even the literature of our own day, it is difficult to avoid seeing in that Mongolian market-place a symbol of our own society, with its iron cage, wherein women are held in bondage, suffering moral starvation, while the thoughtless gather round to taunt and insult their lingering misery. Let any one who thinks this exaggerated and unjust, note the manner in which our own novelists, for instance, past and present, treat all subjects connected with women, marriage, and motherhood, and then ask himself if he does not recognize at once its ludicrous inconsistency and its cruel insults to womanhood, open and implied. The very respect, so called, of man for woman, being granted solely on condition of her observing certain restrictions of thought and action dictated by him, conceals a subtle sort of insolence. It is really the pleased approval of a lawgiver at the sight of obedient subjects. The pitiful cry of Elsie in *The Golden Legend* has had many a repetition in the hearts of women age after age—

"Why should I live? Do I not know
The life of woman is full of woe!
    Toiling on, and on, and on,
With breaking heart, and tearful eyes,
    And silent lips, and in the soul
The secret longings that arise
Which this world never satisfies!"[20]

So much for the past and its relation to the present. Now we come to the problem of to-day. This is extremely complex. We have a society ruled by Luther's views on marriage; we have girls brought up to regard it as their destiny; and we have, at the same time, such a large majority of women that they cannot all marry, even (as I think Miss Clapperton[21] puts it) if they had the fascinations of Helen of Troy and Cleopatra rolled into one. We find, therefore, a number of women thrown on the world to earn their own living in the face of every sort of discouragement. Competition runs high for all, and even were there no prejudice to encounter, the struggle would be a hard one; as it is, life for poor and single women becomes a mere treadmill. It is folly to inveigh against mercenary marriages, however degrading they may be, for a glance at the position of affairs shows that there is no reasonable alternative. We cannot ask every woman to be a heroine and chose a hard and thorny path when a comparatively smooth one, (as it seems), offers itself, and when the pressure of public opinion urges strongly in that direction. A few higher natures will resist and swell the crowds of worn-out, underpaid workers, but the majority will take the voice of society for the voice of God, or at any rate of wisdom, and our common respectable marriage—upon which the safety of all social existence is supposed to rest—will remain, as it is now, the worst, because the most hypocritical, form of woman-purchase. Thus we have on one side a more or less degrading marriage, and on the other side a number of women who cannot command an entry into that profession, but who must give up health and enjoyment of life in a losing battle with the world.

Babel is very eloquent upon the sufferings of unmarried women, which must be keen indeed for those who have been prepared for marriage and for nothing else, whose emotions have been stimulated and whose ideas have been coloured by the imagination of domestic cares and happiness. Society, having forbidden or discouraged other ambitions for women, flings them scornfully aside as failures when through its own organization they are unable to secure a fireside and a proper "sphere" in which to practise the womanly virtues. Insult and injury to women is literally the key-note and the foundation of society.

Mrs. Augusta Webster[22] amusingly points out the inconsistencies of popular notions on this subject. She says:—"People think women who do not want to marry unfeminine; people think women who do want to marry immodest; people combine both opinions by regarding it as unfeminine for women not to look forward longingly to wifehood as the hope and purpose of their lives, and ridiculing and contemning any individual woman of their acquaintance whom they suspect of entertaining such a longing. They must wish and not wish; they must by no means give, and they must certainly not withhold, encouragement—and so it goes on, each precept cancelling the last, and most of them negative." There are, doubtless, equally absurd social prejudices which hamper a man's freedom, by teaching girls and their friends to look for proposals, instead of regarding signs of interest and liking in a more wholesome spirit. We shall never have a world really worth living in until men and women can show interest in one another, without being driven either to marry or to forego altogether the pleasure and profit of frequent meeting. Nor will the world be really a pleasant world while it continues to make friendship between persons of opposite sexes well-nigh impossible by insisting that they *are* so, and thereby in a thousand direct and indirect ways brings about the fulfilment of its own prophecy. All this false sentiment and shallow shrewdness, with the restrictions they imply, make the ideal marriage—that is, a union prompted by love, by affinity or attraction of nature and by friendship—almost beyond the reach of this generation. While we are on this part of the subject it may be worth while to quote a typical example of some letters written to Max O'Rell on the publication of *The Daughters of John Bull*.[23] One lady of direct language exclaims fiercely, "Man is a beast!" and she goes on to explain in gleeful strains that, having been left a small fortune by a relative, she is able to dispense with the society of "the odious creature." Of course Max O'Rell warmly congratulates the "odious creature." "At last," another lady burst forth, "we have some one among us with wit to perceive that the life which a woman leads with the ordinary sherry-drinking, cigar-smoking husband is no better than that of an Eastern slave. Take my own case, which is that of thousands of others in our land. I belong to my lord and master, body and soul; the duties of a housekeeper, upper nurse, and governess are required of me; I am expected to be always at home, at my husband's beck and call. It is true that he feeds me, and that for his own glorification he gives me handsome clothing. It is also true that he does not beat me. For this I ought, of course, to be duly grateful; but I often think of what you say on the wife and servant question, and wonder how many of us would like to have the cook's privilege of being able to give warning to leave."

If the wife feels thus we may be sure the husband thinks he has his grievances also, and when we place this not exaggerated description side by side with that of the unhappy plight of bored husbands commiserated by Mrs. Lynn Linton,[24] there is no escaping the impression that there is something very "rotten in the state of Denmark." Amongst other absurdities, we have well-meaning husbands and wives harassing one another to death for no reason in the world but the desire of conforming to current notions regarding the proper conduct of married people. These victims are expected to go about perpetually together, as if they were a pair of carriage-horses; to be for ever holding claims over one another, exacting or making useless sacrifices, and generally getting in one another's way. The man who marries finds that his liberty has gone, and the woman exchanges one set of restrictions for another. She thinks herself neglected if the husband does not always return to her in the evenings, and the husband and society think her undutiful, frivolous, and so forth if she does not stay at home alone, trying to sigh him back again. The luckless man finds his wife so *very* dutiful and domesticated, and so *very* much confined to her "proper sphere," that she is, perchance, more exemplary than entertaining. Still she may look injured and resigned, but she must not seek society and occupation on her own account, adding to the common mental store, bringing new interest and knowledge into the joint existence, and becoming thus a contented, cultivated, and agreeable being. No wonder that while all this is forbidden we have so many unhappy wives and bored husbands. The more admirable the wives the more profoundly bored the husbands!

Of course there are bright exceptions to this picture of married life, but we are not dealing with exceptions. In most cases, the chain of marriage chafes the flesh, if it does not make a serious wound; and where there is happiness the happiness is dearly bought and is not on a very high plane. For husband and wife are then apt to forget everything in the absorbing but narrow interests of their home, to depend entirely upon one another, to steep themselves in the same ideas, till they become mere echoes, half creatures, useless to the world, because they have run into a groove and have let individuality die. There are few things more stolidly irritating than a very "united" couple. The likeness that may often be remarked between married people is a melancholy index of this united degeneration.

We come then to the conclusion that the present form of marriage— exactly in proportion to its conformity with orthodox ideas—is a vexatious failure. If certain people have made it a success by ignoring those orthodox ideas, such instances afford no argument in favour of the institution as it stands. We are also led to conclude that modern "Respectability" draws its life-blood from the degradation of womanhood in marriage and in prostitution. But what is to be done to remedy these manifold evils? how is marriage to be rescued from a mercenary society, torn from the arms of "Respectability," and established on a footing which will make it no longer an insult to human dignity?

First of all we must set up an ideal, undismayed by what will seem its Utopian impossibility. Every good thing that we enjoy to-day was once the dream of a "crazy enthusiast" mad enough to believe in the power of ideas and in the power of man to have things as he wills. The ideal marriage then, despite all dangers and difficulties, should be *free*. So long as love and trust and friendship remain, no bonds are necessary to bind two people together; life apart will be empty and colourless; but whenever these cease the tie becomes false and iniquitous, and no one ought to have power to enforce it. The matter is one in which any interposition, whether of law or of society, is an impertinence. Even the idea of "duty" ought to be excluded from the most perfect marriage, because the intense attraction of one being for another, the intense desire for one another's happiness, would make interchanges of whatever kind the outcome of a feeling far more passionate than that of duty. It need scarcely be said that there must be a full understanding and acknowledgment of the obvious right of the woman to *possess herself* body and soul, to give or withhold herself body and soul exactly as she wills. The moral right here is so palpable, and its denial implies ideas so low and offensive to human dignity, that no fear of consequences ought to deter us from making this liberty an element of our ideal, in fact its fundamental principle. Without it, no ideal could hold up its head. Moreover, "consequences" in the long run are never beneficent, where obvious moral rights are disregarded. The idea of a perfectly free marriage would imply the possibility of any form of contract being entered into between the two persons, the State and society standing aside, and recognizing the entirely private character of the transaction.

The economical independence of woman is the first condition of free marriage. She ought not to be tempted to marry, or to remain married, for the sake of bread and butter. But the condition is a very hard one to secure. Our present competitive system, with the daily increasing ferocity of the struggle for existence, is fast reducing itself to an absurdity, woman's labour helping to make the struggle only the fiercer. The problem now offered to the mind and conscience of humanity is to readjust its industrial organization in such a way as to gradually reduce this absurd and useless competition within reasonable limits, and to bring about in its place some form of co-operation, in which no man's interest will depend on the misfortune of his neighbour, but rather on his neighbour's happiness and welfare. It is idle to say that this cannot be done; the state of society shows quite clearly that it *must* be done sooner or later; otherwise some violent catastrophe will put an end to a condition of things which is hurrying towards impossibility. Under improved economical conditions the difficult problem of securing the real independence of women, and thence of the readjustment of their position in relation to men and to society would find easy solution.

When girls and boys are educated together, when the unwholesome atmosphere of social life becomes fresher and nobler, when the pressure of existence slackens (as it will and *must* do), and when the whole nature has thus a chance to expand, such additions to the scope and interest of life will cease to be thought marvellous or "unnatural." "Human nature" has more variety of powers and is more responsive to conditions than we imagine. It is hard to believe in things for which we feel no capacity in ourselves, but fortunately such things exist in spite of our placid unconsciousness. Give room for the development of individuality, and individuality develops, to the amazement of spectators! Give freedom in marriage, and each pair will enter upon their union after their own particular fashion, creating a refreshing diversity in modes of life, and consequently of character. Infinitely preferable will this be to our own gloomy uniformity, the offspring of our passion to be in all things exactly like our neighbours.

The proposed freedom in marriage would of course have to go hand-in-hand with the co-education of the sexes. It is our present absurd interference with the natural civilizing influences of one sex upon the other, that creates half the dangers and difficulties of our social life, and gives colour to the fears of those who would hedge round marriage with a thousand restraints or so-called safeguards, ruinous to happiness and certainly not productive of a satisfactory social condition. Already the good results of this method of co-education have been proved by experiment in America, but we ought to go farther in this direction than our go-ahead cousins have yet gone. Meeting freely in their working-hours as well as at times of recreation, men and women would have opportunity for forming reasonable judgments of character, for making friendships irrespective of sex, and for giving and receiving that inspiring influence which apparently can only be given by one sex to the other.[25] There would also be a chance of forming genuine attachments founded on friendship; marriage would cease to be the haphazard thing it is now; girls would no longer fancy themselves in love with a man because they had met none other on terms equally intimate, and they would not be tempted to marry for the sake of freedom and a place in life, for existence would be free and full from the beginning.

The general rise in health, physical and moral, following the improvement in birth, surroundings and training, would rapidly tell upon the whole state of society. Any one who has observed carefully knows how grateful a response the human organism gives to improved conditions, if only these remain constant. We should have to deal with healthier, better equipped, more reasonable men and women, possessing well-developed minds, and hearts kindly disposed towards their fellow-creatures. Are such people more likely to enter into a union frivolously and ignorantly than are the average men and women of to-day? Surely not. If the number of divorces did not actually decrease there would be the certainty that no couple remained united against their will, and that no lives were sacrificed to a mere convention. With the social changes which would go hand in hand with changes in the status of marriage, would come inevitably many fresh forms of human power, and thus all sorts of new and stimulating influences would be brought to bear upon society. No man has a right to consider himself educated until he has been under the influence of cultivated women, and the same may be said of women as regards men.[26] Development involves an increase of complexity. It is so in all forms of existence, vegetable and animal; it is so in human life. It will be found that men and women as they increase in complexity can enter into a numberless variety of relationships, abandoning no good gift that they now possess, but adding to their powers indefinitely, and thence to their emotions and experiences. The action of the man's nature upon the woman's and of the woman's upon the man's, is now only known in a few instances; there is a whole world yet to explore in this direction, and it is more than probable that the future holds a discovery in the domain of spirit as great as that of Columbus in the domain of matter.

With regard to the dangers attending these readjustments, there is no doubt much to be said. The evils that hedge around marriage are linked with other evils, so that movement is difficult and perilous indeed. Nevertheless, we have to remember that we now live in the midst of dangers, and that human happiness is cruelly murdered by our systems of legalized injustice. By sitting still circumspectly and treating our social system as if it were a card-house which would tumble down at a breath, we merely wait to see it fall from its own internal rottenness, and *then* we shall have dangers to encounter indeed! The time has come, not for violent overturning of established institutions before people admit that they are evil, but for a gradual alteration of opinion which will rebuild them from the very foundation. The method of the most enlightened reformer is to crowd out old evil by new good, and to seek to sow the seed of the nobler future where alone it can take root and grow to its full height: in the souls of men and women. Far-seeing we ought to be, but we know in our hearts right well that fear will never lead us to the height of our ever-growing possibility. Evolution has ceased to be a power driving us like dead leaves on a gale; thanks to science, we are no longer entirely blind, and we aspire to direct that mighty force for the good of humanity. We see a limitless field of possibility opening out before us; the adventurous spirit in us might leap up at the wonderful romance of life! We recognize that no power, however trivial, fails to count in the general sum of things which moves this way or that—towards heaven or hell, according to the preponderating motives of individual units. We shall begin, slowly but surely, to see the folly of permitting the forces of one sex to pull against and neutralize the workings of the other, to the confusion of our efforts and the checking of our progress. We shall see, in the relations of men and women to one another, the source of all good or of all evil, precisely as those relations are true and noble and equal or false and low and unjust. With this belief we shall seek to move opinion in all the directions that may bring us to this "consummation devoutly to be wished,"[27] and we look forward steadily, hoping and working for the day when men and women shall be comrades and fellow-workers as well as lovers and husbands and wives, when the rich and many-sided happiness which they have the power to bestow one on another shall no longer be enjoyed in tantalizing snatches, but shall gladden and give new life to all humanity. That will be the day prophesied by Lewis Morris in *The New Order*—

> "When man and woman in an equal union
> Shall merge, and marriage be a true communion."[28]

"DOES MARRIAGE HINDER A WOMAN'S SELF-DEVELOPMENT?"

MONA CAIRD

[*Lady's Realm* 5 (March 1899): 581-83]

Perhaps it might throw some light on the question whether marriage interferes with a woman's self-development and career, if we were to ask ourselves honestly how a man would fare in the position, say, of his own wife.

We will take a mild case, so as to avoid all risk of exaggeration.

Our hero's wife is very kind to him. Many of his friends have far sadder tales to tell. Mrs. Brown is fond of her home and family. She pats the children on the head when they come down to dessert, and plies them with chocolate creams, much to the detriment of their health; but it amuses Mrs. Brown. Mr. Brown superintends the bilous attacks, which the lady attributes to other causes. As she never finds fault with the children, and generally remonstrates with their father, in a good-natured way, when *he* does so, they are devoted to the indulgent parent, and are inclined to regard the other as second-rate.

Meal-times are often trying in this household, for Sophia is very particular about her food; sometimes she sends it out with a rude message to the cook. Not that John objects to this. He wishes she would do it oftener, for the cook gets used to Mr. Brown's second-hand version of his wife's language. He simply cannot bring himself to hint at Mrs. Brown's robust objurations. She *can* express herself when it comes to a question of her creature comforts!

John's faded cheeks, the hollow lines under the eyes, and hair out of curl, speak of the struggle for existence as it penetrates to the fireside. If Sophia but knew what it meant to keep going the multitudinous details and departments of a household! Her idea of adding housemaids and page-boys whenever there is a jolt in the machinery has landed them in expensive disasters, time out of mind. And then, it hopelessly cuts off all margin of income for every other purpose. It is all rather discouraging for the hero of this petty, yet gigantic tussle, for he works, so to speak, in a hostile camp, with no sympathy from his entirely unconscious spouse, whom popular sentiment nevertheless regards as the gallant protector of his manly weakness.

If incessant vigilance, tact, firmness, foresight, initiative, courage and judgment—in short, all the qualities required for governing a kingdom, and more—have made things go smoothly, the wife takes it as a matter of course; if they go wrong, she naturally lays the blame on the husband. In the same way, if the children are a credit to their parents, that is only as it should be. But if they are naughty, and fretful, and stupid, and untidy, is it not clear that there must be some serious flaw in the system which could produce such results in the offspring of Mrs. Brown? What word in the English language is too severe to describe the man who neglects to watch with sufficient vigilance over his children's health and moral training, who fails to see that his little boys' sailor-suits and knickerbockers are in good repair, that their boot-lace ends do not fly out from their ankles at every step, that their hair is not like a hearth-brush, that they do not come down to dinner every day with dirty hands?

To every true man, the cares of fatherhood and home are sacred and all-sufficing. He realizes, as he looks around at his little ones, that they are his crown and recompense.

John often finds that *his* crown-and-recompense gives him a racking headache by war-whoops and stampedes of infinite variety, and there are moments when he wonders in dismay if he is really a true man! He has had the privilege of rearing and training five small crowns and recompenses, and he feels that he could face the future if further privilege, of this sort, were denied him. Not but that he is devoted to his family. Nobody who understands the sacrifices he has made for them could doubt that. Only, he feels that those parts of his nature which are said to distinguish the human from the animal kingdom, are getting rather effaced.

He remembers the days before his marriage, when he was so bold, in his ignorant youth, as to cherish a passion for scientific research. He even went so far as to make a chemical laboratory of the family box-room, till attention was drawn to the circumstance by a series of terrific explosions, which shaved off his eyebrows, blackened his scientific countenance, and caused him to be turned out, neck and crop, with his crucibles, and a sermon on the duty that lay nearest him,—which resolved itself into that of paying innumerable afternoon calls with his father and brothers, on acquaintances selected—as he declared in his haste—for their phenomenal stupidity. His father pointed out how selfish it was for a young fellow to indulge his own little fads and fancies, when he might make himself useful in a nice manly way, at home.

When, a year later, the scapegrace Josephine, who had caused infinite trouble and expense to all belonging to her, showed a languid interest in chemistry, a spare room was at once fitted up for her, and an extraordinary wealth of crucibles provided by her delighted parents; and when explosions and smells pervaded the house, her father, with a proud smile, would exclaim: "What genius and enthusiasm that dear girl does display!" Sophia afterwards became a distinguished professor, with an awestruck family, and a husband who made it his chief duty and privilege to save her from all worry and interruption in her valuable work.

John, who knows in his heart of hearts that he could have walked round Josephine, in the old days, now speaks with manly pride of his sister, the Professor. His own bent, however, has always been so painfully strong that he even yet tries to snatch spare moments for his researches; but the strain in so many directions has broken down his health. People always told him that a man's constitution was not fitted for severe brain-work. He supposes it is true.

During those odd moments, he made a discovery that seemed to him of value, and he told Sophia about it, in a mood of scientific enthusiasm. But she burst out laughing, and said he would really be setting the Thames on fire if he didn't take care.

"Perhaps you will excuse my remarking, my dear, that I think you might be more usefully, not to say becomingly employed, in attending to your children and your household duties, than in dealing with explosive substances in the back dining-room."

And Sophia tossed off her glass of port in such an unanswerable manner, that John felt as if a defensive reply would be almost of the nature of a sacrilege. So he remained silent, feeling vaguely guilty. And as Johnny took measles just then, and it ran through the house, there was no chance of completing his work, or of making it of public value.

Curiously enough, a little later, Josephine made the very same discovery—only rather less perfect—and every one said, with acclamation, that science had been revolutionised by a discovery before which that of gravitation paled.

John still hoped, after twenty years of experience, that presently, by some different arrangement, some better management on his part, he would achieve leisure and mental repose to do the work that his heart was in; but that time never came.

No doubt John was not infallible, and made mistakes in dealing with his various problems: do the best of us achieve consummate wisdom? No doubt, if he had followed the advice that we could all have supplied him with, in such large quantities, he might have done rather more than he did. But the question is: Did his marriage interfere with his self-development and career, and would many other Johns, in his circumstances, have succeeded much better?

"DOES MARRIAGE HINDER
A WOMAN'S SELF-DEVELOPMENT?"

GERTRUDE ATHERTON

[*Lady's Realm* 5 (March 1899): 579]

If a woman deliberately goes in for a career, and her gifts and ambitions are both above the average, she certainly should make up her mind to stand alone. Women are still too concentrative to do two things well. Matrimony in itself is a career, and if the man happens to be interesting the woman is almost sure to give him her best, and put what is left into any work she attempts. Of course, the average woman who writes or paints is either a *dilettante* or is working for bread, and for them matrimony, unless they draw a vicious or dependent being, is rather an advantage than otherwise; they have some one to help them pay the bills, or to encourage and advise them. But when one mounts to the plane of Art the questions of sex and of the ego cease to exist, and if a woman has made up her mind to train her gifts to the highest perfection, and to rise to the first rank, then she must leave personal happiness to other people, and concentrate every faculty upon the extreme development of the one which carries ambition with it.

After all, personal happiness, as distinguished from the content which may or may not succeed it, is a transient thing, whereas an author who really loves her work, and does not create under pressure, is thoroughly happy every time she writes a book. It is a sort of mental passion, and, unlike a succession of love-affairs, is equally fresh and keen each time. One makes one's own world in creating a novel, for instance, and the unexpected—in which I never found the traditional pleasure, for I hate to be bothered—does not exist. If you have a love affair, the man can die, or transfer his affections, or *you* tire—which is more tragic still—or other people worry you about it—to say nothing of the fact that you are a mass of sensitive nerves; but if you go and shut yourself up in some old European city with your work, the world and all its details cease to exist, and you become so detached from practical life that you are incapable of receiving a personal impression.

When I am in the middle of a book I might hear of the death of every relative I have in the world, and it would mean nothing to me whatever. Of course, this means that in time one is less and less capable of receiving personal impressions; one becomes more and more a mere faculty in an increasing state of development; your sense of your own ego becomes smaller and smaller, and your one desire and determination is to do your best by the peculiar twist your brain has taken, and let everything else go.

Now, all this would be very hard on a husband, and I do not think that a woman whose ambitions rise as high, and whose powers of concentration are as great as those I have just described, has any right to marry. When a man offers a woman his name, his affections, and his support, he has a right to expect equal measure in return. If a woman of talent is prepared to give this measure, she must resign herself to being a *dilettante.* If she wants to be great she must go the pace alone and hope for the other happiness in another life.

It is of great advantage to have been married a little while in the beginning, but I do not know how that can be managed satisfactorily, if Fate is not kind enough to take the matter in hand.

"A Young Woman's Right: Knowledge"

Julia M.A. Hawksley

[*Westminster Review* 142 (September 1894): 315-18]

By this I do not mean scholarship. The battle of the higher education of women was long ago fought and won. Every woman who is endowed with the necessary talents and tastes, and can command the needful time and money, may become, so far as study is concerned, almost what she will. Nor is the boon the less because those who as yet avail themselves of their opportunities are an infinitesimal minority. But this is beside my subject.

The knowledge, a claim to which I urge on behalf of all maidenhood, is of a vastly different nature. It is a knowledge which, no more than any other, comes by intuition or by inspiration. It is a knowledge the possession of which would mould differently many lives, change the destinies of sundry families and prevent the wreckage of much faith and hope. It is a knowledge the bestowal of which is at the option of each mother and is the right of every daughter. It is a knowledge which, from the nature of things, is most easily withheld from girls of the upper classes, since theirs are the lives most closely confined within the home radius and sheltered from outside influences. On them, therefore, falls the chief suffering. It is a knowledge the first glimmer of which caused Eve to make herself aprons of fig-leaves, but which does not dawn upon one and another of Eve's descendants until the apron is cast away, and the woman stands helpless and ashamed.

A mere truism is it to say that young women to-day are trained in a far broader and more precocious school than that in which their grandmothers were taught. True, that the blunter words of Shakespeare are expunged from the acting editions, that Sheridan's situations are apt to raise a blush, and that Swift[29] is considered coarse. Yet actual children read newspapers, hear social subjects analysed, and form independent opinions in a manner which, I suppose, would have been considered indecent half a century ago. The older folks, whose youth is visible only through a vista of past decades, but who acquiesce in this *fin-de-siècle* order, certainly, by so doing, afford proof that they have in the interim discovered that their own up-bringing was not unimpeachable. And indeed that present-day life has unique advantages is unquestionable. But still, however much surface-freedom of action, speech, and reading is permitted, there is yet one subject which can happily never become a topic talked or written of publicly in such terms as to be grasped by the untutored mind. The misfortune is that it is also a topic equally tabooed between those to whom, of right, its discussion belongs. Girls are to-day constantly married without any more idea of what matrimony implies than has been imparted by the prurient, whispered gossip of an impure-minded schoolfellow; and frequently—especially, as I have said, in the case of members of high-born families—without even that modicum of enlightenment. This condition of things, moreover, is regarded by many a satisfied matron as proving the perfection of watchful guardianship upon her own part and of sweet pliability upon that of her child.

And why?

Men, we are told, like to perform their own initiation. Men, it is constantly and truly said, prefer girls of innocent mind. In which latter statement, by the by, crops up the old, old confusion between innocence and ignorance. Men desire that their wives should realise nothing of the inner secrets and vast divergences of passing passion and of lasting love. This, too, in spite of, or, perhaps because of, the fact that they themselves almost invariably claim the privilege of ante-nuptial revelation, a revelation not only of theory, but also of practice. For what proportion of bridegrooms could declare that they present the same conditions of physical purity as they demand? And thus, as ever, are the women sacrificed for the men's gratification. Sacrificed in the most cruel, the most needless, the most irrevocable fashion of all. Because sacrificed in ignorance.

For wifehood and motherhood are professions, as truly as are medicine, and literature, and the law. No lad is compelled to make his choice between the half hundred occupations open to him with his eyes shut. Few are educated without some regard to particular gifts, or are subsequently driven into a special calling without the option afforded by the explanation of the step that is being taken. Yet, is it not a fact that there are many women who, if they were informed as to what is implied by wedded life, would fly from the idea; women whose sexual instincts are those of repulsion instead of attraction; women whose mental and spiritual attitude for weeks, months, and even years will, in case of marriage, be but a long shrinking from their own bodies, a loathing of the flesh in which their souls are clothed? Yet women who, until too late, do not know.

Not indeed that such knowledge will always, or perhaps often, prove a deterrent or secure voluntary celibacy. Woman's love, customarily regarded as a beautiful generality, is, in fact, as individually various as all her other idiosyncracies. There is, for instance, the self-denying affection which, itself devoid of passion, will submit to any imposition in order to enhance the happiness or well-being of its object. That is not precisely the same as the love which would face marriage, as it would brave death itself, rather than endure separation. Which, again, is different from the burning passion that looks forward to complete union as to the consummation of its own bliss. Yet still freedom of choice does remain a right, though comprehension may increase self-denial, make pain the alternative of parting, or deepen a sensuous yearning. For with whom can rest the liberty of withholding it?

It is a cult, nowadays, to talk of such ignorance as I have indicated as of unusual and, indeed, of almost impossible preservation. An absurd cult. For at the best, or the worst, what better than ignorance is the information imparted by girlish gossip, mingled with wondering conjecture and hysteric laughter? It is not from so tainted a source that the earliest disclosure of the deepest mysteries of womanhood should reach the uncontaminated mind. Certainly it is not from such a source alone that revelation should be derived before the die is irretrievably cast, and all pre-conceived ideas are merged in an experience which renders speech unavailing. Upon whom, then, does the responsibility lie? Surely upon the mothers and guardians of the young, the mothers who, speaking of that which in all purity they understand, can impart a knowledge which it is not theirs to deny. Passion, which is not and never will be love, would surely be ofttimes restrained from a wretched consummation, the sanctity of the marriage tie would be more regarded, and as a consequence divorce would become a thing of less frequent occurrence, if those women who are parents could be induced to realise and to face their accountability in this matter. They provide for their daughters thorough and fitting teaching as to all things else in heaven and earth. Why not in this, which to many may be the most crucial subject of all? When, before they stand at the altar, girls know to what they will be yielding themselves; when they understand the distinction, the huge distinction, between lust and love, animalism and affection, carnality and comradeship; when they possess the liberty of a comprehending, voluntary choice—then, and not until then, will they have their right.

A girl, four or five days before her marriage, went to her mother and implored to be told what that was which lay before her, to which her vows would commit her. She had heard much that to her seemed horrible to incredulity, repellent beyond words. She was half frantic with a vague dread, worse than any certainty. And she craved to know. But she was laughed at and refused. Why? A bride upon her husband's first approach believed him mad, and in her dread tried to reach a bell and summon help. Why? A man consulting a specialist upon a constitutional sexual ailment, mentioned his wife, who was also his confidante. The doctor deprecated any such confidence towards a wife, whose mind, he considered, should be "like a sheet of white paper." Why?

Because men will to have it so, and mothers shrink from the task—truly a terrible task—involved. Perhaps they forget their own past suffering. Perhaps they are oblivious of the fact that every day women are becoming more sensitive, more highly strung, and therefore more and more capable of mental agony, more and more liable to the tortures of morbidity. However that may be, certain it is that innumerable girls are still the victims, on the one hand, of ignorance, and, upon the other, of that natural inquisitiveness which causes them to seek from corrupt sources the intelligence which they crave.

Nor are the consequences of this reticence upon the part of those who ought to speak confined to such as I have sketched. In too many cases, when a girl, high spirited and healthy, with all her natural instincts in full, though unconscious, play, with a mind either uninformed or misinformed, is flung into the whirlpool of modern life and granted the liberty of present day action, still vaster evil may ensue. The modesty which a few plain, womanly words might have preserved uninjured, and none the less profound because self-revealed, is soiled and undermined by innuendoes and suggestions but half comprehended. Equivocal situations lead to unequivocal results. And the maiden's purity, risked with the audacity of the experimenter, is lost with the irrecoverableness of fate. Only not fate, but ignorance—a remediable ignorance—is the cause.

The matter remains with the mothers—mothers not merely in the carnal, but also in the moral and spiritual sense—those elder women, in fact, in whose hands rest the education of the rising generation. The preservation of true innocence, that horribly maligned but most beautiful word; the dispelling of a blinding mist of misconception; the prevention of untold suffering; all hang upon their decision. Let them grant to their charges the right which those charges cannot claim. Otherwise will the young, rash creatures, in the first flush of unrecognised passion, determine, by a headlong rush into matrimony, the whole course of their lives; or, already in a measure demoralised by a sense of secrecy and wrongdoing, seek enlightenment from unauthorised oracles. Let them give to their daughters a choice, a fair choice, lighted by understanding. Or let them themselves bear the reproach of soiled and strangled virtue, of discovery made too late. But the weight of sin and of pain they cannot assume. Such must for ever lie upon the persons and the souls of those whom they might have saved.

"The Voice of Woman"

H.E. Harvey

[*Westminster Review* 145 (February 1896): 193-96]

It is only during the last twenty years or so that the voice of woman has really been heard in literature. The women who distinguished themselves as writers before that time wrote under the influence of the social laws and literature which had been established by male feeling—because it was their interest to do so. Being entirely dependent on marriage as a profession, the woman of the past found it her interest to train herself in those qualities which made her attractive to men, humility being conspicuous among them. Even Charlotte Brontë, one of the most original and independent of women writers, stoutly maintained the inferiority of women.

This necessity for meeting the demands of the marriage market has given to the sex an artificial character of subservience and servility which I suppose was pleasing to the men of the past, and is still to a large number; but I observe that for the most part the men of the present day are more ready to admire women of an independent turn of mind. The effects of this system showed themselves in many ways, notably in the writings of literary women, who always wrote from a masculine point of view, and preached subserviency to their own sex. A very good example of this style of writing is Mdme. Cottin's *Exiles of Siberia*,[30] in which the author is very careful to point out the superior wisdom of Elizabeth's father as compared with her mother—the mother being, at the same time, all that a mother ought to be. It showed itself in the special training which was formerly given to girls, who were taught chiefly showy accomplishments, which were likely to make them attractive to men, with merely a smattering of serious knowledge. Modesty, gentleness, and humility were much insisted on as suitable feminine qualifications.

It shows itself still in the readiness of women to blame one another, especially those among them who have fallen from the path of virtue, while they overlook the shortcomings of men.

It shows itself in the underhand arts practised by many women, more especially in the working classes, who do not scruple to deceive their husbands in order to carry on in private something which he has forbidden—the man, all the while, believing, in a blustering sort of way, that he is master in his own house. The woman does this in order to preserve the domestic peace, and have her own way at the same time.

The woman who is so indignant when any one tries to prevent her husband beating her is another result of this teaching.

Man has always posed as the protector of the weaker sex; but, with the best intentions, is it possible that he can thoroughly understand the interests of a creature different from himself, without consulting her opinion? The law which denied property to married women proved that he did not. Now, the woman of the present day has suddenly discovered that she has opinions of her own respecting her welfare; and those men and women who deride the extravagance of some of the female writers of our times would do well, before they scoff, to consider calmly what these women have to say, and see if there is any cause for their complaints. Until now, men have had it all their own way in literature; and what they have written about women may be broadly divided under three heads—the first division being by far the largest.

1. Raptures written by men who are in love about the beauty and graces of women.

2. Complaints of married men about the trials of domestic life and the unreasonableness of women. (Good examples may be found in some of Lord Lytton's novels.)[31]

3. Ill-natured sneers at old maids or women who are supposed to wish to marry. (Such as those written by Dickens and Smollett.)[32]

Of course, there are some notable exceptions to this rule, such as Solomon's description of the virtuous woman.[33]

Now, I do not for a moment suppose that the writings which I have mentioned show the average feeling of men towards women. The great majority of the men who are contented with their lot do not find it necessary to say so. We all know that the unfortunate have more to tell than the fortunate. The lover writes because he has not obtained what he desires. But I wish to point out that the women who were dissatisfied with their lot were obliged to make their complaints in private, to each other, because public feeling was such that if a wife did not agree with her husband she was blamed. The woman who complained of ceaseless child-bearing was told by husband and doctor that it was "the will of God" that she should spend her whole life in producing children. We see by the writings of Shakespeare how much meekness and subserviency was expected from a wife in his time. She must be ready to forgive any insult or backsliding on the part of her husband, being herself required to be blameless. No matter how badly he has treated her, she is ready to beg him, on her knees it may be, to receive her back again, because her honour and reputation depend on her being recognised as his wife. There is another, and still more degraded, modern type of heroine, who, I fancy, exists only in the imagination of male poets and novelists. This class of woman does not beg for her reputation; she is ready to sacrifice reputation, honour, happiness, life, everything that is hers, and a good deal that is not hers, for the sake of the man she loves, without receiving anything in return. Such an one is "Joan Haste."[34] But there is no place for self-respect in the manners and customs which owe their being to the marriage laws. Even at the present day, a woman whose husband has been unfaithful to her is allowed no redress. Dr. Johnson distinctly stated that he would not receive back a daughter who left her husband on these grounds, because he considered that it would be her own fault that she had not succeeded in pleasing him![35]

The artificial distinction conferred by society on the married woman as compared with the unmarried, combined with the difficulty of qualifying themselves for other professions, is, of course, the great inducement to marriage with the majority of women, as very many women, who do not care for domestic life, would greatly prefer independence and liberty. But they marry because society expects it of them, and tempts them with the promise of its favours.

The unmarried woman who is deserted by her lover has, of course, always been a scapegoat in the eyes of society, and it is only since George Eliot[36] took up her cause that it has become the fashion to interest ourselves in her. But here I must make a small exception, as there are several very pathetic Scotch and French ballads descriptive of her sorrows. And the most eloquent of these, "Ye Banks and Braes of Bonnie Doon,"[37] was written by a man. In a French ballad in the same style, which is not generally known, we have:

"Je veux que la rose
Soit encore au rosier;
Et que le rosier
Soit encore à planter."[38]

That such a woman, having become an outcast through the fault of a man, should be restored to her place in society by receiving the name of the villain who has injured her, is, I think, the most revolting of the principles which have been evolved from the marriage system. A perfect instance of the absurdity of this rule is *My Little Girl*, by Walter Besant.[39] The heroine has been deceived by a false marriage and deserted. Her betrayer is then ordered to marry her by another woman, who is supposed to be perfect. *They separate directly the ceremony is over.* Note this: the man was not worthy to live with her; and yet it was only by his deigning to confer his name on her that she could regain her self-respect and the respect of others! What a miserable, poor-spirited creature must a woman be who could submit to such a ceremony! But the absurdest part of the story has yet to come; for the poor villain has to be killed off in order to leave the girl at liberty to marry a man who is worthy of her!

We see the same principle illustrated in *The Vicar of Wakefield*,[40] though not so fully.

But now those women who dare to make complaint of existing social institutions are told that they wish to overthrow morality and order, and introduce a state of chaos. The question is, Are we living just now in a state of morality and order? Are there no social laws that press unjustly on the hitherto silent part of the community? Now that so many complaints have been made, all these questions ought to be considered. As women have, on the whole, obediently conformed to the character which was required of them for six thousand years or so, I think that now that they have begun to announce publicly that they have opinions of their own, they are due, at the very least, a fair hearing.[*]

"PLAIN WORDS ON THE WOMAN QUESTION"

GRANT ALLEN

[Fortnightly Review 46 (October 1889): 448-58]

If any species or race desires a continued existence, then above all things it is necessary that that species or race should go on reproducing itself.

This, I am aware, is an obvious platitude; but I think it was John Stuart Mill who once said there were such things in the world as luminous platitudes. Some truths are so often taken for granted in silence, that we are in danger at times of quite losing sight of them. And as some good friends of mine have lately been accusing me of "barren paradoxes," I am anxious in this paper to avoid all appearance of paradox, barren or fertile, and to confine myself strictly to the merest truisms. Though the truisms, to be sure, are of a particular sort too much overlooked in controversy nowadays by a certain type of modern lady writers.

Let us look then briefly at the needful conditions under which alone the human race can go on reproducing itself.

If every woman married, and every woman had four children, population would remain just stationary. Or rather, if every marriageable adult man and woman in a given community were to marry and if every marriage proved fertile, on the average, to the extent of four children, then, under favourable circumstances, that community, I take it, would just keep up its numbers, neither increasing nor decreasing from generation to generation. If less than all the adult men and women married, or if the marriages proved fertile on the average to a less degree than four children apiece, then that community would grow smaller and smaller. In order that the community may keep up to its normal level, therefore, either all adults must marry and produce to this extent, or else, fewer marrying, those few must have families exceeding on the average four children, in exact proportion to the rate of abstention. And if the community is to increase (which on Darwinian principles I believe to be a condition precedent of national health and vigour), then either all adults must marry and produce more than four children apiece, or else, fewer marrying, those few must produce as many more as will compensate for the abstention of the remainder and form a small surplus in each generation.

In Britain, at the present day, I believe I am right in deducing (after Mr. F. Galton)[41] that an average of about six children per marriage (not per head of female inhabitants) is necessary in order to keep the population just stationary. And the actual number of children per marriage is a little in excess of even that high figure, thus providing for the regular increase from census to census and for overflow by emigration.

These facts, all platitudes as they are, look so startling at first sight that they will probably need for the unstatistical reader a little explanation and simplification.

Well, suppose, now, every man and every woman in a given community were to marry; and suppose they were in each case to produce two children, a boy and a girl; and suppose those children were in every case to attain maturity: why, then, the next generation would exactly reproduce the last, each father being represented by his son, and each mother by her daughter, *ad infinitum.* (I purposely omit, for simplicity's sake, the complicating factor of the length and succession of generations, which by good luck in the case of the human species practically cancels itself.) But as a matter of fact, all the children do not attain maturity: on the contrary, nearly half of them die before reaching the age of manhood—in some conditions of life, indeed, and in some countries, more than half. Roughly speaking, therefore (for I don't wish to become a statistical bore), it may be said that in order that two children may attain maturity and be capable of marriage, even under the most favourable circumstances, four must be born. The other two must be provided to cover risks of infant or adolescent mortality, and to insure against infertility or incapacity for marriage in later life. They are wanted to make up the categories of soldiers, sailors, imbeciles, cripples, and incapables generally. So that even if every possible person married and if every married pair had four children, we should only just keep up the number of our population from one age to another.

Now, I need hardly say that not every possible person does marry, and that we do actually a good deal more than keep up the number of our population. Therefore it will at once be clear that each actual marriage is fertile to considerably more than the extent of four children. That is, indeed, a heavy burden to lay upon women. One aim, at least, of social reformers should certainly be to lighten it as much as possible.

Nevertheless, I think, it will be abundantly apparent from these simple considerations that in every community, and to all time, the vast majority of the women must become wives and mothers, and must bear at least four children apiece. If some women shirk their natural duties, then a heavier task must be laid upon the remainder. But in any case almost all must become wives and mothers, and almost all must bear at least four or five children. In our existing state six are the very fewest that our country can do with.

Moreover, it is pretty clear that the best-ordered community will be one where as large a proportion of the women as possible marry, and where the burden of maternity is thus most evenly shared between them.[42] Admitting that certain women may have good reasons for avoiding maternity on various grounds—unfitness, or, what is probably much the same thing at bottom, disinclination—and admitting also that where such good reasons exist, it is best those women should remain unmarried, we must still feel that in most cases marriage is in itself desirable, and that limited families are better than large ones. In other words, it is best for the community at large that most women should marry, and should have moderate families, rather than that fewer should marry and have unwieldily large ones; for if families are moderate there will be a greater reserve of health and strength left in the mothers for each birth, the production of children can be spread more slowly over a longer time, and the family resources will be less heavily taxed for their maintenance and education. Incidentally this will benefit both parents, as well as the community. That is to say, where many marriages and small families are the rule, the children will on the average be born healthier, be better fed, and be launched more fairly on the world in the end. Where marriages are fewer and families large, the strain of maternity will be most constant and most heavily felt; the father will be harder-worked, and the children will be born feebler, will be worse fed, and will start worse equipped in the battle of life.

Hence I would infer that the goal a wise community should keep in view is rather more marriages and fewer children per marriage, than fewer marriages and more children per marriage.

Or, to put these conclusions another way: in any case, the vast majority of women in any community must needs become wives and mothers: and in the best-ordered community, the largest possible number will doubtless become so, in order to distribute the burden equally, and to produce in the end the best results for the nation.

Well, it may be brutal and unmanly to admit these facts or to insist upon these facts, as we are often told it is by maiden ladies; but still, if we are to go on existing at all, we must look the facts fairly and squarely in the face, and must see how modern tendencies stand with regard to them.

Now, I have the greatest sympathy with the modern woman's demand for emancipation. I am an enthusiast on the Woman Question. Indeed, so far am I from wishing to keep her in subjection to man, that I should like to see her a great deal more emancipated than she herself as yet at all desires. Only, her emancipation must not be of a sort that interferes in any way with this prime natural necessity. To the end of all time, it is mathematically demonstrable that most women must become the mothers of at least four children, or else the race must cease to exist. Any supposed solution of the woman-problem, therefore, which fails to look this fact straight in the face, is a false solution. It cries "Peace, peace!" where there is no peace. It substitutes a verbal juggle for a real way out of the difficulty. It withdraws the attention of thinking women from the true problem of their sex to fix it on side-issues of comparative unimportance.

And this, I believe, is what almost all the Woman's Rights women are sedulously doing at the present day. They are pursuing a chimæra, and neglecting to perceive the true aim of their sex. They are setting up a false and unattainable ideal, while they omit to realise the true and attainable one which alone is open to them.

For let us look again for a moment at what this all but universal necessity of maternity implies. Almost every woman must bear four or five children. In doing so she must on the average use up the ten or twelve best years of her life: the ten or twelve years that immediately succeed her attainment of complete womanhood. For note, by the way, that these women must also for the most part marry young: as Mr. Galton has shown, you can quietly and effectually wipe out a race by merely making its women all marry at twenty-eight: married beyond that age, they don't produce children enough to replenish the population. Again, during these ten or twelve years of child-bearing at the very least, the women can't conveniently earn their own livelihood; they must be provided for by the labour of the men—under existing circumstances (in favour of which I have no Philistine prejudice) by their own husbands. It is true that in the very lowest state of savagery special provision is seldom made by the men for the women even during the periods of pregnancy, childbirth, and infancy of the offspring. The women must live (as among the Hottentots) over the worst of these periods on their own stored-up stock of fat, like hibernating bears or desert camels. It is true also that among savage races generally the women have to work as hard as the men, though the men bear in most cases the larger share in providing actual food for the entire family. But in civilised communities—and the more so in proportion to their degree of civilisation—the men do most of the hardest work, and in particular take upon themselves the duty of providing for the wives and children. The higher the type, the longer are the wives and children provided for. Analogy would lead one to suppose (with Comte)[43] that in the highest communities the men would do all the work, and the women would be left entirely free to undertake the management and education of the children.

Seeing, then, that these necessities are laid by the very nature of our organization upon women, it would appear as though two duties were clearly imposed upon the women themselves, and upon all those men who sympathize in their welfare: First, to see that their training and education should fit them above everything else for this their main function in life; and, second, that in consideration of the special burden they have to bear in connection with reproduction, all the rest of life should be made as light and easy and free for them as possible. We ought frankly to recognise that most women must be wives and mothers: that most women should therefore be trained, physically, morally, socially, and mentally, in the way best fitting them to be wives and mothers; and that all such women have a right to the fullest and most generous support in carrying out their functions as wives and mothers.

And here it is that we seem to come in conflict for a moment with most of the modern Woman-Question agitators. I say for a moment only, for I am not going to admit, even for that brief space of time, that the doctrine I wish to set forth here is one whit less advanced, one whit less radical, or one whit less emancipatory than the doctrine laid down by the most emancipated women. On the contrary, I feel sure that while women are crying for emancipation they really want to be left in slavery; and that it is only a few exceptional men, here and there in the world, who wish to see them fully and wholly enfranchised. And those men are not the ones who take the lead in so-called Woman's Rights movements.

For what is the ideal that most of these modern women agitators set before them? Is it not clearly the ideal of an unsexed woman? Are they not always talking to us as though it were not the fact that most women must be wives and mothers? Do they not treat any reference to that fact as something ungenerous, ungentlemanly, and almost brutal? Do they not talk about our "casting their sex in their teeth"?—as though any man ever resented the imputation of manliness. Nay, have we not even, many times lately, heard those women who insist upon the essential womanliness of women described as "traitors to the cause of their sex"? Now, we men are (rightly) very jealous of our virility. We hold it a slight not to be borne that anyone should impugn our essential manhood. And we do well to be angry: for virility is the keynote to all that is best and most forcible in the masculine character. Women ought equally to glory in their femininity. A woman ought to be ashamed to say she has no desire to become a wife and mother. Many such women there are no doubt—it is to be feared, with our existing training, far too many: but instead of boasting of their sexlessness as a matter of pride, they ought to keep it dark, and to be ashamed of it—as ashamed as a man in a like predicament would be of his impotence. They ought to feel they have fallen short of the healthy instincts of their kind, instead of posing as in some sense the cream of the universe, on the strength of what is really a functional aberration.

Unfortunately, however, just at the present moment, a considerable number of the ablest women have been misled into taking this unfeminine side, and becoming real "traitors to their sex" in so far as they endeavour to assimilate women to men in everything, and to put upon their shoulders, as a glory and privilege, the burden of their own support. Unfortunately, too, they have erected into an ideal what is really an unhappy necessity of the passing phase. They have set before them as an aim what ought to be regarded as a *pis-aller*.[44] And the reasons why they have done so are abundantly evident to anybody who takes a wide and extended view of the present crisis—for a crisis it undoubtedly is—in the position of women.

In the first place, the movement for the Higher Education of Women, in itself an excellent and most praiseworthy movement, has at first, almost of necessity, taken a wrong direction, which has entailed in the end much of the present uneasiness. Of course, nothing could well be worse than the so-called education of women forty or fifty years ago. Of course, nothing could be narrower than the view of their sex then prevalent as eternally predestined to suckle fools and chronicle small beer. But when the need for some change was first felt, instead of reform taking a rational direction—instead of women being educated to suckle strong and intelligent children, and to order well a wholesome, beautiful, reasonable household,—the mistake was made of educating them like men—giving a like training for totally unlike functions. The result was that many women became unsexed in the process, and many others acquired a distaste, an unnatural distaste, for the functions which nature intended them to perform. At the present moment, a great majority of the ablest women are wholly dissatisfied with their own position as women, and with the position imposed by the facts of the case upon women generally: and this as the direct result of their false education. They have no real plan to propose for the future of women as a sex: but in a vague and formless way they protest inarticulately against the whole feminine function in women, often even going the length of talking as though the world could get along permanently without wives and mothers.[45]

In the second place, a certain real lack of men to marry, here and now, in certain classes of society, and those the classes that lead thought, has made an exceptional number of able women at present husbandless, and thus has added strength to the feeling that women must and ought to earn their own living. How small and local this cause is I shall hereafter try to show: but there can be no doubt that it has much to do with the present discontents among women. There is a feeling abroad that many women can't get married: and this feeling, bolstered up by erroneous statistics and misunderstood facts, has greatly induced women to erect into an ideal for all what is really a *pis-aller* for a small fraction of their body—self-support in competition with men.

But are there not seven hundred thousand more women than men in the United Kingdom? And must not these seven hundred thousand be enabled to earn their own living? That is the one solid fact which the "advanced" women are always flinging at our heads; and that is the one fallacious bit of statistics which seems at first sight to give some colour of reasonableness to the arguments in favour of the defeminization of women.

As a matter of fact, the statistics are not true. There are not 700,000 more women than men, but 700,000 more *females* than *males* in the United Kingdom. The people who say "seven hundred thousand women," picture to themselves that vast body of marriageable girls, massed in a hollow square, and looking about them in vain across wide leagues of country for non-existent husbands. But figures are things that always require to be explained, and above all, to be regarded in their true proportions to one another. These 700,000 females include infants in arms, lunatics, sisters of charity, unfortunates, and ladies of eighty. A large part of the excess is due to the greater longevity of women; and the number comprises the great mass of widows, who have once in their lives possessed a husband of their own, and have outlived him, partly because they are, as a rule, younger, and partly by dint of their stronger constitutions. Moreover, this total disparity of 700,000, including babies, lunatics, and widows, is a disparity on a gross population of something more than thirty-five million. Looking these figures straight in the face, we find the actual proportion of the sexes to be as 172 males to 179 females. Speaking very roughly, this makes about four females in every hundred, including babies, widows, and so forth, who haven't a complementary male found for them. This in itself is surely no very terrible disproportion. It doesn't more than cover the relative number of women who are naturally debarred from marriage, or who under no circumstances would ever submit to be married. Out of every hundred women, roughly speaking, ninety-six have husbands provided for them by nature, and only four need go into a nunnery or take to teaching the higher mathematics. And if the marriageable men and women only are reckoned in the account, as far as I can gather from existing statistics, the disproportion sinks to a quite insignificant fraction.

Nevertheless, it is a fact, that both in England and America the marriageable men of the middle and upper classes are not to the fore, and that accordingly in these classes—the discussing, thinking, agitating classes—an undue proportion of women remains unmarried. The causes of this class-disparity are not far to seek. In America, the young man has gone West. In England he is in the army, in the navy, in the Indian Civil Service, in the Cape Mounted Rifles. He is sheep-farming in New Zealand, ranching in Colorado, growing tea in Assam, planting coffee in Ceylon; he is a cowboy in Montana, or a wheat-farmer in Manitoba, or a diamond-digger at Kimberley, or a merchant at Melbourne: in short, he is anywhere, and everywhere, except where he ought to be, making love to the pretty girls in England. For, being a man, I, of course, take it for granted that the first business of a girl is to be pretty.

Owing to these causes, it has unfortunately happened that a period of great upheaval in the female mind has coincided with a period when the number of unmarried women in the cultivated classes was abnormally large.

The upheaval would undoubtedly have taken place in our time, even without the co-operation of this last exacerbating cause. The position of women was not a position which could bear the test of nineteenth-century scrutiny. Their education was inadequate; their social status was humiliating; their political power was nil; their practical and personal grievances were innumerable: above all, their relations to the family—to their husbands, their children, their friends, their property—was simply insupportable. A real Woman Question there was, and is, and must be. The pity of it is that the coincidence of its recognition with the dearth of marriageable men in the middle and upper classes has largely deflected the consequent movement into wrong and essentially impracticable channels.

For the result has been that instead of subordinating the claims of the unmarried women to the claims of the wives and mothers, the movement has subordinated the claims of the wives and mothers to the claims of the unmarried women. Almost all the Woman's Rights women have constantly spoken, thought, and written as though it were possible and desirable for the mass of women to support themselves, and to remain unmarried for ever. The point of view they all tacitly take is the point of view of the self-supporting spinster. Now, the self-supporting spinster is undoubtedly a fact—a deplorable accident of the passing moment. Probably, however, even the most rabid of the Woman's Rights people would admit, if hard pressed, that in the best-ordered community almost every woman should marry at twenty or thereabouts. We ought, of course, frankly to recognise the existence of the deplorable accident; we ought for the moment to make things as easy and smooth as possible for her; we ought to remove all professional barriers, to break down the absurd jealousies and prejudices of men, to give her fair play, and if possible a little more than fair play, in the struggle for existence. So much our very chivalry ought to make obligatory upon us. That we should try to handicap her heavily in the race for life is a shame to our manhood. But we ought at the same time fully to realise that she is an abnormality, not the woman of the future. We ought not to erect into an ideal what is in reality a painful necessity of the present transitional age. We ought always clearly to bear in mind—men and women alike—that to all time the vast majority of women must be wives and mothers; that on those women who become wives and mothers depends the future of the race; and that if either class must be sacrificed to the other, it is the spinsters whose type perishes with them that should be sacrificed to the matrons who carry on the life and qualities of the species.

For this reason a scheme of female education ought to be mainly a scheme for the education of wives and mothers. And if women realised how noble and important a task it is that falls upon mothers, they would ask no other. If they realised how magnificent a nation might be moulded by mothers who devoted themselves faithfully and earnestly to their great privilege, they would be proud to carry out the duties of their maternity. Instead of that, the scheme of female education now in vogue is a scheme for the production of literary women, schoolmistresses, hospital nurses, and lecturers on cookery. All these things are good in themselves, to be sure—I have not a word to say against them; but they are not of the centre. They are side-lines off the main stream of feminine life, which must always consist of the maternal element. "But we can't know beforehand," say the advocates of the mannish training, "which women are going to be married, and which to be spinsters." Exactly so; and therefore you sacrifice the many to the few, the potential wives to the possible lady-lecturers. You sacrifice the race to a handful of barren experimenters. What is thus true of the blind groping after female education is true throughout of almost all the Woman Movement. It gives precedence to the wrong element in the problem. What is essential and eternal it neglects in favour of what is accidental and temporary. What is feminine in women it neglects in favour of what is masculine. It attempts to override the natural distinction of the sexes, and to make women men—in all but virility.

The exact opposite, I believe, is the true line of progress. We are of two sexes: and in healthy diversity of sex, pushed to its utmost, lies the greatest strength of all of us. Make your men virile: make your women womanly. Don't cramp their intelligence: don't compress their waists: don't try to turn them into dolls or dancing girls: but freely and equally develop their feminine idiosyncrasy, physical, moral, intellectual. Let them be healthy in body: let them be sound in mind: if possible (but here I know even the most advanced among them will object) try to preserve them from the tyranny of their own chosen goddess and model, Mrs. Grundy.[46] In one word, emancipate woman (if woman will let you, which is more than doubtful) but leave her woman still, not a dulled and spiritless epicene automaton.

That last, it is to be feared, is the one existing practical result of the higher education of women, up to date. Both in England and America, the women of the cultivated classes are becoming unfit to be wives or mothers. Their sexuality (which lies at the basis of everything) is enfeebled or destroyed. In some cases they eschew marriage altogether—openly refuse and despise it, which surely shows a lamentable weakening of wholesome feminine instincts. In other cases, they marry, though obviously ill adapted to bear the strain of maternity; and in such instances they frequently break down with the birth of their first or second infant. This evil, of course, is destined by natural means to cure itself with time: the families in question will not be represented at all in the second generation, or will be represented only by feeble and futile descendants. In a hundred years, things will have righted themselves. But meanwhile, there is a danger that many of the most cultivated and able families of the English-speaking race will have become extinct, through the prime error of supposing that an education which is good for men must necessarily also be good for women.

I said just now that many women at present eschew marriage, and that this shows a weakening of wholesome feminine instinct. Let me hasten to add, for fear of misconception,—I mean, of course, if they eschew it for want of the physical impulse which ought to be as present in every healthy woman as in every healthy man. That independent-minded women should hesitate to accept the terms of marriage as they now and here exist, I do not wonder. But if they have it really at heart to alter those terms, to escape from slavery, to widen the basis of the contract between the sexes, to put the wife on a higher and safer footing, most sensible men, I feel sure, will heartily co-operate with them. As a rule, however, I observe in actual life that "advanced" women are chary of either putting forward or accepting modifications in this matter. They dread the frown of their Grundian deity. They usually content themselves with vague declamation and with erecting female celibacy into a panacea for the ills that woman is heir to, while they refuse to meddle at all in definite terms with the question of marriage or its substitute in the future. While denouncing loudly the supremacy of man, they seem ready to shake off that supremacy only for the celibate minority of their sex, without attempting to do anything for the married majority.

To sum up the point whither this long, and I confess discursive, argument is tending. There is, and ought to be, a genuine Woman Question and a genuine Woman Movement. But that movement, if it is ever to do any good, must not ignore—nay, on the contrary, must frankly and unreservedly accept and embrace the fact that the vast majority of adult women are and will always be wives and mothers (and when I say "wives," I say so only in the broadest sense, subject to all possible expansions or modifications of the nature of wifehood). It must also recognise the other fact that in an ideal community the greatest possible number of women should be devoted to the duties of maternity, in order that the average family may be kept small, that is to say, healthy and educable. It must assume as its goal, not general celibacy and the independence of women, but general marriage and the ample support of women by the men of the community. While allowing that exceptional circumstances call for exceptional tenderness towards those women who are now compelled by untoward conditions to earn their own livelihood, it will avoid creating that accident into a positive goal, and it will endeavour to lessen the necessity for the existence of such exceptions in the future. In short, it will recognise maternity as the central function of the mass of women, and will do everything in its power to make that maternity as healthy, as noble, as little burdensome as possible.

If the "advanced" women will meet us on this platform, I believe that majority of "advanced" men will gladly hold out to them the right hand of fellowship. As a body we are, I think, prepared to reconsider fundamentally, without prejudice or preconception, the entire question of the relations between the sexes—which is a great deal more than the women are prepared to do. We are ready to make any modifications in those relations which will satisfy the woman's just aspiration for personal independence, for intellectual and moral development, for physical culture, for political activity, and for a voice in the arrangement of her own affairs, both domestic and national. As a matter of fact, few women will go as far in their desire to emancipate woman as many men will go. It was Ibsen, not Mrs. Ibsen, who wrote the *Doll's House*. It was women, not men, who ostracized George Eliot.[47] The slavishness begotten in women by the *régime* of man is what we have most to fight against, not the slave-driving instinct of the men—now happily becoming obsolete, or even changing into a sincere desire to do equal justice. But what we must absolutely insist upon is full and free recognition of the fact that, in spite of everything, the race and the nation must go on reproducing themselves. Whatever modifications we make must not interfere with that prime necessity. We will not aid or abet women as a sex in rebelling against maternity, or in quarrelling with the constitution of the solar system. Whether we have wives or not—and that is a minor point about which I, for one, am supremely unprejudiced—we must at least have mothers. And it would be well, if possible, to bring up those mothers as strong, as wise, as free, as sane, as healthy, as earnest, and as efficient as we can make them. If this is barren paradox, I am content to be paradoxical; if this is rank Toryism, I am content for once to be reckoned among the Tories.

NOTES

1. Martin Luther (1483-1546), German Protestant reformer.
2. See Tylor's *Primitive Culture* [author's note]. The complete title of the book by Edward Burnett Tylor (1832-1917) is *Primitive Culture: Researches into the Development of Mythology, Philosophy, Religion, Language, Art, and Custom.*
3. "Glory be to the Father, and to the Son, and to the Holy Ghost; As it was in the beginning, is now, and ever shall be, world without end. Amen." Commonly called the doxology, these lines do not appear in the Old or the New Testament. They date back to the fourth century and first appear in the Divine Liturgy of St. John Chrysostomos.
4. John Milton, from the Preface to Book I, *The Doctrine and Discipline of Divorce* (1644).
5. With regard to the evil effects of ignorance in the mismanagement of young children, probably few people realize how much avoidable pain is endured, and how much weakness in after-life is traceable to the absurd traditional modes of treating infants and children [author's note].
6. See note 8 below.
7. John Stuart Mill, in the *Subjection of Women* (1869), compares women's condition in marriage to slavery. He states in Chapter IV: "Marriage is the only actual

bondage known to our law. There remain no legal slaves, except the mistress of every house."

8. *Sex-Relations in Germany.* By Karl Pierson [author's note].

9. Tertullian (c.155-c.220) was a Carthaginian who converted to Christianity from paganism and became a Christian theologian, apologist, and writer. He makes many negative statements about women in *The Apparel of Women* (197 CE), accusing women of "being the cause of the fall of the human race": "You are the one who opened the door to the Devil, you are the one who first plucked the fruit of the forbidden tree, you are the first who deserted the divine law; you are the one who persuaded him whom the Devil was not strong enough to attack" (Book 1, Chapter 1). In a later passage he blames women for men's lustful thoughts, questioning whether God will not condemn woman as well as man for being the inspiration for his thoughts: "For he [man] perishes as soon as he looks upon your beauty with desire, and has already committed in his soul what he desires, and you have become a sword (of perdition) to him so that, even though you are free from the actual crime of unchastity, you are not altogether free from the odium (attached to it)" (Book 2, Chapter 2).

10. The troubadours in the twelfth and thirteenth centuries were poet-musicians whose lyric poetry was devoted to themes of courtly love and the idealization of women. Minnesingers were twelfth- to fourteenth-century German lyric poets and musicians who continued the tradition of the French troubadours, singing mainly about courtly love.

11. Luther on women and marriage: "He who takes a wife is not entering a life of ease but is creating trouble for himself." "Another very fine factor, one that contributes much toward harmony in the home, is the concerted effort of the wife to regard her husband's will, to do what she knows he likes, and to avoid what she knows he dislikes." "The weakness or frivolousness of the female sex is known. They like to gad about and ask about everything with a prying curiosity." "Men are commanded to rule and to reign over their wives and families. But if woman, forsaking her position (*officio*), presumes to rule over her husband, she then and there engages in a work for which she was not created, a work which stems from her own failing (*vitio*) and is evil." (*What Luther Says: An Anthology,* Compiled by Eward M. Plass. St. Louis, Missouri: Concordia, 1959; numbers 2799, 2830, 2832, 4706.)

12. The Philistine social system refers to values of the ignorant middle class which allegedly is hostile to artistic and cultural values and associated with hypocrisy in sexual relationships.

13. In the Clerk's Tale in Chaucer's *Canterbury Tales,* the nobleman Walter subjects his loyal wife Griselda to a series of tests of her patience and fidelity. Griselda is a sharp contrast to the lecherous Wife of Bath (and seems to be a reply to the Wife's Prologue and Tale).

14. Bebel on *Woman* [author's note]. August Bebel (1840-1913) was a German socialist leader who became a Marxist Socialist under the influence of Wilhelm

Liebknecht. In *Woman and Socialism* (1879), Bebel argues that the social emancipation of women is necessary to overthrow capitalism. The book had many editions and was translated into many languages.

15. Philip Melanchthon (1497-1560) played an important role during the Reformation as Luther's friend and confidant. He systematized Reformation thought with his "Loci Communes."

16. Henry Brooke (1703-83), *The Fool of Quality; or, The History of Henry, Earl of Moreland* (1766). Charles Kingsley (1819-75), a clergyman and novelist, wrote a biographical preface for a new edition of the book which was published in 1860.

17. *Martin Luther; his Influence on the Material and Intellectual Welfare of Germany*—The Westminster Review. New Series, No. CXXIX, January, 1884, pp.38-9 [author's note].

18. Opposing the doctrine of the Roman Catholic Church, Luther contended that marriage was not one of the sacraments.

19. "To have and to hold" are words taken from the Celebration and Blessing of a Marriage found in the *Book of Common Prayer* used by Anglican Church or the Church of England.

20. The lines are said by Elsie in Longfellow's *The Golden Legend* (1852) which was later (1886) set to music by Arthur Sullivan. Prince Henry of Hoheneck is ill and learns he can only be cured by the blood of a maiden who will die for him of her own free will. Elsie, the daughter of one of his vassals, resolves to sacrifice her life for him. When her mother pleads with her not to die, Elsie makes this lament. The Prince is eventually healed miraculously and marries the devoted Elsie.

21. *Scientific Meliorism.* By Jane Hume Clapperton [author's note]. The complete title of the book by Clapperton (1832-1914) is *Scientific Meliorism and the Evolution of Happiness* (1885).

22. Augusta Webster (1837-94), poet.

23. Max O'Rell (1848-1903), *John Bull and his Daughters* (1884).

24. Eliza Lynn Linton (1822-98) wrote anti-feminist articles for the *Saturday Review* which were collected as *The Girl of the Period* (1869). Her later novels attack this so-called girl of the period or Girton girl. (See the introduction to II, 2.)

25. Mr. Henry Stanton, in his work on *The Woman Question in Europe*, speaks of the main idea conveyed in Legouvé's *Histoire des Femmes* as follows:—"Equality in difference is its key-note. The question is not to make woman a man but to complete man by woman." [author's note] Caird probably means Theodore Stanton (1851-1925) who wrote *The Woman Question in Europe: A Series of Original Essays* (1884). Gabriel Jean Baptiste Ernest Wilfrid Legouvé's *Histoire Morale des Femmes* was published in 1854.

26. Mrs. Cady Stanton believes that there is a sex in mind, and that men can only be inspired to their highest achievements by women, while women are stimulated to their utmost only by men [author's note].

27. From *Hamlet* 3.1.62.

28. Lewis Morris (1833-1907), poet.

29. Richard Brinsley Sheridan (1751-1816), English playwright, author of *The Rivals* (1775) and *The School for Scandal* (1777); Jonathan Swift (1667-1745), English satirist, author of *Gulliver's Travels* (1726).

30. Madame (Sophie) Cottin (1770-1807), *Elizabeth, or, The Exiles of Siberia: A Tale Founded upon Facts* (1806). Published in French and translated to English.

31. Edward Bulwer-Lytton (1803-73). His novels of domestic life include *The Caxtons, a Family Portrait* (1849) and *My Novel* (1853). One of his novels about unpleasant women is *Lucretia* (1846), whose vicious heroine poisons her own son.

32. Charles Dickens (1812-70), in his novel *Martin Chuzzlewit* (1844), depicts two marriage-hungry daughters, Mercy and Charity, the daughters of Mr. Pecksniff. Mrs. Sparsit, in *Hard Times* (1854), is an unpleasant widow with designs on Mr. Bounderby. Being left at the altar on her wedding day forever embitters Miss Havisham, in *Great Expectations* (1861). In *Humphry Clinker* (1771), a novel by Tobias Smollett (1721-71), Tabitha, sister to Matthew Bramble, is bent on matrimony.

33. Proverbs 31:10: "Who can find a virtuous woman? for her price is far above rubies" (King James Version of the Bible). Solomon supposedly compiled the proverbs.

34. *Joan Haste* (1895), a novel by H. Rider Haggard (1856-1925).

35. James Boswell, in his *Life of Johnson* (1791), said of Dr. Johnson: "He talked of the heinousness of the crime of adultery, by which the peace of families was destroyed. He said, 'Confusion of progeny constitutes the essence of the crime; and therefore a woman who breaks her marriage vows is much more criminal than a man who does it. A man, to be sure, is criminal in the sight of God; but he does not do his wife a very material injury, if he does not insult her; if, for instance, from mere wantonness of appetite, he steals privately to her chambermaid. Sir, a wife ought not greatly to resent this. I would not receive home a daughter who had run away from her husband on that account. A wife should study to reclaim her husband by more attention to please him. Sir, a man will not, once in a hundred instances, leave his wife and go to a harlot, if his wife has not been negligent of pleasing'" (Spring 1768).

36. George Eliot (Mary Anne or Marian Evans, 1819-80), British novelist. In Eliot's novel *Adam Bede* (1859), the unmarried Hetty Sorrel becomes pregnant and then is condemned to hang for letting her baby die. She is finally reprieved on the scaffold and sentenced instead to be transported.

37. "Ye Banks and Braes o' Bonnie Doon," by Robert Burns (1759-96), is a ballad spoken by a broken-hearted woman who waits in vain for her faithless lover.

38. The French ballad, entitled "A la Claire Fontaine," expresses a sense of nostalgia, a longing to go back to a past time: "I wish the rose/ Were again on the bush;/ And that the rose bush/ Were still to be planted."

39. *My Little Girl*, a novel by Walter Besant (1836-1901) and James Rice (1843-82), was adapted for the stage by Dion Boucicault (1820-90). It was produced at the Court Theatre, February 15, 1882.

40. *The Vicar of Wakefield* (1766) by Oliver Goldsmith (1728-74).

41. Francis Galton (1822-1911), a cousin of Charles Darwin, had among his many interests the study of human intelligence and eugenics. He believed that intelligence and character were innate rather than resulting from environmental factors. This belief led him to propose that human stock could be improved by a selective mating program. He published many books, among them *Hereditary Genius* (1869), *A Theory of Heredity* (1875), and *Natural Inheritance* (1889).

42. Oh, yes, I know all about Malthus; but Mr. Galton has shown that a certain amount of over-population is necessary for survival of the fittest, and that if the best and most intelligent classes abstain, the worst and lowest will surely make up the leeway for them [author's note].

43. Auguste Comte (1798-1857), French mathematician and philosopher.

44. *pis-aller*, the final recourse or last resort (French).

45. A short time ago I received an angry letter from a correspondent in Iowa, full of curious bluster about "doing without the men altogether." Apparently this lady really imagined that the human race could be recruited from the gooseberry bushes [author's note].

46. Mrs. Grundy is a neighbor repeatedly referred to (but never appearing) in Tom Morton's play *Speed the Plow* (1798). She represents conventional social disapproval, prudishness, and narrow-mindedness.

47. George Eliot (Mary Anne or Marian Evans) began to live with George Henry Lewes in 1855 despite the fact that he was still married. She called herself Mrs. Lewes and referred to Lewes as her husband. For this behavior she was socially ostracized.

THE ATTACK ON THE NEW WOMAN WRITERS

To some critics during the 1890s the New Woman was a figure of fun and an easy target of satire. *Punch,* the most famous Victorian comic newspaper, mocked the New Woman in its cartoons and parodied her fiction in its stories. A cartoon appearing in *Punch,* entitled "Donna Quixote," targeted the New Woman in a variety of ways: the "keynote," held aloft by a woman looking suspiciously like George Egerton, suggests Egerton's collection of stories called *Keynotes* as well as the Keynotes Series of books published by John Lane at the Bodley Head. It is also the latchkey whose ownership became a sign of independence for the "revolting daughters."

George Egerton, along with New Woman writers Sarah Grand, Iota (Kathleen Hunt Caffyn, 1855?-1926), and Mona Caird, was a frequent target of critics. Egerton's stories, with their psychological explorations of women and lack of narrative line, were easy to parody. *Keynotes* (1893), Egerton's first collection of stories, was followed by *Discords* (1894); both were published by John Lane. Egerton's *Keynotes* had a frontispiece designed by Aubrey Beardsley, the art editor of the *Yellow Book* from 1894 to 1895. "She-Notes," published in two parts in *Punch* in 1894 and illustrated by a so-called "Mortarthurio Whiskersly," parodies Beardsley's drawings and Egerton's fiction, particularly her story "A Cross Line."

However, not every critic believed that the New Women fiction writers were comic figures to be satirized; some critics accused them of writing neurotic literature that merited condemnation for its unhealthy effect on readers. Such critics argued that the New Woman fiction was excessively introspective, dwelling too much on women's emotions and feelings; it revealed evidence of hysteria and neurosis and exhibited an unhealthy interest in women's sexuality. In his two articles in *Blackwood's* attacking the New Woman and the literature she produced, Hugh Stutfield (1858-1929), who was known primarily as a travel writer, put the New Woman writers in the same company as the decadents and aesthetics. In this group of degenerates he included also writers of the late nineteenth-century problem plays, particularly the Norwegian playwright Henrik Ibsen. Stutfield believed that the so-called decadent and revolting literature produced by these late-nineteenth century writers revealed signs of a diseased imagination and that the public's morbid interest in such literature had national implications.

The final essay in this section, by Cesare Lombroso (1835-1909), while not specifically about the New Woman, provides an insight into the thinking on women by a man of science at the end of the nineteenth century. Lombroso, a professor of medicine and psychiatry at Turin and author of *Criminal Man* (1876), made a scientific study of criminals. He developed the theory that criminal traits are inborn and that criminals are atavistic or evolutionary throwbacks to our ancestral past. In his view apish or savage characteristics lie dormant, appearing in certain people who can be recognized by anatomical signs and criminal behavior. Lombroso posited that criminal behavior was the norm among inferior people. A low threshold for pain, evidence of inferior development, was a characteristic of certain "savage" people. According to Stephen Jay Gould, in *The Mismeasure of Man* (1981), "Lombroso constructed virtually all his arguments in a manner that precluded their defeat... Whenever Lombroso encountered a contrary fact, he performed some mental gymnastics to incorporate it within his system" (125-26). Evidence of such mental gymnastics is evident in "The Physical Insensibility of Woman."

"DONNA QUIXOTE"

[*Punch, or the London Charivari* 106 (28 April 1894): 195]

The dreamy Don who to the goatherds told
Long-winded legends of the Age of Gold,
Finds a fair rival in our later days;
The newest Chivalry brings the newest Craze.
Dear Donna QUIXOTE—and the sex *is* dear,
Even when querulous, or quaint, or queer—
Dear Donna, like La Mancha's moonstruck knight,
Whose fancy shaped the foes he turned to fight,
Mere book-bred phantoms you for facts mistake;
Your *Wanderjahr* will vanish when you—wake!

Yes, there you sit surrounded by wild hosts
Of warring wonders which indeed are *"Ghosts"*:[1]
"Doll's-House" delirium sets your nerves a-thrill,
"DODO"[2] hysteria misdirects your will;
You yearn—indefinitely—to Advance!
You shake your lifted latch-key like a lance!
And shout, "In spite of babies, bonnets, tea,
Creation's heir, I must, I will be—Free!"

Morbid conceptions born of books ferment
In brains a-burn with febrile discontent!

So the dear Don, with dream-disordered head,
His fancy fired with all that he had read—
Enchantments, contests, challenges, and scars—
Found rustic Arragon a world of wars,
Windmills fierce foes, and e'en domestic sheep
Destructive demons. Donna, could you keep
That trim-coiled "hair on"—pray forgive the slang!—
You do in *Dodo!*—let the fads go hang,
And "realise yourself" in natural sort,
For churls and cynics you should make less sport.
These shapes are things of mirage and the mist,
Gendered by genius with a mental twist;
By male hysteria, Amazonian sham,
And the smart world's great *Fin de Siècle* flam!
See Mrs. Cerberus[3] in your cloudy vision,
Keeping the portals of that Home Elysian
Which cranks now call a Hades! Home, sweet home?
Nay, 'tis a gaol to those who long to roam,
Unchaperoned, emancipate, and *free*
With the large Liberty of the Latch-key!
Materfamilias and the chaperon grim,
Of watchful eye, firm mouth, and triple chin,
Are Mrs. GRUNDY's brace of stout supporters,
Three-headed guard of our Revolting Daughters!
You, Donna QUIXOTE, to this ward—or these——
Would but too gladly play the Hercules,
Urged by the CAIRDS, and CRACKANTHORPES, and GRANDS!
These demon-weavers of domestic bands,
Who've snared the Daughter of the Day, and bound her,
As the bard sings, with dark Styx[4] nine times round her,
Do not exist, dear Donna, save in dreams,
Like QUIXOTE's Caraculiambo![5] Gleams
Of common sense and glorious hope illume
(As dawn's first rosy streaks break night's black gloom)
The sex's future. The dull despot, man,
Backed by the bondage of the social plan,
Shall not for ever unrestricted sway.
But Donna dear, not by the masher's way,
Or MILL's or the sham Amazons, or CAIRD's
Or HEDDA GABLER's;[6] not through cranks ill-paired,
Or franchise, or the female volunteers,
EGERTON's phantasies or DODO's jeers,
Shall come the true emancipation. No!

PUNCH, OR THE LONDON CHARIVARI.   [April 28, 1894.

DONNA QUIXOTE.

"A world of disorderly notions *picked out of books,* crowded into his (her) imagination."—*Don Quixote.*

[*Punch* 28 April 1894 (vol. 106, p. 194).]

"Picture by Our Own Yellow-Booky Daubaway Weirdsley, intended as a Puzzle
Picture to preface of Juvenile Poems, or as nothing in particular."
[*Punch* 2 February 1895 (vol. 108, p. 58).]

The *Yellow Book* and the Keynotes Series of novels and short stories, which featured
works by New Women and other advanced writers of the 1890s, were published
by John Lane at the Bodley Head, located in Vigo Street in London.
Aubrey Beardsley was the art editor of the *Yellow Book* from 1894 to 1895.

The Heavenly Twins, or *A Grey Eye or So,*
The Yellow Aster—or the *Yellow Book,*[7]
Latch-keys or key-notes; all the "thrills" that shook
The Master-builder's[8] minx, or moved a soul
Midway between a maniac and troll;
Music-hall freedom, laxity in love,
Affinities that range all rites above;
Soul-swell that outgrows marriage, as a plant
Its pot-bound limitations—all the cants
Of culture's cranks, and extra-ethic dolts,
Whose fetish is the Gospel of Revolts,—
Not these shall shed one single lustrous ray
Of light divine upon the bitter way,
Or help with human melody their songs
Who'd "ride abroad redressing *woman's* wrongs."

Therefore, dear Donna QUIXOTE, be not stupid,
Fight not with Hymen, and war not with Cupid,
Run not amuck 'gainst Mother Nature's plan,
Nor make a monster of your mate, poor Man,
Or like La Mancha's cracked, though noble knight,
You'll find blank failure in mistaken fight.

"SHE-NOTES"

"BORGIA SMUDGITON,
WITH JAPANESE FAN DE SIÈCLE ILLUSTRATIONS
BY MORTARTHURIO WHISKERSLY."

[*Punch, or the London Charivari* 106 (10 March 1894): 109]

"My Soozie! My Toozle! My Soozie!"
It is the voice of a man, and he sings. He has grey eyes, and wears a grey Norfolk-broad. They accentuate one another; the pine-trees also accentuate his fishing-rod. His hum blends with the bleating of the *Bufo vulgaris* and the cooing of *Coleoptera.*
Beside a fallen pine lies a woman (*genus,* in fact, *muliebre*). Where the tree fell there she lies. Her fresh animal instinct sniffs the music-hall refrain; the footlights of the Pavillon Rouge mix rather weirdly with a vision, just rudely interrupted, of terra-cottas from Tanagra. Not every woman thinks of these things in a wood.

The male is a student of the Eternal Femininity. Already, while still out of gunshot, he has noticed her wedding-ring and the diamond keeper. "Talking of keepers," he begins, with the affected drawl now sufficiently familiar to the reader, "are we trespassing here?" She replies in her frank unembarrassed way. "Better ask a p'leeceman," she says. (A lady, obviously! Worth cultivating? Bet your braces!)

"After trout, you know. Any local tips in flies?" A rare smile comes with her ready answer. "'Pick-me-ups' after a heavy night: 'Henry Clays' after lunch; 'spotted cocktails' for the evening. Like a 'coachman' myself; sometimes find them quite killing!" "Happy Coachman!"

A chill comes over the sylvan scene with these reckless words. She has gathered her cream-coloured mittens about her wrists; the contrast at once strikes him; in the subdued evening light he can see that her hands are unwashed. She bows coolly, and is off across the stream like a water-snake.

❋ ❋ ❋

She is lounging nervously on the edge of the parlour-grate. There are two (an acute observer would say three) furrows on her forehead. "Off your pipe, old chappie? Feel a bit cheap?" (It is her husband who speaks in this way.) "Yes, beastly, thanks, old man!" "Try a nip o' whiskey. No soda; soda for boys. There, that's right! Buck up! What's your book?" "Oh! one of WILDE's little things. I like WILDE; he shocks the middle classes. Only the middle classes are so easily shocked!" He smiles, a gentle, dull smile. There is a long pause; he cannot follow her swift eternally feminine fancy. "What's it now, old buffer? A brass for your thoughts!" "I was thinking, little woman, of a filly foal I once had. She grew up to be a mare. I never would have let anyone on God's beautiful earth ride her." "I'd have ridden her!" "No, you wouldn't!" "Yes, I would!" (passionately and concentratedly). "Well, I sold her anyway. Lucky the beast isn't here now to spoil our conjugal unity!" The crisis had past. Another moment and she might have left him for ever lonely and forlorn! But in a twinkling her wild, free instinct doubles at a tangent. With a supple bound she is on his shoulders curling her lithe fishing boots into one of his waistcoat pockets. Surely gipsy blood runs in her veins!

"Oh! I wish I were a devil" (it is the lady speaking); "yes, a d-e-v-i-l!" "But you *are*, old woman, you *are*! And such a dear little devil!" "Say it again, old man!" (kissing him fiercely in the left eye and worrying his ear like a ferret), "I love to hear you call me that. We women yearn for praise!" "You're a rare brick, old dear; and you're never jealous. Look at that photo of the other girl! Some women would have cut up rough about it. But *you*—why, you sent her a quid when she was peckish, and she chewed it for a week! Was there ever such a little chip?"

"SHE-NOTES. PART II"

"BORGIA SMUDGITON"

[*Punch* 106 (17 March 1894): 129]

She is lying on her back in a bog-stream. Strangely enough there are white clouds waltzing along the sky. To her fancy, which is nothing if not picturesque, they are a troop of fairy geese on their way to Michaelmas. No? well then, plainly they are ANTONY and CLEOPATRA. And oh! The dalliance, the wild free life of Egypt! No dinner to order; very little washing on Mondays.

Presto! In imagination she is on stage. She is a *Tableau Vivant!* All the fauteuils have their glasses up. She has pink overalls, with a cestus round her neck. Her lissom limbs scintillate; she dances slightly. KILANYI says she must try and keep still. A moment more and there is a lovely cat-call from the gallery; she can still hear it above the orchestra, as the next tableau is being wheeled on. It *was* a supreme keynote!

And the other women? Crushed, joyless, machines—misunderstood! How can the dense brute male read the enigma of the Female Idea? They think us innocent! not we! but we all keep up the deception and lie courageously. They will never know that we are really primitive, untamable, ineradicable animalculæ.

"Got the blue devils, little witch?" (It is the grey man. He has dropped his drawl and his fly-book. They have been getting on nicely, thank you, since we saw them last.)

"Yes, we are all witches, we women. We can read men but they can't read us." "Can't *I* read you?" "*Me*, the real ineffable *me?* Yes, perhaps just a little. You have a dash of the Everlasting Female in you." As she speaks she rolls up her shawl into an infinitesimal pellet.

"Well, look here" (desperately). "What do you say to a trip in my yacht? Southern seas! Venice! Constantinople! Olympia! And then, when the winds are hushed and the steam is shut off for the night, we would fly with no visible means of locomotion over the silvery deep! You smile? Where is the pain?" "Oh! if I could only have the yacht without you in it!" (He winces.) "Yet, I say, give us women freedom and we would all go one better than NAPOLEON. NELSON knew nothing of the eternal I! Bah! and he was blind in the other." "You strange creature!" "No, not strange; only true. Were I more elusive I might be more fascinating."

A long silence broken only by the chirp of a grasshopper. The air is charged like a battery. It seems that a submarine cable connects these two souls. Nevertheless, she distinctly observes that the grasshopper has strained his Achilles-tendon. Curious that at such a climax the minutest detail should not escape her. Am I right in thinking that no novelist has as yet detected this remarkable phenomenon? He comes nearer (I mean the grey man). His skin beneath his collar blushes a rich cobalt. "Is my little moment up?" he gasps. (His stop-watch is in his trembling hand.) "Lord! What a cheek you have!" "Don't, oh, don't say that!" "Very well, I withdraw it." "But listen!" (she is dropping asleep): "listen, I say!" (she will be snoring directly); "if my moment is really ended—and my stop-watch points to the fact—and if you mean to send me away, *hang something white on the gooseberry-bush* (our *gooseberry-bush*) *to-morrow about the ninth hour*!" She rises and is gone like a water-snake.

❧ ❧ ❧

It is to-morrow about the eighth hour. She is still in bed. There is a nod at the window. It is all right; only a blushing sweet-william. On the mantel-piece is a daguerreotype of her late aunt, in a velvet bodice and other things. But it is not *that* which drives her crazy. It is her husband's cheery pick-axe in the garden. Is he really digging her grave? Why, surely, not; he is simply arranging the onion-bed. Yet what an interesting corpse she would make! The pity is that one can never see one's own corpse in the glass. Stay, is that BETSY? "Oh! BETSY" (the young cook enters demurely for orders), "I wonder had you ever a lover?" "Well, Ma'm, what do *you* think?" "Say, what happened him, anyway?" "Why, he left me, Ma'm, left me for Another; and" (regretfully) "we might have married, and had such *heavenly* twins; and, oh! he *had* such a beautiful crest on his writing-paper!"

A moment's tension follows; the next sees the lady feeling for a coin in her dress-pocket. She spins it deftly. "Heads, he stays! Tails, he goes! Tails! By all that is virtuous."

"BETSY!" (Her voice is firm, like a quickset hedge.) "BETSY! I cannot spare my 'nighty' just now, but your white apron will do as well. You *do* love me, don't you?" (Kisses her.) "Then for *my* sake go and hang yourself for a little while on the gooseberry-bush. Mind! The *gooseberry*-bush!" "Yes, Ma'm."

A rare fidelity! And so few men could have understood or even spelt the why in BETSY!

❧ ❧ ❧

Two hours later she wakes up and remembers the faithful girl! Perhaps it is even now too late! She hurries through her toilet. The daguerreotype shows no sign. Threads of bogwool float persistently in the summer air. She is by the gooseberry-bush with a stout pair of scissors. Too late! The girl is gone! Another hand, a hand that held a stop-watch, has cut her down, and BETSY is by this time a free and unfettered woman, on her way to a yacht.

The grey man, after all, had his consolation.

"Tommyrotics"

Hugh E.M. Stutfield

[*Blackwood's* 157 (June 1895): 833-45]

A most excellent wag—quoted with approval by the grave and sedate "Spectator"—recently described modern fiction as "erotic, neurotic, and Tommyrotic." Judging from certain signs of the times, he might have extended his description to the mental condition in our day of a considerable section of civilized mankind. Our restless, dissatisfied, sadly muddled, much-inquiring generation seems to be smitten with a new malady, which so far bids fair to baffle the doctors. Society, in the limited sense of the word, still dreads the influenza and shudders at the approach of typhoid, but its most dangerous and subtle foes are beyond question "neurotics" and hysteria in their manifold forms.

A wave of unrest is passing over the world. Humanity is beginning to sicken at the daily round, the common task, of ordinary humdrum existence, and is eagerly seeking for new forms of excitement. Hence it is kicking over the traces all round. Revolt is the order of the day. The shadow of an immeasurable, and by no means divine, discontent broods over us all. Everybody is talking and preaching: one is distressed because he cannot solve the riddle of the universe, the why and the wherefore of human existence; another racks his brains to invent brand-new social or political systems which shall make everybody rich, happy, and contented at a bound. It is an age of individual and collective—perhaps I should say, collectivist—fuss, and the last thing that anybody thinks of is settling down to do the work that lies nearest to him. Carlyle[9] is out of fashion, for Israel has taken to stoning her older prophets who exhorted to duty, submission, and suchlike antiquated virtues, and the social anarchist and the New Hedonist bid fair to take their place as teachers of mankind.

It is thought by many that the hour brings forth the man; and just as the world seems most in need of him, a new prophet has arisen to point out some of the dangers which lie in the path of modern civilization. Like most prophets, he raves somewhat incoherently at times and is guilty of much exaggeration, but this is a fault common to nearly all men with a mission. And, when every allowance has been made on this score, we should still be grateful to Dr Max Nordau for his striking and powerful work, "Degeneration."[10] The book has been violently assailed, and portions of it lend themselves readily to hostile criticism. It is certainly not a book *virginibus puerisque*,[11] and it is exceedingly learned and long; but the wealth of epigram, the fecundity of illustration, and the brilliant incisiveness of its style, make it far from heavy reading. A perusal thereof forces one to "devour much abomination," as the Arabs say; but unsavoury topics are at any rate not handled sympathetically, as by decadent essayists and "yellow" lady novelists, but rather in the spirit of fierce hatred and horror which characterise a Juvenal.[12]

And the sum of his matter is this—that ours may be an age of progress, but it is progress which, if left unchecked, will land us in the hospital or the lunatic asylum. Neurasthenia and brain-exhaustion are driving the upper classes among mankind post-haste to Colney Hatch.[13] The causes of our mental disease are the wear-and-tear and excitement of modern life, and its symptoms are to be found in the debased emotionalism apparent in so many of the leading writers and thinkers of our day, who, together with their numerous followers and admirers, are victims of a form of mania whereof the scientific name is "degeneration." Now all this is very sad, and happily only partially true, else the world were indeed in a bad way. If it be the fact that we are in the Dusk of the Nations, that the *Zeitgeist* is poisoned, and that the upper stratum of society in large towns is a sort of hospital of actual or potential epileptics, then are we all doubly and trebly cursed. The pity of it is that Dr Nordau should partially spoil an excellent case by such palpable overstatement. Indeed, an opponent might fairly retort that our learned Teuton's exaggeration and his overstrained pessimism are just as much evidence of a disordered intellect as are the eccentricities of the authors he condemns. Nevertheless, in spite of these faults and certain others of tone and temper, his book remains a memorable protest against the foulness and hysteria which deface modern literature, and the waywardness and maudlin sensibility which impair the intellectual "movement" of the latter half of the century.

I do not propose to follow Dr Nordau in his searching analysis of Continental authors belonging to the decadent or "degenerate" schools. Anybody desiring to acquaint himself with the morbid abominations with which they abound will have his curiosity abundantly satisfied in the pages of "Degeneration." He will find there eloquent expression given to the feeling of loathing, usually inarticulate, with which their works inspire healthy-minded people— a feeling that is aroused less, as a rule, by their immorality than by their unnaturalness, morbidity, and general unwholesomeness. And our pale English imitations of Continental decadentism are almost as objectionable as their originals. They are less highly seasoned, no doubt, because the authors (or their publishers) have still some fear of Mrs Grundy before their eyes, while it is easy to see that they would say a great deal more than they do if they only dared. On the other hand, they display less talent, and they lack the saving merit of originality. Both their style and their matter are borrowed—so much so that our late apostle of æstheticism is said to have earned the admiration of a brother *précieux*[14] because he had "the courage of other people's opinions." Decadentism is an exotic growth unsuited to British soil, and it may be hoped that it will never take permanent root here. Still, the popularity of debased and morbid literature, especially among women, is not an agreeable or healthy feature. It may be that it is only a passing fancy, a cloud on our social horizon that will soon blow over; but the enormous sale of hysterical and disgusting books is a sign of the times which ought not to be ignored.

Continental influence upon our literature is more apparent now than for many years past. The predilection for the foul and repulsive, the puling emotionalism, and the sickly sensuousness of the French decadents, are also the leading characteristics of the nascent English schools. The former, to take a single example, are the direct intellectual progenitors of our æsthetes, whose doctrines Dr Nordau examines at quite unnecessary length. He takes far too seriously their intellectual clowning, their laboured absurdities and inane paradoxes which the vulgar mistake for wit, as well as the assiduous literary and artistic mountebankery with which they have advertised themselves into notoriety. For a while sensible and healthy-minded people regarded with half-amused contempt their antics, and their absurd claim to form a species of artistic aristocracy apart from the common herd, but the contempt has since deepened into disgust. Recent events, which shall be nameless, must surely have opened the eyes even of those who have hitherto been blind to the true inwardness of modern æsthetic Hellenism, and perhaps the less said on this subject now the better.

A somewhat similar, and scarcely less unlovely, offspring of hysteria and foreign "degenerate" influence is the neurotic and repulsive fiction which so justly incensed the "Philistine" in the "Westminster Gazette." Its hysterical origin shows itself chiefly in its morbid spirit of analysis. Judging from their works, the authors must be vivified notes of interrogation. Their characters are so dreadfully introspective. When they are not talking of psychology, they are discussing physiology. They search for new thrills and sensations, and they possess a maddening faculty of dissecting and probing their "primary impulses"—especially the sexual ones. Being convinced, like the ancient sage, that "there is nothing so dreadful in its nakedness as the heart of man,"[15] they endeavour to explore its innermost recesses. They are oppressed with a dismal sense that everything is an enigma, that they themselves are "playthings of the inexplicable"; or else they try to "compass the whole physiological gamut of their being"—whatever that may be. I am quoting from Miss George Egerton's "Discords," a fair type of English neurotic fiction, which some critics are trying to make us believe is very high-class literature. I must confess that I find the characters in these books more agreeable when they are indulging in nebulous cackle like the above than when they are describing their sexual emotions. The cackle means nothing, and at any rate serves—as Balzac said of his unintelligible sentence—*mystifier le bourgeois.*"[16]

It is noticeable that most of these profound psychological creations belong to that sex in which, according to Mrs Sarah Grand, "the true spirit of God dwells," and which, we are assured by another authority, "constitutes the angelic portion of humanity." "To be a woman is to be mad," says the notorious and neurotic Mrs Ebbsmith.[17] Possibly, but the woman of the new Ibsenite neuropathic school is not only mad herself, but she does her best to drive those around her crazed also. As far as the husband is concerned, he is seldom deserving of much sympathy. In morbid novels and problem plays he is usually an imbecile, a bully, or a libertine. An even worse charge has recently been preferred against him: he is apt to snore horribly, thereby inducing insomnia—a disease to which our neuropaths are naturally subject. Indeed, the horrors of matrimony from the feminine point of view are so much insisted upon nowadays, and the Husband-Fiend is trotted out so often both in fiction and in drama, that one wonders how the demon manages still to command a premium in the marriage market. "What brutes men are!" is the never-ceasing burden of the new woman's song, yet the "choked up, seething pit" of matrimony (*vide* the "Notorious Mrs Ebbsmith") is still tolerably full. The latest phase in the discussion of the eternal sex-problem, or marriage question, is a cry of revolt recently sounded in an American magazine by Lady Henry Somerset concerning "the unwelcome child." I do not propose to trench on this very delicate subject further than to mention that a very new woman,[18] a German unit of the angelic portion of humanity, has suggested a highly effective method of dealing with the intrusive little stranger—chloroform. Let us hope, however, that this lady is somewhat in advance even of the "intellectual movement" of the end of the nineteenth century.

The physiological excursions of our writers of neuropathic fiction are usually confined to one field—that of sex. Their chief delight seems to be in making their characters discuss matters which would not have been tolerated in the novels of a decade or so ago. Emancipated woman in particular loves to show her independence by dealing freely with the relations of the sexes. Hence all the prating of passion, animalism, "the natural workings of sex," and so forth, with which we are nauseated. Most of the characters in these books seem to be erotomaniacs. Some are "amorous sensitives"; others are apparently sexless, and are at pains to explain this to the reader. Here and there a girl indulges in what would be styled, in another sphere, "straight talks to young men." Those nice heroines of "Iota's" and other writers of the physiologico-pornographic school consort by choice with "unfortunates," or else describe at length their sensations in various interesting phases of their lives. The charming Gallia,[19] in the novel of that name, studies letters on the State Regulation of Vice, and selects her husband on principles which are decidedly startling to the old-fashioned reader. Now this sort of thing may be very high art and wonderful psychology to some people, but to me it is garbage pure and simple, and such dull garbage too. If anybody objects that I have picked out some of the extreme cases, I reply that these are just the books that sell. That morbid and nasty books are written is nothing: their popularity is what is disquieting. I have no wish to pose as a moralist. A book may be shameless and disgusting without being precisely immoral—like the fetid realism of Zola and Mr George Moore[20]—and the novels I allude to are at any rate thoroughly unhealthy. I would much rather see a boy or girl reading "Tom Jones" or "Roderick Random" than some of our "modern" works of fiction. Their authors, who write as a rule under a sense of moral compulsion, as martyrs, so to speak, to up-to-date indecency, seem to be following the principles laid down by Tennyson in the lines:—

"Author, atheist, essayist, novelist, realist, rhymester, play your part;
Paint the mortal shame of Nature with the living hues of art.
Rip your brother's vices open; strip your own foul passions bare;
Down with reticence, down with reverence—forward, naked, let them stare,
Feed the budding rose of boyhood with the drainage of your sewer;
Send the drain into the fountain, lest the stream should issue pure.
Set the maiden fancies wallowing in the troughs of Zolaism—
Forward, forward, aye to backward, downward too into Abysm."

If this be an accurate description of contemporary literature when "Locksley Hall—Sixty Years After"[21] was written, one shudders to think what it will be like a few years hence! Perhaps, however, the tide will have turned by then, and the British public will be in the middle of one of these periodical fits of morality which Macaulay[22] found so supremely ridiculous. They may be so, but at any rate John Bull[23] the moralist is a less incongruous figure than John Bull masquerading, as of late years, in anarchical rags tricked out with the peacock feathers of æsthetic culture.

Some critics are fond of complaining of the lack of humour in the "new" fiction. But what in heaven's name do they expect? In this age of sciolism, or half-knowledge, of smattering and chattering, we are too much occupied in improving our minds to be mirthful. In particular the New Woman, or "the desexualised half-man," as a character in "Discords" unkindly calls her, is a victim of the universal passion for learning and "culture," which, when ill-digested, are apt to cause intellectual dyspepsia. With her head full of all the 'ologies and 'isms, with sex-problems and heredity, and other gleanings from the surgery and the lecture-room, there is no space left for humour, and her novels are for the most part merely pamphlets, sermons, or treatises in disguise. The lady novelist of today resembles the "literary bicyclist" so delightfully satirised by the late Lord Justice Bowen. She covers a vast extent of ground, and sometimes her machine takes her along some sadly muddy roads, where her petticoats—or her knickerbockers—are apt to get soiled. As Lord Justice Bowen puts it, "cheap thought, like cheap claret, can be produced on an extensive scale. Instruction grows apace; knowledge comes, as the poet says, but wisdom lingers; intellectual modesty and reserve, the sense of proportion and wholesome mental habits of discrimination, all have yet to be acquired."

The pathological novel is beyond question a symptom of the mental disease from which civilised mankind is suffering. And if the nerves of humanity at large were in the same state as those of the characters in erotomaniac fiction, ours would be a decaying race indeed. These "subtle confidences of the neuropath" are all thoroughly morbid, and remind one of a decadent writer's[24] description of the language of the falling Roman empire, "already mottled with the greenness of decomposition, and, as it were, gamy (*faisandée*)"[25] with incipient decay. And if the idioms a nation uses are in any sense an indication of its state of mental health, surely some of our modern jargon gives us occasion for anxiety. As far as our decadent lady novelists are concerned, we may console ourselves with the reflection that there is one failing which they certainly do not share with their foreign originals—over-refinement of style. Whatever else may be said of them, they are, as a rule, robustly ungrammatical.

Along with its diseased imaginings—its passion for the abnormal, the morbid, and the unnatural—the anarchical spirit broods over all literature of the decadent and "revolting" type. It is rebellion all along the line. Everybody is to be a law unto himself. The restraints and conventions which civilised mankind have set over their appetites are absurd, and should be dispensed with. Art and morality have nothing to do with one another (twaddle borrowed from the French Parnassians);[26] there is nothing clean but the unclean; wickedness is a myth, and morbid impressionability is the one cardinal virtue. Following their French masters, our English "degenerates" are victims of what Dr Nordau calls ego-mania. They are cultivators of the "I"— moral and social rebels, like Ibsen, whose popularity rests far less on his merits as a writer than on the new evangel of revolt which he preaches, or like Ola Hansson,[27] whose aim is to go one better than Ibsen.[28] By the way, the "triumphant doctrine of the ego," which Miss George Egerton finds so comforting, appears to be the theory of a German imbecile[29] who, after several temporary detentions, was permanently confined in a lunatic asylum. His writings being thoroughly hysterical and abnormal, he naturally had a crowd of foolish disciplines who considered him a very great philosopher. Indeed, "Degeneration" is worth reading if only to learn of what very inferior clay are fashioned the idols whom modern "culture" worships. Some of them are mentally diseased beyond question; others rhapsodise over, or have even been convicted of, abominable crimes, while their writings are often crazy and disgusting beyond belief. "The only reality is the 'I,'" cries one of them, "a poor shattered ego-maniac," and his English imitators echo him by proclaiming the development of one's personality to be the sole rational aim of life. "I am responsible before but one tribunal, which is myself," cried the Parisian dynamiter Henry, and this is the keynote of all modern egotism....

Hysteria, whether in politics or art, has the same inevitable effect of sapping manliness and making people flabby. To the æsthete and decadent, who worship inaction, all strenuousness is naturally repugnant. The sturdy Radical of former years, whose ideal was independence and a disdain of Governmental petting, is being superseded by the political "degenerate," who preaches the doctrine that all men are equal, when experience proves precisely the opposite, and dislikes the notion of the best man winning in the struggle to live. Individual effort is to be discouraged, while the weak and worthless are to be pampered at the expense of the capable and industrious. State aid is to dispense with the necessity of thrift and self-reliance, for men will be saved from the natural consequences of their own acts. Hence it is that your anarchist or communist is usually an ineffective person who, finding himself worsted in the battle of life, would plunge society into chaos in the hope of bettering himself....

Is it the fact that, as many believe, we have fallen on a temporarily sterile time, an age of "mental anæmia" and intellectual exhaustion? The world seems growing weary after the mighty work it has accomplished during this most marvellous of centuries. Perhaps the great Titan, finding his back bending under the too vast orb or his fate, would fain lie down and sleep a while. Be that as it may, in politics we seem to be losing faith in ourselves, and leaning more and more on the State for aid. In literature the effects of brain-exhaustion are certainly apparent. A generation that nourished its early youth on Shakespeare and Scott seems like to solace its declining years with Ibsen and Sarah Grand, and an epidemic of suicide is to be feared as the result! In no previous age has such a torrent of crazy and offensive drivel been poured forth over Europe—drivel which is not only written, but widely read and admired, and which the new woman and her male coadjutors are now trying to popularise in England. We may hope, however, that the present reaction will only be temporary, and that humanity will recover itself before it is ripe for Dr Nordau's hospital or lunatic asylum. If the world is going backward now, it is only *reculer pour mieux sauter.*[30] For the moment, if it knew the things would pertain to its peace, it would cease to fume and fret; it would seek to calm, instead of further exciting, its agitated nerve-centres, and to regain, if possible, some measure of its lost repose.

To sum up, Dr Nordau has admirably diagnosed the prevailing disease, but he has monstrously exaggerated its universality. The *Zeitgeist* may be poisoned, but not to any great extent, and the *Zeitgeist* can be trusted to find its own antidote before long. In this country, at any rate, amid much flabbiness and effeminacy, there is plenty of good sense and manliness lift, and I never can see the evidence of the moral or material degeneration (in the ordinary sense of the word) of the mass of the population. Luxury may be increasing, but athleticism redresses the balance, and if our young barbarians *are* all at play, why, so much the better. In artistic and ethical matters most people are still what Mr Grant Allen contemptuously calls "average Philistines"—and long may they remain so. In other words, they adhere to the old-fashioned ideas of social order and decency. At the same time, our age, like every other, has its ugly features and its special dangers that threaten it. I know that each generation is apt to think that its own vices and crazes are peculiar to itself. We forget that there were literary fops in the days of Molière, and that fashionable fops, snobs, and money-grubbers there have always been and always will be. Nasty plays and books are nothing new, and the faults and follies of to-day are pretty much those that Juvenal satirised. All this is perfectly true, yet I cannot help thinking that Dr Nordau's charge of "degeneration" (in the specialist's sense) as a malady peculiar to our time is justified by the facts. Never was there an age that worked so hard or lived at such high pressure, and it would be strange indeed if the strain upon our nerves were not beginning to tell. In fact, excessive nervous sensibility is regarded by some as a thing to be admired and cultivated. It is a bad sign when people grow proud of their diseases, especially if the disease is one which, if left unchecked, will poison the springs of national life. That there is a moral cancer in our midst is not to be denied, and that it has its roots deep down in morbid hysteria seems equally clear. That such morbidity is directly fed and fostered by the "new" art and the "new" literature—themselves symptoms of the disease—is a (to me) self-evident proposition. So far our fiction is only "gamy": let us see to it that we do not acquire a taste for the carrion of the French literary vulture.

It is time that a stand were made by sane and healthy-minded people against the "gilded and perfumed putrescence" which is creeping over every branch of art. Concerning fiction enough has been said, but what of the problem play with its medley of social faddists, sots, harlots, and crazy neuropaths who discuss the "workings of sex," or, more unpleasant still, the gospel of sexlessness as preached by Tolstoi and his disciples? No doubt the bulk of the manhood and womanhood of this country are sound enough, but it has been well said that "nations perish from the top downwards." And if the leaders of the intellectual movement of the day, as it expresses itself in contemporary art—those who mould the thoughts and shape the tendencies of future generations—if these are in a sense mentally diseased, is not the whole body politic likely to be soon infected? The remedy is a very simple one, if people would only enforce it. The so-called Philistines are still the large majority of the population, and if only these would resolutely boycott morbid and nasty books and plays, they would soon be swept, for a time at least, into the limbo of extinct crazes. The matter rests largely in the hands of women. I do not wish to say anything unfair, but I think it cannot be denied that women are chiefly responsible for the "booming" of books that are "close to life"—life, that is to say, as viewed through sex-maniacal glasses. They are greater novel-readers than men, to begin with, and their curiosity is piqued by the subjects dealt with in the new fiction and drama, and not a few of them regard the authors as champions of their rights. In all matters relating to decency and good taste men gladly acknowledge the supremacy of women, and we may surely ask them to give us a lead in discouraging books which are a degradation of English literature. Frankly, isn't the whole thing getting slightly ridiculous as well as sickening?

If public opinion should prove powerless to check the growing nuisance, all the poor Philistine can do is to stop his ears and hold his nose until perhaps finally the policeman is called in to his aid. It is always well to dispense with that useful functionary as far as possible, but, if matters go on at the present rate, it may soon become a question whether his services will not again be required. They have proved highly effectual before now, and an occasional prosecution has an amazing moral effect upon the weak-kneed. Above all, it is to be hoped that that much-abused but most necessary official, the Licenser of Plays,[31] will harden his heart and do his duty undeterred by the ridicule heaped upon him by interested persons. Ours is a free country, no doubt, but the claim for liberty to disseminate morbid abomination among the public ought not to be entertained for a moment.

Much of the modern spirit of revolt has its origin in the craving for novelty and notoriety that is such a prominent feature of our day. A contempt for conventionalities and a feverish desire to be abreast of the times may be reckoned among the first-fruits of decadentism. Its subtle and all pervading influence is observable nowadays in the affectations and semi-indecency of fashionable conversation. The social atmosphere is becoming slightly *faisandée*, as Gautier[32] has it. Effeminacy and artificiality of manner are so common that they have almost ceased to appear ridiculous. Table-talk is garnished with the choice flowers of new woman's speech or the jargon of our shoddy end-of-the-century Renaissance. In certain sections of society it requires some courage to be merely straightforward and natural. Personally, I esteem it rather a distinction to be commonplace. Affectation is not a mark of wit, nor does the preaching of a novel theory or crack-brained social fad argue the possession of a great intellect. Whence, then, sprang the foolish fear of being natural, the craving to attitudinise in everything? The answer is plain. It was Oscar Wilde who infected us with our dread of the conventional, with the silly straining after originality characteristic of a society that desires above all things to be thought intellectually smart. "To be natural is to be obvious, and to be obvious is to be inartistic;" and the buffoonery of a worldly-wise and cynical charlatan was accepted by many as inspired gospel truth. Truly, they be strange gods before whom modern culture bows down! But let the Philistine take heart of grace. He is not alone in his fight for common-sense and common decency. That large number of really cultivated people whose instincts are still sound and healthy, who disbelieve in "moral autonomy," but cling to the old ideals of discipline and duty, of manliness and self-reliance in men, and womanliness in women; who sicken at Ibsenism and the problem play, at the putrid eroticism of a literature that is at once hysterical and foul; who, despising the apes and mountebanks of the new culture, refuse to believe that to be "modern" and up-to-date is to have attained to the acme of enlightenment,—all these will be on his side.

"THE PSYCHOLOGY OF FEMINISM"

HUGH E.M. STUTFIELD

[*Blackwood's* 161 (January 1897): 104-17]

The Soul of Woman, its Sphinx-like ambiguities and complexities, its manifold contradictions, its sorrows and joys, its vagrant fancies and never-to-be-satisfied longings, furnish the literary analyst of these days with inexhaustible material. Above all do the sex-problem novelist and introspective biographer and essayist revel in the theme. Psychology—word more blessed than Mesopotamia—is their never-ending delight! And modern woman, who, if we may believe those who claim to know most about her, is a sort of walking enigma, is their chief subject of investigation. Her ego, that mysterious entity of which she is now only just becoming conscious, is said to remain a *terra incognita* even to herself;[33] but they are determined to explore its inmost recesses. The pioneers of this formidable undertaking must of necessity be women. Man, great, clumsy, comical creature that he is, knows nothing of the inner springs of the modern Eve's complicated nature. He sees everything in her, we are told, without comprehending anything, and the worst of it is that often he cannot even express his ignorance in good English. Man possesses brute force, woman divine influence, and her nature is in closer relation with the infinite than the masculine mind. He is an "utter failure," while her womanhood "almost guarantees to her a knowledge of the eternal verities," which he can only hope partially to attain to through woman.

Obviously, therefore, it is to women writers that we must look for the solution of what is termed the "feminine enigma," and more especially to their more recently published works. It is only lately that woman has really begun to turn herself inside out, as it were, and to put herself into her books. A German authoress, whose interesting work I shall deal with presently, observes that the great feminine intellects of former years simply followed in man's footsteps, and philosophised and preached after the manner of the leading male thinkers of the day. A well-known authoress of our time, Mrs Humphry Ward,[34] may be said to do the same. It is quite different with modern women's books of the introspective type. No man, were he the greatest genius alive, could write them, and in them the true spirit of feminism dwells. And yet, in spite of their multitude, the subject of the sex's psychology is so far only scratched. As Mrs Roy Devereux tells us in her book, "The

Ascent of Woman,"[35] "The first loyal luminous word is still to write about woman"; and even this talented authoress has exhausted her energies in framing a few syllables of the message which must be left to some future seer to deliver. Nevertheless it may be hoped that this fascinating science of feminine psychology is now approaching the stage of rapid and continuous development.

In olden days woman was less troubled about the nature of her soul, possibly for the sufficient reason that it was then considered doubtful if she possessed such a thing. Mohammedans, for instance, used to be credited with a disbelief in the existence of the feminine soul. Their Prophet, however, cannot be accused of justifying their scepticism, although Sale[36] tells us that once when he looked down into hell he perceived the majority of its denizens to be women. Doubtless this uncourteous vision occurred to him after a tiff with Ayesha.[37] In much later days a celebrated Archbishop described woman as "a creature that cannot reason and pokes the fire from the top"; and there are people who now urge me to treat the subject of her soul and its attributes after the manner of "Snakes in Ireland"! Again, the American woman is regarded by many people as the highest development of modern feminism, yet she is frequently accused of being soulless. A recent writer in the "Contemporary Review" points out that she has failed to inspire the classical literature even of her own country, as the female characters of the great American novelists were drawn from English or Continental sources; and the reason, he thinks, must be sought in the lack of depth in her nature. An American girl in a recent novel, if I remember rightly, opines that she has no soul, "only digestion." Be this as it may, the average European appears to find the Translantic Undine sufficiently charming. He marries her, even though, owing to her congenital defect, he cannot vivisect her soul in three-volume novels. The American woman, as we see her on this side of the Ocean, is usually an exotic of the "orchidaceous type"; but, speaking generally, we may regard the vexed question of the existence of the feminine soul as being now finally set at rest. In order, however, that there may be no mistake about the matter, the lady writer has for some years past been busily occupied in baring her soul for our benefit. And not only baring it, but dissecting it, analysing and probing into the innermost crannies of her nature. She is for ever examining her mental self in the looking-glass. Her every thought and impulse, her fleeting whims and fancies, along with the deepest fountains of her feeling, and above all her grievances, are set forth in naked black and white. The monotony of her life, its narrowness of interest, the brutality and selfishness of man, the burden of sex, and the newly awakened consciousness of ill-usage at Nature's hands, form the principal subjects of her complaint; and the chorus of her wailings surges up to heaven in stories, poems, and essays innumerable. Their dominant note is restlessness and discontent with the existing order of things; and that there is some reason in it few will be found to deny. Man has no idea what it feels like to be a woman, but it will not be her fault if he does not soon begin in some degree to understand.

The glory of woman in olden days, according to St Paul, was her hair.[38] The glory of the woman of to-day, as portrayed in sex-problem literature, is her "complicatedness." To be subtle, inscrutable, complex—irrational possibly, but at any rate incomprehensible—to puzzle the adoring male, to make him scratch his head in vexation and wonderment as to what on earth she will be up to next,—this is the ambition of the latter-day heroine. She is consumed with a desire for new experiences, new sensations, new objects in life. Like Evadne in "The Heavenly Twins" she "wants to know";[39] to penetrate to the core of truth; to dive deep down into the sacred heart of things, and to learn their true sequence and meaning. But in spite of the awakening of her intellect she remains a being of transient impulses and more or less hysterical emotions. Curiously enough, in all this mystification of hers, which to the uninitiated appears sheer puzzle-headedness, some weird witchery is supposed to lurk. Her lover, poor fellow, is baffled by her elusive and contradictory spirit; he understands nothing of the perpetual conflict within her, and canker of mysterious care that gnaws at her heart, her immense yearnings, and great vague thirst for heaven alone knows what. The dualism of her nature, half instinct, half intellect—for, as Mrs Roy Devereux explains, modern woman is not one incomprehensible, but two incomprehensibles—is all Greek to him. He endures her tantrums as best he may, though his simple self would be better mated with an open-hearted natural woman, who wore her heart upon her sleeve, than with an animated riddle or an enigma in flounces and furbelows. For, be it understood, love itself fails to unravel the mystery of her being, and Mr Spooner's flirtations with Miss Up-to-date in no way give him the key to the feminine abstraction of which she is the external garniture. And it is good for him that it should be so, else he, too, might suffer the pangs of disillusionment. Nowadays, however, the solution of the feminine conundrum is a less hopeless task than formerly for the bewildered and slightly irritated male; and the present year has given birth to at least two books which throw much light upon the subject.

Of these the most remarkable in some respects in the "Ascent of Woman," by Mrs Roy Devereux, to which allusion has been made already. It is, to begin with, a distinctly clever book. It contains much shrewd observation, while the style is polished and epigrammatic to a fault, and replete with the *curiosa felicitas*[40] of decadentism. But it is less with the manner than with some of the matter of these essays that I am now concerned, as much in them will be news to a great many people. They originally bore the title of "*Dies Dominae*,"[41] and they are dedicated to "The most dear vision of Her that shall be."

Signs, I think, are not wanting that the *dies dominæ* will dawn before very long, and in that case "She that shall be" will most probably appear as "She-who-must-be-obeyed."[42] The authoress does not profess to dispel the cloud of mystery which envelops her subject, but she does raise for our benefit a corner of the veil which shrouds the Great Arcanum of the feminine soul. The picture thus revealed is a curious one, and she is aware that her method of presenting it is likely to arouse the resentment of her fellow-women; but she is prepared to face the consequences. There is so much to say about woman which has never yet been said, that the truth that is in her must out; and, like Lucifer the light-bringer, she feels bound to fulfil her mission of illuminating a people that now sit in the darkness of ignorance concerning the psychology of feminism.

The most characteristic portions of the book are those dealing with the great sex-problem, as it is called. "Man," says Mrs Roy Devereux, is apt to "rail at the sexlessness of the New Woman"; but, if we may take her as a trustworthy guide, the charge is a baseless one. For with the awakening of her intellect "there has been a coincident awakening of the senses.... Every problem in heaven and earth is brought to the edge of this newly-acquired consciousness, and the she-animal is abroad cursing man's monopoly of the *joie-de-vivre*." Moreover, the instincts of fidelity are not in her. "To every season its book and its bonnet; why not also its love?"

"So at each renascence of passion her spirit, drifting among the ghosts of disembodied kisses, has a faint foretaste of those yet to come. Nor is this the limit of her consciousness. With that realisation of her nature's complexity comes the prescience that no man will ever learn it through.... It is only the man who 'in love's deep woods will dream of loyal life.'"

This tribute to his constancy will doubtless be as agreeable to the much-abused male as it is unexpected. My only doubt is whether the perfidious creature deserves the compliment. In another strangely eloquent passage, which I quote in full, we have a terrible picture of the tumult raging in the modern Eve's bosom.

"At the moment woman seems still to be floating amid the mists of her lost illusions, on fire with the passion of the impossible, sick unto death of her outworn ideals, and girt about with the incense of strange prayers. Having forsworn the service of love she would still retain the beauty of life, and wander over 'the crooked hills of delicious pleasure' without forfeiting the old-world sanctuary. She would sin and yet not suffer; she would pluck the 'roses and raptures' of passion, and yet be white of soul. But until she learns that love cannot be bought at store prices, she will drift deathwards undelighted and unshriven—a follower after empty symbols and impotent divinities. Yet will this quickened consciousness lead eventually to her perfecting."

To those who, like the writer, were brought up in the Sarah Grandian school to believe in the moral and mental perfection of the modern incarnation of the feminine spirit, these indiscreet revelations came as a sad shock. They appeared originally in the form of an article in the "Saturday Review" entitled "Dies Dominæ; The Value of Love by a Woman of the Day"; and I remember that the editor appended thereto a homily in the form of a rejoinder by Lady Jeune as a wholesome corrective. As might be expected, Lady Jeune disputed entirely the accuracy of the picture. Indeed, to find its counterpart one would probably have to search in the miscellaneous gallery of feminine portraiture with which modern fiction supplies us. I need only mention a few of the types, for their names have become household words: the woman who did, who didn't;[43] who would, who wouldn't, or would if she could; the girl who desires matrimony, but shrinks from its obligations; and the lady who yearns for motherhood, if only it could be managed (*vide* "Keynotes") "without a husband or the disgrace; ugh, the disgusting men!" These searching studies in the sexual emotions of young ladies are, I fear, a source of merriment to the masculine mind, but their popularity with the gentler sex survives alike their constant iteration and the gibes of the scoffer. Age cannot wither, nor custom stale, the infinite variety of the sex-problem novel or essay....

Another treatise, on the same subject, to which I should like to introduce readers of "Maga," is "Modern Woman," by Fru Marholm Hansson.[44]...

Concerning Mrs George Egerton, who is to my mind the ablest of our women writers of the neurotic school, Fru Hansson writes with critical yet sympathetic insight. The authoress of "Keynotes" ("Punch" profanely nicknamed it "She Notes") is essentially a womanly writer. Her gifts are intuitive rather than intellectual, and she owes nothing whatever to the reason or the research of man. Her perceptions are of the nerves, for, like some of her favourite Swedish and Norwegian authors, she personifies our modern nervousness, and her best characters are quivering bundles of nerves. The reader can hardly fail to recognise the autobiographical character of her writings, redolent, as they are, of the spirit of discontent and disillusionment. Stories of the "Keynotes" type, especially the more artistic ones, are monologues, as it were. The writers seem to be relating their own mental experiences, like Marie Bashkirtseff,[45] without any attempt at concealment. The mood varies in these books—sometimes tender, sometimes sorrowful, sometimes vicious, as though the authoress would like to scratch or slap somebody; but they are always purely subjective, or else rapid generalisations from limited experience. Like all introspective work of the kind, Mrs Egerton's appeals to women far more than to men, for her instinct enables her to perceive the fundamental traits of woman's nature. Of these traits the deepest and most ineradicable, it appears, is her "eternal wildness, the untamed primitive savage temperament that lurks in the mildest, best woman." Mrs. Roy Devereux also asserts that woman is at heart a barbarian, and her affinity in many respects to her remote ancestresses is insisted on by other lady writers. Backwards across the ages, remarks one of them, her gaze flashes recognition to "the grand untamed eyes of the primeval woman," whose freedom from the restraints of civilisation some of our *revoltées* would seem to envy. Only one man, we are told, "has had sufficient instinct to bring to light this abyss in woman's nature," a poet named Barbey D'Aurévilly, and he, poor fellow, was never understood. This seems to be the usual fate of people with very complex natures in both sexes. They make a study of incomprehensibility, and raise mystification to the level of a fine art, and then complain because they are misunderstood. It is not quite clear why this somewhat commonplace trait of wildness should be called an "abyss," except that all terms denoting profundity and immensity are deemed appropriate to the feminine soul, which possesses many other fundamental characteristics besides that of wildness. It is volcanic, for instance, in its nature, as may be learned from the neurotic novelists, and as some men, I am given to understand, have occasion to know. I notice, by way of illustration, that one young lady describes herself as "a bundle of electric currents bursting forth in all directions into chaos." This, however, strikes me as a somewhat daring metaphor. Personally, I should be content to liken the spirit of feminism to a river, now flowing tranquilly with every passing sentiment and impression mirrored on its placid surface, now surging tumultuously onwards—but always prodigiously deep.

Another characteristic, according to Fru Marholm Hansson, is beginning to make itself felt, "and that is an intense and morbid consciousness of the ego in woman." Mrs Egerton is, of course, a great believer in the Scandinavian doctrine of the ego. Self-sacrifice is out of fashion altogether in our modern school of novelists, and self-development has taken its place. This consciousness of the self is of recent growth: it was unknown to our mothers and grandmothers, who, says Mrs Devereux, "knew as little about their sensations as a cabbage does about its growth." I have no knowledge of what it feels like to be conscious of your ego, so I must content myself with simply chronicling the phenomenon without commenting upon it. It has always been understood that the best sign of all being right with a man's heart or liver is, that he should not be conscious of possessing such things; and to be conscious of your ego must be a much more serious matter. I remember that Max Nordau classes egomania as among the leading stigmata of degeneration, so doubtless this newly aroused consciousness lies at the root of our modern introspectiveness, and accounts for many of the strange things that neurotic people do both in real life and in fiction....

We have lately been witnessing a slight recrudescence of the Ibsen "boom"; so, being naturally interested in the father of the new psychology, I attended a *matinée* of "Little Eyolf"[46] at the Avenue theatre. I arrived early, but found the house already full. There was a small sprinkling of males, but woman had assembled in force to do honour to the Master who headed the revolt of her sex. The new culture and the newest *chiffon* were alike represented in the audience, proving that intellectual womanhood has listened to Mrs Roy Devereux and once more begun (did it ever cease?) to beautify itself in real earnest. Through a forest of colossal and befeathered hats I obtained occasional glimpses of the stage and the performers engaged in their self-appointed but depressing task—the hero, the usual Ibsenite idiot or travesty of a man, with a chronic but futile appetite for well-doing; his wife Rita, a neurotic "she-animal,"—she, all for the "roses and raptures"; he, preferring the "lilies and languors,"—and the pantomime witch or Rat-wife, who is, according to the critics, "a heavenly messenger," and apparently symbolical of anything you please. Two mortal hours those two poor unbalanced creatures, the Allmers, spent in dismal psychologising and mutual torment and self-torture. The acting was excellent, and it was an intellectual treat to see three such artists as Mrs Patrick Campbell, Miss Robins, and Miss Janet Achurch[47] on the stage together. Everything that art can do was done to infuse life and reality into these doleful marionettes, but the general impression the two Allmers made on my mind was that of a couple of epileptics exercising in the hospital grounds. In particular, Miss Achurch's scream at the end of the first Act, which has been much admired by connoisseurs in painful sensations, recalled vividly to my mind the screeching of a woman whom I once had the misfortune to see fall down in an epileptic fit. However, the audience, or rather some of the female portion of it, seemed at times much affected, and sobs and tears occasionally greeted such passages in the drama as were especially lugubrious. The males, I regret to say, were more disposed to chuckle irreverently, probably because the contemplation of nervous disorders and the whinings of sexual hysteria, and other forms of mental disease, less arouse the sympathy of the dull masculine mind. "Morbid trash," my nearest neighbour ejaculated as we emerged into the comparatively pure atmosphere of a London fog; while I went home and read Max Nordau's chapter on Ibsen in "Degeneration," and felt better.

The author of this dismal and evil-smelling play is certainly one of the portents of the age. He voices better than any one else its morbid tendencies, and, although a man, he is distinctly the founder of the new so-called science of feminine psychology. That is to say, he above all others has directed the energies of the woman psychologist into the channels they now run in. To my humble way of thinking, these semi-insane weaklings and irresponsible neuropaths of the Ibsenite drama are neither admirable nor interesting. They are simply "sick" men and women; degenerates to be shunned, like any other manifestations of disease. And yet they serve as the pattern and type of characters in books and plays innumerable that have taken hold of the public mind. It would be interesting to know how far this literature is the cause, and how far simply the expression, of the morbid tendencies of which I have spoken. The shockingly improper young person in Miss Marie Corelli's "Sorrows of Satan,"[48] who would have flirted with the Devil if that more self-respecting personage had permitted her, attributed her moral downfall to our modern literature of decadence. It was the "satyr-songster," Swinburne,[49] and those wicked women novelists, who wrought all the mischief. Max Nordau thinks that the influence of polite literature on life is much greater than that of life on polite literature. He mentions several instances of fashions being set by books, the most remarkable one being the epidemic of suicide that broke out in Germany after the publication of "The Sorrows of Young Werther."[50] Every one knows that the young men in Byron's time went about wearing low-cut collars and a terrible scowl, denoting their views of the misery and hopelessness of life. These views were probably derived from verses like the following:—

"We wither from our youth, we gasp away—
Sick, sick; unfound the boon, unslaked the thirst.
Though to the last in verge of our decay,
Some phantom lures, such as we sought at first—
But all too late—so are we doubly curst.
Love, fame, ambition, avarice—'tis the same,
Each idle, and all ill, and none the worst—
For all are meteors with a different name,
And Death the sable smoke where vanishes the flame."[51]

This stanza contains as good psychology and as good philosophy as any Scandinavian drama, while there is something almost elevating in the swing and rhythm of the majestic verse compared with the commonplace and the *banalités* of Ibsen's "Ollendorffian" dialogue. No doubt the Byronic morbidity was all affectation, but so to a great extent is the psychology and morbid pessimism of these days. Marie Bashkirtseff was a walking affectation, a mere pose in petticoats, but she succeeded in making herself intensely miserable. And it seems certain that the same process of needless self-torture is at work in some women's minds now. It is difficult to explain on any other hypothesis their craving for the literature of hysteria or decadence—the doleful squalor of Ibsen, the mawkishness of the neurotic fiction writers, or that strange blend of "hoggishness and hysteria," to borrow a truculent critic's phrase, "Jude the Obscure."[52]

I know there are people who say that the whole thing is mere literary and journalistic froth—just as the New Woman was said to be solely a creation of the comic newspapers—and that the sex is no more uneasy in its mind than it was formerly. Surely, however, the evidence is all the other way. The New

Woman is simply the woman of to-day striving to shake off old shackles, and the immense mass of "revolting" literature cannot have grown out of nothing, or continue to flourish upon mere curiosity. Mrs Devereux's chapter on "The Feminine Potential" contains some caustic satire on the sham realism with which some women nowadays saturate their souls, and their "cult of the gutter" is unkindly described as "simply a form of hysteria based upon a morbid appetite for coquetting with sin, so characteristic of the modern woman."

Besides being the outward and visible sign of our modern *malaise* of the nerves, these books are also an undoubted aggravation of the disorder. If one asks what is the good of it all, one is told that it is inevitable. But surely morbidity is a disease which can be combated like other diseases, and equally, on the other hand, aggravated by continually dwelling on morbid subjects. And, after all, the world is not made up entirely of refuse-heaps or hospitals; and no sort of good can come out of this literary scavenging and constant removal of the rags that cover poor humanity's sores. That life is full of suffering, and that women have more than their fair share of it, are facts sufficiently sad in themselves without perpetually harping upon them. Of all regrets, we are told, "the nausea of sex is the vainest, the most futile"; and surely even the lot of women has its compensations. There are still many left who have the pluck to say that, in spite of all temptations to belong to the opposite sex, they prefer to remain as they are. Much has been done already, especially in the way of relaxing certain stupid social conventions, to make their lives freer and happier than they were before, and more, doubtless, will be done in the future. To take one small instance, the bicycle, though in some respects it has added a new terror to life, has certainly done something to take women out of themselves, and thus to lighten the load they bear. I cannot help thinking that if poor Marie Bashkirtseff had only possessed a "bike," it might have prolonged her life by rendering her less self-centred and miserable than she was.

There is much that is pathetic in the self-questioning and the cravings of the type of woman depicted in neurotic fiction. There is a note of infinite weariness, a kind of anæmic despondency, in books of the "Keynotes" class; but there is also a note of real pain. No one can read them without seeing that the writers have felt, and felt deeply; but while their dolefulness may command our sympathy, the expression of it in hysterical or squalid stories is not to be encouraged, for it does but add one grain more to the heap of humanity's woes. The sale of these books by thousands is not a healthy sign. People read them because they are interested in them, and the interest arises from the fact that what they read corresponds to something in their own natures. Fru Hansson tells us that when "Keynotes" was published the critics said that the heroines were exceptional types; but the critics, as usual, were wrong. "'Good heavens! How stupid they are!' laughed Mrs Egerton. Numberless women wrote to her, women whom she did not know, and whose acquaintance she never made. 'We are quite ordinary everyday sort of people,' they said; 'we lead trivial unimportant lives: but there is something in us that vibrates to your touch, for we, too, are such as you describe.'" If so many hysterical people really exist, the best advice that can be given them is to try and cultivate a sense of humour and to "bike" in moderation.

One morbid symptom of our social life is certainly fostered and developed by books of the "revolting" type, and that is the mutual suspiciousness of men and women. Fru Hansson remarks that, in spite of the breaking down of many barriers of social intercourse, there never was a time when the sexes stood wider apart than at present; and when man is represented by so many lady novelists as a blackguard or an idiot, or both, sometimes diseased, always a libertine and a bully, one can hardly wonder at the result. There is no doubt that the literature of vituperation and of sex-mania, with its perpetual harping on the miseries of married life, and its public washing of domestic dirty linen, tends to widen the breach between men and women, and to make them more mutually distrustful than ever.

To institute comparisons between the literary pygmies of these days and the giants of the past may possibly provoke a smile. Nevertheless it may be useful, perhaps, *magnis componere parva*,[53] to see in what qualities we moderns are especially deficient. As far as mere style goes, there are many living writers who are the superiors of Scott, to take a single example. This sounds rank heresy, but it is nevertheless true. But in such larger matters as character-drawing, in breadth of sympathy and observation, and, most of all, in their sense of proportion and the atmosphere of restfulness and restraint which envelops their work, the older authors far surpass their successors. Unlike the latter, the great novelists of this century were never morbid or hysterical, and they maintained a dignified reticence in dealing with delicate subjects. The soul of woman was presented by them in less questionable shape. One cannot imagine Diana Vernon,[54] to take one instance that occurs to me, prattling in public about her sexual emotions. Very possibly she may have been filled, like any young person in modern fiction, with "erotic yearnings for fulness of life," but at any rate she had the good taste to keep them to herself. The feebler literary folk of to-day have departed from these wholesome traditions, and have determined to set themselves free from what one of their number, Mr Grant Allen, calls "the leprous taint of respectability." Not content with the shining examples set them by their great English forerunners, they blindly copy French and Norwegian models, and endeavour to supplement their own lack of talent, and to stimulate the flagging interest of their readers, by concentrating their attention upon whatever is foul and unlovely in life.

I read in the newspapers not long ago that an American lady was fortunate enough to obtain the coveted appointment of Garbage Inspector in the town of Denver, with power to burn and destroy the city refuse; and the thought struck me that it might be well if some enterprising Englishwoman could be found to undertake the post of Literary Garbage Inspector in this country, with authority to relieve the shelves of our circulating libraries of the rubbish under which they groan. I fear, however, the task would be beyond the powers of any single person to accomplish. In the long-run the reading public must always be its own censor of books, with the Press as its most effective auxiliary; and it is the *láches* of the Press that are largely responsible for the vulgarisation of our fiction in the past decade. As far as concerns the past year, it may readily be admitted that both the literature and the drama of 1896 have shown a distinct improvement upon those of two or three years ago. The protests of the Philistines have not been altogether in vain. We have seen less of our so-called realists and second-hand Diabolists, our fishers for grotesque fantasies in the unclean waters of a diseased imagination. The tide of popular taste is flowing in healthier channels, and the change seems to have affected even that most "modern" of poets, Mr John Davidson. We thought he belonged to the anarchical school, but the following verse of his "Ballad of a Workman" seems to prove him a convert to the old-fashioned ideas of discipline and self-restraint:—

"Only obedience can be great;
    It brings the Golden Age again;
Even to be still, abiding Fate,
    Is kingly ministry to men!"

I commend these lines, coming as they do from so unexpected a quarter, to those ladies whose souls are filled with the fret and fury of revolt or the questionings and self-torture of the new psychology. Such sentiments might have emanated from Carlyle himself—so little do they accord with our modern "eleuthero-mania," or the triumphant doctrine of the ego. We seem to have quitted awhile the seductive society of Baudelaire's *surhomme* or the *Urmensch* of Nietzsche,[55] so beloved of the 'Keynotes' novelist, and to be listening once more to the voice of the older prophets. I rather fear, however, lest Mr Davidson may be preaching to deaf ears. Counsels of obedience will be lost upon those watchers for the dawning of the *dies dominæ* who claim, not equality, but admitted supremacy, for their sex. "To be still" is advice no less unpalatable to our neuropaths, male or female, who are so busily occupied in rendering the burden of existence intolerable. It would be well, indeed, if they could be induced to follow it. Both in life and in literature humanity has less need nowadays of mental excitants than of sedatives; and the true prophet of the future will be, not another Ibsen, but one who shall deliver to a disordered world the great gospel of Anti-Fuss.

"THE PHYSICAL INSENSIBILITY OF WOMAN"

CESARE LOMBROSO

[*Fortnightly Review* 51 (March 1892): 354-57]

Incredible as it may appear, it is, nevertheless, the fact that no real data exist concerning the physical and moral conditions of the female constitution. Searching studies have been made of the Bushmen and of the aboriginal Australian races, but, scientifically speaking, little more is known in relation to the admired, adored, despised and misunderstood gentler half of the human race, than if the Dog Star or the planet Mars were its habitat instead of this our earth.

To take a solitary instance: only a short time since, it was discovered that the notions formed of woman's cranial capacity as compared with man's were erroneous, for the simple reason that in establishing the parallel the difference in the respective weight, height, and size of the male and female bodies had not been taken into account. Upon due allowance being made for these variations, it now appears that the capacity of woman's brain is, relatively, very little, if at all, inferior to the capacity of man's. And so disappears a prevalent error founded upon the grossest of "scientific" blundering; but when one considers that this question of the relative cranial capacity of the sexes was one of those to which most attention had been directed, it may be imagined how much of truth is known concerning other peculiarities of the moral and physical constitution of woman.

Thus, upon the subject of feminine sensibility in general, the most authoritative physiological treatises have virtually nothing to say. At the most, their authors may reiterate the common conjecture that women are much more sensitive than men; an opinion which, up to the present, is not confirmed by scientific research.

I have myself used Weber's æsthesiometer to measure the power of tact and sensitiveness to pain at the tip of the forefinger in over a hundred women, and I have found that, except in the case of very young girls, whose tactile sensitiveness is exceedingly developed, women's sense of touch is, in general, nearly twice as obtuse as that of men.

The exact figures in millimetres, are for plebeian women, 2.6 mm.; for women of a superior class, 2.0 mm.; while the average for men is only 1.6 mm. This difference will appear even greater when it is considered that, as shown by inquiries made into the subject under my direction at Turin, the sense of tact is more obtuse in persons presenting a degenerative type of physiognomy, and that such cases are much rarer among women than among men.

With regard to the senses of taste and smell, very little difference between the sexes is discoverable, and, if any exist, it is rather in woman's favour; though even this point is placed in doubt by recent researches.

Passing now to the question of general sensibility, including sensitiveness to pain: by experiments made with the electric algometer it is clearly shown that woman is inferior to man. Among no less than fifty women of the lower classes general sensibility was represented by 90 mm., and sensitiveness to pain by 53 mm.; among an equal number of men of the same condition the figures were respectively 94 mm. and 64 mm. In very young men general sensibility was 95 mm., and sensitiveness to pain 78 mm.; in young girls the figures were 91 and 70 mm.

Thus, judging from results obtained by the algometer women in general are characterized by a marked degree of sensory obtuseness. But should the accuracy of the above figures be doubted (and persons who affect scepticism regarding such results of scientific research are, as I have reason to know, anything but rare), I have sought out still further corroborative data.

From some of the principal surgeons in Europe I have elicited opinions amply confirming me in the above conclusions concerning the manner in which women bear pain during the course of surgical operations effected under the same conditions of age and disease as in the case of an equal number of men. My conclusions are also borne out by a celebrated operation of Dr. Billroth's, who, when he determined upon making his great experiment of the excision of the pylorus, performed it originally upon women, as being less sensitive and better qualified to resist pain.

By Carle I have been informed that the majority of women allow themselves to be operated upon with astonishing insensibility, almost as though the body beneath the surgeon's knife were that of another and not their own. Giordano, too, has assured me that even in the midst of the throes of childbirth, despite their apprehensions, women suffer much less than might be supposed.

One of the most distinguished dentists of Turin, Dr. Martini writes to tell me he has been surprised to observe in his daily practice that women undergo every variety of dental operation with much more courage and facility than men. And Dr. Mela adds that men swoon under the dentist's hands much more frequently than women.

The inferior sensibility of women has been noted, not only by scientists, but by the people, as shown in some of our old Italian proverbs: "A woman has seven skins"; "A woman has a soul, but a little one"; "A woman never dies." Morally, as well as physically, woman's sensibility would seem different from, if not inferior to, man's; for, as Balzac remarks in *César Birotteau*,[56] women apprehend trouble more keenly than men, but feel it less when it actually overtakes them. And, no doubt, the inferior degree of sensibility to moral and physical pain is the chief cause of women's greater longevity. The best authorities on this subject inform us that, during the first twenty years of female life, the mortality is slightly greater than with men; but from twenty to fifty the rate of feminine mortality is much less. Thus the average of woman's life is decidedly longer than man's, leaving out of account the fact, not without bearing on the present argument, that the number of suicides among women is smaller than among men. The greater physical frailty of women, and the extra element of danger to life involved in childbirth, being taken into consideration, the fact of the sex's greater average longevity will appear still more striking, and not to be satisfactorily explained otherwise than by the hypothesis of its inferior sensibility. The moral conditions of woman's life, moreover, are, in the majority of cases, distinctly unfavourable. Reduced to subjection by man, frequently maltreated, and often neglected and abandoned, her lot in middle age is often such as might be expected to shorten her period of existence. Affection is the be-all and end-all of woman's life; and this precious gift is, on the whole, but parsimoniously meted out to her; while, again, to her on the one hand and to man on the other, two weights and two measures are applied and we see that which in the man is deemed but a venial sin, regarded in the woman as an unpardonable crime.

In woman, undoubtedly, the outward expression of moral, if not physical, pain is much more vehement than in the majority of men. This is hinted by our popular Italian saying: "You weep; you are not a man." Or again: "You are a man, and yet are without dignity in your grief." Feminine self-abandonment in moments of painful emotion is due probably to two causes: firstly, the fact that the female brain is known to have less control than the male brain over reflex or semi-reflex actions; and, secondly, the peculiar nature of woman's early training, owing to which, grace and delicacy are expected to be found in her rather than strength or courage. Sooner or later women rarely fail to learn the all-powerful effect of feminine tears, and often succeed, by dint of much practice, in calling them up almost at will. How many cases have been scientifically observed, in which women had the faculty of passing from smiles to sorrow and of weeping, with every appearance of real grief, from one moment to the next!

According to Dr. Tait, speaking at the congress of the French Surgical Society, in 1891, even the sexual sensibility of woman is not on a par with that of man; this being also the case among all animal species. And does not Dante say:—

"... da questo assai ben si comprende
Quanto in femmina fucco d'amor dura
So l'occhio o il tatto spesso nol riaccende."[57]

Again: may it not be argued that the comparative infrequence of cases of sexual psychopathy in women as compared with men tend to denote inferior sensory irritability? Still further, it may be observed that among all peoples, save perhaps the ancient Germans as described by Tacitus,[58] chastity has been regarded mainly as a feminine virtue. Woman, moreover, appears to accept, with equal facility, the *régime* of polygamy in certain lands and of monogamy in others; and, doubtless, a certain physical obtuseness or indifference is at the root of her readiness to put up, according to circumstances, with either system. Herein, too, may be found a reason why, at all times, and among all races, adultery should have been regarded and been punished as a so much more heinous crime in woman than in man. Love, from a certain point of view, appears a more important factor in the problem of woman's life than man's; but it is, nevertheless, an undoubted fact, that the maternal instinct in woman is far more powerful than the erotic tendency, which is, in a so much greater degree, connected with the physical sensibilities. As a gifted gynecologist once expressed it: "Man loves woman for her sex; woman loves in man the husband and the father."

NOTES

1. *Ghosts* (1881) and *A Doll's House* (1879), plays by Henrik Ibsen.
2. *Dodo, a Detail of the Day* (1893) is a novel by Edward Frederic Benson (1867-1940).
3. In Greek and Roman mythology, Cerberus was a three-headed dog guarding the entrance of Hades.
4. Styx, in Greek mythology, is a river of Hades across which Charon ferried the souls of the dead.
5. In Cervantes' *Don Quixote*, the giant Caraculiambro is an imaginary foe whom Quixote seeks to vanquish and send to his lady-love (I, i).
6. *Hedda Gabler* (1890), a play by Henrik Ibsen.
7. *The Heavenly Twins* (1893), a novel by Sarah Grand; *A Grey Eye, or So*, perhaps a reference to Egerton's story "A Little Grey Glove," included in *Keynotes*; *The Yellow Aster* (1894), a novel by Iota (Kathleen Hunt Caffyn); the *Yellow Book* (1894-97), an illustrated quarterly published by Elkin Mathews and John Lane (after October 1894 by Lane alone) and edited by Henry Harland.
8. *The Master Builder* (1892), a play by Henrik Ibsen.
9. Thomas Carlyle (1795-1881), a historian, biographer, and social critic, who believed in a hierarchical society which has leaders and those who can only be content as followers.
10. Max Nordau (1849-1923), born in Hungary, was a physician who played an important role in the Zionist movement, giving the opening speech at the first Zionist Congress. In 1892 he published his book *Degeneration* which angrily attacked much of the culture and many of the intellectuals and writers of the late nineteenth century, including Baudelaire, Wagner, Rossetti, Verlaine, Swinburne, and Nietzsche. Nordau believed that civilization was being threatened by decadence, a loss of vitality, and physical and mental degeneration. In a section on "Egomania" he attacks egotism, particularly Nietzsche's egotistic philosophy which Nordau saw as symptomatic of mental disease.
11. *virginibus puerisque*, for maidens and boys (Latin).

12. Juvenal (60?-140?), Roman satirist who attacked human behavior for being sordid and disgusting and women for possessing almost every vice.

13. Colney Hatch Lunatic Asylum, an institution for the mentally ill in London which is no longer in existence.

14. *précieux*, precious, affected (French).

15. Jeremiah 17:9, "The heart is deceitful above all things, and desperately wicked" (King James Version).

16. *mystifier le bourgeois*, to mystify the middle class (French).

17. Mrs. Ebbsmith, in Arthur Pinero's 1895 play *The Notorious Mrs. Ebbsmith*, wants to live in a free union with a man.

18. Frau von Troll-Borostyani. See the "Quarterly Review" for October 1894 [author's note].

19. Gallia Hamesthwaite, in Ménie Muriel Dowie's novel *Gallia* (1895), selects her husband on the basis of eugenic principles.

20. Both Emile Zola (1840-1902), a French novelist, and George Moore (1852-1933), an English novelist, were naturalist writers.

21. "Locksley Hall Sixty Years After," by Alfred, Lord Tennyson (1809-92), was published in 1886, forty-four years after "Locksley Hall." The poem reflects Tennyson's disillusionment with the optimism and faith in progress he expressed in his earlier poem.

22. Unlike many other Victorian writers, Thomas Babington Macaulay (1800-59) believed that society was improving and that the Industrial Revolution was evidence of that progress.

23. John Bull personifies England or the typical Englishman.

24. Théophile Gautier, quoted in "Degeneration," p. 299 [author's note].

25. *faisandée*, gamy (French).

26. "Degeneration," p. 274 [author's note].

27. Ola Hansson (1860-1925), Swedish poet, prose writer, and critic. In *Dikter* (1884; "Poems") and *Notturno* (1885) he celebrated the beauty and folkways of his native Skåne. In 1887 he published a collection of morbid, erotic sketches called *Sensitiva Amorosa*. His later work reveals an admiration for Nietzsche.

28. "Young Ofeg's Ditties," translated by George Egerton. I have just been reading these "beautiful prose poems," as Miss Egerton calls them, together with Mr Punch's excellent skit thereon, and I am not sure whether the original or the travesty is the more absurd. The author's confused and idiotic babblings mark him out as a worthy disciple and expositor of the mad Nietzsche, whose works Dr Nordau analyses at length. If this is to be the literature of the future, heaven help poor humanity! [author's note]

29. One assumes the reference is to Friedrich Nietzsche (1844-1900), German philosopher, poet, and critic.

30. *reculer pour mieux sauter*, to draw back to jump better (French).

31. The Lord Chamberlain was empowered by Act of Parliament to censor stage performances in Britain. Bernard Shaw's play *Mrs. Warren's Profession* was written in 1893 but did not have a legal public performance in Britain until 1925.

32. Theophile Gautier (1811-72), French poet.

33. George Egerton: "I realised that in literature, everything had been done better by man than woman could hope to emulate. There was only one small plot left for her to tell: the *terra incognita* of herself, as she knew herself to be, not as man liked to imagine her—in a word to give herself away, as man had given himself away in his writing" ("A Keynote to Keynotes," in *Ten Contemporaries,* John Gawsworth, ed., London, 1932).

34. Mrs. Humphry Ward or Mary Ward (1851-1920), a novelist.

35. Mrs. Roy Devereux, *The Ascent of Woman* (1896).

36. George Sale (1697?-1736) translated the Koran into English, adding explanatory notes, as early as 1734. In 1882 *A Comprehensive Commentary on the Qurán Comprising Sale's Translation and Preliminary Discourse* was published. This is perhaps the book by Sale with which Stutfield would have been familiar.

37. Ayesha (611-78) was the chief wife of Mohammed.

38. "But if a woman have long hair, it is a glory to her" (I Corinthians 11:15, King James Version).

39. Evadne Frayling is one of the New Women in Sarah Grand's *The Heavenly Twins* (1893).

40. *curiosa felicitas,* curious fruitfulness (Latin).

41. *dies dominæ,* day of our lord (Latin).

42. In H. Rider Haggard's novel *She* (1887), She-who-must-be-obeyed is the heavily veiled queen Ayesha or She.

43. For example, novels by Grant Allen, *The Woman Who Did* (1895), and Victoria Cross [Vivian Cory], *The Woman Who Did Not* (1895).

44. A reference to *Woman, A Character Study,* by Norwegian writer Laura Marholm, whose name, after marriage, was Laura Marholm Hansson (1854-1928). Marholm Hansson's book tells the fate of several gifted women writers who longed for a more complete and satisfying life and a mate who could be a friend and comrade.

45. Marie Bashkirtseff (1858?-84) was born in the Ukraine and moved to Paris where she studied painting. Her journal, which she began at age fourteen, was published as *I Am the Most Interesting Book of All: The Diary of Marie Bashkirtseff.* Bashkirtseff wrote of the narrowness and emptiness of women's lives caused by the restrictions placed upon them. She died at an early age of tuberculosis.

46. *Little Eyolf* (1894), a play by Henrik Ibsen.

47. Mrs. Patrick Campbell (originally Beatrice Stella Tanner) (1867-1940), Elizabeth Robins (1862-1952), and Janet Achurch (1864-1916) were well-known actresses in London. Robins and Achurch were pioneers in presenting the work of Ibsen on the London stage.

48. In *Sorrows of Satan* (1895), by Marie Corelli, Mavis Clare resists Satan and provides salvation for the hero Geoffrey Tempest.

49. Algernon Charles Swinburne (1837-1909), English poet.

50. *The Sorrows of Young Werther* (1774), by Johann Wolfgang von Goethe, a German poet and dramatist.

51. Lines from Canto Four, Stanza CXXIV, of *Childe Harold's Pilgrimage* (1812), by Lord Byron.

52. *Jude the Obscure* (1895), by Thomas Hardy.

53. *magnis componere parva*, to compare small things to large (Latin).

54. Diana Vernon is a character in *Rob Roy* (1817), a novel by Sir Walter Scott.

55. A *surhomme* is a Superman; Charles Baudelaire (1821-67), French poet. The *Urmensch* or *Übermensch* is the "higher man" or enlightened figure predicted in Nietzsche's *Thus Spake Zarathustra* (1892).

56. *César Birotteau*, by Honoré de Balzac (1799-1850), a French writer.

57. "Through her, one understands so easily/ how brief, in woman, is love's fire— when not/ rekindled frequently by eye or touch," Dante's *Purgatorio*, VIII, 76-79 (translated by Allen Mandelbaum).

58. Publius Cornelius Tacitus, Roman historian and orator, late first and early second centuries C.E.

THE REVOLTING DAUGHTERS

In January 1894, "The Revolt of the Daughters," an article by Blanche Alethea Crackanthorpe, appeared in the *Nineteenth Century*. Although Crackanthorpe was sympathetic to the freedoms desired by young women, the words of her title, transformed into the "revolting daughters," became a familiar catchphrase used by those hostile to the emancipation of their daughters. Crackanthorpe was the mother of Hubert Crackanthorpe, a fiction writer who contributed to the *Yellow Book*. Other mothers, such as Lady Susan Mary E. Jeune (d.1931) and Sarah M. Amos, a prominent suffragist, signed in on the controversies raised by Crackanthorpe's essay.

Among the daughters responding were Gertrude Hemery and Alys W. Pearsall Smith. Pearsall Smith (1867?-1951) was an American, a graduate of Bryn Mawr, a member of the Fabian Society, and the first wife of the philosopher and mathematician Bertrand Russell, whom she married in 1894, the same year that her article appeared in the *Nineteenth Century*.

In 1894 the controversy over the emancipation of daughters and the desirability of their revolt soon spread from the *Nineteenth Century* to other prominent journals, with writers taking a variety of positions on these issues as well as many related topics. Crackanthorpe's essay is printed below, followed by some representative essays which became part of the debate.

"THE REVOLT OF THE DAUGHTERS"

B.A. CRACKANTHORPE

[*Nineteenth Century* 35 (January 1894): 23-31]

These are the days of strikes. No sooner is one happily closed than another, more serious it may be, and farther reaching in its effects, comes up for next consideration. A big trade strike is just ended; another, of a totally different complexion, is fast approaching. Not every one possesses the power to reading sky signs aright, yet for months past very large and plain specimens have been on view. More than one of the public prints has beguiled this year's autumn dulness by opening its columns to a majority of daughters, who have therein detailed their intimate and personal home grievances. They in their turn have been answered by a minority of mothers champing under the sense of the burning ingratitude, and more, the general unseemliness of their offspring. With a frankness that would be indecent were it not absolutely tragic both sets of combatants have exposed to a gaping audience their naked griefs and unveiled wrongs. As the controversy ended precisely where it began, in mere hot statement, no one was any the better, and not a few were considerably the worse. Neither did the question itself get any "forrader" towards solution. This was a large and vulgar sky "skeleton," but others, more subtle, yet to the full as significant, are not lacking.

When an *habitué* of London Society, himself a keen observer of manners, is heard to remark that this question must be ripe, seeing the very large percentage of households where war, open or concealed, exists between mothers and daughters, it is serious. When a leading London doctor confides to a friend that he is much concerned by a new phenomenon in his practice, to wit, the frequent presence in his waiting-room of mothers broken down in body and perplexed in mind over "difficulties" with their grown-up daughters, and of daughters come to consult him privately whose nerves have "gone wrong" because, as they put their case, they are not "understood" nor "sympathised with" by their mothers, this is significant indeed. The evil cannot be lightly laughed away as a passing trouble, to be speedily cured by marriage in the one case, and in the other—where the mothers' inappropriate youthfulness is a chief disturbing cause—by the certain grip of relentless old age. For our own part we believe the psychological moment has arrived in which to probe, to diagnose, and to prescribe for, the hidden disease.

Let it be granted, for the sake of convenience, that the premises above stated are correct, and that a case is so far proven. With whom does the fault lie? on whose shoulders should rest the main burden of responsibility for the dead-lock, if it exists as stated by these experts? In this latest strike we will call the mothers the employers, and the daughters the operatives. The capital of the employers is here represented by a wide experience, which should carry in its train wisdom, far-reaching vision, and a balance of patient staying power which ought never to be wholly drawn out. The operatives bring as their contribution to the carrying out of the existing social contract, youth, vitality, "go," and the muscle strength that enables them to pick themselves up and go home after a deadly encounter, only a surface bruise or two the worse, whilst their elder and less supple opponent has possibly received wounds which, bleeding inwardly, poison the joy of life at its purest source.

For our own part we are prepared to state frankly at the outset that, whilst admitting to the full the provocative nature, the egoism, the governing unreasonableness, which too often characterise the attitude of the daughters during the struggle for supremacy, everything in fact which goes to form that expressive yet inelegant word *tiresome*, we yet find ourselves ranged on the side of the younger generation. Let their case be first stated. They are young. They are vital. The springs of life, the thirst to taste its joys, run very strong in their veins. They desire ardently to try things on their own account. They long for the "unexpected," not always the "properly introduced," still less the "well accredited" of that sage and prudent ambassador their mother. Far from them is the desire for things that are wrong in themselves. They have no unwholesome hankering for forbidden fruit. Their individuality is at this moment the strongest—and the most inconvenient—thing about them. They pray passionately to be allowed to travel ever so short a way alone. Should an obstructive pebble lie in their path and threaten for a moment to upset their youthful equilibrium, they resent hotly the immediate application of the hand of a guardian to the small of their back. So have we seen a rebellious baby, just able to run, hit out impotently, but with deadly intent, at the over-conscientious nurse who stood by ready to "save" it from that wholesome tumble provided by a wise nature as experience-lesson. Girls want to make their own minor mistakes and not to be strictly limited by unwritten law to producing feeble imitations of their mothers' best copies. And why not, since mistakes have to be made? No one is worth a thought who has not made them, and he, or she, who has lost the capacity for their manufacture, as an occasional indulgence, is far on towards old age. To look upon trivial errors, whether of speech, manner, or action, as *anathema maranatha*[1]—and this is the real bogey of the good mother—is but to make complacent display of her own limited intelligence. Other and graver plaints has the daughter, plaints which perhaps she has never actually formulated, but of the existence of which she is intensely subconscious. Does uncongenial atmosphere go for nothing as a shaping influence? What of the suffering of a girl on whom tricksy Nature, or some remote ancestress, has bestowed a romantic, gipsy-minded personality, and who finds herself in a well-ordered and accurately balanced entourage where this side of her—a side she can no more help than the colour of her hair or the shape of her nose—is conscientiously repressed, disapproved of, and ignored?

We have of late years elected to educate everybody, our daughters included. Girton and Newnham,[2] the "halls," and all kinds of minor establishments of a like kind fill the land. "Higher Education," "University Extension," are common form, whilst diplomas of proficiency—not, be it observed, of efficiency—are more plentiful than were blackberries last year. The attempt to open wide the doors one side the house, and to hermetically close them the other, is a trifle illogical, and no one but politicians anxious to buy votes and not eager to pay the full price, or women who demand heaven and earth at the same moment, would make such an attempt. Wisely or foolishly—it is yet an open question—we have said that our daughters are to know. They, in their turn, insist that they shall be allowed the free use of the weapon with which we ourselves have furnished them. Are they to be blamed for this?

It is not so usual now as it was twenty years ago for the head of a middle-class household to cheerfully spend a thousand pounds or more on each boy's training, first at a public school, then at a University, to "fit him for taking his place in the world," whilst his daughters, were they many or few, had to put up with equal shares in the talents of one lady with the indulgence of occasional snap-shots at music and dancing masters. The injustice of his proceeding is, at this time of day, more visible to the naked eye, though we fear the practice is not altogether obsolete. For our own part we have no hesitation in saying that the girl who sees her brothers equipped for any professions they may choose, whilst she herself is confined to the single one of marriage, is a really ill-used person. Marriage *is* the best profession for a woman; we all know and acknowledge it; but, for obvious reasons, all women cannot enter its strait and narrow gate. When the moment comes in which the daughter sees clearly that success for her, if it comes at all, must come on other lines, and that the sense of modest achievement alone gives zest and fire to life, can it be gainsaid that if she then goes to her father and says, "Give me a portion, a fraction of what you have laid out on Dick and Tom, to enable me to make my experiment, to try to do *my* little bit of world's work," and he refuses her on the score that a woman's place is entirely at home till she is called higher by a husband, she has a very real grievance indeed?

So far, and it is a long way, in their plea for a larger liberty, not license—the liberty that claims the right to be an individual as well as a daughter—we are entirely with the girls in their revolt. Justice, however, now demands that the mirror should be presented to them with a stern command that they do take a long look therein. It will not be a beautiful vision that will meet their gaze. For inner barrenness of spirit, manifesting itself in ugly outside action, few things can match the ruthless young daughter pulling her own way against her mother, and generally getting it too. She is, by reason of her youth, perfectly insensible to, absolutely regardless of, the agony she is causing and the wounds she is inflicting. For the time being she presents to the observer a curious mental compound of which the fundamental basis is egoism. Such imagination as she possesses is so self-centered, its light so turned on the point she desires either to secure or to avoid, that it stands her in no stead at all as an illuminator of her own or other people's conduct. During this state she distinctly becomes that hideous product, a non-human *thing*, governed only by its own innate stubbornness (this a quality, by the way, too often pinnacle-placed by women of all ages, who christen it firmness, and then chant secret psalms in its honour). This is indeed a parlous state, and the animating spirit possessing her for the time being is not to be exorcised save by prayer and fasting. It may be that the true vision of herself is withheld from her for many a long day, but it comes at last, possibly when the little drama is repeated—with this little difference, that she now fills the other rôle. For time always calls to a reckoning. Accounts in that book are never crossed off unpaid, and it is only the fool who says in his heart, "For me there is no judgment-day."

The Attitude of the Mothers

Ce n'est que le premier pas qui coûte[3] is a fiction familiar to most of us. We have often found, to our cost, that bad as was the first step, those that come after were a hundred-fold darker and more slippery. So will it be with the New Strike. "Flags are Flying," Björnson's title,[4] becomes now very apt. The tom-tom is heard at the street-corners calling out the younger levies, who answer in glad haste; whilst far away in upper chambers sit the legitimate rulers of the rebels in deep consultation—anxious, waiting, determined. No wonder they wear a care-lined air. For in their souls they know full well that whatever the results may be—whoever stands or whoever falls—the responsibility of the situation is their own. A little more magnanimity, a larger sense of the rights of the individual, although the individual in question be that sacred product their own daughter, a little more of that most difficult of all forms of altruism, the tucking-in of their own skirts to make room for the new-comers, and the present dead-lock would never have arisen at all. This is their burden, and a pretty heavy one it proves. They would not be the mothers of their own daughters if they were deficient in stubbornness. Watch them as they sit round the table with tightened lips and mouths that have a comic resemblance to the steel-clasped bag of our youth—how viciously it used to snap!—note the angry sparkle in their eyes, and then marvel at the thought that in spite of all the outward show of righteous wrath these women are in their hearts enduring the torture of remorse for neglected opportunities and wasted chances.

Can it be denied that mothers are oftentimes mortally stupid? Their intentions are, indeed, excellent, but only to supply another illustration of the proverb. For stupid it is not to recognise facts and tendencies, which, after all, are but facts in their first stage; still more stupid is it when to ignore them is no longer possible, not to admit their consideration frankly, and to let conduct be guided, nay, altered thereby. Principles make excellent consulting physicians, but it would fare ill with many of us in the affairs of life were we to be deprived of those useful general practitioners, tact and expediency. Let mothers, especially "good" mothers, practise in secret the art of contemplating their daughters as part of a vast "collective" youth, and not as highly specialised young females on whom no wind is to blow roughly, whose ears are to be stuffed with medicated cotton-wool, and whose sight is to be ever safeguarded by good substantial blinkers well tied on by the prudent parent. Let us again protect ourselves by repeating that we are *not* writing of girls in their teens, but of women turned twenty. With sons this course has to be taken, as every mother of sons knows. Often the lesson is bitter and hard, but the wiser and more catholic the woman, the quicker she will be in mastering it. Her best-loved son must have his *wanderjahre.* She cannot hold him back. She can only gaze after his retreating form from the watch-tower of her love; too often he departs with never a backward glance at her. But in her heart a silent witness speaketh, telling her to have patience, for he will return in the end. Why not allow the possibility that nice girls, well-disposed girls, may also desire a mild sort of *wanderjahre* period, during which they, too, want not to break fences, but to get occasional glimpses of the landscape beyond the family domain? Blunders not a few they may make, but not of the kind that need be counted with. The far-seeing mother will consent to sit a quiet and smiling spectator when her daughter ventures on small, or even comparatively big, social experiments. She will not employ her leisure moments in crushing every troublesome symptom of individuality, nor in flat-ironing the surface creases that may from time to time appear. She will be slow to blame and quick to praise. A saving sense of humour, if the gods have smiled at her birth, will help her greatly, for we do not for a moment pretend that this will be the happiest or most careless period of the mother's reign. But if she has made a friend of her girl *in childhood*—and it is vain to think this can be done later on—nothing will really come between them. Yet, after all, in any collision between them, her suffering is a hundred times acuter than that of her daughter, for, unfortunately, women are addicted to feeling more and not less as they grow older, and if, as has been well said, in every contest only one of the combatants is booted and spurred, it must be admitted that more often than not these advantages remain with the daughter.

Once, a mother, Celtic and nervous edged, suffering from friction with her elder daughter, Saxon and stolid, addressed herself in her tribulation to the sage of the household, who happened in this instance to be its youngest member, aged fourteen. "Mother," said the child, after listening sympathetically to the plaint, "do you think you love Mary quite enough? She needs loving." Thus out of the mouth of the babe and suckling dropped the word of truth which furnishes a key to part, though by no means to the whole, of the situation.

So much for the lighter aspects; when we come to the other and graver side, it is, we fear, a serious indictment that many mothers have to meet. We would ask them what have been the methods they have chosen by which to rear and train their difficult young? How much personal time, personal influence, and personal effort have they expended on the task during the critical years which lie between ten and seventeen—the only moulding time in a girl's life? Would thirty hours a week cover it? Would twenty? Would ten? Have they not rather—we write of the majority—selected from the very moment of birth the very best outside help they could obtain, beginning with the certified wet-nurse and ending with the diplomaed lady who, for a hundred a year, undertakes the herculean task of administering tongues and social wisdom in equal doses to her charges, the mothers themselves falling the while into the sin that most easily besets them—namely, that of overlooking the work instead of bearing a hand in it?

When, if ever, did real friendship between them and their daughters begin? What are the guiding principles of conduct they have been careful to instil—no, to get instilled—into them during the few years when alone the process is easy of accomplishment? And, lastly, in every conflict of opinion that may have arisen since, what has been the true motive at the back which underlies their disapprobation and commands both the quantity and the quality of their frowns?

The moment has come for the secrets of the maternal heart to be disclosed. Is it not true that the marriage "ring" is the governing authority which the mothers acknowledge and obey, although not for a moment will they admit it? The things that make or mar a girl's chances *there* are the mother's realities. We believe that the mother we describe would prefer her daughter to steal spoons (she would carefully return them next morning) to her committing any social misdemeanour, of no moment whatever, which should militate against these chances. To take an example. A girl wants exceedingly to hear Chevalier sing. This innocent desire can only, we will suppose, be gratified by a visit to a music-hall in charge of a brother. Now music-halls are not "nice" places[5]—a nice girl, *i.e.* a promising candidate in the marriage market, must on no account be seen in one. The domestic fiat is pronounced; the girl rages inwardly over the shams that govern her life. There is her sister, only a year or two older, who married but a few months ago—she is free to visit a music-hall with her husband and friends. "Where is truth?" cries the girl.

When it comes to actual marriage—we feel we are here on very delicate ground, but forward we must go—the mother we describe makes but one inquiry, after ways and means are satisfactorily established. Is the man free *now* from entanglements of any kind, and can he be depended upon to remain so? Of the girl's passionate ideals, of her hot burning heart, of the purity she brings as a flame to the altar—for, in spite of the sound of laughter in the air, we maintain that to many a girl marriage is still a sacrament— the mothers recks not at all. Her "knowledge of the world" enables her to assure her daughter that "Mr. Jones will make a good and 'dependable' husband." Is it too much to say that many mothers would be exceedingly shocked if their daughter came to them saying she would like to be assured that the man she was about to marry had no "past" to bury? And yet here the girl's instinct is surely a right one, for if the "burying the past" means the putting aside a woman who has faithfully filled the place of wife and mother for many years, that girl is not far wrong who feels that, under these conditions, she is after all but the lawful mistress, the other remaining the unlawful wife. Not so very long ago a mother anxious to secure the best *parti*[6] of many seasons achieved at last this signal triumph, and bore him triumphantly away for her daughter from a horde of angry rivals. At the close of the interview which took place between her gratified self and the half-indifferent son-in-law-to-be he remarked carelessly, "Well, you had better take ——'s," mentioning the name of a legal expert, "opinion as to whether I am free or not," which the lady did, her daughter lending no unwilling hand. Together they sought the gentleman of the long robe, and being satisfied that the thing was sufficiently "safe," the wedding came off. (Admission to the church was by ticket only, lest unwelcome and uninvited guests should present themselves.) It is almost a satisfaction to remember that the last stage of that marriage was even worse than the first. Repulsive as this story is, it is true.

Not a little curious is it that the mothers who so carefully shield their daughters from the faintest breath of adverse criticism before marriage appear to be absolutely indifferent to what is said openly of these same daughters when marriage has set them free. Is this a reality, or is it a monstrous unreality, leading to every kind of social hypocrisy? On all sides we are told that society, both at the top and at the bottom, is rotten to its core. These are the factors that go to produce such rottenness. It has been suggested that nothing but a clean sweep of it can purify the stable, and that a boat should be started, say, every Wednesday morning from Tilbury Dock, bearing one week its load of West-End loungers, and the next a like load of East-End loafers, the cargo to be discharged in mid-ocean. So would the "impossible" elements of our civilisation be happily disposed of, "scum" and "dregs" alike, and the way at last left clear for the onward march of the resolute and the purposeful of all classes. Over-population being the problem of the hour, this experiment might be worth the trying.

Salvation comes from within always and everywhere. Since the capitalists have failed them, the operatives must work out their own. Then perhaps shall we have the woman of to-morrow, pure of heart and fearless of speech, who demands of herself and of every one else, not a flimsy and superficial "correctness," but that inward sincerity which enables her both to say and to hear, "I have erred," with equanimity. Of this woman it will truly be said, Blessed are the pure in heart, for God-like possibilities will be plain to her clear vision, not only in the suffering pavement-dweller, but, far harder still, in the lady of high place, set with every outward circumstance of prosperity, who decorates herself with lovers as lightly as with the diamonds in her hair.

We are told that, in view of the threatened "Union of Daughters," "mothers' meetings" will shortly be organised not only in Mayfair and Belgravia,[7] but throughout the provinces. We should like to suggest the following as test questions to be set at each meeting. On their right answering would, to our mind, depend the placing of each individual mother on the alternative "wise" or "foolish" list.

(1) Give an example of a possible difference of opinion between mother and daughter, and state the line of least resistance you would be prepared to adopt.

(2) If your daughter, turned twenty years of age, should desire to pursue an acquaintance which you, from instinctive or sentimental reasons (reasons

which might be absolutely just), did not consider a valuable one for her, would you, or would you not, make it difficult for her to try its value for herself?

But all these well-meant efforts may fail, and, as in other strikes, a Board of Conciliation may be the only way of meeting the difficulty. Delegates from both camps will doubtless be eager to attend. But where is the President to come from who will be acceptable to both camps? Would Mr. Gladstone crown the glories of his long life by accomplishing this Union of Hearts as his final public act? Or, failing him, would the Archbishop of Canterbury (in his robes), and carrying Dodo of Lambeth as text-book,[8] undertake the task?

One word more. As during the late coal strike entire districts in the midlands remained wholly unaffected by it, work going forward continuously the while, and the harmonious understanding between masters and men remaining unbroken, so in what we have fancifully called the New Strike, we are thankfully aware that there are whole strata of society in which no difficulty has arisen nor, in all probability, ever will arise. Such a state of things is only to be reached by the mothers recognising betimes that loyal friendship is the only lasting basis for this as for all other human relationships. There lies the root of the matter. Not of the happy households where this truth obtains are these pages written.

"A Reply From the Daughters"

Alys W. Pearsall Smith

[*Nineteenth Century* 35 (March 1894): 443-50]

Now that the mothers have been heard upon this subject, it seems only fair that the daughters should be heard also. If it is true that there is any widespread revolt of a race of beings so proverbially dutiful as daughters, it can only be because there is at bottom a sufficient reason and a crying need. And who so fitted to tell of this need and explain this reason as the daughters themselves?

In a conversation not long ago with a witty but rather ill-natured friend, we happened to speak of a large family of daughters whom we both knew.

"They are charming girls," she said, "but I wonder why they have been left to wither on the parent stem?"

The expression struck me unpleasantly. "Withering," I said to my self, "are unmarried girls at home in danger of withering?" And I was forced to acknowledge that it was only too true. I could recall to my mind at once at least a dozen instances of girls I knew who were, it seemed to me, slowly but surely withering in ideas and interests, and whose lives were becoming less and less fruitful and more and more limited day by day.

Then came the question why this was, and the answer seemed to me a revelation of the whole difficulty in regard to this revolt of the daughters—the underlying cause of all the trouble. These girls are withering because they are not allowed to live their own lives, but are always compelled to live the lives of other people. They have no chance of self-development, no work or pursuits of their own; their especial talents are left to lie dormant, and their best powers are allowed no sphere of action. They must continually crush back the aspirations of their own natures, and must stifle the cry of their own individuality. And I said to myself, "No wonder they wither, and no wonder they revolt."

The time of unmarried daughters at home is often entirely spent in domestic and social duties or pleasures, agreeable or distasteful as the case may be, imposed upon them by the authority of those around them. Their individuality is absorbed in the family life, and they are not allowed to develop their own interests and pursuits. It is thought quite enough for them to be carried along in the current of the family pursuits, and to be interested only in the family interests. And then in later years when the family life ceases, as it inevitably must sooner or later, these girls, perhaps by this time middle-aged women, will be left quite forlorn, with narrowed ideas and circumscribed faculties, and with no resources of their own upon which to depend. Their "withered" lives, cut off from the parent stem, become mere cumberers of the ground, a weariness to themselves and a care to their friends....

They must arrange the flowers, help with the housekeeping, pay the family calls, entertain the family visitors, always be at hand, well-dressed, cheerful and smiling, like household angels, as they are often called, without any personal preferences or pursuits, ready to meet every call, and to contribute to everyone's pleasure but their own. All this, it is true, is a part, and a very essential part, of the duty belonging to an unmarried daughter at home; but it is only a part. The tyranny of it comes in when it is considered to be all. It is the fact that she must always be "on tap," if we may use the expression, that makes this life so hard and dull in its effects. Under such circumstances the girl can never sit down to read or write without fear of being disturbed; she can never undertake any definite work or pursuit, lest it might interfere with some of these unceasing claims. She never, in fact, has an hour that she can call absolutely her own, free from the danger of interruption. There is always something wanted by somebody, and a girl of average conscientiousness would feel very selfish should she refuse to meet these unceasing claims, even though most of them may be very unimportant, and although she herself may have on hand at that very moment some important work of her own. Her brother, who is reading at home in his vacation, is never to be disturbed; but that, of course, is because he is reading for his examinations, and expects to do something afterwards. But are the girls who are not going in for examinations, and who never expect to do any great things, not to be allowed some definite time for study and self-improvement, or for some outside philanthropic work?

Among all the girls I know there is scarcely one who is not especially interested in something outside the family life, and who is not longing to be allowed a little time to devote to it. One would like to study botany, another wants to do literary work, another longs to be allowed to paint, while still another is secretly preparing for the higher local examinations, and, to do her work, is obliged to get up at five every morning. From the fear of seeming selfish, or in dread of the opposition they will be sure to meet, none of these girls have as yet dared to insist on their own personal rights; and I doubt if their parents even so much as suspect that their daughters have any real interests or pursuits of their own at all.

A lady said lately, in speaking of her career in life, that when a girl she had an insatiable desire for study, but that after her schoolroom days were over, her family strongly objected to her taking time from the family life for this purpose, and she was therefore compelled to adopt the plan of secretly rising several hours before the rest of the household that she might secure the necessary time for her work. She said that, as a consequence, by afternoon she was utterly worn out, not being very strong, and was obliged to take a regular afternoon nap. Not knowing the cause, no one objected to this. It was considered in the family that she was delicate, and must on no account be disturbed in this daily nap. Whereas had she wished to take the hours devoted to this nap for her study, and had so been able to sleep until the usual time in the morning, she would have been indignantly reproved for her selfishness. For her surface need of a nap she found sympathy and consideration, for her vital need of study she found only reproof. And her case is only a sample of thousands.

Some years ago a friend of mine was among a company of girls who were studying in one of the earliest colleges for women, and it occurred to her to ask them whether they had had the sympathy of their families and friends in their college career. Almost without exception each girl present said that she had had to fight for her liberty to go to college every inch of the way, and that all her family and friends had looked upon her as a monster of selfishness for persisting in carrying out her purpose. And I know at this moment any number of girls who have failed in a similar fight, from want of courage to resist the opposition by which they were confronted, and who have lived disheartened lives every since.

In the matter of marriage every girl has an acknowledged right to determine her own life. Why not, then, let her have some little right to arrange her life when she does not marry? Some day her parents must leave her, and if they do not leave her with a husband and children to fill her life, is it not important that they should be able to leave her with some pursuits and interests of her own to occupy her and make her happy?

Grown-up sons are started off in an independent career of their own, with the good wishes and kindly help of all their family and friends, and are afforded every facility for the development of any especial talents they may possess, or for the pursuit of any career they may choose. Grown-up daughters, on the other hand, often with equal and perhaps greater talents, and with at least as high purposes as their brothers, are condemned to a life of dependence at home, their energies limited to the social and domestic duties of the household, all their talents cramped and thwarted, and every impulse to do something for the world outside treated as unwomanly and revolutionary.

The suffering endured by many a young woman under these circumstances has never yet been told. Possessing no money in her own right, and obliged to beg, too often from an unwilling father, for all she gets, a girl of character, as she grows into maturity and lives on as a woman in her father's house, suffers from a sense of bitter humiliation that no one who has not experienced it can understand. Many young women under these circumstances would gladly engage in any honourable labour, however menial, that would enable them to be independent and to own themselves. But this, of course, "is not to be thought of for a moment." Could the parents of these daughters, who have never thought of them as independent beings, but only as appendages to themselves, created for the purpose of ministering to their pleasures, and waiting upon their fancies—could they for one single moment get a glimpse into the hearts of their quiet, uncomplaining daughters, they would be astonished and perhaps horrified. "What can our daughters want more than they have now?" they would ask. "They have a good home and every comfort, and the society of their parents' friends; perhaps a carriage to drive in and horses to ride. What more can they possibly desire?" To such parents I would reply: Your daughter wants herself. She belongs to you now, and can walk only in your paths, and enjoy your pleasures, and live your life. She wants to belong to herself. She has paths of her own she longs to walk in, and purposes of her own she is eager to carry out. She is an independent being, created by God for the development of her own talents, and for the use of her own time. Her capacities were not given to her parents, but to herself; her life is not their possession, but her own; and to herself God looks for an account of it. Put yourselves in her place, and ask yourselves how you would like to have no independence, but be obliged to live always someone else's life, and carry out only someone else's purposes. You have had aims and purposes in your lives, and have been free, perhaps, to carry them out. Can you dare, as mere human beings like themselves, to lay hands upon the mature lives of your daughters and say, "It shall be as we please, not as they please"? If they yield to your demands it can only be at the expense of a grievous waste of energies and capabilities that were meant by God to accomplish, through their instrumentality, some personal and instrumental work for Him. But this is an aspect of the question that very few adequately realise. There is no sadder sight in the world than that of a wasted life. And when this waste is the result of carelessness or selfishness on the part of the strong towards the weak, it becomes no less a tragedy even although it is done under the name of parental love. Such tragedies are no fiction, but the very common occurrence of everyday life around us. How wanton is the waste continually going on in the lives of thousands of women, whose powers, by a long course of trivialities and mental starvation, deteriorate year after year, until they themselves and all their friends suffer incalculable loss.

It is, indeed, in the name of unselfishness that women are urged to this sacrifice. But is it a true unselfishness to suffer one's life to be wasted in passing trivialities that leave one unfit for higher duties? Is it not rather a form of weak selfishness that, from a desire to win the approbation of those around one, or to avoid their censure, will consent to sacrifice the truest and deepest impulses and capacities of one's nature in order to minister to passing and trivial demands? And is it not likely to end in a far worse selfishness, when the day comes in which those to whom they have sacrificed themselves must inevitably suffer from the cramped and starved natures that such sacrifices produce? They have become unfitted for struggling with life and with the wider needs that come with increasing age, and are a burden and a drag where they were meant to be a prop and a comfort.

A great deal is said about the duty and the beauty of "self-sacrifice," and as it is mostly said to the female part of creation, it is not to be wondered at that a conscientious girl feels herself to be a monster of selfishness if she ventures for a moment to assert her right to live her own life in her own way, should that way differ in the least from the ways of those around her.

Now the expression "self-sacrifice" possesses two widely different meanings, and the trouble is that the emphasis is generally put upon the wrong one. The difference is shown by the two little words "to" and "for." Self-sacrifice *to* is very different from self-sacrifice *for*. When a man throws himself before the Juggernaut car[9] and is crushed to death, he has sacrificed himself "to" an idol; when he loses his life to save the life of another, he has sacrificed himself "for" that other. The wrong self-sacrifice is where we sacrifice ourselves "to" the whims or fancies or passing pleasure of those around us. The right self-sacrifice is where we find it necessary, for the best good of ourselves and others, to sacrifice ourselves "for" their and our highest good. The wrong self-sacrifice is often easier at the passing moment than the right, but in the long run it is sure to become a yoke of dreadful bondage. It is often easier for a sister to sacrifice herself "to" her selfish brother, by giving way to his selfishness, than it would be to sacrifice herself "for" him by withstanding it. But by choosing the easier way she increases his selfishness, until it destroys all respect and affection. To help those we love, we must sacrifice ourselves not "to" but "for." Present attentions or services are not always the test of the truest devotion. There is a self-abnegation that is only a magnified selfishness, and there is an apparent selfish regard to one's own character and development that is in reality the truest unselfishness. The girl who insists upon an opportunity for self-development and training at, perhaps, the cost to her parents of some present passing pleasure, will in the end bring far more interest and satisfaction into their lives than the one who has wasted her days of development in sacrificing all her highest powers "to" the petty occupations and amiabilities demanded from her, often so unthinkingly, by the home circle.

A woman with a definite purpose in life creates an atmosphere about her that cannot fail to impart a higher moral tone to those with whom she comes in contact, while without such a purpose she is liable to become a dead weight upon them, paralysing their energies and hindering their work. Girls need to realise this, and to be awakened to the sense of their responsibilities. For, after all, every woman, whether married or unmarried, is a human being, distinct from every other human being, and, as such, has her own individual and distinct duties and responsibilities, which she cannot and ought not to shift from her own shoulders. She cannot lay them on her parents, nor her husband, nor her friends, even should they desire and demand it. It must rest at last between her own soul and God alone. He has made her, not a puppet nor an idiot, but a rational free agent; and no false ideal of self-sacrifice can release her from this sacred responsibility. Any unnecessary suppression of her God-given powers, any stinting of her highest development, is nothing less than sacrilege against the Creator who took pleasure in endowing her with powers to work for Him.

The Bishop of Winchester, in an address to some young men and women, lately said some memorable words on this subject. After speaking of their opportunities and their capabilities, he urged upon them their responsibilities in the following words:

> Find out your work, your own personal work, and then set yourself to do it. But you may ask "What is your work?" I reply that it is that which you think of and feel after most frequently and most lovingly, the work that you are conscious of being best fitted to do. It is, however, almost better to choose the wrong work than not to begin any. To lounge and loiter through life has not only an unspeakable baseness with it, but it is environed with the subtlest dangers.

What these dangers are anyone can divine who will carefully study the wasted and withered lives around them.

But there is another aspect, apart from that which affects merely the home or the individual life, in which we must consider this question. No one of us can live to herself nor die to herself, nor even to her family. We are each a part of the society around us, of the nation to which we belong, of the world in which we live. And we must consider the claims that these have upon us, when we are trying to decide what our duty really is. Women must be taught to realise the solidarity of the human race, and to recognise the fact that we are all members one of another, and that if one member suffers all must necessarily suffer with it. No woman can permit her life to be dwarfed and thwarted without inflicting an injury not only upon herself and upon her family, but also upon the community in which she lives; and no woman can develop herself and make the most of all her powers without bestowing a positive benefit upon her friends and neighbours, and also upon the world.

Let every girl then claim her right to individual development, not merely for her own welfare and enjoyment or for that of her family, but chiefly that she may become a more perfect instrument to perform her allotted part in the world's work. It must be a matter of principle, not a matter of self-indulgence. She must be able to say not merely, "I want to do this or that," but "I believe I ought to do it." It is as fatal to a woman to live her life merely for her own enjoyment as it is for her to sacrifice her own life to other people's enjoyment. She must sacrifice herself, not *to* people, but *for* principles. She must ask herself frankly and honestly, "Have I any worthy purpose in my life? Am I doing the best with such powers as God has given me, or am I allowing them to be unused and wasted? Am I growing stronger and better with each year, or am I narrowing and deteriorating? Shall I be able rightly to fulfil my duties to the world in which I live if I allow myself to be frittered away in little nothings, and fail to strengthen and develop all my powers? Is it not my duty, even for the sake of others, to realise my best and highest self, and to make the most of all my capacities?"

If the community were only alive to its own highest interests, it would hail with heartiest welcome the advent of girls such as these, and all true lovers of humanity would reach out a hand to help them break through the trammels of prejudice or conventionality that have hitherto held them in check.

Hundreds of avenues are opening for the girls of to-day in which they can get the development and find the work they need. It ought, therefore, to be a matter of principle for every girl who has reached maturity to consider what is her own especial gift or capability; and, having discovered it, she ought to be as conscientious in trying to carry it out as she would be conscientious in carrying out any of the domestic duties which hitherto may have seemed to her to have been the only career allowed her.

The revolt of the daughter is not, if I understand it, a revolt against any merely surface conventionalities, that are after all of not much account one way or another, but it is a revolt against a bondage that enslaves her whole life. In the past she has belonged to other people, now she demands to belong to herself. In the past other people have decided her duties for her, now she asks that she may decide them for herself. She asks simply and only for freedom to make out of her own life the highest that can be made, and to develop her own individuality as seems to her the wisest and the best. She claims only the ordinary human rights of a human being, and humbly begs that no one will hinder her.

"The Revolt of the Daughters"

May Jeune

[*Fortnightly Review* 55 (February 1894): 267-76]

If the article by Mrs. Crackanthorpe, in the *Nineteenth Century*, represents a true picture of the mental attitude of the daughters of England, we are indeed on the verge of a social revolution. It has come quickly, and without premonitory symptoms, for no note of discord has been struck hitherto to warn us of the impending "strike." To us unsophisticated mothers, living happily in the blind ignorance of the passionate discontent burning in the bosoms of our daughters, the announcement of an organised series of "mothers' meetings," to protest against the movement, comes as a cruel surprise for apparently the strike is developing rapidly, and increasing in supporters, and we are totally unprepared with any organisation to resist its onslaught. In an hysterical and sentimental age like the present, what chance of success, what hope of sympathy can we expect against a crusade waged by everything that is strong, vital, beautiful, and interesting? An army of youth, sentiment, and ignorance, with no sense of proportion, and no knowledge of life, rises in its might to redress the grievances of girls caused by the failure and obstinacy of foolish mothers: the tocsin sounds; and we are told to beware, for the days of the "Know-nothings" are numbered at the hands of the would-be "Know-alls." Truly a terrible problem is added to the many which already beset the vexed question of the emancipation of women; but it is one that all thoughtful people who have interested themselves in the matter have long anticipated, only it has come rather sooner than was imagined; and if Mrs. Crackanthorpe and her followers represent anything like a large proportion of dissatisfied women, the question is a very serious one. We are, however, optimistic enough to believe that it is only one of the many phases which a new social question always assumes at its initiation, and that its supporters have assigned an importance to it altogether disproportionate to its significance.

When the question of higher education of women was taken up in England, it was opposed by many, not from any rooted antipathy to improve the position of women, but from an instinctive conviction that when once they could claim anything like an intellectual equality with men, they would not rest content with the subordinate position they had formerly occupied, and would soon claim equal rights. And their instincts have proved correct, for with women's intellectual development has also come their entry into the arena of men's work, and their successful struggle with men in many of its branches. The recognition by law that a woman's earnings were her own, and to be protected from her husband, was the crowning act of her emancipation; and though there are privileges still withheld from her, every year brings her nearer to the full realisation of her desires. Were we prepared to go into the question of how women have borne the responsibilities they have won, it would not be difficult to show that they have felt their power, and have conducted themselves with patience and dignity, disposing of the world-accepted dictum that the monopoly of wisdom and self-control is that of the stronger sex. But our aim lies in another direction, and deals solely with the effect which better education, more freedom, and an earlier knowledge of life are likely to exercise over a class of women who have hitherto been overlooked. We shall endeavour to point out that, though it must undoubtedly influence and alter their lives, the difference it will make is neither so serious nor so subversive of the traditions of the past as we are told.

Let us admit that there are certain households where mothers and daughters do not "hit it off," and that there are girls who from constitutional causes are hysterical, and find their home surroundings uncongenial; but this is no development of later days. We speak, alas, of many years' experience, and are prepared to affirm that there are no greater number proportionately now than forty years ago. Among the middle classes, indeed, there are many less, because the better education of women has enabled thousands to go afield, and expend their superfluous energy; or their unsatisfied yearnings, in good, honest, solid work, which, while acting as a safety valve, has enabled them to earn their own living. The nervous and hysterical young woman has, and will always exist, and is the result of no system, but one of those excrescences which appear from time to time in nature, as well as in the family, and which every observer of life sees round him in every quarter. The increase of amusement, late hours, great excitement, and the press of modern life have increased the number of such women, and with life as full as it is, their numbers will not diminish.

We hardly feel sure that we know the girls of whom Mrs. Crackanthorpe writes, but we will take it that she means girls of those classes who from position and fortune form a large portion of English society, and are over twenty years of age. Why twenty should be the age at which a revolt from maternal control supervenes we cannot understand, or why a girl is better able to judge what is wise and prudent at that time than at eighteen. Everything is a matter of degree. Some girls are as wise and discreet at sixteen as at twenty-six; but

no girl can have the knowledge of life and of the world, which is her only protection, until she has had the experience which age alone can bestow. Modern education opens girls' minds and develops them intellectually, but such
knowledge is purely theoretical and of no practical use to them as regards
their own conduct. Were they allowed to shape their life on theories evolved
from what they learn from books, they would be better without any education
whatever.

It would be idle to deny that the girl of to-day is a different creature to that
of forty years ago. The scheme of her education, her *entourage*, are absolutely
changed, and she lives in an atmosphere which is liberal in thought as well as
in conversation; and no girl now is as ignorant of life as her mother was when
she was the same age; but the fact that the sphere of her life and knowledge
is broader does not, we maintain, make her impatient of the restraint that is
both necessary and desirable. There are not many girls who sigh for the forbidden fruits of amusement, or consider themselves ill-used because music
halls, plays which deal with equivocal subjects, and books which treat of the
relation of the sexes are withheld from them. Nor do we see where the grievances arise, if there are any, of which girls complain. It is very difficult to picture a happier life or one of greater freedom than they now enjoy, or one
more replete with varied interests and pursuits. If a girl is intellectually
inclined, a university career is open to her, where she can distance her male
competitors. If athletic, she can take her part in all the sports and pastimes
formerly the sole monopoly of her brothers. If sentimental or of a humanitarian disposition, she can find ample scope for her powers in work among
the poor and in nursing. If frivolous, there never was an age when society was
pleasanter or more delightful for girls, or when there were fewer restrictions
of their enjoyment, and those only of such a nature as to prevent them going
"too far ahead" until they have acquired some moral ballast. Some girls, more
emancipated than others, sigh for latchkeys and wish to be allowed to pursue
their occupations and amusements without any chaperone—in short for the
perfect freedom which marriage alone should give a woman. These forbidden liberties constitute, no doubt, a formidable list, but to the calm maternal
mind they appear not only obvious but most necessary, and contrasting our
own youth with that of our daughters, we find it difficult to imagine anything
more antipodean than the relative positions. The freedom which girls are
permitted now, even in the strictest households, is as much as is good or
wholesome for them during the early years of their life, and were the
restraints relaxed the ultimate results would be indeed disastrous. Most mothers have realised that the result of education and the spirit of the age is
against placing any vexatious restrictions on their daughters, who in their
choice of girl friends, of amusements, in their variety and quantity, as well as
in the very much wider social intercourse with men which they enjoy, seem to
have shown both wisdom and tact.

There are, and must always be, questions in which the mother's experience and love will clash with her daughter's inclinations, and where her indulgence must stop short, but they are of such importance as to put them beyond discussion, and to a mother and daughter who get on well together they present no grievance.

Mrs. Crackanthorpe opens a totally new aspect of the relations between mother and daughter, for we confess, until some premonitory rumblings of the storm reached our ears, and before we had read her paper, one felt inclined to be grateful to one's girls that, considering the independence and enfranchisement of their lives, they were as lenient to our shortcomings and old-fashioned notions as they are. If there are homes where a system of repression exists, and where all individuality is stamped out, they are surely the exceptions, and, as with all other minorities, a struggle for supremacy must ensue; though even in such cases we are old-fashioned enough to believe that the fault is on the right side. But we do not desire to hold a brief for the mothers only, and are ready to admit that where the shoe pinches it may oftener than not be the mother's fault. Mothers too often grow older than need be, and forget that they have lives around them full of the keen impulses of youth, and of youth's capacity for drinking deep the cup of pleasure and yet being unsatisfied, and, more often than not, they have failed to be friends to their girls. It is very difficult to have perfect friendship without equality, and in that lies the secret of the difficulties which often arise. The mother must perforce be the ruler, and it needs almost superhuman tact, temper, and discretion to hold the reins and yet not appear to drive. There is no relation, no position, in life so theoretically perfect as that of a mother, and yet there is none so full of difficulties. The mother, in giving them birth, gives all the devotion, love, nay, almost passion, of her life to her children. Her sole object is their welfare, their affection her reward. A good mother is the most unselfish of human beings, and during childhood and youth all that is most precious in her to bestow she lavishes upon them, and for no inconsiderable period she is everything to her children; the embodiment of wisdom, beauty and love, and beyond her there is nothing perfect or divine. While it lasts there is nothing out of heaven so perfect; but into her Eden the serpent comes, and brings with him knowledge and dreams and ideals, and a world outside the childhood's world of mother's love opens and her children discover that in the new world there are pleasures that compare not unfavourably with the world they have lived in up till now. Their affection is not weaker or less real, but the positions are altered, and side by side with the trust and absorbing love of a child grow up other desires, other interests. It is then that the turning-point in both their lives comes, and if the mother, out of her love, can develop the wisdom that shows her that the moment has arrived when she is no longer to be the divinity of her children's dreams, but the guardian angel of their opening lives, then all may be well. But it needs both love and patience, for it is hard to realise the change and to accept the fact that the young individualities growing up around her are as distinct and irrepressible as her own.

This, however, is what every woman who loves her children has to endure, and she must stand by and see them learn life from their own experience, for hers is old-fashioned and out of date; and she, like the mother hen, can only go with her ducklings to the edge of the pond and cackle anxiously from the bank as they revel in their new-found liberty. The time for enforcing obedience, for prohibition is long past, the spirit of the age is changed, and the wise mother sits by watching the enterprises and the experiments which are being carried out gaily under the eyes of the person who is popularly supposed to wield the rod which destroys and paralyzes the daughters' confidences.

Although such may be the theory about the position of the mother and the militant daughter of the nineteenth century, no civil war is being waged in English households, for though the positions are altered, no change has come over the real love and affection that reign between the two. Now, more than at any other epoch, is the mother the friend of the girl, for though there are exceptions (and where do they not exist?), we maintain that there is a greater camaraderie between them, the result of their altered relations, than was ever possible before.

While mothers retain their youth and enjoyment of life much longer, girls grow older more quickly, so that a perpetual levelling-up process is being carried on, which diminishes the distance between them. The old system of severity and repression is past, and, whatever other feelings may have survived, that of fear has disappeared, and the frankest discussion takes place between the conflicting parties on any questions which involve the maternal or paternal control. Equality is the cry of the day in every class, and equality is nowhere more flourishing than in a happy household. In the present state of things, unless this was the case, we should not have to deal with the question as a phase of modern life, but we should long ago have been compelled to reorganize our whole family system. Mothers are accused of being stupid, wanting in magnanimity, narrow, and unsympathetic, and, like the Master Builder, are supposed to dread the pressure of the younger generation, who in their ruthless egoism are trying to sweep away the most precious traditions of their sex and give full play to what is an "inconvenient individuality." There are "mothers and mothers," but we prefer to leave the "and mothers" to "dree their weird,"[10] and ask our readers to consider carefully whether we are not right in our contention that the relation of mother and daughter is incomparably happier now and more on an equal footing than at any other time, and that the vast majority have long ago learnt that to enforce obedience and control by right of motherhood in these times is the most hopeless and fatal mistake.

In Mrs. Crackanthorpe's indictment against mothers, the real grievance lies in the charge that they oppose the freedom desired by their daughters because it diminishes their chance of making good marriages, and that the "marriage-ring is the authority which mothers acknowledge and obey, although not for one moment will they admit it." Well, we are not going to deny that accusation, nor do we see any reason to be ashamed of the admission. We will go still further, and declare that if the opinion of men is to be of so much importance in framing the characters and making the lives of girls in England what they have been, we are glad of it, and pray for the continuance of such an influence. To deny that marriage is the object of woman's existence is nonsense; long ago it was the only aim a woman had, and her training, education, and life were framed on that supposition. That there were many women who could not and did not marry, and led very miserable lives, does not disprove it; but that woman was created for the purpose of being the wife and mother of mankind no one can deny, and that none of the discoveries of science or any attempt to solve the mysteries of life have brought her one bit nearer the knowledge of how to unburden herself of these responsibilities, is also a fact. Such being the case, why should we always affirm with such vehemence that it is not so? It cannot be a cause of shame, nor is it a disgrace; it is a fact immutable and unchangeable as any in nature. It is an instinct that is inherent in women and shows itself in the love of the little child for her doll, and the unbidden blush which rises to the cheek of every girl when the mysteries of life are beginning to be unfolded to her, and her heart tells her that there is a deeper and more passionate love outside her home. Since the creation of all things woman has joyfully fulfilled her mission and will so continue, those only protesting to whom the opportunity has not come, or to whom independence constitutes the crowning joy of life. Far from joining in Mrs. Crackanthorpe's cry against the influence the marriage market has on the action of mothers, we think, within limits, it is a good one. Every woman wishes for the happiness of her daughters, and knows that in a happy union, where there is sympathy in tastes and character, the real happiness of life is to be found; and in training her daughter for that career, and in doing what she feels will facilitate that object, she is only doing her duty and seeking her girl's welfare. No one blames a mother for educating her daughters well, for selecting desirable companions, for dressing them well, and for endeavouring to find them pleasant society and amusements, and why, when the most important event of their life is impending, should it be a crime for her to desire that they should marry well? Any happily married mother must earnestly desire the same good fortune for her girl, and she is perfectly justified, within legitimate limits, in endeavouring to put such happiness in her way. We are very fond of protesting and declaring that we only seek the happiness of our daughters, but that on that one subject we are indifferent provided, &c., &c. Let us be quite honest and say we care more about that subject than almost any other, and that we want our girls to marry, and marry well, and marry the best men, because we know that they will be the happier and better women for it. The whole subject has got overladen with so much sentiment and mawkish delicacy that, whatever people's private opinions and wishes may be, they have not the courage to speak them out. There is no question of greater interest and anxiety to parents than the question as to who is to be their son's wife, and there is nothing a mother will not do to secure for him the girl on whom he has set his affections; and yet, with regard to her daughters, she must and should appear perfectly indifferent as to whether they marry, and above all, never commit the unforgivable crime of trying to help them in the most momentous hour of their life.

However indifferent a mother may appear to be, or pretend she is, it is impossible for her not to feel the keenest desire that her girl should make a good marriage, and everything that she can do to insure it we may be certain she will do, and be justified. The mother of whom Mrs. Crackanthorpe speaks is unhappily not a fiction; there have been, there are, and always will be, alas! women and girls who are ready to sell themselves as long as rank, wealth, and position are the sole objects a woman aspires to in marrying. If the position is only well gilded there will always be aspirants, but that is not the result of modern training or influence. Such a marriage-market has always existed. Of the mother, with her knowledge of life, we will not speak, for there is nothing to be said in extenuation, but of the girl one must always remember she is ignorant, and often weak, and has the example before her of many women who have done the same, and have, with an unpromising future before them, not only made themselves happy, but their husbands better men. A girl will always justify her action by the hope that, in the surroundings of a happy, peaceful life and the influence of a better woman, a man will *ranger* himself and become a good husband and father. The risk is great and the result always doubtful, but there are sufficient examples of such cases to make her feel that the experiment need not be a failure. Men cannot and will not, at least as society is at present constituted, bring a blameless past to the altar, but they may make expiation for their past by fidelity and devotion to the woman they marry; and unless a man is lost to every sense of honour, he does not disappoint the woman in her expectations. There are some men so completely outside the pale of morality as to be worthless in every way, but of the majority may we not reasonably admit our position to be a fair one?

In the face of the greater emancipation desired by girls, which would, if permitted, lead to grave scandals, it seems a little superfluous that they should expect so high a standard of morality from men; and if the concession of the Wanderjahr is made to them, we shall see the positions reversed, and find men exacting a standard of purity from women the existence of which is now taken as a matter of course.

It is exceedingly difficult and invidious to say what the age should be (if there is any) at which the restraints which, we think, are necessary for young girls should be relaxed. There is obviously a period when, if a woman does not marry, she may be allowed freedom both in regards the way in which she will live her life and as to the maternal control, but we should say not before she is twenty-five. We know that the acquisition of a privilege, when it comes in the order of things, is not so precious as when wrested in conflict, and the enfranchisement which a woman attains by age is somewhat tainted, and not of the same value in her eyes. It has, in reality, a value far greater than it would have had in earlier days, for she has learnt something of life, and experienced some of its difficulties, and she is better able to appreciate the proportionate value of what she acquires, and will not run a-muck, outraging and violating every rule of conduct and decorum—which she would, in all probability, do if she were eighteen or twenty. We do not say this from a disbelief in the inherent purity of girls, but with the ignorance of youth, the strength of its impulses, the unscrupulousness of men, and the varied temptations of life, how could we trust any girl, left to herself, to sail safely through the troublous sea on which she would embark?

There is, however, another aspect of the question which is graver and still more delicate. We do not imagine that the proposed enfranchisement of girls is to be limited to the life they wish to lead or the companions they associate with. If a girl is to be left to exercise her own discretion in such things, it can be only after a fuller knowledge of life and its problems have been unfolded to her, for she could not be launched on her new career without full instruction in the mysteries of the Book of Life. To be safe, she must know how to protect herself, and that power can only be acquired after full initiation in that knowledge which hitherto she had been carefully guarded from. Superficially, the proposed change in the life of young girls appears comparatively small, but if one analyses its effect it means a complete upheaval of all the traditions of the past. The new school with regard to the position of women holds that absolute knowledge of life can not only do no harm, but is necessary and just, and should not be withheld from the girl of to-day, and that instruction in its mysteries is as important a part of her curriculum as any other subject. If knowledge meant absolute protection from temptation and evil, it might be argued that girls thrown early on their own resources, and from circumstances obliged to face the world, would be better able to carry out their career safely if warned of certain obvious dangers to be avoided. But such cases are the exception, for with the majority of girls the home is still a haven of safety, the mother is counsellor and friend, and we have to legislate for the community at large. We are told that there is no innocence in ignorance, and that girls would be wiser, more discreet, and less likely to fall into temptation if they knew more. If the programme of the new reformers were carried out, the complete destruction of the present system as to the bringing up of girls would make some changes necessary. For if we are to give girls the freedom of married women without the protection of the husband, we must find his substitute, and from a fuller knowledge of life that substitute must come.

Will anyone calmly say that such a change is possible or desirable in any of its aspects? Do we wish to see our girls half men in theory and half women in inexperience and ignorance, with a superficial smattering of knowledge grafted on to the restless impulses and vague curiosity of youth—with all the romance, all the illusions of life dispelled, and with neither the constitution nor capacity of men to carry out their careers, and, above all, bereft of the sweet gift of purity which hitherto has constituted their greatest charm? What advantage is it to a woman to know the dark ways of life and their dark shadows, as well as all the byways of vice and wickedness, for we may rest assured that women, like their mother Eve, will not be content with a little knowledge, but will probe as deeply as is possible and will eat the fruit of the tree of knowledge to their fill? Why is the rosy morning of life, with its joys, its interests, its indescribable longings, to be but a dream of the past, and why must the girl step from the threshold of her girlhood into womanhood surrounded by the cloud of a knowledge which makes her sad and old before she is young? For we believe that the majority of women would, if asked, declare that such knowledge only brought sorrow and often horror. The days of youth are few, alas! and why shroud them sooner than need be with instruction that is the painful necessity of later life?

Were we to appeal to the creature whose influence has created this false atmosphere around women, we have little doubt that his reply would be that what women must learn of life and all its shadows had best be taught by their safest counsellor and friend, their husband. We fear we shall be considered but very poor champions of our sex in avowing this, but we prefer our daughters should be as little versed in the knowledge of life as their foremothers were. No doubt we shall lose something of the robust intellectual self-reliance of emancipated girls, but we shall always have with us the daughters of our hearts, ignorant, wilful, perhaps not always prudent, but with the better armour that innocence, romance, and a belief in the illusions of life must always ensure. The problem is so difficult, so complex, so full of pitfalls, that if we really come to analyse all the criticisms and suggestions which are made, we find that no one has ventured seriously to attack the system. It is very pleasant to break a lance against existing customs, and many have been shivered by the reformer's onslaught, but the position, the education, the training of our girls are far more momentous than any social tradition yet assailed; and mothers, though they do not yet "scent the battle from afar," or are gathering themselves in conclave "in upper chambers, anxious, waiting, determined," are perfectly conscious of their difficulties and of the new questions created by the changes which education and the growing dislike of all control have brought about. The whole fabric of the love between mother and daughter is not to be shattered because the restrictions against hearing Mr. Chevalier sing, seeing *The Second Mrs. Tanqueray,* and reading *Dodo* and *The Heavenly Twins* are being enforced. That love has existed and will continue as long as women do not forfeit the friendship and confidence which it is a girl's instinct always to give to her mother; and the wise mother, having gained her affection, will have no difficulty in steering clear of the rocks and shoals which ever underlie the smoothest currents of the waters of life.

"THE REVOLT OF THE DAUGHTERS. AN ANSWER—BY ONE OF THEM"

GERTRUDE HEMERY

[*Westminster Review* 141 (June 1894): 679-81]

Our thanks are due to Lady Jeune for her admirable article in the February number of the *Fortnightly Review.*

She takes up the cudgels on behalf of girls warmly—halfway, but only halfway. She would treat them very much as one treats caged birds—viz., by opening the prison-door for a little and letting them flutter round and round the room, at the same time preventing all possibility of their soaring away from that narrow boundary into the free, fair world without!

Lady Jeune admits that the position of woman is greatly improved and that they now enjoy numerous privileges denied them heretofore. And, admitting this, she would have them sit down, with meekly folded hands, dutifully content with the success they have already won. It says much for the courage and determination of women that they refuse thus to stand still; that, having advanced so far and so well, they see no reason why they should not continue advancing and reaping fresh laurels.

Lady Jeune regrets that "some girls sigh for latchkeys, and wish to pursue their occupations and amusements without any chaperone—in short, for the perfect freedom that marriage alone should give a woman."

If we are worthy to have our freedom at all, why stop short at a latchkey and other appurtenances of freedom?

Lady Jeune fears that, if girls are allowed their freedom too early, they will make grave blunders in decorum. Not so; being thrown on their own resources, and having only their own self-respect and dignity to protect them, they are more likely to be mindful of their conduct than girls more carefully guarded; and, even if this early emancipation were to have the effect of making them self-opinionative and aggressively assertive at first, contact with the world's rough edges, and the daily endeavour to force a path through its thorns, would soon reduce them to a becoming humility without destroying their self-reliance.

Our world is a very wise, moral world, taking it on the whole, and not so much a pit for the unwary as a benevolent and wholesome instructor to all who profit by its teachings.

I am only eighteen years old, and can boast of a latchkey, and am never chaperoned; and, speaking from my own experience, I think I may venture to assert that any young girl who takes the moulding of her life into her own hands, and asserts her right as an individual to the exercise of individual thought and action, will never have occasion to regret the step. She will attain an experience of the world that will strengthen her character, bring out all her graver, nobler qualities, and render her a being well worthy "man's" respect and reverence!

And, what is more, she will learn during her brief apprenticeship to form a higher estimate of man himself; when, instead of being protected and shielded from him, she stands and fights the battle of life side by side with him, she will discover how much her conduct influences his; how, instead of turning in contempt (as Lady Jeune fears) away from this real flesh and blood woman with her independent aspirations, he will instinctively turn to her, and allow all that is purest and best in his own nature to respond to hers.

It has always been contended that women have great influence over men, and yet, notwithstanding, until a few years back, they were caged up in conservatories, veritable hothouse plants, very lovely to look upon, but on no account to be spoken to or touched; and that profane creature "man" was trotted around to bow down at Purity's shrine! Purity! There can be no purity where there is no knowledge.

Those women who face the world bravely every day, seeing its dark as well as its bright side, mingling with its many helpless miseries, in the midst of its many temptations, and passing through all unscathed—these, I repeat, are the pure women to whom man may well bend the knee. The others are mere ignoramuses.

Lady Jeune would not have girls taste of the "tree of knowledge" until they are five-and-twenty, and here again I think her somewhat mistaken. If a girl be brought up in her mother's secluded convent school until she has reached the sober age specified, her views and ideas, moulded in the before-mentioned school, will by that time have arrived at maturity; she will have come to her own narrow, ignorant conclusion on things; and when the real, practical truth is forced upon her, she will suddenly realise that she lives in a very dark and miserable world, and that "mankind" is one of the greatest evils every perpetrated! And we cannot well blame her for so thinking. The mother brings her up in a little fairyland of her own, encourages her in bright dreams of an ideal existence; then suddenly, without one word of warning, dashes her little invention to the ground, leaving the girl to face a very grim and stern reality with none of the experience that enables the parent to discern the bright side of things and enjoy it.

Lady Jeune's plea is very weak and unconvincing—viz, that she would keep girls from scanning the "Book of Life," as it would "darken their lives, and fill some of them with sorrow and horror." This is mere false delicacy; such knowledge, if instilled early into the young mind, would be received with no such mawkish sentimentality. The woman would be quick to recognise the responsibilities of her womanhood; she would not lose one iota of her love and respect for "man" through learning that, by a law of Nature, he is more open to temptation and more prone to sink under it than she herself; and "man," in his turn, would not deem her wanting in purity because she possessed that broad-minded tolerance and keen sympathy that knowledge, not ignorance, teaches.

I say, by all means let girls go and see *The Second Mrs. Tanqueray.* The play itself is one of the highest moral lessons a girl can take to heart. The same can be said of Mr. Chevalier's songs, *Dodo* and *The Heavenly Twins.* They will each tend to impress girls with a graver consideration of "human life" and its many problems.

If I ever have children of my own, I shall deem it my first and sacred duty to bring them up daily and hourly to a just and practical knowledge of the world into which they are born. I shall let them see every side of human nature, that they may contrast the good and the evil, and derive a moral therefrom. I shall try and impress upon them the seriousness of "life," and the many responsibilities it entails. I shall make no difference in my treatment of either sex. Sons and daughters shall grow up in the love and esteem of each other, each sex looking up to the other, and recognising the good, true, sterling qualities of each. And I shall confidently expect my girls to develop into living, loving examples of womanhood, purified by contact with the world in which they live, and worthy to be admitted to man's most enduring, most reverent friendship.

"The Evolution of the Daughters"

Sarah M. Amos

[*Contemporary Review* 65 (April 1894): 515-20]

Daughters are not revolting, but being evolved, and the evolution may be looked upon with great placidity. Their progressive assertion of themselves is no new factor, although a certain Class in English Society (fond of spelling themselves with capitals) have for some generations past shut their daughters up and shut their own eyes, and they are now obliged to open their eyes while their daughters open the doors and windows. From the beginning it was not so. The heroic times of English history produced women whose names are famous, and also show more and more, the more deeply and intimately they are studied, how well instructed, how sensible and capable, English women and girls used to be. And indeed they still are. Although the day when dames and demoiselles of high degree may admit to their company the men who lightly injure poorer women and girls when occasion offers, the layers of society they think beneath them are, on the whole, more careful than they are in this respect, and have been able, therefore, to keep more of their personal freedom. The Classes do not realise how free these other women are. I remember being present at a meeting called to consider the education of working girls, where a man who bears an honoured name for his goodness, his enlightenment, and his knowledge of working-class problems, delivered an eloquent speech, much of which was based on the supposition that milliners' girls, and domestic servants, and map-painters, *et hoc genus omne*,[11] were always chaperoned to and from their classes by their mothers' matronly servants. Those of us who were teaching them and knew the good homes from which they came, and the struggles they made to get their education after their working hours were over, and the security in passing through the streets which their business-like air and self-respect gave them, smiled behind his back, and thought that the day was coming when education would free even the poor over-chaperoned girls with whom he was accustomed to mix.

Let us go what is called a little lower down. In the factory districts of England, machinery evolved the daughters long ago. It is a long time since the ordinary north-country factory girl was by custom under the control of her parents after the age of fifteen or sixteen; and yet those who work among factory operatives, if they chance to know the morals of Mayfair, will tell you that the factory girls have the advantage in most of those things which denote true womanliness as dissociated from questions of polish and culture. The time of stress there, thirty years ago, showed the English factory girl to be made of as fine stuff as her sister who lived in the times, three hundred years ago, when the struggles were military instead of economical. The habits of economic independence and of freedom in the streets did not make the Lancashire cotton operative a less good woman or a less good daughter in the time of the cotton famine.

The common plea for ignorance in girls is based upon the pessimistic theories that men will never be pure, while at the same time they will always require women to be pure; and that women will sometimes be able to make something out of so bad a bargain. I think this is a slander on men. A large mass of them are good; that is to say, they have known evil from their first schoolboy days, have known it in the way most likely to make them impure—

as a secret to be hidden from the mothers and sisters. They have yet hugged to their hearts the idea of a pure manhood, have gone through agonies of false shame in order to hold to their ideal, and are to be blamed, if at all, chiefly because they have allowed the impure among them to impose upon the world the damnable doctrine that purity is impossible, unknown, and even undesired among men.

Of course, the impure wish to impose this doctrine upon the world. They have been weak and do not wish to think themselves weaker than others; or wicked, and have sought and known only like-minded companions, and have deceived themselves; or they have been diabolical, and want to drag others down to their own pit of destruction.

The reason why girls have been so protected is that there were such men, and a better way had not been thought of. Common sense would suggest the diminution of the dangerous class, and it is not a counsel of perfection to preach the possibility of this. Civilisation works wonders. But few years elapsed between the day when English settlers in Fiji went in dread of their lives and of being eaten, and the day when an English governor gave the same natives a constitutional government. So the men in our midst who now devour the daughters of the poor may, by right treatment, be made civilised members of a civilised society.

So far the evil-doers have been the talkers, and the good, both men and women, have not realised the consequences of their silence. They have allowed their good to be evil spoken of, and the liberty of women to be curtailed, in the vain hope of evading the tongues of the evil-minded. Meanwhile you could not long have such a class as the free factory girls of England without the infection of freedom spreading upwards. It has already spread through the middle classes, and by many an agency is spreading through the professional classes, until at last it has touched "Society." It has come to stay.

But in Society it has, for the first time, come across a fully organised foe. The club man and the military man stand each shoulder to shoulder with his friend, and he is not without women allies. The women whose youth was kept "guarded" till they were flung, ignorant, helpless and friendless, into the arms and to the cruel tender mercies of debauchees, have often been so hardened by their misery, so bewildered by the social approval of their immolation, so destroyed in their whole being by the concealment of the woe imposed upon them by Society, that they have no character left to make them champion the cause of their daughters. They go astray like sheep, and cannot imagine a state of society in which the men would be in a position to ask with justice for pure wives. It is such poor victims as these who counsel that girls should to all eternity be flung gagged to wolves, in the hope that the wolves may turn fleecy by companionship.

The day, if there ever was such a day of ignorance of evil among boys, died, at latest, when the first boys' school was opened in England, and the night is not yet past. The day of ignorance among girls died, at latest, when it was admitted that they were to be educated. We talk nonsense when we talk of ignorant boys and girls. Girls are often ignorant, it is only too true, of what would be useful and protective to them; they are ignorant of what their mothers ought to teach them; they are ignorant of the holy elevating aspects of their woman's lives; but they are, more or less dimly, well acquainted with what is debasing, terrifying, distressing; with what would render them more easily victims, less certainly the elevators of society.

The crying need is of such physical and moral instruction for both boys and girls as will make the world safe for both alike to be free in. We do not want our sons to have the freedom to embitter their lives with memories of degradation. We do not want our girls to be free to rub shoulders with the degraded; but we do not think—and our daughters go further and *know*—that a better world will not be produced by a mixture of licence and slavery. The girls are going on ahead of us; and they are good girls, and the world will be the better for them. The boys now are not so ashamed to acknowledge that they are good too.

I was once present at a meeting of lawyers to discuss bankruptcy laws, where an eminent man, not noticing the presence of a woman, defended legal frauds, instancing the fraud practised upon an ignorant girl when she signed her settlements, with phrases about her children in law-English, the night before her marriage. The whole company accepted it as a joke, and I thought the doctrine and its ground worthy of each other.

But the daughters, right through the nation, have done with frauds. They intend to know in future who they are, where they are, and what they are doing; and such knowledge is their birthright. For us mothers it remains (we ourselves having walked the same road in its earlier reaches) to see them well equipped, to give them all the help and companionship we can, and then to wish them God-speed. We shall entreat our boys to walk hand in hand with them. We shall tell our husbands—those fathers who seem so forgotten in this controversy—that on their training of our sons, on their example, on their courage, nay, on their loyalty to their daughters, depend greatly the speed and security with which our young people will form the new society.

We parents can blight and dwarf and mildew the young plants; we cannot stop their growth.

Even "Society" has more than accepted nursing as a noble profession for women. The nurse comes from every grade, is met in every hovel and every drawing-room; her freedom, her happy independence, her own and others' sense of her value; her accepted knowledge of the darker sides of life—in all of which respects she is rivalled by that mighty host of sisters and deaconesses and "church-workers" of all sects—have their instructive and incitive influence on the home daughters. If Society wants *them* to be ignorant and uninterested, like the legendary English lady, it must arrange terms with the hospital, the sick-room, the parish priest, the social reformer. Meanwhile, our girls will learn, will throw off their swaddling clothes. I believe myself that the passing of the Married Women's Property Act in 1872 was only a first step in a change which will give women that equal control of property which will harbinger or accompany the establishment of their social and political equality; and when that is gained we shall begin to discern the heights to which a society may climb which expects noble lives from all its members alike. I and the many women who think with me have known already many girls who use their latchkeys to come and go on errands of sisterly mercy, and who have been refreshed themselves by many a trip in joyful company of their sisters and their brothers and their friends, with or without chaperones as convenience may suggest, and to whom and to their brothers the words "latchkey" and *"Wanderjahr"* have conveyed nothing but sweet and wholesome suggestion; and the more girls follow such an example, with the full concurrence of parents who trust them, the better it will be for all concerned. Freedom brings responsibility, and responsibility breeds prudence. The jeer of the profligate, the hesitation of the disloyal father, will be silenced in no long time. The tender apprehension of the mother will be over-weighted by her growing experience of her daughters' considerate prudence; and our poor rich girls will come to have as happily responsible and as free a life as their sisters on whom the blessing of toil rests.

A great deal of the ill-health of our delicate girls arises from repression of their young energy. The boys, too, would be hysterical if their youth were hedged in with so many conventional restraints, that there would be no room left for self-restraint, if everything they wore, every word they spoke, every youthful grace and beauty, every intellectual endowment, were habitually looked upon and openly spoken of as making them more saleable articles. These things belong only to the ages of slavery, and I would once and for all protest that where there is a "market," marriage in its true sense cannot be said to exist. Marriage is the free union of the free, taking upon themselves such limitations of their freedom as will lead them into the highest realms of liberty. Liberty implies law, discerned to be the best for ourselves and our neighbours, the guarantee of personal and national freedom. This is the sort of freedom, this is the sort of liberty, which has become a part of the Englishman's very self-consciousness, and it is the same liberty which our girls are claiming, are taking, and are using well. It seems certain that the result must be to restrain the licence into which some men have turned their liberty. In fulfilling the logical sequence which must give to a nation free women to stand by the side of free men, our English girls are also carrying on the destined work of England for the world.

With grievous and daring exceptions, the example and influence of England have, on the whole, brought hope and light and order to brutalised and enslaved nations—at least to the men of those nations. Here and there, even in the darkest recesses of Paganism, a hint, a gleam, of the freedom which Christianity means for women has reached the most down-trodden and tortured of the women of the world. They groan with a new apprehension of their misery; and it will lie in the hands of our daughters, freed themselves, to carry freedom to other women.

The result of endeavouring to keep the restrictions of women's freedom, which the vices of the courts of a hundred years ago rendered necessary, has been to produce plague-spots as virulent in poison as even the history of the Roman Empire can show. The women who have broken through the conventional barriers have been, and are, the women whom England delights to honour. But there is unnecessary pain and suffering in breaking through barriers, and the fathers and mothers of England will be kind and wise if they consult with their sons and daughters in what direction the new generation may best broaden the path for the new order.

Certainly the restrictions which produce the feeble-witted, earthbound Dodo, must give way to the freedom which will give the angels in our houses room to grow their six strong wings—two for personal dignity and beauty, two for spiritual elevation, and two with which to fly on serviceable errands for humanity.

NOTES

1. Anathema is an Aramaic phrase found in I Corinthians 16:22; it is a curse or denunciation. The term maranatha is translated "Our Lord will come." The terms together are a threat against those who do not love the Lord and a prayer that our Lord will come.
2. Girton and Newnham are women's colleges at Cambridge University.
3. *Ce n'est que le premier pas qui coûte,* It's only the first step that counts (French).
4. *Flags are Flying in Town and Port* (1884), a novel by Bjørnstjerne Bjørnson, Norwegian writer and winner of the Nobel Prize for Literature in 1903.
5. Music Halls, whose atmosphere was considered unsuitable for young women, sometimes had a promenade for prostitutes.
6. *parti,* a good match (French).
7. Mayfair and Belgravia are exclusive neighborhoods in London.
8. The father of Edward Frederic Benson, who wrote the witty novel *Dodo, A Detail of the Day* (1893), was Edward White Benson. The elder Benson became Archbishop of Canterbury in 1882 and thus lived at Lambeth Palace.
9. The Juggernaut car carries the idol of the Hindu deity Krishna in an annual procession. Worshippers supposedly threw themselves under the wheels of the car to be crushed.
10. "dree their weird," endure their fate (Scottish).
11. *et hoc genus omne,* and this entire class or kind (Latin).

PART THREE
DRAMA

INTRODUCTION

In the late nineteenth and early twentieth centuries, well-known playwrights created variations of the New Woman for the stage. Henrik Ibsen's Nora in *A Doll's House* (1889) and Hedda in *Hedda Gabler* (1891), and George Bernard Shaw's Vivie in *Mrs. Warren's Profession* (written 1893; performed privately 1902) and Barbara in *Major Barbara* (1905), were all types of the New Woman. Sydney Grundy, a prolific but less significant playwright, created a satiric version of the New Woman and the aesthete when he staged his play *The New Woman* in London in September 1894 at the Comedy Theatre. Produced just months after Sarah Grand had named the New Woman, the play was a great success with the audience, revealing that the New Woman was already in the minds of many a comic figure who could be easily caricatured and mocked. The New Women in Grundy's drama are strident and aggressive while their male companions are languid and effeminate. Dr. Mary Bevan, Enid Bethune, and Victoria Vivash are "real" men's worst nightmare. They burst onto the stage in the midst of an argument over whether women need more sexual freedom or men less—an issue that was debated by the New Women writers in their essays and fiction. In fact, the books the fictional women of the play write have titles that sound suspiciously like ideas found in the writings of Sarah Grand, with her demand for a higher standard of morality for men, Mona Caird, with her marriage problem novels, and George Egerton, with her desire to liberate women sexually. Gerald Cazenove, under the influence of another New Woman, Mrs. Sylvester, has become feminized. His sitting room is "effeminately decorated" and has the "stench of flowers." Sylvester points out to Colonel Cazenove the gender crossing advocated by Enid, one of the New Women: "Her theory is, that boys ought to be girls, and young men should be maids." The Colonel responds that "these people are a sex of their own, Sylvester. They have invented a new gender."

Grundy allays the fears aroused by such gender crossing by restoring several of the women to their traditional sphere by play's end. He exposes the New Women as fraudulent posers who, despite their education, intellectual pretensions, and literary works, are just as desirous of marriage as women have always been. And Gerald, after spending time with Margery, a woman whose traditional femininity makes her attractive to all the men, eventually realizes what "real" men have always known—that a woman is desirable not for her brains and accomplishments but for her submission and charm. In contrast to the stated desires of the New Women of the play, Margery wants a man she can love, honour, and obey.

Grundy further satirizes the New Women by characterizing them as intellectual lightweights whose feminist theorizing leads to heated discussions over such topics as whether women should have latchkeys and whether they ought to become as degenerate as men. Mrs. Sylvester, who is writing a book on the ethics of marriage, begins by writing the conclusion before she has formed the arguments. Her topic is particularly apt since she neglects her husband and pursues Gerald while they are collaborating on the marriage book. Percy Pettigrew, with his languid boredom and inane remarks about art, is a caricature of the aesthete, another target of Grundy's satire. Percy tells the women that for pure art one must go to Athens or the Music Halls, an interesting juxtaposition of sites, and in Trixy Blinko, a popular entertainer in the Music Hall, he finds "the prevailing characteristics of Hellenic culture." The New Women and aesthetes that Grundy gives to his audience are represented less as serious people to be feared than as destabilizing elements to be ridiculed as foolish posers.

The unregenerate Colonel Cazenove, with a wild sexual past of which he is proud, represents the ideal masculine male. Despite her earlier protests against a man who is "reeking with infamy" being allowed to marry a "pure girl," Enid is charmed by the Colonel. She has no problem in accepting his marriage offer after she pretends not to believe the stories of his peccadilloes. She discounts women's claim to purity: "You simply can't believe a word they say!" Most of the characters by play's end are exposed as affecting a belief in advanced ideas and new sexual roles while retaining traditional ideas about love, marriage, and relationships. Although the audience may have feared that the New Woman with her masculine behavior might feminize men, the play demonstrates that men still desire a sweet womanly wife and that all women really need is a husband.

Sydney Grundy (1848-1914)

Sydney Grundy was born in Manchester, the only son of Charles Sydney Grundy who was once the mayor of Manchester. Grundy was educated as a lawyer and practised law in Manchester until 1870, when he turned to writing drama. His first play was *A Little Change* (1872). Grundy wrote primarily comedies and farces, many adapted from the French, and, later in his career, sentimental melodramas. Among his plays are *A Pair of Spectacles* (1890), *The Degenerates* (1890), and *Sowing the Wind* (1893). He also wrote the libretto for *The Vicar of Bray* in 1892, and the same year *Haddon Hall*, for music by Sir Arthur Sullivan. He was unmarried.

The New Woman

An Original Comedy, in Four Acts
[London: Chiswick Press, 1894]

Characters

Gerald Cazenove
Colonel Cazenove
Captain Sylvester
James Armstrong
Percy Pettigrew
Wells
Servants
Margery
Lady Wargrave
Mrs. Sylvester
Miss Enid Bethune
Miss Victoria Vivash
Dr. Mary Bevan

Acts 1 and 2: At Gerald Cazenove's
Act 3: Drawing-room at Lady Wargrave's
Act 4: An Orchard at Mapledurham

ACT I

Scene.—Gerald Cazenove's *Chambers. A sitting-room, somewhat effeminately decorated. The furniture of the boudoir type, several antimacassars and a profusion of photographs and flowers. The main entrance, R. at back, in the flat. Doors, R. and L.,
window, L. of flat.*

A knock is heard off, as curtain rises. Enter Wells, *L., crosses stage and opens door
in flat. Enter* Colonel Cazenove *and* Sylvester.

Colonel: Is my nephew at home?

Wells: No, Colonel; but I expect him every moment.

Colonel: Very well; I'll wait. [*Exit* Wells, *door in flat.*] Bah! what a stench of
flowers! [*Opens a window and throws out a bunch of lilies standing on the table
below.*] Sit down, Sylvester—if you can find a chair to carry twelve stone.

Sylvester: Really, I feel a sort of trespasser.

Colonel: Sit down.

Sylvester [*sits*]: I don't know Cazenove very well—

Colonel: I'm much in the same case. Since he came up to town, I've only
called upon him once before. By Jove, it was enough. Such a set as I met
here!

Sylvester: I understood that he was up the river.

Colonel: Came back yesterday. Hope it's done him good. After all, he's my
nephew, and I mean to knock the nonsense out of him.

Sylvester: Colonel, you're very proud of him; and you have every reason to
be. From all I hear, few men have won more distinction at Oxford.

Colonel [*pleased*]: Proud of him? My dear Sylvester, that boy has more brains
in his little finger than I have—gout. He takes after his aunt Caroline.
You remember Caroline?

Sylvester: Oh, I remember Lady Wargrave well.

Colonel: Wonderful woman, sir—a heart of gold—and a head—phew! Gerald takes after her. At Oxford, he carried everything before him.

Sylvester [*laughing*]: And now these women carry him behind them!

Colonel: But he's a Cazenove! He'll come right side up. We Cazenoves
always do. We may go under every now and then, but we come up again!
It's in the blood.

Sylvester: According to my wife—and Agnes is a clever woman in her way—

Colonel: Don't know her.

Sylvester: His cultivated spirit and magnetic intellect are one of the bright-
est hopes for the social progress of our time—[*Laughs.*] whatever that
may mean!

Colonel: Does it mean anything? That is the sort of jargon Gerald was full
of, when I saw him last. But he'll get over it. Intellectual measles.
Oxford's a fine place, but no mental drainage.

Sylvester: I can form no opinion. I hadn't the advantage of a university training.

Colonel: I had. I was rusticated.[1] We Cazenoves always were—till Gerald's time. But he'll redeem himself. We Cazenoves have always been men, except one. That's my sister, Caroline; and, by Jove, she's the next best thing—a woman. [*Rising, in his enthusiasm—the antimacassar slips on to the seat.*]

Sylvester: A real woman.

Colonel: Caroline's a heart of gold—

Sylvester: Yes, so you said.

Colonel: Did I? I beg your pardon. [*Sits on the antimacassar, instantly springs up, and flings it into a corner. Points to that covering* Sylvester's *chair.*] Throw that thing away!

Sylvester: All right. I'm used to 'em. We grow 'em at our house. [*Looks round.*] I might be sitting in my wife's boudoir! Same furniture, same flowers, same photographs—hallo, that's rather a pretty woman over there! [*Crosses.*]

Colonel: A pretty woman, where? [*Crosses.*] No, not my style!

Sylvester: Ha! ha!

Colonel: What are you laughing at?

Sylvester: My wife! I didn't recognize her. [*Goes about examining photographs.*]

Colonel: Ten thousand pardons! I had no idea—

Sylvester: Bless me, my wife again!

Colonel [*looking*]: That's better. That's much better.

Sylvester: It's an older photograph. Agnes was quite a woman when I married her, but she grows more and more ethereal. Philosophy doesn't seem very nourishing.

Colonel: She's a philosopher?

Sylvester: Haven't you read her book? "Aspirations after a Higher Morality."

Colonel: The old morality's high enough for me.

Sylvester: I've tried to read it, but I didn't succeed. However, I've cut the leaves[2] and dropped cigar ash on the final chapter. Why, here she is again!

Colonel: *Three* photographs? And you're not jealous?

Sylvester: My dear Colonel, who am I to be jealous?

Colonel: Her husband, aren't you?

Sylvester: Yes, I am Mrs. Sylvester's husband. I belong to my wife, but my wife doesn't belong to me. She is the property of the public. Directly I saw her photograph in a shop-window I realized the situation. People tell me I've a wife to be proud of; but they're wrong. Mrs. Sylvester is not my wife; I am her husband.

Colonel [*taking up a book*]: This is what comes of educating women. We have created a Frankenstein. "Man, the Betrayer—A Study of the Sexes—By Enid Bethune."

Sylvester: Oh, I know her. She comes to our home.

Colonel: And has a man betrayed her?

Sylvester: Never. Not likely to.

Colonel: That's what's the matter, perhaps?

Sylvester: Her theory is, that boys ought to be girls, and young men should be maids. [Colonel *throws down the book*.] That's how she'd equalize the sexes.

Colonel: Pshaw! [*Takes up another book*.] "Ye Foolish Virgins!—A Remonstrance—by Victoria Vivash."

Sylvester: Another soul! She's also for equality. Her theory is, that girls should be boys, and maids should be young men. Goes in for latchkeys[3] and that sort of thing.

Colonel [*throws down the book*]: Bah! [*Takes up a third*.] "Naked and Unashamed—A Few Plain Facts and Figures—by Mary Bevan, M.D." Who on earth's she?

Sylvester: One of the plain figures. *She* comes to our house, too.

Colonel [*reads*]: "The Physiology of the Sexes!" Oh, this eternal babble of the sexes! [*Throws book down*.] Why can't a woman be content to be a woman? What does she want to make a beastly man of herself for?

Sylvester: But my wife isn't a woman.

Colonel: None of them are, my boy. A woman, who *is* a woman, doesn't want to be anything else. These people are a sex of their own, Sylvester. They have invented a new gender. And to think my nephew's one of them! [*Strides up and down, seizes another antimacassar and flings it into another corner*.]

Sylvester: Oh, he's young. Don't despair!

Colonel: I don't despair! Do you suppose this folly can continue? Do you imagine that these puffed-up women will not soon burst of their own vanity? Then, the reaction! then will come *our* turn! Mark my words, Sylvester, there'll be a boom in men! [*Rubbing his hands*.]

Enter Gerald, *door in flat*.

Gerald: Good afternoon. I'm sorry to have kept you waiting. [*Shakes hands with* Colonel.]

Colonel: Here you are, at last.

Gerald [*shaking hands with* Sylvester]: How's Mrs. Sylvester?

Sylvester: I was just going to ask you. You see more of her than I do.

Gerald: We are collaborating.

Colonel: In the Higher Morality?

Sylvester: How are you getting on?

Gerald: Oh, we are only on the threshold. I finished the first chapter about daybreak.

Colonel: That's how you waste the precious hours of night? Gad, sir, when I
was your age—

Gerald: That was thirty years ago. Things have changed since then.

Colonel: And they haven't improved.

Gerald: That is a question.

Colonel: Oh, everything's a question nowadays! Nothing is sacred to a
young man fresh from Oxford. Existence is a problem to be investigated;
in my youth, it was a life to be lived; and, I thank Heaven, I lived it. Ah,
the nights *I* had!

Sylvester: Would it be impertinent to inquire upon what subject my wife is
engaged?

Gerald: Our subject is the Ethics of Marriage.

Sylvester: Of my marriage?

Gerald: Of marriage in the abstract.

Colonel: As if people married for ethics! There is no such thing, sir. There
are no ethics in marriage.

Gerald: That is the conclusion at which we have arrived.

Colonel: You are only on the threshold, and yet you have arrived at a conclusion?

Gerald: So much is obvious. It is a conclusion to which literature and the
higher culture inevitably tend. The awakened conscience of woman is
already alive to it.

Colonel: Conscience of woman! What are you talking about? I've known a
good many women in my time, and they hadn't a conscience amongst
'em! There's only one thing can awaken the conscience of woman, and
that is being found out.

Gerald: I am speaking of innocent women.

Colonel: I never met one.

Gerald: Yet—

Colonel: Tut, tut, sir; read your Bible. Who was it had the first bite at the
apple? And she's been nibbling at it ever since!

Gerald: Well, well, uncle, you don't often come to see me; so we won't
argue. Can I prevail on you to stay to tea?

Colonel: To stay to *what,* sir?

Gerald: Tea. At five o'clock, I have a few friends coming. Mrs. Sylvester—
[Sylvester *puts down photograph and turns.*]—Miss Bethune—Miss Vivash—

Sylvester: And Dr. Mary Bevan?

Gerald: Yes, I expect Miss Bevan.

Colonel: "Naked and Unashamed?"

Gerald: They may bring Percy with them.

Colonel: Percy?

Gerald: Percy Pettigrew.

Colonel: A man? An actual man? A bull amongst that china?

Sylvester: Well, hardly!

Colonel: You know him, Sylvester?

Sylvester: They bring him to our house.

Gerald: Nobody has done more for the Advancement of Woman.

Sylvester: By making a public exhibition of the Decay of Man.

Gerald: Sylvester, you're a Philistine. I won't ask you to stay.

Sylvester: Man the Betrayer might be dangerous, amongst such foolish virgins.

Colonel: The danger would be all the other way. I am not sorry *I* shall have protection. My sister, Caroline, will be here at five.

Gerald: Aunt Caroline! [*A little nervously.*]

Colonel: I came to announce her visit.

Sylvester: Lady Wargrave has returned to England?

Colonel: After ten years' absence. She has been travelling for her health, which was never too robust; and since Sir Oriel's death, she has been more or less a wanderer.

Gerald: I knew she had arrived, but I postponed presenting myself till I was summoned. My aunt has the kindest of hearts—

Colonel: A heart of gold, sir.

Gerald: And a pocket too. Nobody knows that better than I do. Since my parents' death, she has been father and mother, as well as aunt, to me. But there was always something about aunt that made one keep one's distance.

Colonel [*in a milder voice than he has yet used*]: And there is still, Gerald.

Gerald: Then I'm glad I've kept mine.

Colonel: You acted very wisely; I happen to know she wished her arrival kept secret and to descend upon you like a *dea ex machina*.[4] Caroline always had a sense of dramatic effect. But how the deuce did you know of her return?

Gerald: Oh, very simply. Margery told me.

Colonel: Margery!

Gerald: Aunt wrote to summon her to resume her duties.

Colonel: But Margery's at Mapledurham. Caroline was stopping with some friends in Paris, and Margery was sent on to her father's.

Gerald: Six weeks ago.

Colonel: Why, you know all about it.

Gerald: Yes, I was staying there when she arrived. I have been rusticating for the last six weeks. It's so much easier to write in the fresh air.

Sylvester: You have been writing down at Mapledurham?

Gerald: That's what I went for.

Colonel: For six weeks?

Gerald: Six weeks.

Colonel: And you have only finished the first chapter?

Gerald: It's so difficult to write in the fresh air. One wants to go out and enjoy oneself. And then old Armstrong's such a jolly old boy.

Sylvester: Armstrong, of Mapledurham? The farmer? Oh, I know him well. I go there for the fishing.

Colonel: Then, do you know Margery?

Sylvester: Margery? No.

Gerald: How that girl sculls!

Colonel: Oh, Margery was rowing?

Gerald: Do you know, uncle, she can almost beat me?

Colonel: But what an arm she has!

Gerald: And when she feathers—[*Pantomime.*]

Colonel: Ah! when she feathers—[*Double pantomime.*]

Gerald: What a voice, too!

Colonel: Hasn't she!

Gerald: So musical! When she sings out, "Lock, ho!"

Colonel [*imitating*]: "Lock, ho!"

Gerald: No, not a bit like that—more silvery!

Colonel: Not a bit! more silvery!

Both [*pantomiming*]: "Lock, ho!"

Sylvester: Who's Margery?

Colonel: Oh, my dear fellow, just your sort—*my* sort—well, hang it, every man's sort! Margery is—oh, how can I explain? If I'd seen a Margery thirty years ago; well, I should never have been a bachelor! Margery is— come, Gerald, what *is* Margery? Margery is a woman, who—Well, Margery's a woman! That's all Margery is!

Gerald: Old Armstrong's daughter. We grew up together. When I was very young, I was considered delicate, and I was sent to the farmhouse at Mapledurham. When I went to Eton, Lady Wargrave took Margery into her service. There she has remained—

Colonel: And she is coming with your aunt to-day. [*Knock at door in flat. Re-enter* Wells, *followed by* Mrs. Sylvester, *with a small portfolio.*]

Wells: Mrs. Sylvester! [*Exit, door in flat.*]

Mrs. Sylvester [*stops short on seeing* Sylvester]: Jack!

Sylvester: This is an unexpected pleasure. [*A cold matrimonial kiss.*] Colonel Cazenove—my old Colonel. Mr. Cazenove I think you know.

Mrs. Sylvester: Well, of course, Jack! How ridiculous you are! Should I be here if I didn't know Mr. Cazenove?

Sylvester: I haven't the least notion. I only know you wouldn't be at home.

Mrs. Sylvester: I was in all the morning.

Sylvester: I had business at the Horse Guards.[5] I shall be home to dinner, though.

Mrs. Sylvester: Oh dear, I wish I had known that. There's only mutton.

Sylvester: The same mutton?

Mrs. Sylvester: What do you mean by same?

Sylvester: I mean the mutton I had yesterday.

Mrs. Sylvester: Did you have mutton yesterday?

Sylvester: No matter; I'll dine at the club.[6]

Mrs. Sylvester: Thank you, dear.

Sylvester: Good-bye. [*Kiss.*] Good-bye, Mr. Cazenove.

Colonel: I will come with you. [*To* Gerald.] I am due at your aunt's.

Gerald: But I shall see you again presently?

Colonel: If I am visible behind Caroline. Madam, your servant. [*Aside to* Sylvester.] Cheer up, Sylvester! I'll join you at the club, and we will wind the night up at the Empire.[7] [*Exit after* Sylvester, *R. of flat.*]

Mrs. Sylvester: That is so like a man! Doesn't say he's coming home, and then expects six courses and a savoury!

Gerald: There is a difference between cold mutton and six courses, to say nothing of the savoury.

Mrs. Sylvester: It is a fine distinction, and in no way affects the validity of my argument.

Gerald [*smiling*]: You mean, of your statement.

Mrs. Sylvester: Husbands are all alike. The ancient regarded his wife as a slave, the modern regards her as a cook.

Gerald: Then they are *not* alike.

Mrs. Sylvester [*emphatically*]: A man thinks of nothing but his stomach.

Gerald: That is another proposition.

Mrs. Sylvester: You're very argumentative to-day. I haven't seen you for six weeks, and you've come home in a nasty, horrid temper!

Gerald: I have been working so hard.

Mrs. Sylvester: Why is your face so brown?

Gerald: Well, of course, I went out.

Mrs. Sylvester [*takes his hand*]: And why are your hands blistered?

Gerald: I had a few pulls on the river; and being out of training—

Mrs. Sylvester [*innocently*]: Were you stroke? [*Holding his hands.*]

Gerald: Not always. [*Bites his lip.*]

Mrs. Sylvester: Oh, then you weren't alone?

Gerald: I met an old friend up the river.

Mrs. Sylvester: Now I understand why you didn't write to me. [*Drops his hand and turns away pettishly.*]

Gerald: About the book? [*She gives him a quick glance.*] Oh, I had nothing to say, except that I was getting on all right. I've written the first chapter. [*Produces MS.*]

Mrs. Sylvester: And I've written the last. [*Opening portfolio.*] Connoting the results of our arguments.

Gerald: But where are the arguments?

Mrs. Sylvester: We'll put those in afterwards. [Gerald *looks at her.*] That's how Victoria always writes her novels. She begins at the end.

Gerald: But this is a work of philosophy.

Mrs. Sylvester [*pouting*]: Oh, you *are* disagreeable!

Gerald [*putting MS. aside*]: Don't let us talk philosophy to-day. I want to talk to you about something else.

Mrs. Sylvester [*cheerfully*]: Yes!

Gerald: I have something to tell you.

Mrs. Sylvester: Interesting? [*Smiling.*]

Gerald: I'm in love.

Mrs. Sylvester: Oh! [*From this point her manner changes.*]

Gerald: Yes, in love, Mrs. Sylvester—in real love.

Mrs. Sylvester: What do you call real love?

Gerald: Something quite different from what we had supposed. We've been on the wrong tack altogether. We have imagined something we have labelled love; we have put it into a crucible, and reduced it to its elements.

Mrs. Sylvester: And we have found those elements to be, community of interest and sympathy of soul.

Gerald: But unfortunately for our theory, the thing we put into the crucible wasn't love at all.

Mrs. Sylvester: How do you know?

Gerald: I didn't, till last week.

Mrs. Sylvester: It was at Mapledurham you made this discovery?

Gerald: At Mapledurham.

Mrs. Sylvester: And your friend?

Gerald: She was the revelation.

Mrs. Sylvester: I thought it was a woman.

Gerald: That word just describes her. She is a woman—nothing more or less. Away went all my theories into air. My precious wisdom was stripped bare before me, and in its nakedness I saw my folly. Not with laborious thought; but in one vivid flash I learned more than I ever learned at Oxford.

Mrs. Sylvester: Really?

Gerald: A woman! that is what one wants—that's all. Birth, brains, accomplishments—pshaw! vanities! community of interest—sympathy of soul? mere dialectics! That's not love.

Mrs. Sylvester: What *is*, then?

Gerald: It defied analysis. You can't put love into a crucible. You only know that there is something empty in you; and you don't know what fills it; but that's love. There's no mistake about the real thing.

Mrs. Sylvester: Is she good-looking?

Gerald: In *my* eyes.

Mrs. Sylvester: A lady?

Gerald: In social station, beneath me. But what's social station?

Mrs. Sylvester: This is infatuation. Some riverside coquette—

Gerald: Simplicity itself.

Mrs. Sylvester: Of course you think so; but you don't know women. The simple woman hasn't yet been born. This isn't love, Mr. Cazenove. This is the temporary victory of the baser side of your nature. The true alliance is the union of souls.

Gerald: Of man and woman.

Mrs. Sylvester: But of soul and soul; not a mere sensual temptation.

Gerald: Nor is this. A week ago I thought so. I know better now.

Mrs. Sylvester: Happily the weeks are not all over yet. In a few more you will have forgotten her as completely as she will have forgotten *you*.

Gerald: In a few more, I hope that she will be my wife.

Mrs. Sylvester: You contemplate a *mésalliance*?[8]

Gerald: There is no *mésalliance* where there's love.

Mrs. Sylvester: You, of whom everyone expects so much, to throw away your opportunities, and to begin your life hindered and hampered by a foolish marriage.

Gerald: If she will only marry me.

Mrs. Sylvester [*looks at him, pained*]: I may still be your friend? [*Offers him her hands, which he takes a little reluctantly.*]

Re-enter Wells.

Wells: Lady Wargrave. [*Exit.*]

Enter Lady Wargrave *leaning on the* Colonel's *arm. She walks with a crutch-stick, and is followed by* Margery, *who carries a cushion.* Mrs. Sylvester *retires up, so that she is not immediately seen by* Lady Wargrave.

Gerald [*a little tentatively*]: My dear aunt! [*They shake hands.*]

Lady Wargrave: You may kiss me. [*He kisses her, then casts a glance of gratitude at* Margery. *Meanwhile* Margery *has prepared a chair for her, into which she is placed by* Gerald *and the* Colonel, *who is now subdued and deferential, in marked contrast to his last scene.* Margery *takes up her position in the background.*]

Colonel: I was so fortunate as to meet the carriage.

Lady Wargrave: Theodore was late as usual.

Colonel: Only ten minutes, Caroline; but, as you know, time, tide, and your aunt wait for no man.

Lady Wargrave: Now, Gerald, let me look at you. Your face to the light, please. [Gerald *stands for inspection. She takes a long look through her eye-glass.*] I don't like that necktie.

Gerald [*smiling and bowing*]: It shall be changed to-morrow, aunt.

Lady Wargrave: To-day. [Gerald *bows. She takes another look.*] That will do, Gerald. [Gerald *salutes. She drops her glasses.*]

Colonel: Stand at ease! Dismiss!

Lady Wargrave: Theodore, this is not a barracks!

Colonel: True. [*Bows.*] *Peccavi!*[9]

Lady Wargrave [*addressing* Gerald]: I need hardly say with what pleasure I have followed your career at Oxford. It is worthy of a Cazenove.

Colonel: Brilliant—magnificent!

Lady Wargrave: It is worthy of a Cazenove; that is all [Colonel *subsides, bowing.*]

Gerald: Yes, aunt, I flatter myself—

Lady Wargrave: Don't do that. You did your duty. Nothing more.

Gerald: By the way, did you receive my poem?

Lady Wargrave: Poem?

Gerald: That won the Newdigate.[10] I sent you a copy—to Rome.

Lady Wargrave: Ah, I remember; I received the document. Tell me, were there many competitors?

Gerald: A dozen or so.

Lady Wargrave: Is it possible that Oxford can produce eleven worse poems than yours?

Gerald: My dear aunt!

[Colonel *turns aside, chuckling, and finds himself face to face with* Margery, *laughing; both become suddenly serious.*]

Mrs. Sylvester [*advancing*]: It is a work of genius—none but a true poet—

Lady Wargrave [*half rising*: Margery *steps forward to help her*]: I ask your pardon. Gerald, you haven't introduced me!

Gerald: Forgive me, Mrs. Sylvester—forgive me, aunt, but in the excitement of seeing you—

Lady Wargrave: Sylvester!

Colonel: Wife of my old lieutenant. Captain now.

Lady Wargrave: Wife of Jack Sylvester! I am pleased to meet you. I have known your husband almost from a boy. But I don't see him. [*Looking round.*]

Gerald [*confused*]: He has just gone.

[Lady Wargrave *looks from one to another. Slight pause.*]

Mrs. Sylvester: Mr. Cazenove and I are collaborating.

Lady Wargrave: Oh! Captain Sylvester's wife is collaborating with *you?*

Gerald: On the ethics of marriage.

Mrs. Sylvester: Viewed from the standpoint of the higher morality.

Lady Wargrave: Ah! [*Drops back into her seat, helped by* Margery.] That will be a

very interesting work. [Margery *retires up.*] Did you do very much down at
   Mapledurham?

Gerald: Not *very* much, I'm afraid.

Mrs. Sylvester: Mr. Cazenove met a friend up the river.

Lady Wargrave: A friend? Margery, you didn't tell me that.

Margery [*advancing, and with a slight curtsey*]: I didn't know, my lady.

Mrs. Sylvester: An old friend.

Colonel: Perhaps the old friend was Margery herself?

Mrs. Sylvester [*perplexed and curious*]: Your maid was at Mapledurham?

Lady Wargrave: Her father lives there. Theodore, don't you think Margery
   looks all the better for her holiday?

Colonel [*with enthusiasm*]: If it is possible—

Lady Wargrave: Theodore! [*Aside to him, stopping his mouth with her fan.*]

Colonel [*subsides*]: Peccavi! [*Sotto voce.*][11]

Lady Wargrave: Doesn't she look brown?

Gerald: Well, up the river everybody does. It was hot weather, too.

Lady Wargrave: It must have been. You should have seen her hands. They
   were all over blisters.

Colonel: Ah, that was the rowing! [*Pantomime as before.*]

Lady Wargrave: Margery! [*Margery casts down her eyes.*] You were rowing?

Margery: Sometimes, my lady.

Mrs. Sylvester: Stroke. [*Looking at Gerald.*]

[Lady Wargrave, *watching* Mrs. Sylvester, *motions to* Margery, *who retires up.*]

Colonel [*aside to* Lady Wargrave]: Caroline, you took the water very neatly.

Lady Wargrave [*aside to* Colonel]: The higher morality has caught a crab.

Mrs. Sylvester [*gathers up MS. into her portfolio*]: I will not trespass any longer,
   Mr. Cazenove. No doubt, your aunt has much to say to you.

Gerald: But won't you stay to tea?

Mrs. Sylvester: Thanks. Captain Sylvester dines early.

Colonel [*aside*]: At the club!

Mrs. Sylvester: Good day to you, Lady Wargrave. [Lady Wargrave *is about to
   rise.*] Pray don't rise. [*Bows to the* Colonel *and goes to door in flat where* Gerald *is waiting for her.*] Don't trouble; I know my way. [*Exit.*]

Lady Wargrave: Poor Sylvester! He was such a nice boy! [Gerald *comes down.*]
   Gerald, can Margery wait in the next room? [Gerald *opens door R. Exit*
   Margery *R.*]

Gerald [*returning*]: And how have you been, aunt? You never mentioned
   your health in your letters. Are you better?

Lady Wargrave: I mustn't complain; but Providence is really most unjust.
   Here am I, who have lived a life of temperance, in my old age—

Colonel: Middle age, Caroline! [*Bowing.*]

Lady Wargrave [*smiling*]: A chronic invalid; while this old transgressor who has denied himself nothing [Colonel *grins*], and committed every sin in the Decalogue [Colonel *chuckles*], is as hale and as hearty as I am infirm.

Colonel: Never felt better, never!

Lady Wargrave: But how have you been, Gerald? *We* belong to the past—

Colonel: Caroline!

Lady Wargrave: *You* belong to the future, and the future belongs to you.

Gerald: Oh, I've been all right! [*A little recklessly.*]

Lady Wargrave: Quite sure you suffer from nothing?

Gerald: What do you mean?

Lady Wargrave: Your letters have told me a great deal—more than perhaps you know; but I have read them very carefully; and when you asked me to come home—

Gerald: I didn't, aunt.

Lady Wargrave: Between the lines.

Gerald [*laughing*]: What did I say to you between the lines? [*Kneeling by her.*]

Lady Wargrave. You told me that you had learned everything Oxford has to teach worth learning, and that you were in danger of becoming—well [*laying her hand on his head*]—shall we say, *tête montée?*

Colonel: Yes, Caroline! I should certainly say, *tête montée.*

Lady Wargrave: Cure yourself, Gerald. Knowledge is not wisdom [*stroking his head*]. Forgive me, dear; but I have known so many men who have never survived the distinctions of their youth, who are always at Oxford, and even in their manhood play with rattles. Now, forget Oxford—go into the world—lay books aside, and study men.

Colonel: *And* women.

Lady Wargrave: Yes—and *women.* [*Knock without.*]

Gerald [*rising*]: Just what I'm doing!

[*Female voices in altercation. Re-enter* Wells, *door in flat.*]

Wells: Miss Bethune, Miss Vivash.

Enter Enid *and* Victoria, *in hot argument. They take opposite sides of the stage and continue the discussion without taking the slightest notice of anybody.* Lady Wargrave *looks from the one to the other in amazement. Exit* Wells, *door in flat.*

Enid: I can't agree with you! Say what you will, I can't agree with you!

Victoria: That doesn't alter the fact. A woman has just as much right to a latchkey as a man.

Victoria: That's ridiculous!

Enid: Rudeness is not argument!

Victoria: Why make distinctions?

Enid: I make no distinctions. I admit that a woman has just as much right to come home with the milk as a man: but I say, a man has no right to come home with the milk; and I say more—no woman who respects herself has any *desire* to come home with the milk!

Victoria: Bother the milk! It isn't a question of milk. It's a question of making artificial distinctions between the sexes.

Enid: I say that there ought to be *no* distinction! Why should a man be allowed to commit sins—

Victoria: And woman not be given an opportunity?

Enid: Then do you *want* to commit sins?

Victoria: I want to be allowed to do as *men* do.

Enid: Then you ought to be ashamed of yourself; there!

Victoria: I only say, I ought to be allowed.

Enid: And *I* say that a man, reeking with infamy, ought not to be allowed to marry a pure girl—

Victoria: Certainly not! *She* ought to reek with infamy as well.

Enid: Victoria! [*Knock without.*]

Victoria: What is the difference between man and woman?

Enid: There is no difference!

Re-enter Wells, *door in flat.*

Wells: Dr. Mary Bevan. [*Exit* Wells.]

[*Enter* Dr. Mary Bevan.]

Victoria: Why should a woman have children and a man have none?

Enid: But a man has children!

Doctor: Only vicariously.

Victoria: Here's Dr. Mary! [*Rushing up to* Doctor. Enid *has rushed up to the other side of her.*]

Doctor [*pragmatically*]: But I am not without hope that, when the attention of science is directed to the unequal incidence of the burden of maternity, some method of re-adjustment may be devised.

Lady Wargrave [*who has risen*]: Pardon me, ladies; but if you are about to consult your physician, you would no doubt prefer to be alone. [*They turn and see her for the first time.*]

Victoria: Pray, don't move.

Gerald: My aunt, Lady Wargrave. Colonel Cazenove.

Doctor: These matters are best discussed openly. A morbid modesty has too long closed our eyes. But the day of awakening has come. Sylvester, in her "Aspirations after a Higher Moralilty," Bethune, in her "Man, the

Betrayer," Vivash, in her "Foolish Virgins," have postulated the sexual problem from every conceivable point of view; and I have myself contributed to the discussion a modest little treatise—

Enid: No, no, not modest!

Victoria: Profound!

Doctor: "Naked and Unashamed!"

Enid: Man has done all the talking up to now—

Victoria: He has had things all his own way—

Doctor: And a nice mess he's made of them!

Enid: Now it is our turn.

Victoria: We mean to put things right!

Doctor: Man has departed. Woman has arrived.

Lady Wargrave: Excuse my ignorance, but I have been away from England for so many years. Can this be the New Woman I have read about?

Colonel: Everything's New nowadays! We have a New Art—

Enid: A New Journalism—

Victoria: A New Political Economy—

Doctor: A New Morality—

Colonel: A New Sex!

Lady Wargrave [*smiling*]: Ah!

Doctor: Do you object to modernity?

Lady Wargrave: I've only one objection to new things; they are so old.

Victoria: Not the New Woman!

Lady Wargrave: No; she is generally middle-aged. [Colonel *turns to* Gerald, *to hide his chuckles.*]

Enid: Then, do you take Man's part in the discussion?

Lady Wargrave: I take no part in it.

Doctor: Do you deny that Woman has arrived, Man has departed?

Lady Wargrave: I don't wonder at it. But Man has an awkward habit of coming back again.

Trio: Never!

Lady Wargrave: Then Woman will go after him. [Colonel *roars out aloud—the Women survey him with disgust.*]

Re-enter Wells, *L., and whispers to* Gerald.

Gerald: Tea is quite ready, ladies!

Enid: Ah! a cup of tea!

[*Exit L., followed by* Victoria, Doctor Mary *and* Wells.]

Lady Wargrave: Theodore, your arm. These ladies interest me. Besides, they sadly want a chaperone.

Colonel: They want a husband—that's what *they* want, badly!

Lady Wargrave: Gerald, call Margery. [Gerald *goes to door R.*] Well, they are looking for one. [*Glancing after* Gerald.]

Colonel: And they've found *you*, Caroline.

[*Exeunt both, laughing, L. Each time the door, L., is opened, a babel of female voices is heard from within, and such phrases as "Peter Robinson's," "Swan and Edgar's," "Stagg and Mantle's," are distinctly audible above the clink of teacups, etc.*]

Re-enter Margery, *R., she goes straight to* Lady Wargrave's *chair, and is about to carry the cushion into the room, L., when* Gerald, *who has stood back, watching her, advances.*

Gerald: Margery! [Margery *drops the cushion and turns.*] Thank you! God bless you!

Margery: For what, sir?

Gerald: You have not told my aunt.

Margery: Of course I haven't told her! [*Slight pause.*] May I go?

Gerald: Not yet. Margery, can you ever forgive me?

Margery: For being a man? Oh yes!

Gerald: Can you ever respect me again?

Margery: I do respect you, sir.

Gerald: Not as I do you, Margery. You don't know what you did for me that day. If you had rounded on me, I should not have cared—but to be silent—to do nothing—to forgive me!

Margery: I had a reason for forgiving you.

Gerald: What?

Margery: That's my business.

Gerald: But, Margery, you do forgive me?

Margery: Don't let's talk about it:

Gerald: *Really* forgive me?

Margery: Really!

Gerald: Prove it to me.

Margery: How can I?

Gerald [*still holding her*]: Be my wife!

Margery [*recoiling*]: Mr. Cazenove!

Gerald: My name is Gerald.

Margery: Mr. Gerald!

Gerald: Gerald! Call me so, Margery.

Margery: I couldn't, sir. Don't ask me!

Gerald: Then you refuse me? [Margery *is silent—she turns away.*] Well, I don't deserve you.

Margery [*approaching him*]: Oh, don't think I mean that! Do you suppose you are the only man that's ever made love to me? It's a man's business to make love; and it's a woman's business to stop him—when he makes love too hard. But if we can't be lovers, Mr. Gerald, we can be friends.

Gerald: It's got past friendship with me, Margery. Since I came back to town, everything's changed. My pursuits all feel so empty and so meaningless; every woman I meet seems different from what she was: and oh, how different from *you*!

Margery: Gentry *are* different. We're different breeds. That's why we can't be lovers.

Gerald: We can be man and wife!

Margery: Isn't that being lovers?

Gerald: In my case, it would be!

Margery: Hush! Mr. Gerald, that's impossible. My lady will be asking for me. Let me go!

Gerald: Not till I've told you how I love you, Margery. Seeing you again is breathing the pure air. It seems a younger and a sweeter world, now you have come again. Nothing else matters. All my life beside appears a folly and a waste of time. My real life was lived with you down yonder, out in the fields, and rambling through the woods and listening to the music of the weir. The life that we began together so pleasantly, cannot we live together to the end? I was quite honest when I said I loved you. And couldn't you love *me*,—just a little bit?

Margery: You oughtn't to ask that!

Gerald: I mean to have an answer.

Margery: Please, Mr. Gerald, don't! It makes it very hard for me—

Gerald: Answer me! Could you love me, Margery?

Margery: Oh, what's the use of asking? You only want to make me tell a lie.

Gerald: Answer me!

Margery: I *have* answered you!

Gerald: Margery, then you do!

Margery: That is what made it easy to forgive you. Now let me go.

Gerald: Not till you've said that you will be my wife.

Margery: Oh, Mr. Gerald:

Gerald: Gerald! say Gerald!

Margery: It's no use. I can't!

Gerald: Say you will marry me!

Margery: If you will let me call you "Mr. Gerald." [*Embrace.*]

Colonel [*off, opens door L.*]: Margery! where are you?

Re-enter L., just as Margery *is withdrawing from* Gerald's *arms, stands thunderstruck. Exit* Margery, L.

Gerald: It's all right, uncle.

Colonel: All right, you call it? Look here, you young cub! None of your higher morality with Margery!

Gerald: I tell you, it's all right. Margery's going to be your niece—my wife.

Colonel: Margery, your wife! [*Slight pause.*] You're a damned lucky dog!

Gerald: That I am, uncle!

Colonel: 'Gad, sir, you're a man; and I thought you were a monkey. I congratulate you!

Gerald [*shaking hands*]: *You* don't object then?

Colonel: I thought a Cazenove would come right side up.

Gerald: But what will aunt say?

Colonel [*suddenly collapses*]: I was forgetting Caroline!

Gerald: She must be told.

Colonel: But cautiously. Courage! I'll back you up!

Gerald: I'll tell her now!

Colonel: Stay! Don't do anything rash! I wouldn't risk a private interview. Safety in numbers.

Gerald: I will tell them all!

Colonel: Sht! what a bomb-shell! Courage!

Gerald: Courage, yourself! You're shaking all over.

Colonel: No matter. I'll stand by you!

Lady Wargrave [*opening door, L.*]: Gerald!

Colonel: Form square! Prepare to receive cavalry! [*Retires up.*]

Re-enter Lady Wargrave, *L.*

Lady Wargrave: Where are you? Why have you deserted me? To leave me at the mercy of that crew! My poor, dear, Gerald! however did you get into this set?

Gerald: It was my poem did it.

Lady Wargrave: I thought, that crime would bring its punishment. Now, they're upon the marriage service! As though *that* concerned them! Gerald, if you marry any of that tribe, you'll really break my heart! [Colonel *comes down R. of* Gerald.]

Gerald: I hope I shall never do that!

Lady Wargrave: Marry a *woman*, whatever else she is.

Colonel [*aside to* Gerald]: Courage!

Gerald: Or isn't, aunt! [*Effusively.*]

Colonel [*aside to* Gerald] Caution! [*Retires up.*]:

Lady Wargrave. Or isn't!

The door L. is thrown open, and re-enter Dr. Mary, Enid, *and* Victoria, *all talking, followed by* Margery, *who takes up her original position at the back.*

Doctor: "Obey," forsooth!

Victoria: To promise to love is ridiculous, for how can one control the mysterious expansions of the heart?

Doctor: It is the brain that loves. A still more complicated mechanism.

Enid: It is impossible to honour a man who has invariably lived a revolting, ante-nuptial life—

Victoria: But to "obey!" [Colonel *works down stage, interested.*]

Doctor: Lady Wargrave, even *you* surely wouldn't promise to "obey" a man?

Lady Wargrave: Not till he asked me, certainly.

Colonel: Ha! ha! [*The trio turn on him; he retires up.*]

Lady Wargrave: Gerald, I must be going.

Doctor: So must I.

Enid: And I.

Doctor: I have a clinical lecture—

Victoria: I have an engagement.

Gerald: One moment, ladies! Stay one moment, aunt! Before you go I want to tell you all of *my* engagement.

Lady Wargrave: Your engagement, Gerald?

Gerald: Yes, I am going to be married. [*Pause.*]

Enid [*with jealousy*]: To Agnes Syl—? Oh, I forgot; she's married.

Lady Wargrave: To whom? [*All stand expectantly.*]

Gerald: To Margery. [*All stand transfixed. Exit* Colonel, *door in flat.*]

Doctor: Mr. Cazenove, I offer you my congratulations. Having a clinical lecture to deliver, you will excuse me if I say good afternoon.

Enid: Wait for me, Doctor. [*Exit* Dr. Mary, *door in flat.*] You have my best wishes. [*Exit, door in flat.*]

Victoria: And thank you for the plot of my next novel. [*Exit, door in flat.*]

Lady Wargrave: Gerald, is this a trick?

Gerald: No, aunt; it is the truth.

Lady Wargrave: And you, a Cazenove! It is out of the question! I won't permit it! I forbid it, Gerald!

Gerald: But, my dear aunt, you said only just now—

Lady Wargrave: No matter!

Gerald: Marry a woman—

Lady Wargrave: Don't repeat my words! A Cazenove marry Margery! Ridiculous!

Gerald: But, aunt—

Lady Wargrave: Silence! You said just now, you hoped that you would never break my heart. Well, Gerald, you have broken it. A Cazenove!

[*Exit, door in flat.* Margery *takes up the cushion, and is about to follow.*]

Gerald: Put that thing down. [*She puts it down.*] You are mine now; not hers.

Margery: Yes, Mr. Gerald.

Gerald [*sits, drawing her to him*]: For better, for worse, Margery.

Margery: For better, for worse.

Gerald: You are not frightened?

Margery: Not now, Mr. Gerald.

Gerald: Then call me, Gerald.

Margery: Gerald! [*Dropping on her knee by his side.*]

Gerald: *You*'re not afraid to make those promises!

Margery: No, Gerald!

Gerald: To love—to honour.

Margery: And obey! [*Looking up at him.*]

ACT II

Twelve months have elapsed.

Scene.—*Study at* Gerald's, *opening upon a little boudoir, through curtains which are drawn across part of the stage at back. Doors, R., and L.U.E. Mantelpiece, between doors, R.*

   Gerald *discovered, seated at a writing table, with his back to the curtains, writing busily.* Margery's *head appears through the curtains, which she holds closely round it, so that only her face is visible. She watches* Gerald *for a few moments, with a broad smile on her face.*

Margery: Bo! [*Withdraws her head.*]

Gerald [starts and looks round]: Margery, of course!

   [*Resumes his writing. A peal of laughter behind the curtains, and* Margery's *head reappears, laughing.* Gerald *throws down his pen.*]

Margery [*running in*]: Did I startle you?

Gerald: Not much; I'm getting used to it.

Margery: Well, don't be cross!

Gerald: I'm not cross, dear; but these repeated interludes make composition rather difficult.

Margery: Oh, bother! you've been all the morning at that stupid book, and I'm so happy, I can't help it. Kiss me, and say that you forgive me!

Gerald: Of course I forgive you!

Margery: Kiss me, then!

Gerald: My dear—

Margery: Gerald! will you kiss me?

Gerald [*kisses her*]: How many times does that make?

Margery: Only three this morning. You used to like kissing me.

Gerald: Yes, dear, but—

Margery: What?

Gerald: This isn't writing my book.

Margery: No, but it's being happy, and that's worth all the books that ever were written.

Gerald: Yes—being happy—that's the great thing. [*Sighs.*]

Margery: Why do you sigh?

Gerald. Did I sigh? [*Smiling.*]

Margery: Yes.

Gerald: I didn't know I sighed. Writing's hard work.

Margery: Then put the book away! [*Thrusts the MS. aside.*] I've such news for you!

Gerald: News?

Margery: Such good news. Guess what it is. I'll give you three tries.

Gerald [*deprecatingly*]: Margery!

Margery: You'll never guess!

Gerald: Then what's the use of trying?

Margery: Because I want you to guess wrong.

Gerald: I shan't do that!

Margery: You will! I'm sure you will!

Gerald: I'm sure I shan't, because I am not going to guess at all.

Margery [*grimaces*]: Cross again! You'd better not be, or you know the penalty!

Gerald: Come! what is the good news?

Margery: That's the good news. [*Gives him a card.*]

Gerald [*with real pleasure*]: Margery!

Margery [*pouting*]: You might have guessed!

Gerald: A card from Lady Wargrave! And addressed to you!

Margery: Asking us to a party at her house.

Gerald: Don't say a party, Margery!

Margery: Well, isn't it a party?

Gerald: Call it an At Home.

Margery: Oh, that's another lesson! Never call things by their right names, it's vulgar!

Gerald: This is an olive-branch, and no mistake! So aunt is thawing at last.

Margery: Stop a bit, Gerald!

Gerald: Wait a moment, Margery!

Margery: Is that another lesson? Never use one syllable when two will do? Very well, Gerald, I'll remember that. But what do you mean by olive-branch?

Gerald [*looks at her, and sighs again*]: Oh, never mind!

Margery: Yes, tell me. I want to make sure as I go along.

Gerald: An overture—a sign of reconciliation—like holding out your hand.

Margery: Ah, now I understand! But what a funny thing to call it—olive-branch! [*Bursts into a peal of laughter.*]

Gerald [*shivers slightly and goes over to the mantelpiece. Aside*]: It didn't sound like that in Mapledurham! [*Conquering himself, returns to her.*] I'm so glad aunt's come round. You don't know how it's worried me—her estrangement.

Margery: They've all come round now. They've all recognized me. Oh, I'm so happy, Gerald! It isn't half as hard to be a lady as I thought!

Gerald [*thoughtfully*]. Of course you'll have to answer this!

Margery: Of course!

Gerald: Show me the answer when you've written it!

Margery: Oh, I shan't spell it wrong!

Gerald: No, dear, but—

Margery: I know what you mean. I might use all short words instead of long ones. [Gerald *laughs.*] Don't be afraid: I'll pick the longest in the dictionary. [*Kisses him.*] Ah, Gerald, dear! short words were good enough for you once! [*Archly.*]

Gerald: I dare say.

Margery: Yes; when you said, "I love you, Margery!" Say it again!

Gerald: Margery, what nonsense!

Margery: That's what I like—nonsense. Say it again!

Gerald [*with effort*]: I love you, Margery. [*Sits, and resumes his pen.*] Now, let me get on with my work!

Margery [*goes L. Aside*]. Somehow it didn't sound like that in Mapledurham. [*Brightly.*] Well, I suppose his head's full of his book. I wish mine was of mine. Oh, those French verbs! and what's the use of them? Why isn't English good enough for England?

Enter Wells, *L.*

Wells: Captain Sylvester. [Gerald *flings down his pen in despair. Exit* Wells, *L.*]

Enter Sylvester.

Margery: Ah, I'm so glad you've come! [*Crosses to him.*] I wanted somebody to talk to. Gerald's so busy! [*Takes* Sylvester's *hat and stick.*]

Sylvester: Busy? then I'm afraid I intrude.

Gerald [*resignedly*]: Oh, not at all! [*Sees* Margery *at back, who has put* Sylvester's *hat on, very much askew, and is marching up and down with the stick under her arm.*] Good gracious, Margery!

[Margery *laughs.* Sylvester *laughs.* Gerald *goes up, snatches the hat and stick, and turns to put them down.*]

Margery: Cross again! [*As Gerald turns again, he finds himself face to face with her, holding her mouth out.*] Penalty!

Gerald: It is for Captain Sylvester to forgive you.

Sylvester: Anything. Mrs. Cazenove can do no wrong. [*Bows. Margery curtseys.*] But where's Agnes? Happening to pass this way, I thought I might perhaps give her a lift home.

Margery: Oh! Gerald expects Mrs. Sylvester—

Gerald: Later on, later on!

Sylvester: Then may I wait for her?

Gerald: Oh, certainly! [*Taking up MS.*] If you'll excuse me going on with my work. I've been a good deal interrupted. [*Goes to door, R.*]

Sylvester: By all means, if I may talk to Mrs. Cazenove!

[Gerald *bows stiffly and exit, R., watched by* Margery, *who makes a grimace to audience.*]

Margery: I believe Gerald's jealous!

Sylvester [*laughing*]: Of *me?*

Margery [*laughs*]: Just fancy anyone being jealous of *you!* [*Laughs loudly, then stops suddenly.*] Hush! I forgot! We musn't make so much noise. Clever people don't like noise.

Sylvester: Music is noise to some people. I like it!

Margery: Ah, but then you're not clever!

Sylvester [*laughing*]: I'm afraid not!

Margery: There's a pair of us!

Sylvester: And what a pleasure it is to meet somebody who's not clever. Mrs. Cazenove, I think cleverness is the most boring thing in the world. This planet would be quite a pleasant place but for the clever people.

Margery: Do you mean my husband?

Sylvester: I was thinking of my wife; she's one of them. I'm not. I'm only Mrs. Sylvester's husband.

Margery: Are you sure you're that?

Sylvester: I have always been under that impression.

Margery: A husband who isn't master of his wife isn't half a husband.

Sylvester: I am content to be a fraction!

Margery: But you're a cipher.

Sylvester: You're frank, Mrs. Cazenove.

Margery: I only say to your face what everybody says behind your back.

Sylvester: What do they say?

Margery: That Mrs. Sylvester's too much alone.

Sylvester: Never. She's always with your husband!

Margery: Well?

Sylvester: As long as *you* don't object—

Margery: Object? Not I! But that's a very different thing!

Sylvester: How so?

Margery: I am my husband's wife, and I am not afraid of any woman in the world.

Sylvester: You have no need to be. [*With admiration.*] And in your pre-eminence resides my safety, Margery.

Margery: I'm not Margery now!

Sylvester [*seriously*]: I ask Mrs. Cazenove's pardon. [*In a casual tone.*] You don't object to the collaboration, then?

Margery: I think it's fun! They are so serious over it. As if the world depended on a book! As if there were no Providence or anything, and they two had to keep creation going by scratching upon little bits of paper! I love to watch them, biting at their pens, and staring at that little crack up there. [*Looking at the ceiling.* Sylvester *looks also.*] I often think to myself, you may well look—there's something there that'll keep the world going round, just as it is, long after your precious book is dust and ashes.

Sylvester: Then you do watch them, Margery—Mrs. Cazenove?

Margery. Oh, often, from my room. [*Indicates curtains.*] But I can scarcely keep from laughing all the time. Some day I mean to have such fun with them! I mean to steal in here, [*business*] and put my hand out, so—and just when they are putting the world right, say Bo!

[*Runs back, and bursts into a peal of laughter.* Sylvester *laughs also.*]

Re-enter Wells, L.

Wells: Miss Vivash! [*Exit* Wells, L.]

Enter Victoria.

Victoria: Good morning, dear. [*Kisses* Margery.] What! Captain Sylvester! you here, and Agnes not?

Margery: Mrs. Sylvester is coming!

Victoria: No need to apologize! A wife is just as much entitled to entertain another woman's husband as a husband to entertain another man's wife. You're getting on, dear. That's philosophy!

Margery: Gerald is in the next room!

Victoria: Then it's not philosophy!

Margery: I'll go and wake him up. [*Exit, R.*]

Victoria; Humph! [*Sits.*] Well, how long do you give it?

Sylvester: Do you mean philosophy?

Victoria: The Cazenove *ménage.* Another six months? These love-matches are honeymoon affairs. When once that's over, there's an end of everything.

Sylvester: But is it over?

Victoria: Everybody's talking. Cazenove is bored to death.

Sylvester: I don't think his wife is.

Victoria: Ah, that will come in time; and when it does, I mean to take Margery in hand. She is neglected shamefully. *She* hasn't discovered it yet, but all her friends have.

Sylvester: They're generally first in the field.

Victoria: If a husband ignores his wife, the wife is entitled to ignore her husband. What would a man do under the same circumstances?

Sylvester: Is not the question rather, what a man *ought* to do?

Victoria: That is Utopian. We must take the world as we find it.

Sylvester: I'm afraid Mrs. Cazenove won't be an apt pupil.

Victoria: No spirit—no proper pride. But things can't go on as they're going long. Margery is on the edge of a volcano. I give it six months.

Sylvester: Is it as bad as that?

Victoria: Never at home—and when he is— "in the next room." Never takes her anywhere, and I don't wonder at it. Margery is too *gauche* for anything. But what could be expected, when a man throws himself away in that manner? Bless me, there were other women in the world!

Sylvester: Oh, plenty, plenty.

Victoria: Unluckily, he's found that out. [*Aside.*] That's one for *him*!

Sylvester: Indeed!

Victoria [*gives him a glance of contempt, and produces a cigarette case*]: Do you mind tobacco?

Sylvester: Not at all. I like it.

Re-enter Margery, *R.*

If Mrs. Cazenove—

Margery: Gerald's so busy, will you please excuse him?

Victoria: Certainly. Will you join me? [*Offers case.*]

Margery: Thank you, I can't smoke.

Victoria: Then you should learn at once. [*Puts a cigarette in her mouth.*] Could you oblige me with a light? [Sylvester *strikes a match.*] Thanks. [*Lights up at the wrong end of a gold-tipped cigarette.* Margery *stands, arms akimbo, surveying her.*]

Margery: Do you like smoking?

Victoria: No, but I smoke on principle!

Sylvester: On the wrong principle!

Victoria: I beg your pardon. Men smoke cigarettes.

Sylvester: Yes, but they light them at the other end. [Victoria *takes the cigarette out of her mouth and looks at it.* Margery *and* Sylvester *burst out laughing. She throws it away viciously.*]

Re-enter Wells, *L.*

Wells: Miss Bethune. [*Exit* Wells, *L.*]

Enter Enid.

Enid: How are you, dear? [*Kisses* Margery.] Victoria! [*Goes to* Victoria, *who presents her cheek.*]

Sylvester [*to* Margery]: Now you have company, I'll say good-day. I've waited for my wife quite enough!

Margery [*with outstretched hand*]: But you will come and see me again soon? [Enid *and* Victoria *exchange glances.*]

Sylvester [*holding her hand, and in a lower voice*]: Shall you be in to-morrow?

Margery [*frankly*]: Yes. [Sylvester *smiles and presses her hand; she sees her mistake.*] If Gerald is.

[Enid *and* Victoria *are exchanging whispers.*]

Sylvester [*drops her hand; aside*]: Women are like Bradshaw[12]—a guide and a puzzle! [*Exit, L.*]

Enid: Does Captain Sylvester often call, my dear?

Margery: He has done lately.

Enid: Quite a change for him! He must occasionally meet his wife!

Victoria [*who has gone to the mantelpiece for a match*]: Now that that man has gone—[*Lights another cigarette.*]

Enid: Victoria!

Victoria [*offering case to* Margery]: Can't I prevail on you?

Margery [*takes one*]: Well, I don't mind trying. [*Lights hers from* Victoria's, Victoria *putting the case on the table.*]

Enid: How *can* you, Margery? I call it shocking! To take a nasty, evil-smelling thing like this [*taking a cigarette out of* Victoria's *case*]—and put it to your lips—brrh! [*Shudders, but puts it in her mouth.* Margery *presses her burning cigarette against it till it is alight.*] Don't, Margery, don't! I call it horrid—most unladylike!

Margery: Now puff!

[*All three sit and puff vigorously.* Margery *perched on table.*]

Victoria: Well, dear, and how are you getting on?

Margery: Oh, famously!

Enid: I hope you've taken my advice to heart!

Victoria: And mine! Have you a latch-key yet?

Margery: Oh, yes!

Enid: Margery, you shock me!

Margery: Well, you're easily shocked!

Victoria: You have a latch-key? [*Triumphantly.*]

Margery [*simply*]: Yes, we have a latch-key!

Both [*in different tones*]: *We?*

Margery: What would Gerald do without one?

Victoria [*with contempt*]: Gerald!

Margery: When he comes home late.

Enid: *Does* he come home late?

Victoria: All men do!

Enid: *Before* marriage. Would that were *all* they did. [*Mysteriously.*] Has he told you everything?

Margery: He's told me everything I've asked him.

Victoria [*with curiosity, putting down cigarette*]: What have you asked him?

Margery: Nothing!

Enid: Margery! [*rises*] it's such women as you on whom men prey! [*Turns off.*]

Victoria [*rises*]: And it's such men as him that women marry! [*Turns off.*]

Margery: When they get the chance! [*Grimace at audience.*]

Re-enter Wells, *L.*

Wells: Colonel Cazenove.

[*Enid hides her cigarette behind her back;* Margery *flings hers away, jumps down and runs to meet him. Exit* Wells, *L.*]

Enter Colonel.

Margery: Uncle! [*Flings her arms round his neck, and give him three smacking kisses.* Colonel *smiles all over his face.* Enid *and* Victoria *exchange shrugs.*]

Colonel: Bless me! what a smell of tobacco! [*Looks about, sniffing, sees* Victoria.] Ah, the foolish—beg pardon!—Miss Vivash! [*Bow.*] Dear me, something burning! [*Sniffs.* Victoria *sits again.*]

Enid [*confused*]: Yes, Mr. Cazenove—the next room—

Colonel [*seeing her*]: Man the Be—Miss Bethune, I think?

[*Holds out his hand.* Enid *has to change the cigarette into her left hand behind her back; shakes hands, then turns to wipe the nicotine from her lips, unconsciously presenting the burning cigarette to* Colonel's *eyeglass.* Margery *laughs.* Colonel *grins at audience.*]

Colonel: I thought something was burning. [*Enid throws cigarette into the grate, and covers her face.* Colonel *lifts his finger.*] And you said Mr. Cazenove!

Enid: Well, it wasn't a story. He *is* in the next room.

Colonel: So man has not a monopoly of the vices!

Enid: We're none of us perfect!

Colonel: No, [*rubbing his hands*] thank Heaven! It's the spice of the old Adam that makes life endurable!

Margery [*again embracing him*]: Oh, I'm so happy, uncle!

Enid [*aside*]: Wish she wouldn't do that!

Margery: Oh, so happy!

Colonel: So am I, Margery. What did I always say? Caroline's a heart of gold. I knew she would come round. I always said I'd stand by you and Gerald.

Margery: Uncle!

Colonel: I always said so!

Margery: You ran away!

Colonel: Yes, but I said so. Then you have got her card?

Margery [*nodding her head*]: Yes! [*Jumps up and gives him another kiss.*]

Enid [*aside, jealously*]: I do wish she wouldn't.

Colonel: My doing, Margery—my doing!

Enid: I have a card as well!

Colonel: My doing, Miss Bethune!

Enid: I've just been ordering my gown!

Colonel [*gallantly*]: I trust it will be worthy of the wearer. [*Bows. Enid smiles.*]

Margery: Have *you* a card, Miss Vivash?

Victoria [*who has sat very quietly, now rises*]: If you'll excuse me, dear, I'll say good-morning!

Margery [*shakes hands*]: Must you go? [*Exit Victoria, L.*]

Margery: Excuse *me*, uncle. Gerald doesn't know you're here! [*Exit, R.*]

Colonel: Miss Vivash—?

Enid: Don't trouble, Colonel! She resents an escort. I have no patience with Victoria. Trying to be a man!

Colonel: And making only a *succès d'estime!*[13]

Enid: I like a woman to be womanly!

Colonel [*aside*]: The best of 'em.

Enid: I don't mean weak—like Agnes. She goes to the other extreme. Do you know, I'm getting very anxious about Agnes!

Colonel: Mrs. Sylvester?

Enid: Haven't you noticed anything? Of course not! You men never do!

Colonel: I am afraid I must plead guilty!

Enid: Haven't you observed how much she and your nephew are together?

Colonel: But they're collaborating.

Enid: Ah, Colonel, when a man collaborates with a woman, a third person ought always to be present.

Colonel: To protect the man?

Enid [*tapping him, playfully*]: You are incorrigible!

Colonel [*cheerfully*]: I always was, and at my age reformation is out of the
  question!

Enid: Oh, you are not as old as all that!

Colonel: Guess.

Enid: Fifty!

Colonel [*pleased*]: Add six to it!

Enid: Six!

Colonel [*aside*]: She might add eight.

Enid: I don't believe it, Colonel.

Colonel [*aside*]: *Quite* the best of 'em! [*Sits.*] So you have appointed yourself
  the third person?

Enid: It's time someone did.

Colonel: A sort of Vigilance Committee,[14] eh?

Enid: I simply take the interest of a friend in Agnes.

Colonel: And what is the result of your observations?

Enid: I have come to a terrible conclusion.

Colonel: You alarm me!

Enid: That she is a poor, tempted creature.

Colonel: Bless me! I never regarded her in that light before. I thought the
  boot was on the other leg. [*Corrects himself hurriedly.*] Foot!—foot! [*Indicat-
  ing* Enid's, *which she is carefully showing; aside.*] Very neat foot she has!

Enid: Men always stand by one another, so should women. Agnes must be
  protected against herself!

Colonel: Then it's herself, after all? I thought you meant my nephew.

Enid: So I do. She is the moth—he is the candle.

Colonel: Really!—

Enid: Oh, you men, you men! You're all alike—at least, I won't say all!

Colonel: You say so in your book!

Enid [*pleased*]: You've read my book?

Colonel [*evading the question*]: "Man, the Betrayer?"

Enid: Well, you know, Colonel, one has to paint with a broad brush. [*Pantomime.*]

Colonel: Yes, when one paints with tar! [*Aside.*] Very nice arm, too! [*Aloud.*]
  Look at your title!

Enid: "Man, the Betrayer!"

Colonel [*aside*]: Don't know any more!

Enid: A mere figure of speech!

Colonel [*admiring her*]: Figure?

Enid: Mere figure!

Colonel: Damned fine figure, too! [*To himself, but aloud.*]

Enid: Colonel!

Colonel: Ten thousand pardons! I was thinking of something else. Pray forgive my bad language!

Enid: Oh, I'm used to it! Victoria's is much worse!

Colonel: Miss Vivash!

Enid: Vulgar-minded thing! Learned French on purpose to read Zola's novels.[15] I don't suppose that even *you* have read them.

Colonel: Oh, haven't I? Every one!

Enid: I don't believe it, Colonel!

Colonel: I'm a shocking old sinner! I never professed to be anything else!

Enid: I simply don't believe it! You men exaggerate so! You make yourselves out to be so much worse than you are. Whereas we women pretend to be so much better. That's the worst of us! We are such hypocrites! Oh, if you knew as much about women as *I* do—

Colonel [*aside, much interested*]: Now I'm going to hear something. [*Meanwhile* Margery *has crept in, R., behind them. She flings her handkerchief over the* Colonel's *eyes, and ties it in a knot behind his head, then skips away from him. Rising.*] You rascal! It's that Margery! I know it is! Where are you? [*Groping about,* Margery *evading him, and in shrieks of laughter.*] Margery, if I catch you!

Margery: But you can't!

[Enid *has risen to evade the* Colonel, *who is groping all over the room—a sort of blind man's buff—all laughing.*]

Colonel [*seizing Enid*]: I've got you!

[*Kisses her.* Enid *shrieks.* Margery *roars.* Colonel *tears off the handkerchief and stands aghast.*]

Re-enter Wells. *L.*

Wells: Lady Wargrave.

[*Sudden silence. Exit* Colonel, *R.* Enid *runs out, C., in confusion.*]

Enter Lady Wargrave, *L., and comes down.*

[*Exit* Wells, *L.* Enid *re-appears C., and runs across stage behind* Lady Wargrave, *and off, L.* Margery *stands confused, not knowing how to greet* Lady Wargrave.]

Lady Wargrave [*putting out both hands*]: Margery! [*Holding both* Margery's *hands*].

Margery: Oh, Lady Wargrave!

Lady Wargrave: Aunt. I've called to make amends to you.

Margery: Amends?

Lady Wargrave: For my neglect. [*Kisses her.*] Forgive me, Margery, but your marriage was a shock to me. However, I've got over it. Perhaps, after all, Gerald has chosen wisely!

Margery: Thank you for your kind words. I knew you had got over it.

Lady Wargrave: Of course! you had my card.

Margery: I knew from uncle, too. How good of him to bring it all about!

Lady Wargrave: Theodore!

Margery: I mean, to reconcile you!

Lady Wargrave: My dear Margery, your uncle has never presumed to mention the subject?

Margery: Oh, what a story he has told us! he said it was *his* doing.

Lady Wargrave: No doubt. When you know Theodore as well as I do, you will have learnt what value to attach to his observations!

Margery: Won't I pay him out? [*Shaking her fist.*]

Lady Wargrave: Never mind your uncle. Tell me about yourself—and about Gerald. I hope your marriage has turned out a happy one.

Margery: Yes—we're as happy as the day is long.

Lady Wargrave: That is good news. Then you haven't found your new position difficult?

Margery: Oh, I'm quite used to it! I'm not a bit shy now. Of course I put my foot in it—I make mistakes sometimes; but even born ladies sometimes make mistakes.

Lady Wargrave: Yes, Margery. [*Bending her head slightly.*] And Gerald?

Margery: Is the best husband in the world to me. Of course, he's very busy—

Lady Wargrave: Busy?

Margery: With his book; and sometimes I can't help annoying him. That's nothing. We haven't had a real cross word yet.

Lady Wargrave: Does he write very much?

Margery: Oh, morning, noon, and night. He's always got a pen in his hand. I often say I wonder he doesn't wear the ceiling out with looking at it. [*Laughs.*]

Lady Wargrave: That isn't writing, Margery.

Margery: No, but it's thinking—and he's always thinking. [*Falls into a reverie.*]

Lady Wargrave: Do you go out much?

Margery: We went out a good deal at first, but we got tired of it. I like home best; at any rate, Gerald does. I rather liked going out. Oh, I'm quite a success in society.

Lady Wargrave: Indeed?

Margery: Of course, aunt, I'm not clever; but I suppose I'm witty without knowing it!

Lady Wargrave: Witty?

Margery: At any rate, I make the people laugh. Isn't that being witty? Then *I* laugh as well, although I don't know what I'm laughing at, I'm sure! [*Laughs.*] Oh, everybody laughs at me—but Gerald. And he's thinking of his book!

Lady Wargrave: Do you have many visitors?

Margery: Oh, yes! Miss Vivash—Miss Bethune—Dr. Mary—Mrs. Sylvester—and uncle. They're often coming. As for Mrs. Sylvester, she almost lives here!—oh, and Captain Sylvester, he's taken to calling lately!

Lady Wargrave: In future, dear, you'll have another visitor. I see I have neglected you too long. And you must come and see me. We'll go out together.

Margery: Oh, that *will* be nice! Then you have *quite* forgiven me?

Lady Wargrave: But not myself!

Margery [*embracing her*]: Oh, why is everyone so good to me?

Re-enter Gerald, *R., followed by* Colonel.

Gerald: Aunt, this is kind of you! but you were always kind.

Lady Wargrave: Not always. I ought to have paid this visit earlier. I made a mistake, Gerald, and I have come to acknowledge it.

Colonel [*laying his hand on* Lady Wargrave's *shoulder in an access of enthusiasm*]: Caroline, you're a trump!

Lady Wargrave: Theodore!

Colonel: No other word for it! I always said you'd come round!

Lady Wargrave: Never!

Colonel: Always!

Lady Wargrave: Theodore, you *never* said so!

Colonel: To myself. [*Turns off.*]

Gerald: Better late than never, aunt. And thank you for the card for your At Home. [*Talks to* Lady Wargrave.]

Margery: Oh, uncle, you're a shocking old story, aren't you?

Colonel: What have I been saying now?

Margery: You said it was *your* doing!

Colonel: So it was!

Margery: Aunt vows you'd nothing to do with it at all!

Colonel [*taking Margery aside*]: Caroline's a heart of gold; but your aunt must be managing! So I let her manage, and I manage *her.*

Margery: You? [*Smiling.*]

Colonel: But I do it quietly. I influence her, without her knowing it. Sheer force of character. Chut! not a word! [*Backing away from her, signalling silence; backs into* Lady Wargrave.] Ten thousand pardons! [*Bows profusely.*]

Lady Wargrave: Really, Theodore!

[Margery goes up, stifling her laughter; he shakes his handkerchief at her.]

Re-enter Wells, *L.*

Wells: Mrs. Sylvester!

Enter Mrs. Sylvester, *she hesitates, on seeing* Lady Wargrave. *Exit* Wells, *L.*

Gerald: Pray come in, Mrs. Sylvester. You know my aunt.

Mrs. Sylvester: I think we've met before.

Lady Wargrave: Yes, at my nephew's chambers. I remember perfectly. You were engaged upon some work or other.

Gerald: It's not finished yet. I am so interrupted! [*Glancing at* Margery *who has crept down behind* Colonel.]

Margery [*whispering in* Colonel's *ear*]: Who kissed Miss Bethune? [Colonel *starts guiltily*; Margery *roars.*]

Gerald [*angrily*]: Margery! [Margery *runs out, L.*]

Lady Wargrave: Not finished yet!

Mrs. Sylvester: But we have made great progress.

Lady Wargrave: And are you satisfied with what you have done?

Gerald: It is certainly interesting.

Lady Wargrave: It is not enough for me that a work of my nephew's should be interesting! Tell me, as far as you have gone, do you think it is worthy of a Cazenove?

Gerald: It is the work of my life.

Mrs. Sylvester: And of mine!

Lady Wargrave: As far as you have gone. But what is to be the end of it?

Gerald: Ah, we've not got there yet.

Lady Wargrave: Would you admit a third collaborateur?

Mrs. Sylvester [*alarmed*]: Who?

Lady Wargrave: An *old* woman.

Gerald: Lady Wargrave's joking!

Lady Wargrave: Oh, I could put an end to it, I think!

Mrs. Sylvester: We don't know what the end will be ourselves.

Lady Wargrave: There I have the advantage. If I can help in any way, my experience is always at your service. Meanwhile, I fear I am another interruption. Theodore, your arm!

Gerald [*follows them to door, L.*]: Thank you so much for coming. [*Holding his hand out.*]

Lady Wargrave [*taking it*]: And for going? [*Exit with* Colonel, *L.*]

Mrs. Sylvester: What does she mean?

Gerald: Thank her for going?

Mrs. Sylvester: And the end of it?

Gerald: Aunt always talks in riddles!

Mrs. Sylvester: Is it a riddle?

Gerald [*avoids her eyes*]: Come, let us get to work. I've done hardly anything today. It's first one interruption, then another. [*Sits.*]

Mrs. Sylvester: We should be quieter at our house.

Gerald: There's your husband!

Mrs. Sylvester: Always a husband!

Gerald: Or a wife. Ah, me! [*Sits with his head between his hands, staring at vacancy;* Mrs. Sylvester *watching him sympathetically.*]

Mrs. Sylvester [*comes and kneels by him*]: Gerald! [*He starts slightly.*] You are not happy. You have realized the truth.

Gerald: What truth?

Mrs. Sylvester: Your marriage was a mistake from the beginning.

Gerald: Not from the beginning. It started right enough, but somehow it has taken the wrong turn.

Mrs. Sylvester: It was wrong from the first. Mine was the true ideal. The thing that you thought love was a mere passion—an intoxication. Now you have come back to your better self you feel the need of sympathy.

Gerald: No, no; my love was real enough, and I love Margery still; but love doesn't seem to bear the wear and tear of marriage—the hourly friction—the continual jar.

Mrs. Sylvester: There is no friction in true marriage, Gerald. You say you love your wife, and it is good and loyal of you to deceive yourself; but you can't deceive me. Haven't I made the same mistake myself? I was a thoughtless, inexperienced girl, Jack was a handsome, easy-going man. We married, and for a year or two we jogged along. But I grew up—the girl became a woman. I read, I thought, I felt; my life enlarged. Jack never reads, never thinks—he is just the same. [*Rising.*] I am not unhappy, but my soul is starved—[*goes to mantelpiece and stands looking at him*]—as yours is!

[*Pause.* Margery's *face appears between the curtains at the back, wearing a broad smile. She grimaces at them, unobserved, and remains there; then looks at* Gerald *with a long face of mock sympathy.*]

Gerald: Well, we must make the best of it!

Mrs. Sylvester: Yes, but what is the best? [Margery *grimaces at her.*] Is our mistake so hopeless, irremediable? After all, is not true loyalty to oneself?

Gerald [*looks at her*]: You think so?

Mrs. Sylvester: Or what becomes of our philosophy?

Gerald: Yes, what becomes of it?

[*Another pause.* Margery *laughs almost audibly. During the next passage the laugh subsides into an expression of perplexity.*]

Mrs. Sylvester: What is a promise when the heart's gone out of it?

Gerald: Surely it is a promise.

Mrs. Sylvester: To an empty phrase must one sacrifice one's life? Must one stake everything on the judgment of one's youth? By the decision of a moment must one be bound for ever? Must one go through the world "with quiet eyes unfaithful to the truth?" Does one not owe a duty to one-self? There can be but one answer!

Gerald [*absently*]: Margery! [Margery *winces as if struck—quite serious now. Then with energy.*] But, Agnes, Margery is impossible! She's no companion to me! I am all alone! Her very laughter grates upon me! There's no meaning in it! It is the laughter of a tomboy, of a clown! And she will never learn! She's hopeless, Agnes, hopeless! [Margery *drops back horror-struck, but her face disappears only by degrees.* Mrs. Sylvester *lays her hand on him. Another pause. The curtains close.*] What is one to do? [*Rising.*]

Mrs. Sylvester: We are face to face with the problem! Let us confront it bold-ly. Gerald, do you love me? [*A thud behind the curtains.* Gerald *starts guilti-ly. Pause. They stand looking at one another.*]

Gerald [*in a whisper*]: What was that? [*Goes cautiously and draws curtains back, discovering* Margery *stretched senseless on the floor.*] Margery!

ACT III

A Fortnight Later.

Scene.—*Drawing-room at* Lady Wargrave's. *Main entrance C., Conservatory R. Entrance, L., to an inner room. Fireplace, R., up stage, near which is* Lady War-grave's *chair, with the cushion of Act I.*

The stage is discovered half-filled with Guests, who stand and sit in groups, including Colonel, Captain *and* Mrs. Sylvester, *and* Gerald. Lady Wargrave *is receiving her guests. A buzz of general conversation; and a band is heard playing in the inner room, loudly at first, but softly after the picture is discovered.*

Servant [*at entrance C.*]: Miss Vivash and Mr. Pettigrew!

Enter Victoria, *followed leisurely by* Percy, *a very young man who is always smil-ing to himself, unconsciously.*

Victoria [*going straight to* Lady Wargrave *and grasping her hand*]: Good evening, Lady Wargrave, I have taken the liberty of bringing a friend whose name is no doubt known to you—Mr. Percy Pettigrew. [Percy *bows distantly, smiling.*]

Lady Wargrave: Pettigrew, did you say?

Percy: Percy *Bysshe* Pettigrew. [*Smiling.*]

Lady Wargrave: Of course! *two* of your names are *quite* well known to me; it is only the surname that is unfamiliar.

Percy [*smiling*]: Pettigrew! [*Turns off.*]

Gerald: One of my Oxford friends.

Lady Wargrave [*aside to him*]: One of those who are always at Oxford?

Victoria: His "Supercilia" are quoted everywhere.

Lady Wargrave: His—?

Gerald: A column Percy does for "The Corset."

Victoria: A newspaper devoted to our cause.

Gerald: "The Corset" is Percy's organ.

Lady Wargrave: Ah, his rattle!

Servant: Dr. Bevan.

Dr. Bevan [*shakes hands with* Lady Wargrave]: I hope I am not late; but I was detained at the hospital. Most interesting case, unhappily unfit for publication.

Servant: Miss Bethune. [*Exit Servant.*]

Enter Enid.

Colonel [*to* Sylvester]: The best of 'em! [Enid *shakes hands with* Lady Wargrave.] Ah, what a pity, what a pity, Sylvester!

Sylvester: What is a pity, Colonel?

Colonel: That such a figure should be wasted!

Sylvester [*in a matter of course voice*]: I prefer Mrs. Cazenove's. [*Turns off. Colonel eyes him curiously. The other Guests should be so arranged that each man is surrounded by a little group of women.*]

Percy [*the centre of one group, lolling lazily, always smiling with self-complacency, suddenly sits up and shivers*]: No, no! don't mention it. It bores me so. [*Shivers.*]

Chorus: And me! [*All shiver.*]

Victoria: The stage has ever been Woman's greatest foe.

Guest: For centuries it has shirked the sexual problem.

Sylvester [*who has strolled up*]: But doesn't it show signs of repentance?

Percy: The theatre is dying.

Sylvester: Death-bed repentance, then. That's the one problem it discusses.

Guest: It is the one problem in life.

Percy: The theatre is dying! Dixi![16] [*Leans back again.*]

Doctor: The novel will sweep everything before it.

Sylvester: You mean, the female novel?

Doctor: Nothing can stop it.

Sylvester: No, it stops at nothing.

Doctor: Nor will it, till the problem is solved. That solution, I venture to predict, will be on the lines of pure mathematics.

Sylvester: Really? [*Smothering a yawn.*]

Doctor: I put the proposition in this way. The sexes are parallel lines.

Sylvester: Which are bound to meet.

Doctor: I must not be taken to admit, that there is any physiological necessity.

Voices: Certainly not.

Doctor [*to* Lady Wargrave, *who is passing*]: I am sure, Lady Wargrave must agree with us.

Lady Wargrave: What is that, Doctor?

Doctor: That there is no physiological necessity—

Lady Wargrave: To discuss physiology? I am quite of your opinion. [*Passes on.*]

Enid [*who is in a group surrounding* Colonel]: That's where we differ. What is *your* view, Colonel?

Colonel: My dear Miss Bethune, there is no occasion for Man to express any view, when Woman expresses them all. First, you must reconcile your internal differences.

Voice: But we can't.

Colonel: To begin with, you must make up your minds whether you wish to regenerate us or to degrade yourselves.

Enid: Regenerate you, of course.

Colonel: Miss Vivash prefers the alternative.

Enid: That is Victoria's foible.

Colonel [*gallantly*]: I can admit no foible in a lady.

Enid: At any rate, we are agreed on the main point—the equality of the sexes.

Colonel: That, alas, is impossible.

Voice: Impossible?

Colonel: Whilst Woman persists in remaining perfect.

Victoria: Cannot Man emulate her?

Colonel: I am afraid his strength is only equal to the confession of his unworthiness.

Enid: You would confess that? Then you agree with me, that a woman is entitled to know the whole of a man's past?

Lady Wargrave [*who has joined them*]: Would it not be more useful if she knew something of his future?

Enid: Women have futures; men have only pasts.

Doctor [*still in* Sylvester's *group*]: It stands to reason—pure reason—there ought not to be one law for women and another for men.

Sylvester: You mean, that they ought both to be for women?

Doctor: I mean, that the institution of marriage is in urgent need of reconsideration.

Sylvester: The sooner, the better.

Doctor: I am glad you think so.

Sylvester: When the institution of marriage is reconsidered, man will have another chance. [*Exit, R.*]

Lady Wargrave [*who has joined* Percy's *group*]: What do I think of the New Woman? There is no New Woman; she is as old as Molière. [*Stands listening, amused.*]

Chorus: Molière!

Victoria: A pagan!

Percy: A frank pagan. For pure art we must go to Athens.

Chorus: Athens!

Percy: Or the Music Halls. Have you seen Trixy Blinko?

Chorus: Trixy—oh, charming—sweet!

Percy: In her alone I find the true Greek spirit. What were the prevailing characteristics of Hellenic culture? [*A sudden silence.*] Breadth and centrality, blitheness and repose. All these I find in Trixy.

Chorus: Little dear!

Lady Wargrave: Somewhat *risquée*, isn't she?

Percy: To the suburban mind. [Lady Wargrave *bows and turns off.*]

Servant *enters, L.*

Servant: Signor Labinski has arrived, your ladyship.

[*Exit, L.* Lady Wargrave *speaks to one or two of the Guests, and the company disperse, most of them going off, L., but a few, C., and others into the conservatory. During this general movement, the music off, is heard louder.* Colonel *is left with* Dr. Mary.]

Colonel: Nonsense, my dear Doctor—The fact's just this. The modern woman is prostrated by the discovery of her own superiority; and she is now engaged in one of those hopeless enterprises which we have regretfully abandoned. She is endeavouring to understand *herself.* I offer her my respectful sympathy. [*Bows and sits, C.*]

Doctor [*sits by him*]: The truth amounts to this: the one mitigating circumstance about the existence of Man is, that he occasionally co-operates in the creation of a Woman.

Colonel: His proudest privilege! The mystery to me is, that you ladies haven't found it out before.

Re-enter Enid, *C.*

Doctor: Yes, but you shirk the question!

[Colonel *is fanning himself, helplessly.*]

Enid [*aside*]: A man in distress! I must help him! [*Advancing sweetly.*] What were you saying, Doctor? [*Sits on the other side of* Colonel.]

Colonel [*aside*]: Bethune! the best of 'em!

Doctor: You know, from your own experience, that marriage is not a necessity.

Colonel: No, it's a luxury—an expensive luxury.

Enid: Oh, surely that depends upon the wife.

Doctor: It is she who has to associate with him.

Enid: And considering what his past has been—

Colonel: Suppose it hasn't!

Doctor: But it always has!

Enid: I should be sorry to think that.

Doctor: Take the Colonel's own case.

Colonel [*alarmed*]: Doctor!

Doctor: Do you deny that you have had a past?

Colonel: Oh, a few trifling peccadilloes!

Enid: Then you must never marry.

Colonel: Am I to have no chance of reformation?

Enid: It is your own fault.

Doctor: Entirely.

Colonel: One moment, my dear ladies! Excuse me pointing out, that, in the last resort, there must always be a female accomplice!

Enid: Poor, tempted creature!

Colonel: *Tempted* by a *man!*

Doctor: We all have our weak moments. [*Sighs.*]

Enid: All of us! [*Sighs. As the pair sit with their eyes cast down, silent,* Colonel *looks from one to the other in dismay, then steals off, R.*]

Colonel [*at door*]: Getting dangerous! [*Exit R. When they look up, each with a languourous glance, they find themselves languishing at one another; both rise.*]

Enid [*putting her arm round* Doctor's *waist*]: My dear, we are missing the music! [*Exeunt, L.*]

Re-enter Mrs. Sylvester *and* Gerald, *C. Movement of other Guests across stage, during music.*

Mrs. Sylvester: Where have you been? I have seen nothing of you. What have you been doing?

Gerald: Thinking.

Mrs. Sylvester [*jealously*]: Of whom?

Gerald: Of Margery. [*Movement of* Mrs. Sylvester.]

Mrs. Sylvester: Has she said anything?

Gerald: No, not a word.

Mrs. Sylvester: Of course, she heard?

Gerald: What did I say? What did I do? What must she think of me? I can't bear this suspense. For the last fortnight, she's been another woman. So grave—so thoughtful—so unlike herself. There is no laugh to grate upon me now. What would I give to bring it back again?

Mrs. Sylvester: Is it she only who has changed?

Gerald: Ever since I saw that figure on the ground, I can see nothing else. And it is I who brought it to the dust—I, who had sworn to cherish it. Yes, you are right; I too am different; I see things from a different point of view. And when I think of Margery's young life, so full of hope and joy—Margery, who never asked to be my wife—Margery, whom I compelled to marry me—with all the joy crushed out of her—I feel too much ashamed even to ask forgiveness. And as I watch her move about the house—silent and sorrowful—I ask myself, how much did Margery give up for me? I took her from the station of life in which she was born, and in which she was happy. I set her in another and a strange one. Was mine the only sacrifice? How much of friendship and of old association did she resign for my sake? My life continued as it was before—I had my old friends and my old pursuits. What had she? Nothing—but my love. And I took it away from her. Because she made a few mistakes, and a few people laughed—a few more didn't call—and I mistook a light heart for an empty head. What do all these things matter? what is a man worth who set such things above a love like hers?

Mrs. Sylvester: This is pure pity, Gerald.

Gerald: Pity for myself.

Mrs. Sylvester: She was no wife for you. She could be no companion.

Gerald: If she was no companion, did I make her one?

Mrs. Sylvester: Need you tell *me* all this?

Gerald: Yes, Mrs. Sylvester, it's best I should. I came to tell it you.

Mrs. Sylvester: Not Agnes now!

Gerald: Forget my folly, and forget your own.

Mrs. Sylvester: Mine was no folly. I, at least, was sincere; the love that isn't based on sympathy is a mere passion.

Gerald: And the love that has no passion in it, isn't worth the name!

Mrs. Sylvester: That's your idea?

Gerald: And what is yours? Let us be frank.

Mrs. Sylvester: Oh, frankness, by all means.

Gerald: Forgive me; but we're face to face with truth. Don't let us flinch from it. We have both made the same mistake—not in our marriages, but in despising them. What we want in a partner is what we lack in ourselves. Not sympathy only, but sex. Strength requires gentleness, sweetness asks for light; and all that is womanly in woman wants all that is manly in man. You think your husband is no mate for you. What I have missed in Margery, have you not missed in him?

Mrs. Sylvester [*after a pause*]: I understand. It is over.

Gerald: It is for you to say. We have gone too far together for either of us to turn back alone. I have not only made my own hearth desolate, but yours. I owe you all the reparation I can make. I only want you to know the truth. What is left of my life you may command, but my heart is not mine to bestow.

Mrs. Sylvester [*turns up, to hide her emotion, and tries to go into the room, L., but half-way she falters and puts out her hand*]: Gerald!

[*He goes to her and offers her his arm. Exeunt* Gerald *and* Mrs. Sylvester, *L. Other Guests cross the stage. Enter* Margery, *C. Finding herself opposite* Lady Wargrave*'s chair, takes a long look at it, then moves the cushion, and gradually gets into her old position behind it. Music heard off, softly, during this passage.*]

Margery: Yes, this is how it ought to be. It looks a different world altogether—the real world—the world, when Gerald loved me! [*Comes down and sits, in a reverie.*]

Re-enter Sylvester, *R.*

Sylvester: Alone, Mrs. Cazenove? It isn't often that I find you alone. I've seen nothing of you lately. You've always been out when I've called.

Margery: I was in once.

Sylvester: Only once.

Margery: It was enough.

Sylvester: You are cruel.

Margery: Are you looking for your wife?

Sylvester [*laughs*]: Agnes and I go very different ways.

Margery: I think you're going the same way, both of you.

Sylvester [*still laughing*]: But in opposite directions. Mrs. Cazenove, you're quite a philosopher. Why have you grown so serious all at once?

Margery: I'm older than I was.

Sylvester: Only a fortnight since you were all vivacity.

Margery: One can live a long time in a fortnight.

Sylvester: I hope these ladies haven't converted you.

Margery: Yes; I am a new woman.

Sylvester [*laughs*]: Your husband had been reading you his book!

Margery: A good deal of it.

Sylvester: What is it all about? If I am not too curious.

Margery: It's about love.

Sylvester: I thought it was about marriage.

Margery: Aren't they the same thing? He says they are, and I agree with him. And then he says [*half to herself*] that, when the love is gone, so is the marriage—and I think he's right! [*Loses herself in thought.*]

Sylvester [*gazes at her for some moments, then unable to restrain himself*]: Ah, Margery! if Heaven had given me such a wife as you—

Margery [*rises*]: Heaven didn't, and there's an end of it.

Sylvester [*rises*]: Forgive me! how can I help admiring you?

Margery: Can't you admire me without telling me? It's well to make the best of what we have, instead of trying to make the worst of what we haven't.

Sylvester: I must be silent!

Margery: Or not talk in that way. [*Moves away.*]

Sylvester [*following, in an outburst*]: Gerald doesn't love you [*movement of Margery*]—oh, you said that just now! you mayn't know that you said it, but you did! My wife doesn't love me—I don't love my wife—and yet I must say nothing.

Margery: What's it to me that you don't love your wife?

Sylvester: I love *you*, Margery.

Margery: I knew that was coming.

Sylvester: Honestly love you! I admired you always. It was an empty admiration, perhaps—the admiration a man feels for twenty women—but it grew solid; and the more you repulsed me, the more you attracted me. You mayn't believe me, but at first I wanted you to repulse me; then it got past that; and when I saw you sitting there alone—living over in your mind your wasted life—I loved you, and the words sprang to my lips. Nothing could keep them back! I love you, Margery—nobody but you! Why should your life be wasted? Why should mine?

Margery: Well, have you finished?

Sylvester [*seizing her*]: No!

Margery: I can guess the rest. You say Gerald doesn't love me, you don't love your wife, and your wife doesn't love *you*; but you forget one thing— that *I* don't love you either.

Sylvester: Not now, but by-and-by. Margery, I would make you love me—I would teach you!

Margery: So, I'm to *learn* to be unfaithful, is that it? As one learns music? No, Captain Sylvester! Suppose two people are so much in love that they can't help it, Heaven is their judge, not me. But to *begin* to love when they *can* help it—not to resist—to *teach* themselves to love—that's where the wrong is, and there's no gainsaying it.

Sylvester: Suppose your husband left you?

Margery: I would have no other!

Sylvester: Why not?

Re-enter Gerald, *L.*

Margery: Because I love him, and I don't love you!

[Margery's back is towards Gerald, *so that she doesn't see him; but* Sylvester *is facing him and sees him.]*

Gerald [*coming down to* Margery]: What has he said?

Margery: Nothing for your ears!

Sylvester: Yes, for all the world's! I'll tell you!

Margery: I forbid you! Leave me with my husband. [Sylvester *hesitates a moment, then exit, C.*]

Gerald: Margery, speak! I have a right to know.

Margery: You have no right!

Gerald: You will not tell me?

Margery: No!

Gerald: Then *he shall!* [*Advances on her.*]

Margery: Stand back! You shall not go!

Gerald: What, you defend him?

Margery: Against you, I do! Who are you to question him? Are your own hands clean?

Gerald [*drops back as if struck*]: Margery!

Margery [*holding out her hand*]: Good-bye!

Gerald: Good-bye?

Margery: I'm going home.

Gerald: To Mapledurham?

Margery: We'll say good-bye now.

Gerald: Here—Margery?

Margery: You needn't be afraid. There'll be no scene; I've done with tears.

Gerald: You're [*chokes*] going to leave me?

Margery: Yes.

Gerald: For a few days, you mean?

Margery: I mean, for ever. Gerald, I've had enough of half a home and only half a heart. I'm starving, withering, dying here with you! They love me there! Let me go back to them! Oh, what a world it is! To think that one can get the love of any man except the man one loves!

Gerald: You have it, Margery!

Margery [*fiercely*]: I haven't.

Gerald: If you only knew—

Margery: I know I haven't! what's the use of words? Do you think a woman doesn't know when she's not loved, or is? When you first said you loved me, down in the fields yonder, do you suppose you took me by surprise? You had no need to swear. I knew you loved me, just as certainly as I know now you don't!

Gerald [*much moved*]: Oh, what a scoundrel I was, Margery!

Margery: No man's a scoundrel to the woman he loves. Ah, it was easy to forgive your loving me. But I'll do something that is not so easy. I will for-

give you for *not* loving me. It's been a struggle. For the last fortnight I
haven't said a word, because I wasn't master of myself, and I didn't want
to speak till I'd forgiven you. I wasn't listening, Gerald. Heaven knows I
would have given all the world not to have heard a word; but when you
spoke my name, I couldn't move. The ground seemed slipping underneath my feet, and all the happiness of all my life went out of it in those
three words, "Margery's hopeless, hopeless!"

Gerald: Don't! don't! you torture me!

Margery: Yes, Margery *is* hopeless. Every scrap of hope has gone out of her
heart. I heard no more. It was enough. There was the end of all the
world for me. [Gerald *groans*.] But it was well I heard you. I should have
gone blundering along, in my old madcap way, and perhaps not found it
out till I had spoilt your life. It's well to know the truth; but, Gerald dear,
why didn't you tell it *me* instead of her? Why didn't you tell me I was no
companion? I would have gone away. But to pretend you loved me, when
you didn't—to let me go on thinking you were happy, when all the time
you were regretting your mistake—not to tell *me*, and to tell someone
else—oh, it was cruel, when I loved you so!

Gerald: How could I tell you, Margery?

Margery: How could you tell *her*? How could she listen to you? I forgive *you*,
Gerald—I didn't at first, but now I understand that there are times when
one's heart is so sore, it must cry out to somebody. But *she*—

Gerald: It was my fault!

Margery: You are mistaken there. It was your voice that spoke them, but the
words were hers. It's she who's robbed me of your love! It isn't I who've
lost it; she has stolen it!

Gerald: No, no!

Margery: Be careful, or she'll steal your honour too. Don't trust to her fine
phrases. She deceives herself. She wants your love, that's what that
woman wants: not to instruct the world—just to be happy—nothing more
or less; but she won't make you happy or herself. If I am no companion,
she's a bad one!

Gerald: You wrong her, Margery—indeed, you do! *I* was the culprit—

Margery: Have some pity on me! Don't let the last words I shall hear you say
be words defending her! Think what she's done for me! Think how you
loved me when you married me—think what our two lives might have
been, but for her—think what mine *will* be! for mine won't be like yours.
Your love is dead, and you will bury it, but mine's alive—alive! [*Breaks
down.*]

Gerald: And so is mine!

Margery [*springs up*]: Don't soil your lips with lies! I've borne as much as I
can bear. I can't bear that!

Gerald: If you will only listen—

Margery: I have heard too much! Don't speak again, or you will make me hate you! My mind's made up. I have no business here! You are above me. I'm no wife for you! I'm dragging you down every day and hour.

Gerald: Margery! you shall not go!

Margery [*flinging him off*]:To-night and now! Good-bye! [*Rushes into conservatory, R.*]

Gerald: What right have I to stop her? [*Goes up, leans upon chair.*]

Re-enter Sylvester, *C.*

Sylvester: Now, Mr. Cazenove, I am at your service.

Gerald: You are too late. [*Exit. C.*]

Sylvester: So, he won't speak to me. But I will make him. If he thinks I am caught, like a rat in a trap, he's made a mistake. There'll be a scandal—well, so much the better! Better that they should know the truth all round.

Re-enter Mrs. Sylvester, *L.*

Mrs. Sylvester: Ah, you are here! I've been looking for you everywhere.

Sylvester: Looking for *me?*

Mrs. Sylvester: I want you to take me home.

Sylvester: I've something to say to you. Sit down.

Mrs. Sylvester: Not to-night. I'm tired.

Sylvester: Yes, to-night. What I'm going to say may be everybody's property to-morrow. I choose that you should know it now.

Mrs. Sylvester: I don't understand you.

Sylvester: But you shall. I've often heard you say that a loveless marriage is no marriage. Well, ours is loveless enough, isn't it?

Mrs. Sylvester: It has been.

Sylvester: It is! I've never understood you; and if there was any good in me, you've never taken the trouble to find it out.

Mrs. Sylvester: I can't bear this now.

Sylvester: You must. Don't think I'm going to reproach you. I take all the blame on myself. What if I were to tell you that you've made a convert to your principles where you least expected it?

Mrs. Sylvester: What do you mean?

Sylvester: That it's best for us both to put an end to this farce that we're living. I mean, that I love another woman.

Mrs. Sylvester [*rising*]: You!

Sylvester: Perhaps that seems to you impossible. You thought, perhaps, that I was dull and stupid enough to go on with this empty life of ours to the end. I thought so too, but I was wrong. I love this woman, and I've told her so—

Mrs. Sylvester [*with jealousy*]: Who is she?

Sylvester: And I would tell her husband to his face—

Mrs. Sylvester: Then she is married?

Sylvester: As I tell *you.*

Mrs. Sylvester: Who is she, I say?

Sylvester: Margery.

Mrs. Sylvester: Margery! Are you all mad, you men? What is it in that woman that enslaves you? What is the charm we others don't possess? Only you men can see it; and you all do! You lose your senses, every one of you! What is it in her that bewitches you?

Sylvester: What you've crushed out of yourself—your womanhood. What you're ashamed of is a woman's glory. Philosophy is well enough in books; but in a woman a man wants flesh and blood—frank human nature!

Mrs. Sylvester [*laughing, hysterically*]: A mere animal!

Sylvester: A woman.

Mrs. Sylvester: Well, you have found one.

Sylvester: Yes.

Mrs. Sylvester: Take her, then! go your way!

Sylvester. I will. [*Exit, C.*]

Mrs. Sylvester: This world was made for such as you and her!

Re-enter Margery, *R., cloaked.*

We have no place in it—we who love with our brains! we have no chance of happiness!

Margery: What chance have we? we, who love with our hearts! we, who are simply what God made us—women! we, to whom love is not a cult—a problem, but just as vital as the air we breathe. Take love away from us, and you take life itself. You have your books, your sciences, your brains! What have we?—nothing but our broken hearts!

Mrs. Sylvester: Broken hearts heal! The things that *you* call hearts! One love is dead, another takes its place; one man is lost, another man is found. What is the difference to a love like yours? Oh, there are always men for such women as you!

By degrees re-enter omnes[17] *R., L., and C., gradually, except* Gerald.

Margery: But if the love is not dead? if it's stolen? what is our lot then—ours, whose love's alive? We, who're not skilled to steal—who only want our own—

Mrs. Sylvester: Not skilled to steal! have you not stolen mine?

Margery: I have one husband, and I want no other! [*Murmurs.*]

Lady Wargrave [*restraining her*]: Calm yourself, dear!

Margery: I have been calm too long!

Lady Wargrave: Remember, you are my niece.

Margery: That's what I do remember! [*Murmurs continue.*] I am Gerald's wife! That's what she doesn't forgive me! [*Addressing* Mrs. Sylvester.] You call yourself a New Woman—you're not New at all. You're just as old as Eve. You only want one thing—the one thing every woman wants—the one thing that no woman's life's worth living without! A true man's love! Ah, if we all had that, there'd be no problem of the sexes then. I had it once. Heaven help me, I have lost it! I've done my best—it isn't much, but it's the best I can. I give it up! If you have robbed me of his love, my own is left to me; and if the future's yours, the past is mine. He loved me once, and I shall love him always! [*Exit, C.*]

ACT IV

A Month Later.

Scene:—*An orchard at Mapledurham. Farmhouse at back, C. Paths off, R. and L. front. A cluster of trees, R., at back. A few stumps of trees to serve as seats.*

Margery *discovered, standing on a ladder placed against one of the trees, gathering apples, which she throws into a basket below. She is dressed in peasant costume.*

Enter Armstrong, *C.*

Armstrong: Margery!

Margery: Yes, dad!

Armstrong [*comes underneath the tree and roars with laughter*]: Here's a slice of luck! That fellow in London wants the grey mare back again!

Margery [*who has come down*]: The grey mare, father?

Armstrong: Old Dapple! you remember her?

Margery: Of course! but what about her?

Armstrong: Bless me, haven't I told you? I sold old Dapple to a chap in London.

Margery [*reproachfully*]: You sold old Dapple?

Armstrong: She's too good for hereabouts. True, she's a splint on the off leg, but what's a splint? I sold her without warranty, and buyer took her with all faults, just as she stood.

Margery: Well, dad?

Armstrong: Darn me, if the next day he didn't cry off his bargain!

Margery [*thoughtfully*]: Poor Dapple!

Armstrong: Oh, says I, if you're not satisfied with her, I am. So, there's your money; give me back my mare. An Armstrong doesn't stand on warranties.

Margery: No, daddy dear, and you don't mind the splint?

Armstrong: But Margery, you should have seen the screw he got in place of her! Ha, ha! she was *all* splints!

Margery: He's found that out?

Armstrong: And wants the old mare back! at my own price!

Margery: This *is* good news! For we were getting hard up, weren't we, father?

Armstrong: Ah, farming isn't what it used to be; and now that you won't let me take in visitors—

Margery: I never stopped you.

Armstrong: How about Captain Sylvester?

Margery: Oh, him!

Armstrong: He's an old customer; and always seemed a civil-spoken gentleman enough.

Margery: Too civil!

Armstrong: That's more than you were, Margery. You'd scarce say a word.

Margery: He came for no good.

Armstrong: There's no harm in trout fishing—unless it's for the trout.

Margery: I was the trout.

Armstrong: You? Go on! That's the way with you girls! You think all the men are after you. I'm sure he said nothing to hurt you.

Margery: But he has written since.

Armstrong [*scratches his head*]: I didn't know he's written.

Margery: Nearly every day.

Armstrong: Those letters were from him? I thought they were from—[*Hesitates.*]

Margery: No! From Captain Sylvester.

Armstrong: Of course you haven't answered them?

Margery: Only the last.

Armstrong: I shouldn't have done that.

Margery: Yes, you would, dad!

Armstrong: Well, you know best. You always went your own way, Margery, and it was always the right road.

Margery: Where shall I put these apples?

Armstrong: Nay, I've the broadest shoulders. Give me a hand; I'll take 'em.

[Margery *helps him to put the basket on his shoulders. Exit, C.]*

Margery: Dear old dad! We leave our parents, and we return to them; they let us go, and they take us back again! How little we think of their partings, and how much of our own! [*Sits*, R.]

Enter Sylvester, *L. front.*

Sylvester: I saw you in the apple-tree, and took a short cut.

Margery: You got my message then?

Sylvester: How good of you to send for me! So then my letters have had some effect?

Margery: I sent for you because I want to speak to you.

Sylvester: And I to you. Margery, I've left my wife.

Margery: Yes, so I heard.

Sylvester: She was no wife to me. For years our marriage has been a mockery, and it was best to put an end to it. Now I am free.

Margery: Because you've left your wife?

Sylvester: It's no use beating about the bush. Things have gone too far, and I'm too much in earnest. She loves your husband. It is common talk. I've shut my eyes as long as possible, and you've shut yours; but we both know the truth.

Margery: That you've deserted her!

Sylvester: What if I have?

Margery: Go back.

Sylvester: Back to a wife who is no wife!

Margery: Back to the woman you promised to protect, and whom you left when she most needed you.

Sylvester: Because I love you, Margery!

Margery: That love won't last long. Love can't live on nothing!

Sylvester: There is no hope for me?

Margery: No, not a scrap!

Sylvester: Then what do you propose? To sacrifice your life to an idea—to be true to a phantom? You owe no faith to one who is unfaithful. Think! You are young—your real life lies before you—would you end it before it's begun? A widow before you're a wife?

Margery: I *am* a wife, and I shall not forget it. If I have lost my husband's love, at least I'll save his honour. A public scandal mayn't mean much to *you*, but it means your wife's ruin—it means Gerald's. Gerald shall not be ruined! You *shall* go back to her!

Sylvester: Is it a challenge?

Margery: Challenge or not, you *shall!* It is ignoble to desert her so! You are a coward to make love to me! If her love was unworthy, what is yours? Is it for you to cast a stone at her? See! Read your letters! [*Producing a packet.*] Letters to me—love-letters! Letters to a woman you didn't respect in her grief and persecuted in her loneliness—a woman who would have none of you—who tells you to your face you're not a man! Your love's an insult! take the thing away! [*Turns off. Pause.*]

Sylvester: Do you propose to send those to my wife?

Margery: No! but I want to make you realize you need more mercy than you show to her. These letters were written for my eye alone; to open them was to promise secrecy.

Sylvester: Why have you kept them, then?

Margery: To give them back to you. [*Gives him the packet. Another pause.*]

Sylvester: Margery, everything you say and do makes it more hard to go away from you.

Margery: You're going, then?

Sylvester: Your words leave me no choice.

Margery: Where are you going? to her?

Sylvester: I don't know yet. I don't know if I'm welcome. [*Playing with the packet, mechanically.*]

Margery: That rests with you. You say, she's been no wife to you; but have you been a husband to her?

Sylvester: Why do you take her part? She's injured you enough.

Margery: Yes; she has injured me; but now I know what it is to live without love, and to want it, I can pardon her. Can't you? [*Goes to him and gives him both her hands.*] Forgive her, Captain Sylvester—freely as I do you— give her the love that you have offered me—and you will find your wife's a woman just as much as I am.

Sylvester: Margery—I may call you "Margery?"

Margery: I'm "Margery" to everybody now.

Sylvester: If there were more women like you, there would be fewer men like me. [*Exit, L.*]

Margery [*looks after him, then goes, R. front and looks again*]: He'll go back to his wife; and if she isn't happy, it's her fault. [*Exit, R.*]

Re-enter Armstrong, *showing out,* C., Lady Wargrave *and the* Colonel.

Armstrong: This way, my lady. I'll send Margery to you. [*Exit Armstrong, R.*]

Colonel: This must be put right, Caroline.

Lady Wargrave: I mean to put it right.

Colonel [*severely*]: A Cazenove living apart from his wife!

Lady Wargrave: It is sad—very sad.

Colonel: More than that, Caroline—it's not respectable.

Lady Wargrave: That doesn't trouble *you.*

Colonel: It shocks me. The institution of marriage is the foundation of society; and whatever tends to cast discredit on that holy "ordnance" saps the moral fibre of the community.

Lady Wargrave: Did you say, "ordnance?"

Colonel: I did say, "ordnance." It was a slip of the tongue.

Lady Wargrave: You are not used to ordinances.

Colonel: What do you mean, Caroline? Wasn't I baptized—wasn't I confirmed?

Lady Wargrave: There is another ceremony which, during a somewhat long career, you have systematically avoided.

Colonel: A mere sin of omission, which even now it is not too late to repair. I am a young man still—

Lady Wargrave: Young man?

Colonel: Comparatively. And everything in the world is comparative. What cannot be undone in the past can at least be avoided in the future.

Lady Wargrave: What is the matter with you, Theodore? You have suddenly become quite a moral martinet, and have developed such a severity of aspect that I scarcely know my own brother.

Colonel [*aside*]: Shall I tell her? Dare I? Courage!

Lady Wargrave: I think I liked you better as you were. At any rate, I was used to you.

Colonel: How peaceful it is here, Caroline—how sylvan!

Lady Wargrave: Yes, it's a pretty place enough.

Colonel: It might have been created expressly for the exchange of those sacred confidences which are never more becoming than when shared between a brother and a sister.

Lady Wargrave: Good gracious! you are growing quite sentimental! I have no confidences to make.

Colonel: But *I* have.

Lady Wargrave: Theodore! What fresh iniquity—?

Colonel: Caroline, I am going to be married. [*Blows his nose vigorously.*]

Lady Wargrave [*astounded*]: Married!

Colonel: To-morrow.

Lady Wargrave: To whom, pray?

Colonel: Miss Bethune.

Lady Wargrave: Give me my smelling salts.

Colonel [*gives her them*]: Enid! Pretty name, isn't it? Enid! [*Smiling to himself.*]

Lady Wargrave: No fool like an old fool!

Colonel: Fifty-six.

Lady Wargrave: Eight.

Colonel: But don't tell Enid, will you?

Lady Wargrave: There are so many things I mustn't tell Enid!

Colonel: No, Caroline; I've made a clean breast of it.

Lady Wargrave: *Quite* a clean breast of it?

Colonel: Everything in the world is comparative.

Lady Wargrave: Then, Miss Bethune has renounced her opinions?

Colonel: Oh, no; she's too much of a woman for that.

Lady Wargrave: How can she reconcile them with your enormities?

Colonel: My peccadilloes? Oh, she doesn't believe them—or she pretends she doesn't—which is the same thing. She says we men exaggerate so; and as for the women, you simply can't believe a word they say! [*Chuckles in his old style.*]

Lady Wargrave: At any rate, she means to marry you?

Colonel: Upon the whole, she thinks I have been rather badly used. [*Chuckles again.*]

Lady Wargrave: To marry! after your experience!

Colonel: Way of the world, my dear. My poor old adjutant! went through the Mutiny[18] unscathed, and killed in Rotten Row![19]

Lady Wargrave: Well, it was quite time that you had a nurse! [*Rising and going R. front to meet* Margery.]

Colonel: Caroline's taken it very well. Nothing like courage in these matters—courage! "Nurse" was distinctly nasty; but that's Caroline's way.

Re-enter Armstrong, *R., followed by* Margery.

Armstrong: Found her at last, my lady.

Lady Wargrave: Leave us together, Armstrong. [*Margery drops a curtsey.*]

Armstrong: Come with me, Colonel. If you'll step indoors, I'll give you a glass of ale that'll do your heart good.

Colonel [*putting his arm through* Armstrong's]: Caroline takes it very well. [*Quite forgetting himself.*]

Armstrong: My lady's very welcome.

Colonel [*hastily withdrawing his arm*]: No, no, no! I was talking to myself. [*Exit* Armstrong, *C., roaring. Aside, glancing at* Lady Wargrave.] Nurse! [*Exit, C.*]

Lady Wargrave: Margery, I've come to scold you.

Margery: Yes, my lady.

Lady Wargrave: Aunt. Come and sit down by me. [*Draws her towards seat under the tree, L.* Lady Wargrave *sits*—Margery *at her feet.*] Yes, Margery, to scold you. Why did you not confide in me? If you had only told me of your troubles, this would never have happened. It was undutiful.

Margery: No, aunt. There are some troubles one can confide to nobody—some griefs which are too sacred to be talked about.

Lady Wargrave: And is yours one of them? You are young, Margery; and youth exaggerates its sorrows as well as its joys. Nothing has happened that cannot be put right, if you will only trust me and obey me.

Margery: I owe my obedience elsewhere.

Lady Wargrave: And do you think that you have paid it?

Margery: Yes.

Lady Wargrave: Gerald *desired* you to leave him?

Margery: No; but I read his thoughts—just as you used to say I could read yours—and I obeyed his wishes.

Lady Wargrave: Then if he wished you to return, you would come back?

Margery: Not if he'd been talked over; not if he asked me to go back to him because he thinks it his duty, or I want him. I don't want duty; I want love.

Lady Wargrave: You wouldn't see him, if I sent him to you?

Margery: What is the use of seeing him? You can send Gerald, but not Gerald's heart. I have done all I can—I can't do any more. I've saved his honour— I've resigned his love. All I ask is, to be left alone with mine. [*Turning away.*]

[*Lady Wargrave* rises, *and as* Gerald *advances, retires into the house, C.*]

Gerald: Margery!

Margery: Gerald!

Gerald: I am not here to ask you to come back to me. How can I say what I have come for? I have come—because I cannot keep away from you. To ask for your forgiveness—

Margery: You have that.

Gerald: And, if it's possible, some place in your esteem. Let me say this, and I will say no more. If, for a little space, my heart strayed from you, Margery—if, for a moment, words escaped my lips which cannot be recalled, that is my only infidelity. You understand me?

Margery: Yes.

Gerald: That's what I came to say—that's all!

Margery [*giving him her hand*]: Thank you for telling me.

Gerald [*holding her hand*]: Not all I want to say, but all I must. I am no longer a free man. My lips are sealed.

Margery: What seals them?

Gerald: Haven't you heard? Sylvester's left his wife—and it is all my doing.

Margery: No, it is his.

Gerald: His?

Margery: I may tell you now. He left his wife, not through your fault or hers, but to make love to me.

Gerald: He has been here?

Margery: But he has gone.

Gerald: Where?

Margery: To his wife. I sent him back to her.

Gerald: Then, I am free!

Margery: Yes, Gerald.

Gerald: Free to say how I love you—how I have always loved you! Yes, Margery, I loved you even then—then when I spoke those unjust, cruel words; but love's so weird a thing it sometimes turns us against those we love. But when I saw you, there upon the ground, my heart turned back to you—no, it was not my heart, only my lips that were unfaithful! My heart was always yours—not half of it, but all—yours when I married you, yours when you said good-bye, and never more yours, never as much as now, now I have lost you.

Margery: You have not lost me, if you love me that much! [*Throwing her arms round him.*]

Gerald: Margery!

Lady Wargrave *and* Colonel *re-enter, quietly, C., and stand, looking on, at back, amongst the trees.*

Gerald: My wife again!

Margery: But, Gerald, remember I am nothing more. I don't think I shall ever be a lady.

Gerald: Always in my eyes!

Margery: No, not even there. Only a woman.

Gerald: I want you to be nothing less or more—only a woman!

[*About to kiss her.* Lady Wargrave, *at back, bows her head, with her fan half spread before the* Colonel's *face.* Gerald *kisses* Margery.]

CURTAIN

Notes

1. The usual meaning of rusticated is to go to the country but, here, it means to suspend or send down from the university for bad behavior or grades.

2. Because books were printed on single sheets which were then folded and bound, one had to cut the pages before reading.

3. latchkeys, or doorkeys, whose ownership was an indication of a woman's freedom to come and go.

4. *dea ex machina,* A goddess or god (deus) in a Greek play who was brought to the stage in a mechanical device to intervene; hence, an improbable way to untangle the plot (Latin).

5. The Horse Guards is a building opposite Whitehall in London which served as the headquarters for the Horse Guards, the personal escort of the British sovereign.

6. The club is a private men's club where members could eat and from which women were excluded.

7. The Empire was a music hall in Leicester Square.

8. *mésalliance,* a marriage to someone socially inferior (French).

9. *Peccavi!,* I have sinned! (Latin).

10. Newdigate: a prize given at Oxford University for the best poem on a set subject.
11. *Sotto voce*, in an undertone (Italian).
12. Bradshaw, a travel guide to Europe.
13. *succès d'estime*, a limited success (French).
14. Vigilance Committee, a group which would report on indecency in the arts.
15. Zola's novels were considered indecent and shocking.
16. *Dixi!*, I have spoken! (Latin).
17. *omnes*, all (Latin).
18. The Indian uprising of 1857 which was suppressed by the British.
19. Rotten Row was a fashionable place to ride in Hyde Park, London.

FURTHER READING

I. NEW WOMAN FICTION

The following list is selective and is intended to be a guide for readers to additional fiction, primarily novels, by New Woman writers. Modern reprints of a work are noted.

Allen, Grant. *The Woman Who Did.* London: John Lane, 1895; Oxford: Oxford University Press, 1995.

Brooke, Emma Frances. *A Superfluous Woman.* 3 vols. London: W. Heinemann, 1894.

—. *Transition.* ["By the author of *A Superfluous Woman*"]. London: W. Heinemann, 1895.

Caird, Mona. *The Daughters of Danaus.* London: Bliss, Sands and Foster, 1894; New York: Feminist Press, 1989.

—. *The Pathway of the Gods.* London: Skeffington, 1898.

—. *Whom Nature Leadeth.* [By G. Noel Hatton]. 3 vols. London: Longmans, Green, and Company, 1883.

—. *The Wing of Azrael.* 3 vols. London: Trübner, 1889; 1 vol., New York: Lovell, 1889.

Cholmondeley, Mary. *Red Pottage.* London: Edward Arnold, 1899; New York: Penguin Books—Virago Press, 1985.

Cross, Victoria [Annie Sophie Cory]. *The Woman Who Didn't.* London: John Lane, 1895.

—. *Six Chapters of a Man's Life.* London: Scott, 1903; New York: Kennerley, 1908.

D'Arcy, Ella. *Monochromes.* London: John Lane, 1895.

—. *Modern Instances.* New York and London: John Lane, 1898.

Dixon, Ella Hepworth. *My Flirtations.* [By Margaret Wynman]. London: Chatto and Windus, 1892; Philadelphia: J.B. Lippincott, 1893.

—. *The Story of a Modern Woman.* London: W. Heinemann, 1894; New York: Cassell, 1894; London: Merlin Press, 1990.

Dowie, Menie Muriel. *Gallia.* London: Methuen and Co., 1895.

—. *A Girl in the Karpathians.* London: G. Philip, 1891; New York: Cassell, [1891].

Egerton, George [Mary Chavelita (Dunne) Bright]. *Discords.* London: J. Lane, 1894; Boston: Roberts, 1894.

—. *Keynotes.* London: E. Mathews and J. Lane, 1893; Boston: Roberts, 1893.

—. *Keynotes and Discords.* London: Virago Press, 1983.

—. *Symphonies.* London: J. Lane, 1897; London and New York: 1897.

—. *The Wheel of God.* London: Richards, 1898; New York: Putnam, 1898.

Gissing, George. *The Odd Women.* London: Lawrence and Bullen, 1893; New York: Penguin Books, 1983.

Grand, Sarah [Frances Elizabeth (Clarke) McFall]. *Babs the Impossible.* New York and London: Harper, 1900; London: Hutchinson, 1901.

—. *The Beth Book.* London: W. Heinemann, 1898; New York: Dial Press, 1980.

—. *The Heavenly Twins.* 3 vol. London: W. Heinemann, 1893; Ann Arbor: University of Michigan Press, 1992.

—. *Ideala: A Study from Life.* (Published anonymously). Warrington: Privately printed, 1888; London: E.W. Allen, 1888; New York: Appleton, 1893.

—. *Our Manifold Nature: Stories from Life.* London: Heinemann, 1894; Freeport, NY: Books for Libraries Press, 1969.

Hardy, Thomas. *Jude the Obscure.* London: Osgood, McIlvaine, 1895.

Hunt, Violet. *The Maiden's Progress.* London: Osgood, McIlvaine, 1894; New York: Harper, 1894.

—. *A Hard Woman.* London: Chapman and Hall, 1895; New York: Appleton, 1895.

Iota [Kathleen Mannington (Hunt) Caffyn]. *Children of Circumstance: A Novel.* London: Hutchinson, 1894; New York: D. Appleton, 1894.

—. *A Yellow Aster.* London: Hutchinson and Co., 1894; New York: D. Appleton, 1894.

Schreiner, Olive. *Dreams.* London: T.F. Unwin, 1891; Boston: Roberts, 1891.

—. *The Story of an African Farm.* [By Ralph Iron]. London: Chapman and Hall, 1883.

Sharp, Evelyn. *At the Relton Arms.* London: J. Lane, 1895; Boston: Roberts, 1895.

—. *Rebel Women.* New York: John Lane Company, 1910.

Syrett, Netta. *Nobody's Fault.* London: John Lane, 1896; Boston: Roberts, 1896.

—. *The Tree of Life.* London and New York: John Lane, 1897.

Wotton, Mabel. *Day-Books.* London: John Lane, 1896.

—. *A Girl Diplomatist.* London: Chapman and Hall, 1892.

—. *A Pretty Radical, and Other Stories.* London: David Stott, 1890.

II. Selected Secondary Sources

Ardis, Ann L. *New Women, New Novels: Feminism and Early Modernism.* New Brunswick, NJ and London: Rutgers University Press, 1990.

Beckson, Karl. *London in the 1890s: A Cultural History.* New York and London: W.W. Norton and Company, 1992.

Beetham, Margaret. *A Magazine of Her Own? Domesticity and Desire in the Woman's Magazine, 1800-1914.* London and New York: Routledge, 1996.

Bonnell, Marilyn. "The Legacy of Sarah Grand's *The Heavenly Twins:* A Review Essay." *English Literature in Transition, 1880-1920* 36 (1993): 467-78.

—. "Sarah Grand and the Critical Establishment: Art for (Wo)man's Sake." *Tulsa Studies in Women's Literature* 14.1 (Spring 1995): 123-48.

Casford, Ethel Lenore. *The Magazines of the 1890s.* Language and Literature Series Vol.1, No. 1. Eugene, OR: University Press, September 1929.

Cunningham, A.R. "The 'New Woman Fiction' of the 1890's." *Victorian Studies* 17 (December 1973): 177-86.

Cunningham, Gail. *The New Woman and the Victorian Novel.* New York: Harper and Row, 1978.

Daims, Diva, and Janet Grimes, ed. *Toward a Feminist Tradition: An Annotated Bibliography of Novels in English by Women 1891-1920.* New York and London: Garland, 1982.

Dowling, Linda. "The Decadent and the New Woman in the 1890s." *Nineteenth Century Fiction* 33 (1979): 434-53.

Gardiner, Juliet. *The New Woman.* London: Collins and Brown Limited, 1993.

Harrison, Fraser, ed. *The Yellow Book: An Illustrated Quarterly.* London: Sidgwick and Jackson, 1974.

Huddleston, Joan. *Sarah Grand: A Bibliography.* St. Lucia, Australia: University of Queensland, 1979.

Jackson, Holbrook. *The Eighteen Nineties: A Review of Art and Ideas at the Close of the Nineteenth Century.* New York: Alfred A. Knopf, 1925.

Kersley, Gillian. *Darling Madame: Sarah Grand and Devoted Friend.* London: Virago, 1983.

Knapp, Shoshana Milgram. "Revolutionary Androgyny in the Fiction of Victoria Cross." *Seeing Double: Revisioning Edwardian and Modernist Literature.* Ed. Carola M. Kaplan and Anne B. Simpson. New York: St. Martin's Press, 1996. 3-19.

Kucich, John. "Curious Dualities: *The Heavenly Twins* (1893) and Sarah Grand's Belated Modernist Aesthetics." *The New Nineteenth Century: Feminist Readings of Underread Victorian Fiction.* Ed. Barbara Leah Harman and Susan Meyer. New York and London: Garland, 1996. 195-205.

Ledger, Sally. *The New Woman: Fiction and Feminism at the Fin de Siècle.* Manchester: Manchester University Press, 1997.

Ledger, Sally, and Scott McCracken, eds. *Cultural Politics at the Fin de Siècle.* Cambridge: Cambridge University Press, 1995.

Mangum, Teresa. "Style Wars of the 1890s: The New Woman and the Decadent." *Transforming Genres: New Approaches to British Fiction of the 1890s.* Ed. Nikki Lee Manos and Meri-Jane Rochelson. New York: St. Martin's, 1994. 47-66.

—. *Married, Middlebrow, and Militant: Sarah Grand and the New Woman Novel.* Ann Arbor: University of Michigan Press, 1998.

McCullough, Kate. "Mapping the 'Terra Incognita' of Woman: George Egerton's *Keynotes* (1893) and New Woman Fiction." *The New Nineteenth Century: Feminist Readings of Underread Victorian Fiction.* Ed. Barbara Leah Harman and Susan Meyer. New York: Garland, 1996. 205-23.

Mix, Katherine Lyon. *A Study in Yellow: The Yellow Book and its Contributors.* Lawrence: University of Kansas Press, 1960.

Miller, Jane Eldridge. *Rebel Women: Feminism, Modernism, and the Edwardian Novel.* London: Virago, 1994.

Nelson, Carolyn Christensen. *British Women Fiction Writers of the 1890s*. New York: Twayne, 1996.

Powell, Kerry. "New Women, New Plays, and Shaw in the 1890s." *The Cambridge Companion to George Bernard Shaw*. Ed. Christopher Innes. Cambridge: Cambridge University Press, 1998. 76-100.

Pykett, Lyn. *The "Improper" Feminine: The Women's Sensation Novel and the New Woman Writing*. London and New York: Routledge, 1992.

—, ed. *Reading Fin de Siècle Fictions*. London and New York: Longmans, 1996.

Rubenstein, David. *Before the Suffragettes: Women's Emancipation in the 1890s*. New York: St. Martin's Press, 1986.

Showalter, Elaine. *A Literature of Their Own: British Women Novelists From Brontë to Lessing*. Princeton, NJ: Princeton University Press, 1993.

—. *Sexual Anarchy: Gender and Culture at the Fin de Siècle*. New York: Viking Penguin, 1990.

Stetz, Margaret. "New Grub Street and the Woman Writer of the 1890s." *Transforming Genres: New Approaches to British Fiction of the 1890s*. Ed. Nikki Lee Manos and Meri-Jane Rochelson. New York: St. Martin's, 1994. 21-45.

Stubbs, Patricia. *Women and Fiction: Feminism and the Novel 1880-1920*. Brighton: Harvester Press, 1979.

Sutherland, John. *The Stanford Companion to Victorian Fiction*. Palo Alto, California: Stanford University Press, 1989.

Todd, Janet, ed. *British Women Writers: A Critical Reference Guide*. New York: Continuum, 1989.

Vicinus, Martha. Introduction to *Keynotes and Discords*. London: Virago Press, 1983.

White, Terence de Vere. *A Leaf from the Yellow Book*. London: Richards Press, 1958.